History of the Clan Lundy, Lundie, Lundin

History of the Clan Lundy, Lundie, Lundin

*One of the most ancient families
of the Kingdom of Scotland*

*A history and genealogy
from the 11th Century to the present day*

Robert Alan Lundie Smith

**With Illustrations
by Isobel Mary Lundie (Smith)**

The Grimsay Press
2005

The Grimsay Press
an imprint of
Zeticula
57 St Vincent Crescent
Glasgow
G3 8NQ

http://www.thegrimsaypress.co.uk
admin@thegrimsaypress.co.uk

ISBN 1 84530 023 8 Paperback
ISBN 1 84530 024 6 Hardback

The cover photographs were taken by the author with the kind permission of Mr and Mrs E. Sherry, the current proprietors of Lundin tower. They have requested for it to be made known that Lundin Tower is their home, and a private residence, and unsolicited visits are unwelcome.

Dedicated to the memory of
Col. Alexander Robert Taylor Lundie, O.B.E., M.C., M.D., Bsc., M.B.
ChB., DTM&H., F.R.C.Path (1916-1988),
and his wife Helen Elizabeth Lundie (nee Wilson) M.A., DipEd.
(1918-2005).

Acknowledgments

The information contained within these pages has come from many sources, and been compiled with advice of a number of people. I would like to give my thanks to the following institutions and individuals who have all in some part aided the research for this work. I would particularly like to thank all those persons who have taken the time to respond to my enquires surrounding the Lundie family history, and thus help a great deal in placing and preserving all of this knowledge in one place. Many such persons worked at the institutions shown below, and so appear un-named.

Institutions and organisations

Aberdeen Art Gallery
The Baronage Press
The British Library
The Church of Scotland
The Free Church of Scotland
The National Library of Scotland
The National Archives of Scotland
North Leith Parish Church
The Scottish National Portrait Gallery
Scottish Heraldry Society
The University of Liverpool
The University of St. Andrews
The University of Glasgow

Individuals

Jack Blair, author of the "Blairs of Balthaylock and their Cadets"
Carolyn Bruce
Charlie Dunoon, researcher for Bordernet sites
Dorothy Kindley
Alexander Stewart Lundie, my uncle
James Paterson Lundie
Hazel Lundie, my great aunt

John Lundie, and Jane Scanu (m/s Lundie), my mother's cousins
Stuart Morris, elder of Balgonie
Stuart Morris, younger of Balgonie
Gordon MacGregor, author of "The Landed Families of Perthshire."
Mr and mrs E. Sherry, proprietors of Lundin Tower
Graham Smith, my father
Isobel Mary Smith, m/s Lundie, my mother and illustrator
of many of the figures in the book
Graham Welsh, author of "The Lundins of Fife"

Note that the order of names signifies no ranking of the magnitude of assistance,
but is simply arranged alphabetically.

Contents

List of Illustrations

Front Cover: Central - Lundin Tower. Background - The view South over the old Barony of Lundin from the top of Lundin Tower, looking towards Largo Bay, The Firth of Forth, and Edinburgh.

Back Cover: The view east over the old Barony of Lundin from the top of Lundin Tower, looking towards the Hill of Largo Law

Illustrations in figure numbers 1, 3, 6, 10, 11, 12, 14, 15, 18, 19, 20, 21, 22 and 23 were kindly drawn and specifically provided for this publication by Mrs I. M. Smith, m/s Lundie, 2004.

Introduction

It is a common misconception that Scots of the surname Lundie, Lundy and Lundin, have different origins, and that Lundins descend from a family from Fife; Lundies from a family from Lundie near Doune in Perthshire, or Lundie in Angus; and persons of the name Lundy are assigned as either one or the other. In fact they all share common descent from Phillip de Lundin, the progenitor of the family. In 1164, Phillip, a chamberlain to King Malcolm IV of Scotland, was granted the Barony of Lundin in Fife. The name of the lands is supposed to be of Gaelic origin. Some say it comes from the Gaelic for 'Gods Meadow,' (Leann dhe, Linn-De or Lunndaidh, depending where you look). Others have suggested that the name comes from the Gaelic Linn and Dun, and means the fort of the pool. Whatever the actual meaning, it is from these lands that the family took its name. Chalmers in his *Caledonia* writes "The Latin name of the charters is Lundin; the English name of common life is Lundie, the usual appellation of the lands." These two clearly defined spelling variants have resulted in the surname of the family that descends from Phillip de Lundin alternating between the two surnames, and intermediate forms of them both. For example, the Barons of this land, starting with Phillip, were the Lundins of Lundin; by 1300, we see them using the name of Lundy of Lundy; two hundred and fifty years later they are using Lundie of Lundie; and by 1700, the family reverts back to Lundin of Lundin. It should however be noted that persons with these surnames of Scottish origin should not be confused with those of Scandinavian and Irish origin, where Lundie and Lundin are quite common surnames, but have no connection with those of the Scottish family.

The history of many of the great houses and families of Scotland are well documented in literature, and, in this cyber age, by clan associations and individuals on the Internet. The family of Lundie (Lundy, Lundin, Lundyn) is described, by Sir Robert Douglas in his Baronage, as one of the most ancient in Scotland; its history however up until now is almost un-documented. Most lists of Scottish Clans and families seem to omit this family. The few books that do include details; with one notable exception, *Lundins of Fife*, by G. T. Welsh; provide very little information. In fact the short paper by Welsh is the only text so far printed that was solely dedicated to this family's history. This lack of documentation of the Lundie family is quite remarkable given, as shall be discussed in full later, the fact that members of this family have occupied many high offices in Scotland; including those of Lord High Treasurer, Chancellor, Chamberlain, Hereditary Doorward (personal body guard to the King), and Member of the Council of Regents of the Kingdom. They have performed duties as hosts, ambassadors and representatives of the Sovereign; voted for Wallace as Protector of Scotland, fighting by his side in Scotland's fight for Independence; and played an important role in the reformation of the church in Scotland. Indeed many of the heads of "Great" families of Scotland, have direct descent from this house through marriage with daughters of the various branches of the Lundie family. By taking what has been written by historians so far, it has really only been through reading the histories of these other families and noting their intermarriage with Lundies, that one could form an idea of their high social standing and historical importance.

Initially when researching the history of this family, much of the information I obtained was from the few sentences that appeared here and there with the odd Lundie reference in the great number of volumes that have been written upon the history and genealogy of Scotland and its other families and clans. This allowed one only to see a fragmented backbone of the genealogy of this family, but with very little historical information, and many conflicting details.

Thankfully, although historians have not written much on this family, there remains, if one takes the trouble and has the time to look, in the archives of Scotland, many many details of this family, enough perhaps to fill several times the volume I have managed to write so far. Sources such as The Registers of the Privy Council of Scotland, The Great Seal of Scotland, The Exchequer Rolls of Scotland, The Accounts of the Lord High Treasurer of Scotland, Deeds, Sasines, Retours, not to mention all of the charters documented in collections that belonged to the religious houses of Scotland, those granted by the various monarchs of Scotland, and those held by the National Archives of Scotland, to name but a few, have provided invaluable resources to be able to write the most comprehensive history of this family, around 840 years since it was founded.

It should be noted that it is not the case that this family were altogether forgotten when compiling the histories of Scotland's great families, and that not all the blame should be laid at the door of the historian. On the 3rd of June 1766, Sir Robert Douglas wrote to James Lundin Drummond, the Earl of Perth, with regards including the history of the Lundin family in 'his book' (Sir Robert Douglas wrote The 'Scot's Peerage' and 'Scot's Baronage'). He was asking the Earl for assistance in this matter. Sir Robert clearly thought that this family was of note enough to be included in his work. Sadly, for unknown reasons, he was not able to include them; perhaps he did not get the assistance he required. Sir Robert's works, which document many of the great families of Scotland, are now a wonderful reference source of Scottish noble society. Had the Lundie family been included in such a text, perhaps their history would be far more widely known. Note should also be made of the Rev. A. T. Grant. This man made comprehensive notes on many of the families of Scotland, and the Gifts and Donations collection number 50, at the National Archives of Scotland, contains many of the notes he made. One section of this collection, GD50/185/57, is his notes on the Lundie family. It is not known why he compiled all of these notes, but they were never written up, and never published.

This book is arranged in seven sections.

Section One, "*The Origins of the Family*," details the progenitor of the Lundie (Lundin, Lundy) family, Phillip de Lundin, and his suggested ancestry, dating back to the Norman Conquest of England in 1066.

Section Two, "*The Barons of Lundie*," concentrates on the senior line of the family, that of the Lairds of Lundie in Fife, (that family of Lundie/Lundin/Lundy of that Ilk), tracing their genealogy and history from 1164 to the present day.

Section Three, "*Other Baronial Branches*," details the history of the four branches of the family that were to hold Baronies in Scotland other than Lundie: These are the Houses of Balgonie and Benholm, who were descended from the family of Lundie of that Ilk, Conland, descended from Balgonie, and Gorthie, who it is thought also descends from Lundie of that Ilk.

Section Four, "*Other Landed Branches*," features the details of eighteen further cadets of the Lundie family who were all at some time holding an estate in Scotland. It should be noted that none of the Landed Lundies continue to hold lands in Scotland.

Section Five, "*Other Well Documented Branches*," includes an account of several families whose genealogical link to the various branches documented in the previous sections is either not known, or not certain, but whose family history and genealogy has been well documented. In most cases these families prominence comes from members' associations with Clerical, Medical and Military careers.

Section Six is entitled *"Families Associated By Region"*. Although the Lundie/Lundy/Lundin surname in Scotland is now very uncommon, to simply list all of the Lundie/Lundy/Lundin birth, marriage and deaths in the different Scottish Parishes would be a volume in itself. This would of course be ignoring all the descendants of this family that now live in other countries. However, there are several areas of Scotland where Lundie inhabitants (whose genealogical link to the families described in the previous sections is as yet undetermined) have appeared in documents other than just the Old Parish records. It is in this penultimate section that these person's details are listed. They are detailed by area as in many cases the people featured for the different areas are in all probability related to some close degree, but the documentation to prove this is not available, or has not yet been found. The perfect example of this would be for the Lundies in the Souther-Fawfield area of the Parish of Kilconquhar, Fife; and those in the Parish of Pittenweem, in Fife. The records show several different Lundy/Lundie/Lundin generations in these areas, but with no documented link between them. As my intention is to create the most complete account of the family as I can, such a history would be incomplete without including these details.

Section Seven, *"Well Documented Individuals,"* is almost self-explanatory. This section describes the details of Lundies, Lundys and Lundins, whose biographical details can be found documented in the records I have consulted, but appear as distinct individuals, with no connection to any of the previous families described. With such an arrangement I hope to include as much of the information I have come across on the Lundie family.

When reading the rest of the text in this book, it is important to consider the spelling used in the various extracts from old documents, and in the main body of the text. At a first glace, the reader may wonder why from page to page the spelling of the same name or place changes, and some of the old fashion Scotch language quoted is on the face of it hard to read. It is not only the case that the spelling of the Lundie surname has changed over the years, but the spelling of many names and places has altered over the last 900 years as well. Going back but only a few centuries, the spelling may be different from document to document, or even from sentence to sentence. I have consciously chosen not to homogenise this account, by changing all first names, surnames and place names to the same modern spelling everywhere in the text. Instead I have tried to use on all occasions the spelling used by the particular source from whence the relevant information came from. One reason for this choice is the fact that the homogenisation of the Lundie/Lundin/Lundy surname, where it has been featured in other works, has led to the belief that the three surnames are in fact three different families. When quoting from old texts I have also chosen not to convert them into modern language in case anything is lost in my interpretation.

In a final note, as many of the people who have written to me, whilst in the process of researching this text, have been interested not only in the family history and how they could relate their own families to the landed families, but also tartan and clan crests; I will give a brief overview of tartans and crests &c. Throughout this text, as I have done thus far in the introduction, I will refer to the Lundie family. This however does not make it incorrect to speak of the Lundie Clan. There is no difference between the two terms, but in general it seems as if for Lowland origins, family is preferred over Clan, so I shall stick with that tradition. As said earlier, it has been very rare to see Lundie/Lundin/Lundy in a list of Scottish Clans, but over that last year or so, I have tried in someway to rectify this. The Chief of the family (or clan) would have been the Laird of Lundie. However, the family sold the Barony of Lundie in 1755. A generation later the head of the family succeeded to the Earldom of Perth, assumed the name of Drummond, and in the following generation the male line died out. As well as this family having no chieftain, this is also a family without a Clan tartan. By the time families began wearing specific weaves of Tartan, the Lundie family had sold all its lands and apart from those taking the name of Drummond, had lost its social position. As the location of the seat of this family, and most of the lands that were held by it, was in Fife, the recommended tartans for this family are the Fife district tartans of Duke of Fife and Dundee. With regards to arms and clan crests, details of the armorials used by the heads of the various Lundie branches are included at the end of the relevant sections of the main body of text.

Section One

The Origins of the Family

What is known for certain is that the Lundie family of Scotland descend from Phillip de Lundin, the 1ˢᵗ Laird of Lundin. There were however a couple of other families around at the time he was given the grant of Lundin by King Malcolm the IV., who also bore variations of the Lundin surname, and Phillip has been linked to them both. This section describes the suggested Norman ancestry of Phillip de Lundin, which links him to these other families, and the other Lundins or Lundies, contemparory with him.

The First Laird of Lundin – Phillip de Lundin

In September 1164, King Malcolm IV of Scotland granted to Phillip the chamberlain, and his heirs, Lundin in Fife. This was granted in exchange for the service of one knight. A transcription of this charter, signed in Aberdeen, is given below.

Malcolmus Rex Scottorum, Episcopis, Abbatibus, Comitibus, Baronibus, Justiciis, Vicecomitibus, Prepositis, Ministries et omnibus probis homnibus totius Scotie, salutem. Sciant presentes et posteri me dediss et concessiss et hac mea Cart confirmasse in Feudo et Hereditate Philippo Camerario et Heredibus suis Lundin in Fif cum suis Pertinentiis per ractas diuisas. Quare volo et precipio ut ipse Philippus et Heredes eius predictum Feudum teneant de me de Heredibus meis in Feudo Hereditate, plenarie, libre et quiete, honorifice, cum omnibus Litertatibus et Rectitudinibus ad idem Feudum pertinentibus in bosco et plano, in Terris et aquis, in Campis, Pratis, Pascuis et in omnibus aliis rectis pertinentiis suis. Per seruitium unius militis. Testibus Andrea episcopo de Caten', Ada comitissa, Engelramo cancellario, Comite Dunecano, Gillebride comite de Angus, Comite Morgano, Comite Phillipo de Coleuill', Willelmo de Haia, Johanne de Vallibus, Willelmo de Lindisi, Malisio filio Leodi, Gillandro filio Alfwini, apud Aberdon.

Registra Regnum Scottorum, I. 270-271.

It has been suggested that Phillip was also the Phillip the chamberlain who appeared as a witness to a Charter of a grant to Dunfermline Abbey, during the reign of King David I of Scotland. The charter in question dates from 1128 – 1136, and was signed in Dunfermline (*ESC*, No. 103).

Upon receiving the grant of Lundin, Phillip thus became Phillip de Lundin, from whence his descendants take their surname.

The Door-wards of All the King's Palaces in Scotland

MALCOLM DE LUNDIN.

In the time of William the Lion, there are two families designated as 'de Lundin'. The first is that of Phillip de Lundin, associated with Lundin in Fife. The second is that of Malcolm de Lundin, who held the lands of Lundin (Lundie) in Forfar. It is commonly perceived that Malcolm and Phillip were brothers, with Phillip being granted Lundin in Fife, and Malcolm being granted Lundin in Forfar, by Malcolm IV. However, there appears to be no direct evidence to support this. Chalmers in his *Caledonia*, would suggest that the two families were originally connected, as Phillip de Lundin's son Walter is found to be holding the land of Benvie, which is near to Lundie in Forfar. Dr. Eason in his *Incholm Chartularies*, suggests that Malcolm was Phillips son. One piece of evidence that might suggest a strong relationship between Phillip and Malcolm, can be seen from a charter granted by Thomas de Lundin, son of Malcolm, to the monks of Cupar of a mark of silver, to be paid yearly by him and his heirs out of his lands of Balmerinach, in consideration of the burying-ground which he had located before the church-door, where he desired he might be buried, (*Chart. Cupar*, No. 51). Malcolm de Lundin held the office of Door-ward (Hostiarius) during the reign of William the Lion. This office was to be held by his son Thomas de Lundin, and grandson Allan de Lundin. The importance of this particular charter is that it is witnessed by Walter, Hosiarius, de Lundin; Walter de Lundin being the son of Phillip de Lundin. If Phillip's son is also holding the Door-ward's office, one which is known to be hereditary in Malcolm de Lundin's family, there must be a strong connection between the two.

Whether or not one can say Phillip and Malcolm were brothers or not, a discussion of Malcolm de Lundin's descendants, of the name de Lundin should be included.

Malcolm de Lundin married a daughter and heiress of Gilchrist the third Earl of Mar (*Scots Peerage*, V. 572). He was appointed by King William the Lion (1165-1214) to the office of Door-ward of all the King's palaces, 'Hostiarius'. It is often claimed that he was the first door ward of Scotland (*Scots Peerage*), an office that became an hereditary honour. What exactly this claim means is not clear. Certainly Malcolm, his son Thomas, and grandson Allan held the office of Hostiarius, but there had been persons described as Hostiarius prior to Malcolm. The Act's of William I (*Reg. Regn. Scot.* II. page 38-9) includes a short but interesting discussion on the position of the Durward in the Scottish Court. It concludes with the idea that the King possessed many Doorwards or Body guards, but the office held by Malcolm and his descendants was "an ancient and honourable office," the duties of which they did not actively carry out (i.e. were not the King's bodyguards themselves) but had these tasks performed by various deputies.

Malcolm had issue.
1   *Thomas de Lundie*, who succeeded his father.
2   *Ewen* (*Lundins of Fife*).

THOMAS DE LUNDIE, THE DOORWARD.

As just described, Thomas's Grandfather was the 3rd Earl of Mar. The 3rd Earl was succeeded by his son, Glichrist 4th Earl of Mar, who died without issue, and was succeeded to the Earldom by Duncan, son of Morgund 2nd Earl of Mar. Thomas de Lundie, on account of his mother felt he was the next blood heir to Glichrist and so contested Duncan's claims. Thomas also claimed that Duncan, and his father, were illegitimate. The claims were supported by the King. The dispute was settled with a compromise with Thomas receiving around half of the land of the Earldom of Mar (*Historic Earls and Earldoms*). He possessed with it a castle at the Peel of Lumphanan, and another at Coull (*Reg. Regn. Scot.* II. page 38-9).

Thomas made several grants to Religious Houses. 'Thomas de Lundie, the son of Malcolm, and the King's Doorward', granted to the monks of Scone the church of Eycht in Marr, with its pertinents (*Chart. Scone*, No.

29-58). He granted to the monks of Cupar a mark of silver, to be paid yearly by him and his heirs out of his lands of Balmerinach, in consideration of the burying-ground which he had located before the church-door, where he desired he might be buried, (*Chart. Cupar*, No. 51). This charter was confirmed by King William on the 3rd of April 1196 – 1207 (*Reg. Regn. Scot. II.*, No. 414). According to Chalmers in his *Caledonia* the ground referred to before the church door of the Abbey became the burial place of the family of Lundin. It is here where Thomas's son Alan was buried in 1275, (*Fordun* 1. x. c. xxxv). The comments by Barrow in the Acts of William I (*Reg. Regn. Scot. II.* page 414) would suggest that the burial ground was located in the cloister before the church door. If Thomas died within the Kingdom of Scotland, he was to be buried there. Thomas granted the church of Kinnernie in Cluny and Midmar, Aberdeenshire, to the Abbey of Arbroath, on the 22nd March 1205-7, (*Arbroath Liber.*, I. No. 59). The grant was confirmed by King William on the same date (*Reg. Regn. Scot.* II. No. 452; *Arbroath Liber.*, I. No. 60; *Chart. Arbroath*, No. 88, 89). He granted the wood of Trustach in Banchory-Ternan, in the Mearns, to Arbroath Abbey by a charter dated between 1203 and 1212 (*Arbroath Liber.* I. No. 65; *Chart. Arbroath*, No. 94). The grant was confirmed by King William I between 1212 and 1213 (*Reg. Regn. Scot.* II. No. 506; *Arbroath Liber.* I. No. 66). Thomas appears as a witness to one of the charters of King William, dated 5th April 1201-1202. The charter was a confirmation of a grant made by the Earl of Strathearn of the lands of Ardunie, Craig, Dubheads and Madderty, to the Abbey of Inchaffray (*Reg. Regn. Scot.* II. No. 427; *Inchaffray Liber.* 70-1, No. 73). In 1211, Guthred, son of Donald Mac William, led a rebellion through Ross and Moray. King William sent an army of 4,000 men to subdue this rebellion, and capture Guthred. The leaders of the Army were the Earl of Athol, the Earl of Buchan, Malcolm Morigrond son of Morgrund Earl of Mar, and Thomas de Lundin (*Chron. Bower*, I. 532; *Reg. Regn. Scot.* II. page 63; *Medieval Scotland*, page 175). In 1220 Thomas was one of the *Magnates Scotiæ*, who ratified the marriage of Alexander II. with Johanna of England (*Caledonia*). Thomas married Margaret or Christina daughter of Malcolm 2nd Earl of Athol (*Scots Peerage*, I. 418) . They had two children:

1 **Sir Alan Lundie, the Durward.** who succeeded his father.
2 **Colin de Lundyn**, (*Scots Peerage*, I. 418)

SIR ALAN DE LUNDIE, THE DOORWARD.

Upon the death of his father, Sir Alan became Durward of Scotland; he held this office from 1233 to his death in 1275. The lineage between Alan, his father Thomas, and his grandfather Malcolm can be seen from one of Alan's father's charters to the Abbey of Arbroath, and Alan's later confirmation of this: "Thomas de Lundin, filius Malcomi de Londia Hostiarius, D. Regis Scotie" granted mortifications to the abbacies of Cupar and Aberbrothock. This was confirmed by "Alanus Hostiarius Regis, comes Atholie, son to Thomas" (*History of Fife and Kinross, Sibbald*). He is often referred to as Alan the Durward. He also claimed the title of Earl of Athol (as can be seen from his designation in the aforementioned confirmation) from 1233 to 1235. This was on account of his first wife Isabella, countess of Athol, the daughter and heiress of Henry, 3rd Earl of Athol (*Scot's Peerage*, I. 422) . His second wife was Marjory, the natural daughter of King Alexander II.

Allan was clearly an ambitious man. Firstly he undertook to further his claim over the whole of the lands of Mar and in 1257 he claimed the title of Earl of Mar for himself. He even concerned the pope in this matter (*Scots Peerage*, V. 575). In that same year a papal prescript was issued, directing an inquest to be held, proceeding on the narrative that "Our beloved son, the nobleman Alan, called the Durward, hath signified to us that, whereas the nobleman William of Mar, of the diocese of Aberdeen, hath withheld the Earldom of Mar, of right belonging to the aforesaid Alan, and the same doth occupy to the prejudice of the said Alan, and that Morgund and Duncan, deceased, to whom the said William asserts his succession to the said earldom, were not begotten in lawful matrimony." These efforts were unsuccessful (*Historic Earls and Earldoms*). He did however gain many other titles. He was Royal Judiciary of Scotia (Scotland north of the Forth) between 1244 and 1251, again between 1256-1257, and was certainly holding the post in 1264 (*Scots Peerage*, II. 255). Alexander II bestowed upon him the title of Earl of Kintyre O'Neil, which was an ancient Thanage. There is debate about whether a Colin Durward was Lord of O'Neil in 1234. Sometime between 1249 and 56, Alan gave £1 2s. p. a. from his land of Skene to the Bishops of Aberdeen, in exchange for 2nd teinds of O'Neil (*Medieval Scotland*, p. 74; [*Aberdeen Reg.*, I, p. 17]). Sir Alan Durward founded amongst other institutions on these lands, the Hospital at Kincarden. He dedicated the hospital to God and the Blessed Mary, and conferred upon it the patronage of the church of Lonfanan, and its chapel of Fothery (Fordie). Alan also had control of the Thanage of Dull. The exchequer rolls of Scotland record Alan as owing 26s.8£d. from the fermes of Dull in 1264 (*Exch. Roll Scot.* I., 3. 48). Alexander II also granted to Alan the Lordship of Urquart. Although a castle was known to be there in the time of William the Lion, Sir Alan Durward is believed to be the founder of the first stone castle on this site. He also built the Castle of St. Monance.

King Alexander II died in 1249, and was succeeded by his son, by Mary de Coucy, Alexander III, who was aged only eight at the time. Alan, being the young king's uncle, was appointed one of the council of Regents. In 1251, Alexander travelled to York. King Henry of England thereupon gave his daughter Margaret in marriage to Alexander. The Scottish nobility at this point seems to have divided in to two factions. One of them, sometimes called the English Party, was headed by Sir Alan, and included such other nobles as Walter the High Steward; the other, the national party, was headed by John Comyn, and included Gamelin, Bishop-elect of St. Andrews, and William Bondington, Bishop of Glasgow.

In January, 1252, the King Alexander and Queen Margaret returned to Scotland from England. Upon their return, Chancellor Robert Kenleith, Abbot of Dunfermline, was accused by the Comyn party of attempting to use the great seal to legitimise Marjory, Sir Alan's wife, as daughter of King Alexander II. This would of course have made her heir to her young brother Alexander III. It is said that Sir Alan had tried to have Margaret legitimised by the Pope as well. When Edward I of England was invited to select the legitimate heir following the death of "Margaret, the Maid of Norway" (1286-1290), granddaughter and sole heir of Alexander III, among the 13 candidates was one of Alan and Marjory's heirs, Nicholas de Soulis, by their daughter Ermenguarde. Had it been possible to prove Marjory's legitimacy, his would have been the senior claim. After these accusations were made, Chancellor Robert and other members of the 'English' Party were removed from office, and Comyns put in their place (*Medieval Scotland*, 133-5)

Sir Alan, in 1255, gained possession of the King, capturing him in Edinburgh, and taking him to Roxburgh. By this act Sir Alan again held the power in Scotland. King Henry of England subsequently visited in September of that year, and supervised the issuing of a decreet by Alexander, that the Comyns, and other Lords of that party should be removed from the King's Council. This advantage was short lived. In 1257, Bishop Gamlin travelled to France and attended the Papal court. Here he was confirmed in his office as Bishop of St. Andrews, and also had his opponents in Scotland, namely Sir Alan and his allies, excommunicated. This sentence was published in Scotland, whereupon Walter Comyn, the Earl of Mentieth, captured the King's person at Kinross, and took him to Stirling Castle. Sir Alan is then said to have fled the country (*The Completion of the Medieval Kingdoms*, 248). Alan must have returned by 1258, as he, along with Bishop Gamlin of St. Andrews, the queen mother, John of Acre, Alexander Comyn, Earl of Buchan, the Earl of Mar, and four other persons took care of the King (*The Thirteenth Century*, 592). The young King is known at sometime to have stayed with his Uncle in his castle of St. Monance.

On the 1st of October 1265, Haakon of Norway landed in the west of Scotland, and took hold of the Island of Bute and Arran. The Norwegians then landed at Largs in Cunninghame. The battle of Largs subsequently ensued, whereupon the Scots defeated the Norwegians. The Norwegians retired to the Orkneys where Haco died, the Scots got control of the Hebrides from Norway, and the King of the Isle of Mann submitted to the King of Scotland. After the battle of Largs, Sir Alan was sent along with the Earl of Mar and the Earl of Buchan, to reduce to submission the men of the Western Isles, who had sided with Haakon of Norway (*Scots Peerage*, II. 255; *Fordun*, ed Skene, I. 301).

Sir Alan Durward died in 1275. He had one son, Thomas de Londonia, who predeceased him (*Chart. Arbroath*, No. 20), and three daughters, between whom his lands were divided. However in 1296 King Edward of England gives a grant of Alan Durward's lands to Sir David of Brechin (*Scots Peerage*, II. 218). Alan Durward is credited with founding a number of buildings. The Kirk in Lundie village Forfar was built around this time by the Durward family.

1   ***Thomas de Londoniia***, who predeceased him.
2   ***Lora, countess of Athol***: A daughter by his first wife (*Scot's Peerage*, I. 422).
3   ***Ermenguarde***, who married William de Soulis (*Scots Peerage*, I. 6).

   i   Nicholas de Soulis, a competitor for the Scottish crown in 1291. He married Margaret Comyn, fifth Daughter of Alexander Comyn, Earl of Buchan. They had three sons (Scots Peerage, VIII. 250):-

a   William Soulis, the conspirator

b   Sir John Soulis, killed at Dundalk

c   Thomas Soulis, died at a similar time to his brother, Sir John.

4   *Anne*, who married Colban MacDuff, 8th Earl of Fife (*Scots Peerage*, IV. 11).

The name of Durward carried on after Alan's death, for example around 1420 an Isabel Durward, heiress of Lintrathen married Sir Walter Ogilvy of Carary (*Scots Peerage*, I, 111), from which union the Earls of Findlater descend. The Annals of Dunfermline list a David Durward of Dunduff around 1231. This could be an unknown brother of Alan. With respect to the Barony of Lundie, in the time of David II, it was in the possession of the Countess of Stratherne, after whose death it passed to a Robert Lyle (Lyill), who was given a charter of it by Robert III (*Ind. Rec. Chart. 1309-1413*, 51, 139). Lundie later passed to a branch of the Duncan family, and it was the family of Duncan of Lundie that built Lundie Castle in Lundie Angus; a castle that no longer stands.

Heraldry

The arms of Alan Durward are recorded in several of the ancient Scottish armorials. The Lindsay Armorial of 1542 includes the arms of '*Lord Durward of Auld*,' showing a shield of arms *Argent*, a chief *Gules*. The Slains Armorial of 1565 shows the arms of *Lord Durward* as *Argent*, a chief *Gules*: and Nisbet in his *System of Heraldry* describes Alan Durwards arms as *Argent* on a chief *Gules*, a lion passant guardant *Argent*.

Norman Origins – de London, de Londoniis, de Londres

According to Sir James Balfour Paul, in his *Scot's Peerage* (I, 11), Malcolm de Lundin, the first Hereditary Door-ward, was the son of Thomas de Londoniis. The Londoniis (de Londres, de Londia) family came to Scotland from England and Wales.

WILLIAM DE LONDRES

Son of Simon de Londres, he was one of the Norman Knights who accompanied Robert Fitz Hamon in the conquest of Glamorgan around the time of 1090. Sir William received, after the victory over the Britons in Glamorgan, the Lordship and castle of Ogmore and the castle and Manor of Dunraven. The castle of Ogmore was founded by Sir William. In 1094 Sir William led a strong force into Kidwelly and Ystrad Tywi. He built a castle at Kidwelly to secure his gains. In 1106 he was granted by Henry I of England the Lordship of Ewenny. He built a Priory church at Ewenny. He soon after built the castle of Ostermouth. He was also Lord of Ogwr. He had at least two sons, Maurice de Londres, and Richard de Londres:

MAURICE DE LONDRES

Maurice was his father's heir, and inherited his estates, and was thus Lord of Ogmore. The Lordship and Lands of Kidwelly that his father had gained, had sometime previous been granted by Henry I. to Roger, Bishop of Salisbury. In 1128 he was denounced in a Bill of Pope Honorius II for robbing and defrauding the Church of Llandaff and for plundering and killing itinerant merchants at Llandaff. In 1141 he donated the Priory church at Ewenny to the Abbey of St. Peter of Gloucester. He also made donations of the Church of St. Bridget with the Chapel of Ogmore de Llanfey, the Church of St. Michael of Colwinstone, the Church of Oystermouth in Gower, the Church of St. Illtyd of Pembrey, and the Church of St. Ishmael.

1126, 10 years after his father had begun to establish a castle at Ogmore, Maurice started the foundations of a stone keep with six-foot thick walls. By 1130 Maurice had gained back the lands, castle and Lordship of Kidwelly. In 1136 he took part in the battle of Maes Gwenllian, which was fought as part of an uprising following the death of Henry I. Here Maurice, Lord of Kidwelly, Ormore and Carnwallon, led the Norman army. Princess Gwenllian, one of the reminants of the various Royal Houses of Wales, led the opposing army. The Normans triumphed, and Maurice beheaded the princess on the battlefield. Maurice died in 1149. His tomb is in the Priory church of Ewenny. His eldest son, William, succeeded his estates. He was succeeded in turn by his son, Thomas. Thomas's heir was his daughter Hawise, by Eva de Tracey. She married twice, firstly to Patrick de Cadurcis (or de Chaworth), grandson of Patrick de Cadurcis of Brittany (who came to England with William the Conqueror); and secondly to Walter de Braose. She was the last of this branch of the de Londres family, and, on her death in 1274, the estates passed on to her son by the first marriage, Patrick de Cadurcis. Her son married Isabel, daughter of William de Beauchamp, Earl of Warwick, and their daughter Maud married Henry, Earl of Lancaster (Henry IV), the de Londres estates thus passing to the Duchy of Lancaster.

Association with Scotland

THOMAS DE LONDONIA

He came to Scotland from England, and it is believed his ancestor was William de Londres the 1st lord of Kidwelly. He obtained from David I. the manor of Lessedwyn (Lessuden) in Roxburghshire, where he settled with his followers. It is most likely, by examination of dates, that Thomas was the son of William de Londres. He could have been no less than his grandson. According to Chalmers (*Caledonia*), Thomas de London married a widow, whose name was Lovel, and who possessed some lands in his vicinity; out of which she gave the monks of Jedburgh that portion which was called Uchtredsxaghe. Thomas is also believed to have married the daughter of Uchtred de Molla (Mow), Morebattle, Roxburghshire, who was in turn the son of Liulf de Mow, who may also have been the son of Maccus (*Reg. Regn. Scot.* II., page 282-3, 334-5). Out of the lands of Lessuden, Thomas granted the church of Lessedwyn to the monks of Dryburgh; This grant was later confirmed by his great grandson, Robert de Londoniis; King William I; and by Jocelin, the bishop of Glasgow (*Chart. Dryburgh*, 39-41). A charter by King William I, confirming the properties and privileges of Jedburgh Abbey, shows that Margaret, Spouse of Thomas de London, with consent of Thomas, and her son Henry Lovel, had previously granted Outerside in Roberton, to the Abbey.

Thomas had issue:

1 *Maurice de London* (*Caledonia*). Succeeded his father, of whom next.

2 *Malcolm de Lundie*, (*Scots Peerage*, I, 11). Laird of Lundie in Forfar.

3   Phillip de Lundin, 1st laird of Lundin in Fife. Implied as son of Thomas as the possible brother of Malcolm

4   Uchtred de Londoniis, (implied). An Uchtred de London is made reference to in a charter of confirmation by King William I. It confirmed 140 acres of land in the hanger of Tottenham, for a rent of one mark of silver each Michaelmas. The land had previously, during the reign of Malcolm IV or before, been held by Uchtred (Whetredus de London') (*Reg. Regn. Scot.* II. No 57). Given that Thomas de Londonia's father-in-law was Uchtred de Mow. It is quite probable that Uchtred de Londoniis would be his son.

5   Eschina de Londonnniis de Molla (*Scots Peerage*, I, 11). She was the granddaughter of Uchtred of Mow. She was married three times. Her first husband was Robert de Croc. Her second husband was Walter Fitz Alan, the first Hereditary High Steward of Scotland. Around 1161 Walter the Steward was granted Mow by Malcolm IV, due to his marriage to Eschina de Londoniis, the heiress of Mow. Her grandfather Uchtred had previously granted the church of Mow to Kelso Abbey during the reign of David I (*Lawrie Charters*, No 196). The grant was confirmed by William I. between 1180 and 1185 (*Reg. Regn. Scot.* II., No. 245); and Eschina herself confirmed it by three charters, the first dated the 31st of January 1186, and the last being after 1198 (*Kelso Liber.*, No. 146-8). Sometime between 1173 and 1177 William I confirmed a grant made by Eschina and her husband Walter the Steward, to the Priory of Paisley, of one ploughgate of arable in Mow, by the marches measured and preambulated, with pasture for 500 sheep and for as many animals are allowed with one ploughgate in that town (*Reg. Regn. Scot.* II., No. 184). There are two charters of Eschina de Molle in *Paisley Registrum* Nos. 74 and 75. Her husband Walter died in 1177, and the second of these charters is dated sometime after his death.

The historian, George Macaulay Trevelyan, wrote a few poetic lines concerning Walter Fitz Alan and Eschina de Molle. He describes "Eschine de Londonia, lady of Molla," the wife of the Steward as "beautiful and worthy of her lord. . . The woman, veiled in the obscurity of eight centuries . . . the ideal lady. Norman, by no means, she; ~ Scoto-Saxon, with eyes softly blue;

some Celtic fervour and devotion spiritualising her face; her aspect generous, and features pearly fair, with the rosy flush of Northern breezes, like a soft dawn, lighting them into the purest human sweetness; reasonable and benign; no fickle impulses, no exacting egotism, no self-worship; a woman of household pleasures ~ to be loved by her husband with a constant love, to be tenderly revered by his vassals. Her brown lashes droop not coyly: they are lifted with modest, serene trust in herself and in her world. Her thoughts keep company with her."

Eschina and Walter had issue, and from their marriage descend the Royal House of Stewart.

i   Alan Fitz Walter, Second Hereditary High Steward of Scotland, married Eve, and had issue:

a   Walter Stewart, Third Hereditary High Steward of Scotland. Married Beatrix, daughter of Glichrest 4th Earl of Angus. Walter died in 1241. His great-great-grandson was Robert II of Scotland, the first of the Royal House of Stewart.

b   David Fitz Alan

c   Simon, progenitor of the Boyd family.

d   Aveline, married Duncan Mac Gilbert, First Earl of Carrick.

ii Marjory, married Robert de Montgomery

After the death of Walter Eschina married for a third time, to a man who is designed Henry de Molla. The second and third charters of confirmation by Eschina, of the church of Mow to the Abbey of Kelso, feature her husband Henry. The later of these charters dates from after 1198.

MAURICE DE LONDON

He succeeded his father, and was in turn succeeded by his son Richard.

RICHARD DE LONDONIIS

Richard was married to Matilda de Ferrers, by whom he had his heir and successor Robert de Londoniis. Richard granted half a ploughgate in Lessudden, to Melrose Abbey. This was later confirmed by King William I (*Reg. Regn. Scot.* II., No 86), between 1165 and 1171. Richard's son Robert later confirmed the charter with further grants of land (*Melrose Liber.*, No. 88).

ROBERT DE LONDONIIS

The lineage from Thomas to his great grandson Robert is well known due to a charter from the reign of William the Lion, where Robert de London confirmed to the monks of Dryburgh the church of Lessedwyn, for the safety of the souls of William the Lion, Richard his own father, and Matilda his mother (*Chart. Dryburgh*, No. 39.) The church had originally been granted by Robert's great-grandfather, Thomas de Londonia. Robert appears designed: "Robertum de Londonia, filium de Richardi, filii Mauritii, filli Thome de Londonia" (*History of Fife and Kinross, Sibbald*). King William confirmed this grant sometime between 1165 and 1174 (*Dryburgh Liber*, No. 55; *Reg. Regn. Scot.*, II., No. 121). Sometime in King William's reign, Robert granted to Walter of Berkley (a kinsman of his) one ploughgate in Lessudden. (*BM Loans*, 29/355; *Reg. Regn. Scot.*, II., pages 209, 234). The relationship between Walter and Robert may go back a few generations. Uchtred de Mow, his great-great grandfather quite possibly had a sister Cecily, who married Robert de Berkley. A charter granted by King William I. confirming the property and privileges of Dunfermline Abbey, dating from between 1165 and 1168, includes a Toft in Edinburgh, where at that time, Roberus de Londoniis was living (*Reg. Regn. Scot.*, II., No. 30).

A seal of Robert de London from around 1165 still exists. It is around 2 and 3/8 inch in diameter. The shield depicts a man on a horseback to sinister, in armour, surcoat, cap-shaped helmet with nasale, sword, convex shield ornamented within a bordure. Horse of large proportions pacing, the poytrail adorned with pendants. The Legend reads 'SIGILLVM ROBBERT DE LVNDRES,' (*Scottish Heraldic Seals; Liber.Melros.* plate 76).

1   *Seal of Robert de Londonniis, drawn after the Liber Sancte Marie de Melros. Munumenta vetusitora Monasterii Cisterciensis de Melros, plate 76*

It is important that Robert de London, son of Richard de London, is not confused with Robert de London, illegitimate son of King William the Lion. They are contemporaries of each other, alive during the reigns of King William the Lion and Alexander II. As will be discussed later, Robert de London, illegitimate son of King William the Lion, is believed to have married the heiress of the family of Phillip de Lundin, and taken his name from her. Although some sources might suggest that they were one and the same person (*History of fife and Kinross, Sibbald*), charters from the time can be found that are witnessed by both Robert de Lundyn, and Robert de

London, the King's son, (*Chart. Inchcolm*, No. 15.; *Chart. Arbroath*, No. 6). In the charters of King William and Alexander II, Robert de London, son of King William, and brother of King Alexander is designed in charters as such, so is clearly discernable. Robert, son of Richard de Londoniis, appears as a witness in a number of charters of King William II; the earliest dates from between 1172 and 1174; the latest 1205 (*Reg. Regn. Scot.* II. Nos. 139, 244, 266, 267, 268, 269, 281, 286, 301, 310, 327, 333, 342, 416, 447, 455, 456, 457, 458; page 401).

NESSIUS DE LONDONIIS

We should also make quick mention of Nesius de Lundon. Who it should be suggested descends from this family. He was a contemporary of Malcolm and Phillip de Lundin. A seal of his from between 1165 and 1214 is still in existence. The shield, similar in nature to that of Robert de London, depicts a man on horseback to sinister, possibly in chain armour, with a flat helmet, a sword in right hand, and shield on breast, (*Scottish Heraldic Seals*). According to Sir James Balfour Paul in his *Peerage*, (I, 450) Nessius de London, had a son John de London, who was the father of a John Moray. Sometime between 1156 and 1214, Nessius granted a charter to his cousin Alan, of 'the half town of Smithetun, to be holden by him and his heirs, of the granter and his heirs, for the foreign service offering to a half plough gate of land and for a pound of pepper at the feast of St. Michael yearly' (*Calendar of Deeds*, 1165 – 1214, No. 21). This charter shows Nessius' seal. Could the Allan referred to be Allan Durward?

JOHN DE LONDONIIS

Son of Nessius de Londoniis, he appears as a witness to many charters in the reign of King William I. Between 1173 and 1193 he appears as a witness to at least twenty charters of King William himself, the earliest being between 1173 and 1177; the last being no later than 1193 (*Reg. Regn. Scot.* II. Nos. 147, 170, 178, 180, 181, 184, 194, 195, 197, 200, 206, 214, 226, 230, 231, 232, 233, 234, 244, 249). In these charters he is predominantly designed as "*de Londoniis*" but also appears designed as "*de London,*" "*de Loundoun,*" "*de Lundon',*" "*de Lundoniis,*" and "*de Lond'.*" Sometime between 1189 and 1198, John '*de Lundin*' witnessed a charter by Roger, bishop elect of St. Andrews, concerning the church of Hadinton; and around

1200, John de Lundoniis witnessed a grant to Arbroath Abbey.

Section Two

The Barons of Lundie

The House of Lundie, Chiefs of the Lundie family.

From 1164 to 1755 the Barony of Lundin/Lundie/Lundy in the Parish of Largo, and Sheriffdom of Fife, was held by the same family; a family which took their name from the land; that of Lundie/Lundy/Lundin of that Ilk (of that Ilk meaning of that place). This is the senior line of the Lundie family, from where all of the other branches or houses descend; as such the Lairds/Barons of Lundie were considered the heads or cheifs of the whole Lundie family/clan. This section of the book describes the lineage and history of the Lairds of Lundie, from the original grant of the land and Barony in 1164, to its sale in 1755,and to the current senior representative of the family.

Lundie/Lundy/Lundin of that Ilk

PHILLIP DE LUNDIN, THE CHAMBERLAIN

As described in the previous section, Phillip, chamberlain to Malcolm IV., was given a charter of Lundin in 1164. He was a witness to a great many charters of King William the Lion (*Reg. Regn. Scot.* II., Nos. 347, 370, 373, 378, 382, 391, 392, 401, 404, 405, 411, 413, 414, 415, 416, 418, 426, 427, 446, 453, 458, 464, 473, 493, 578). The latest of which dates from 1210 (*Reg. Regn. Scot.*, No. 493). He was succeeded to Lundin by his son Walter.

WALTER DE LUNDIN, LORD OF LUNDY

Sometime between 1166 and 1171, at Edinburgh Castle, King William the Lion re-granted Lundin to Walter; confirming the grant made by King Malcolm IV of Lundin to Walter's father Phillip.

W Rex Scott episcopis abbatibus comitibus baronibus justiciariis vicecomitibus et omnibus probis hominibus totius suae salutem. Sciant presentes et posteri me dedisse et concessisse, et hac carta mea confirmasse, Waltero, filio Philippi camerarii, Lundin in Fif cum omnibus justis pertinenciis suis per rectas divisas suas Tenedum sibi et heredibus suis de me et heredibus in feudo et hereditate libere et quiete plenarie et honourifice cure omnibus liberatibus et rectitudinbus ad idem feudum pertinentibus in bosco et plano in pratis et oascuis in terris at aquis in campis et moris et in omnibus aliis rectis pertinenciis suis per servicum unius militis Quare volo et firmiter praecipio Walterus et heredes sui praedictum feudum teneant de me et heredibus meis ita libere et quiete sicut alii milites liberius et quietius feuda sua de me tenent in regno Scocie sicut carta regis M fratis mei testator et confirmat. Testibus, Engelramo episcopo de Glasgu, Nicholao cancellario, comite Waldevo, comite Dunecano, Ricardo de Morvill constabulario, Waltero filio Alani dapifero, Roberto Avenel, Willelmo de Mortimer, Radulfo de Clere, Waltero de Berkelai, Ricardo clerico. Apud castellum puellarum

(*Reg. Regn. Scot.* II., No. 150; *Scotland from the earliest times to 1603*, page 86).

In 1178, Walter, son of Phillip of Lundin granted a charter in favour of the Abbot and Canons of St. Mary of Stirling, of four oxgangs of arable and one toft in the town of Balcormok (Balcormo), in Largo, Fife, with common pasture for 500 sheep, 20 cows, one plough team of oxen, for horses, and free of multure on the abbeys own lands.

DONATIO QUATUOR BOUATARUM TERRARUM DE BALCORMOK

Walterus filius Philip de Lundin, vniuersis sancte matris ecclesie filiis salutem: Sciant presentes et futuri me dedisse et concessiss et hac carta mea confirmasse Deo et ecclesie Sancte Marie de Striuling et abbati et canonicis ibidem Deo seruientibus quatuor bouatas terre cum plenario tofto in villa de Balcormok, et communem pasturam totius terre mee, quicunque eam tenuerit, vbicunque propria animalia siue hominum meorum pascunt, nominatim quingentis ouibus et viginti vaccis, et vni carucate boum et equis et ceteris que ad hec pertinent, et propriam multuram dominii quietam, et tres acras prati, sciut eas perambulaui, pro salute anime mee, et anime patris mei, et pro animabus antecessorum meorum, ad tenendum de me et heredibus meis in perpetuam elemosinam, in aquis et pascuis, ita liber et quiete et honourfice sicut aliqua elemosina in tota terra ab omni seruicio liberius et quietius et honorificentis tentur et possidetur: Testibus hiis, Johanne abbate de Calcho, R. abbate de Abirbrothok, Dunecano comite, Michaele clerico, Petro de Oppido, Willelmo filio Thore, Macbeth de Mestrin, Patricio filio eius, Ace de Sterueling, Radulpho presbytero, et aliis.

(*Cambuskenneth Registrum*, No. 36; *NAS*, RH1/2/18/1).

A charter of William the Lion, sometime between 1189 and 1195 confirmed the donation). A transcript of the confirmation by King William is given below. This confirmation was witnessed by his father, Phillip de Lundin.

CONFIRMATIO WILLELMI REGIS SUPER PREDICTA TERRA DE BALCORMOK

Wilelmus Dei gracia Rex Scotorum omnibus probis hominibus tocius terre sue, clericis at laicis, salutem. Sciant presentes et futuri me concessisse et hac carta mea confirmasse Deo et ecclesie Sancte Marie de Striueling et canonicis ibidem Deo seruientibus donationem illam quam Walterus filius Philippi de Lundin eis fecit de quatour bouatis terre cum uno plenario tofto in villa de Balcormac, cum cummuni pastyra totius terre sue, ita quod propria animalia ipsius Walteri siue hominum suorum pascunt habebunt predicti canonici pasturam, nominatim ad quingentas oues et ad viginti vaccas et ad unam carucatam boum et ad eqous ad cetera que ad hec pertinent; tenendam sibi de predicto Waltero et heredibus suis in liberam et quietam et perpetuam elemosinam cum propria multura dominii sui libera et quieta, ita libere et quiete, plenarie et honorifice sicut carta predicti Walteri testatur, saluo seruicio meo. Testibus, Comitibus Gilleberto, Ricardo de Prebenda clerico meo, Roberto de Quenci, Philippo de Valoniis camerario meo, Alexandro vicecomite meo de Striueling, Philippo de Lundin, Radulfo de Camera, Ricardo filio Hugonis, apud Striueling.

(*Registrum Regnum Scottorum.* II. 369; *Cambuskenneth Registrum,* No. 38)

In the same period, King William confirmed a grant by Walter of Lundin, of 20 acres of arable on the north side of the loch of Lundin, Fife, with one toft which Gillemur held, from the smith's house to the high road, to St. Andrews Cathedral. A transcript of the charter of confirmation is given below. The original charter by Walter de Lundin is to be found in *St Andrews Liber.*, 263-4. This grant was later confirmed by King Alexander II (*St Andrews Liber.*, 235).

Willelmus Dei gracia rex Scotorum . Episcopis abbatibus . Comitibus . Baronibus Justiciis vicecomitibus . prepositis ministris . et omnibus probis hominibus tocius terre sue clericis et laicis salutem . Sciant presentes et futuri me dedisse et concessisse et hac carta mea confirmasse Deo et ecclesie Sancti Andree et canonicis ibidem Deo seruientibus et seruituris in liberam et perpetuam elemosinam . pro salute anime mee et predecessorum et heredum meorum ecclesiam de Eglesgirg cum terra abbacie et cum omnibus eidem ecclesie iuste pertinentibus et cum cappella Sancti Reguli et dimidia carucata eidem capelle pertinente . Et ecclesiam de Inchethore cum omnibus iustis pertinenciis suis . Concedo eciam eisdem canonicis . et hac carta mea confirmo ex donacione Comitis Dunecani . ecclesiam de Sconin cum terra eidem ecclesie pertinente et cum omnibus iustis pertinenciis suis . Et ecclesiam de Marchinche cum capella de Katel . et cum terra ad eandem capellam iuste pertinente et cum omnibus iustis pertinenciis suis . Et ecclesiam de Cupre cum terris et decimis . et cum omnibus aliis iustis pertinenciis suis . Ex donacione Malcolmi comtitis de Atthol' . ecclesiam de Dul . cum capell*is* et terris et omnibus aliis iustis pertinenciis suis . preterea ex donacione Comitis Morgunt

: ecclesiam de Tharflond cum omnibus iustis pertinenciis suis . et cum una carucata terre saluo inde seruicio meo et cum molendio ineadem terra fundato : et cum decima de omnibus redditibus suis . Ex donacione Neisi filii Willelmi . ecclesiam de Louchres cum capellis terris decimis et omnibus iustis pertinenciis suis . Ex donacione Umfredi de Berkeli ecclesiam de Coneued cum terris et decimis . et omnibus aliis iustis pertinenciis suis . Et ex donacione Ricardi Maluuel . ecclesiam de Thanetheis cum omnubus iustis pertinenciis suis . Et ex donacione Walteri de Lundin : viginti acras terre iuxta lacum suum de Lundin a parte aqilonali cum una tofta quam Gillemur tenuit scilicet a domo fabri usque ad uiam et cum communi pastura . Et ex donacione Merleswani ecclesiam de Kennakin cum decimis et omnibus aliis iustis pertinenciss suis . et cum terris quas Simeon prysbyter cum acclesia tenuit . Scilicet Chenoch et uallem a speluncca Mandrethin usque ad metam occidentalem ipsius uallis Pettenduem at Petthaschen : quam Merleswanus eidem ecclesie optulit . et quartam partem Drumchatin . et quartam partem Fanclarathin . et quandam terram que dicitur Chenmochaueth per rectas diuisas suas . in pratis . in moris et cum communi pastura et cum omnibus ad eandem terram iuste pertinentibus. Quare uolo et precipio ut prenominati canonici omnia prescripta ita libere quiete . plenarie . et honorifice teneant . et possideant . sicut alias elemosinas suas liberius quiecius . plenius et honourificenius . tenent et possident . et sicut carte donotorum testantur . Saluo seruicio de terris hac inscriptis : de quibus seruicium habere debo Testibus . Matheo Aberdenensi episcopo . Johanne episcopo de Dunkeldin . Hugone cancellario meo . Ærkenbaldon abbate de Dunfermelin . Comite Dunecano . Comite Gilleberto . Wilelmo de Lindeseya . Willelmo de Moreuill' . constabulario . Roberto de Lundoniis . Malcolmo filio Comitis Dunecani . Willelmo Cumin' . Willelmo de Haya . Dauid de Lindes' . Philippo Marescallo. apud Perth .

(*Registrum Regnum Scottorum.* II. No. 333; *St Andrews Liber.*, 231)

Walter de Lundin also granted to St. Andrews Cathedral Priory the lands of Adhebrecces (*St. Andrews Liber.* 264). King William confirmed this grant sometime between 1173 and 1178 (*Reg. Regn. Scot.* II., No. 167).

One charter of great importance, and one which I have not seen presented in previous discussions of the early Lundies, is a charter by Walter, designed Lord of Lundy, and his spouse Christina, to the Abbey of Inchcolm. The charter grants to the Abbey, as a pledge of fraternity from Walter and his spouse, fifteen silver shillings yearly from their mill of Lundy. A transcription is given below.

Omnibus Christi fidelibus literas istas visuris vel audituris Walterus Dominus de Lundy et Cristiana sponsa sua Salutem. Noveritis nos divine caritatis intuitu dedisse concessiss et hac carta nostra confirmass Deo et Ecclesie Sancti Columbe de Insula et canonicis ibidem servientibus et imperpetuum seritiris in pignore fraternitatis nostre quindecim solidosargenti singulis annis imperpetuum in molendino nostrede Lundy in puram et perpetuam elemosinam percipiendon per manum illius qui dictum molendinum de nobis vel successoribus nostris pro tempore tenuerit scilicet septem solidos et sex denarios ad assumptionem beat Marie virginis et septem solidos et sex denarios ad festem Sancti Baldredi. Quod si ad dictos terminos predictos denarios idem moram fecerit in solvendo dictorum canonicorum nuncium honeste exhibebit usque ad dictorum denariorum plenarium soluitonem. Quare volumus et precipimus ut dicti canonici dictos quindecim solidos ita libere quiete et honorifice de nobis et successoribus nostris imperpetuum sicut aliqua elemonsina melius quietius et honorificentius ab aliquo milite vel Barone in Regn. Scocie dature et possidetur. In curius Rei testimonium presenti Scripto Sigillun nostrum apponi fecimus. Hiis testibus Radulpho capellano, Petro filio nostro et herede, Thome at Archibaldo filiis nostris, Johanne filio, Abraham Senescallo nostro, Hugone Bolte Roberto Maimunde et multis aliis.

(*Inchcolm*, No III)

The charter dates from between 1178 and 1214. It is followed by a Precept by Walter, again designed Lord of Lundy, instructing John, his miller, to pay the fifteen shillings to the Abbey. What is most important is the details this charter gives on the children of Walter and Christina. We find details of Peter (Petro) their son and heir, and two younger sons, Thomas and Archibald. The editor of the Inchcolm charters suggests also that John is the son of Walter. From the transcription this is hard to follow, as from the transcribed text he would seem to be the son of Abraham, their steward. However, having not seen the original charter myself, and the author of that text having done so, one must initialy assume the layout of the charter itself lends to this conclusion, or the printed transcription in *Inchcolm* is incorrect.

Around 1250 Walter of Lundin granted to Philip of Feodarg the lands of Balcarmok (Balcormo), excepting the four oxgangs which had been granted to the Abbey of St Mary of Stirling. This charter was witnessed by Sir Alexander Comyn, Earl of Buchan; Sir William of Brechin; Sir William Comyn; Sir Phillip of Malevile; Hugh de Grey and others (*Scots Peerage*, VI. 170; 269 *NAS* GD160/269, No.5). Philip de Feodarg was Walter's cousin, (*East Neuk of Fife*) and was the progenitor of the family of Meldrum.

Between 1214 and 1249 Walter of Lundyn, and Christian his wife, grant to the Monks of Arbroath a chalder of grain 'pro sua fraternitate', the witnesses being John Wischard, vicecomes de Moernes and his son John.

The Christina referred to in these charters, the spouse of Walter, was the daughter of Hugo de Benne, and the heiress of Benholm. Through this marriage the Lundies obtained the Barony of Benholm (*NAS Benholm Charters*). A few centuries later, the laird of Lundy was to pass this lands to a younger son, and from him descended the cadet family of Lundie of Benholm, and details of them can be found in that particular chapter.

Walter and Christina had issue:

1   **Peter de Lundin.** In the charter by his parents to the Abbey of Inchcolm, of 15 silver shillings yearly, Peter is described as their heir.

2   **Thomas de Lundin.** He is found in charters confirming grants of his father, and is commonly thought to have succeeded him. His full details will be discussed shortly.

3   **Archibald de Lundin.**

4   **John de Lundin.** A John de Lundy is witness to a donation by Sir Alexander Seaton to the Abbey of Dunfermline, sometime before 1246 (*Douglas's Peerage*, p 702; *Dunfermline Chartulary*)

There are a number of other persons around in this period designed 'de Lundin,' who may well be other children or close kin of Walter de Lundin.

a ***William de Lundin****.* In 1192, according to Sir Robert Sibbald's History of Fife and Kinross, a William de Lundin was Chancellor to King William. A 'Willo' sponsa de Lundin appears around this time as witness to a charter to a Roger Mortimer de Soules (St. Andrews Liber. 42). William de Lundy is said to have been a witness to a charter of King William the Lion to Phillip de Seaton (Douglas's Peerage, p 701). In some texts, Walter, son of Phillip the chamberlain is called William, so William the chancellor may well just be Walter.

b ***Adam de Lundin****.* In 1194 King William I confirmed to Adam, son of Odo the steward, the grant made to Odo by Gilchrist, the abbot, and the convent of the culdees of St. Andrews. This confirmation was witnessed by both Phillip de Lundyn and Adam de Lundin.

Wilielmus dei gratia Rex Scotorum, Episcopis, Abbatibus, Comitibus, Baronibus, justiciis, vicecomitibus, ministris et omnibus probis hominibus totius terre sue, clericis et laicis, salutem. Sciant presentes et futuri me concessisse et hac carta mea confirmasse Ade filio Odonis Senescaldi donationem illam quam Gilchrist' abbas et conventus kyldeorum de Sancto Andrea [fecerunt], predicto Odoni dapifero nostro de Kynkel et Petsprochyn et Petkynninn. Tenendum sibi et heredibus suis de predictis kyldeis et ecclesia eorum, per rectas divisas suas et cum omnibus ad predictas terras juste pertinentibus, in feodo et hereditate, ita libere et quiete, plenarie et honorifice, sicut carta prefati abbatis et conventus kyldeorum testatur, salvo servitio meo. Testibus, Comite Duncano justicia, Ricardo de prebenda clerico meo, Philippo de Valoniis camerario, Malcolmo filio Comitis Duncani, Wilielmo Cumyn, Wilielmo de Haya, Umfrido de Berk', Dauide de Haya, **Philippo de Lundyn, Adam de Lundin'**, Rogero de la Kernel. Apud Forfar.

(*Registrum Regnum Scottorum*. II. No. 347)

c **Alexander de Lundin.** He appears as a witness to charters in the reign of King Alexander II of Scotland (*Liber. Melros,* 232). He had at least one son

> *i*   *Robert de Lundin.* Sometime in the reign of King Alexander II, Robert, son of Alexander de Lundin, granted a charter to the Abbey of Melrose. The charter (shown below) includes part of Robert's seal. The seal shows no shield, but depicts an ornament with a crescent and star.

OFIRMACO ROB DE LONON DE TRA DE LECELAVE

Omibz hoc scriptum visuris eul audituris Robertus filius Alexandre de Lunde saltm in dno. Nouitis me concessiss i hac psenti carta mea confirmass deo i ecclie beate Marie de Melros i monachis ibidem deo suientibz. in libera puram i ppetuam elemosinam ; illam donacom quam pat meus eis fecit de tra suasita in lekehalu que ei data suit a Waltero de Burdun et Mabilla uxore eius in eschambia. prout carta puts mea testature. Ego uero et heredes mei tota pdeam tram cu omibz liberatibz i asiamentis suis deif monachis cont amnes homies ac feminas warentiza bim ac defendemus. In cui rei testimoni psenti scripto sigillum meu apposui Testibus dno Nicholao Corbeth, dno Robt de Nesbith, dno Nicholao de Ruthirford i aliis.

(*Liber. Melros.,* No. 301)

d **Allan Lundie.** He was granted 'ane half of ane devach of land of Benhame, in Kincardineshire,' by Christian, daughter of Hugo de Benhame. The charter was confirmed in 1390 by King Robert II (*Ind. Rec. Chart. 1309-1413*, 125). He is noted as a Kinsman of Thomas de Lundy. (*Short Memoir of James Young*).

THOMAS DE LUNDIN

Thomas probably succeeded his father as he is found confirming his grants. In the reign of King William the Lion, sometime between 1195 and 1214, Thomas the son of Walter de Lundin, confirmed his father's grant of land in Balcormak (as seen under Walter's description) to the Abbot and Canons of the church of St. Mary of Stirling.

ALIA CARTA DE BALCORMOK

THOMAS filius Walteri de Lundin, vniuersis sancte matris ecclesie filiis salutem: Sciant presentes et futuri me concessiss et hac carta mea confirmasse Deo et ecclesie Sancte Marie de Stiueling et abbati et canonicis ibidem Deo seruientibus quatuor bouatas terre cum plenario tofto in villa de Balcormock, et comunem pasturam totius terre mee quicunque eam tenuerit, vbicunque propria animalia siue hominum meorum pascunt, nominatim quingenitis ouibus, et viginti vaccis, et vni carucate boum, et equis et ceteris que ad hec pertinent, et propriam multuram dominii quietam, et tres acras prati sicut pater meus eas perambulauit pro salute anime mee et anime patris mei et pro animabus antecessorum meorum: ad tenedum de me heredibus meis in perpetuam elemosinam, in aquis et pasuis, ita libere et quiete honorifice sicut carta predicta patris mei Walteri testatur; hiis testibus, Phillipo de Stichill, Dauid de Balcormock, Andrea de Stradhelm, Galfredo de Maleuile, Galfrido vicecomite de Karell, Edwardo filio Patricii de Steruelin, et multis aliis.

(*NAS*, RH1/2/18/2; *Cambuskenneth Registrum*, No. 36)

Sometime between 1203 and 1214, an Alan de Walchope witnessed a charter by Thomas de Lundin. On the 20th of March, 1215, Robert de London (designed as the Kings brother), and one Thomas de London, were witnesses to a charter by King Alexander II. This charter was also witnessed by: Robert the elect of Ross; William de Boscho, Chancellor; Earl Malcolm of Fife; Philip de Valoniis, Chamberlain; Thomas de C....., Walter C...., and Malcolm the Butler. A transcription is given below:

"confirming to the brethren of the Temple of Solomon of Jerusalem all the rights and liberties which Kings David, Malcolm, and his own father William had granted them, as their authentic writs testify, to wit that all the men of the brethren should have the King's peace, and intercourse with all his subjects in buying and selling their merchandise free of bane and toll and duties of passage; that none inflict or consent to the infliction of injury on them, that their cause be first heard in judgement, and that they first receive their right; that no one bring a man of these brethren to judgment, if his masters are unwilling to stand pledge for him, unless he be a convicted thief etc. that they have all the liberties in all parts of Scotland which they have in other countries; that none take a pledge from them or their men unless for his lord's fine; and that if any one of them ignorantly take money out of their own land it shall be restored to them immediately without any fine"

(*NAS*, GD119/2; *"Scottish Handwriting, 1150-1650"*, no. 4, G.G. Simpson; *"Knights of St John of Jerusalem"*, J.H.J (1983), pp. 41-3).

Sometime before 1214, 'Thomas de Lundyn de Fyf' is witness to a charter by William son of Patrick, of a grant of the church of 'Herisille' to the church and nuns of St. Mary of 'Calderstrem' (*Calendar of Charters*, 1165-1214, No. 44). In 1217, Thomas de Lundin witnesses a charter by Richard, son of Hugh de Camera, with consent of A, his spouse, and Richard, his heir, in favour of abbey of Inchcolm of an oxgang of land in the territory of Fordell next to the sea between lands of Dalgetty and Louhild, and a toft and croft in town of Fordell. This charter was also witnessed by; Hugh, bishop of Dunkeld; William, abbot of Holyrood; Patrick, abbot of Dunfermline; and Alexander, sheriff of Stirling (*NAS*, GD172/1). In 1220, he granted a charter to the convent of North Berwick of 12 acres in Aithernie (Easter Kilmux). This land was part of the Barony of Kincrag which was annexed to Lundin, and which a descendant of Thomas had a charter of in 1488 (*East Neuk of Fife*, p 39, 45, 47). Sometime around 1233, Thomas was Sheriff of Fife. He appears designed as such as witness to a charter of Sayer de Quinci, Earl of Winchester, to the Abbey of Dunfermline (*Douglas's Peerage*, p 702; *Dunfermline Chartularys*).

ROBERT DE LONDON

The descent of the house of Lundin from William the Lion has been briefly touched upon in section one. In 1669 the family of Lundin were granted, by King Charles II., the right for the head of the house to display the arms of Scotland on their shield. This right was due to direct descent from William the Lion. The descent has been said to be through the marriage of the heiress of the house of Lundin of Lundin in Fife to a natural son of William the Lion. Only six other families in Scotland are permitted to bear the Royal arms of Scotland on their shields. The exact relationship between Thomas de Lundin, just described, and the heiress of Lundin, is not known. Her name remains lost in the past. Some texts claim that the descent from Robert de London is false, and the re-grant of arms, so to bear the Royal arms, was allowed due to the powerful connections of the Laird of Lundin in 1669; at that time John Drummond, later to be the Earl of Melfort, who married the heiress of Lundin; rather than an accurate pedigree. However, a letter written over 50 years prior to this, by Sir James Lundie of that ilk, to King James VI of Scotland, concerning the Laird of Largo, includes details of the family's descent from Robert de London ("*Original Letters relating to Eclesiastical affairs*", No. 557). A full transcription of this letter is given later in this section under the details of James Lundie of that Ilk, concerning a feud between the Lundies and the Laird of Largo. Sadly it seems that many of the early charters of this family are lost. So confirming the claim by Sir James Lundie in his letter, and disproving other sceptical historians, is now perhaps impossible, but there is no reason to doubt his word in this letter, as his aim is to complain about the laird of Largo, not obtain new arms. The National Archives of Scotland, in the Drummond of Lundin collection, do hold some of the early Lundin papers. In this collection is a charter to Robert de London, son of King William the Lion, and his heirs. This charter is discussed shortly.

Between 1189 and 1195, King William granted to his son Robert, one full toft in his burgh of Montrose, viz the tort between that belonging to Alexander Sheriff of Stirling and that belonging to Jocelin the King's Doorward. This was to be held in free burage, as any of the King's barons held their tofts in that burgh.

Willelmus Dei gracia Rex Scotorum omnibus probis hominibus tocius terre sue, clericis et laicis, salutem. Sciant presentes at futuri me dedisse et concessisse et hac carta mea confirmasse Roberto de Londoniis filio meo unum plenarium toftum in burgo de Munros, scilicet illud toftum quod est inter toftum Allexandri vicecomitis de Striuelyn et toftum Jocelini hostiarii mei. Tenedum in liberum burgagium de me et heredibus meis in feodo et hereditate ita libere et quiete plenarie et honorifice sicut sicut aliquis baronum meorum aliqoud toftum in aliquo burgorum meorum quiecius plenius et honorifice tenet. Testibus Hugone cancellario meo, Comite David fratre meo, Willelmo de Morauill constabulario, Alano filio Walteri dapiferi, Adam Syreis, Rogero de Mortimer. Apud Munros.

(*Reg. Regn. Scot.* II., No. 351; *Arbroath Liber.* I., No. 304)

On the 8th of July, sometime between 1195 and 1210, at Stirling, William, King of Scots, granted a charter to Robert of London, his son, and his heirs, of the royal forest of Ouethe (in Dunfermline). The charter specifies that no person is to fell timber or hunt in the forest without Robert's prior permission. Anyone found guilty of felling or hunting without his permission would suffer the King's forfeiture of ten pounds.

W Dei Gracia Rex Scott Omnibus probis Hominibus Tocius Terre sue Clericis et Laicis Salutem Sciant presentes et futuri me Concessisse et Hac Carta mea confirmasse Roberto de Londoniis filio meo et heredibus suis in forestum forestum meum de Uueth sicut illud habui in forestum die qua illud dedi Quare probibeo firmiter ne Quis in foresto illo sine eorum licentia secet aut uenetur super meam plenarium forisfacturam decem lirarum. Testibus Phillipo de Valoniis Camerario meo, Willilmo de Boscho Clerico meo, Alexandro Vicecomitte meo de Striuelin, Ricardo filio Hugonis, Herberto de camera. Apud Striulin. viij die Julii.

(*Reg. Regn. Scot.* II. 428; *NAS*, GD 169/260/2; *Dunfermline Registrum*, No. 57; *NLS, MS. Adv.* 34.1.3a; *NLS, MS.* 29.4.2 VI ; *NLS MS.* 34.3.25, p182-8).

This is the charter referred to previously that is held in the Drummond of Lundin Collection at the NAS. There would seem to be little reason for the Lundin's to hold such a charter if there was no connection to Robert de London. Sometime before 1211 Robert granted this forest to Dunfermline Abbey. A charter of his shows that Robert of Londoun, illegitimate son of William, king of Scots, granted; for the souls of himself, his brother Alexander, his grandmother the Countess of Kellie, and his ancestors, in discharge of a claim of 6 merks due to monks of Dunfermline; from the royal lordship of Killin, to the Church of Holy Trinity of Dunfermline and monks thereof, the whole of Uueth, granted previously by King William the Lion to Robert. This charter being witnessed by William, bishop of St Andrews; Richard, bishop of Dunkeld; Thomas, prior of St Andrews; John, prior of May; Alexander, prior of the island of St Columba; Malcolm, Earl of Fife; Walter Olifart; Hingelgram Baillol; William del Bois, king's clerk; Alexander, sheriff of Stirling; Galfridus of Inverkunniglas; John of Morravia; Simon Malleverer and William Avenal (*NAS*, GD160/269; *Dunfermline Registrum*, No. 167). This grant was confirmed by King William sometime between 1208 and 1211 (suggested as 1211 by Barrow), (*Reg. Regn. Scot.*, II., No 495).

Prior to 1214, Robert granted the church of Ruthven, to Arbroath Abbey (*Arbroath Liber.*, I., No. 61). This charter was confirmed, sometime between 1196 and 1214 (Suggested by Barrow to be 1204 or 1205), by King William I.

> W. Dei gratia Rex Scott omnibus probis hominibus tocius sue clericis et laicis salutem. Sciant presentes et futuri me concessisse et hac carta mea confirmasse Deo et ecclesoe Sancti Thome de Abirbrothoc et monachis ibidem Deo serientibus donacionem illam Robertus de Lundris eis fecit de ecclesea de Rothen cum omnibus pertinenciis suis. Tenendam in liberam et puram et perpetuam elemosinam ita libere et quiete plenaire et honorfice sicut Carta predicti Roberti iuste testatur. Testibus Phillipo de Valoniis Camerario meo, Ricardo Reul, David de Haya, Roger de Wiltona, David de Marescallo, Bricio Judice. Apud Forfar. primo die Februarii.

> (*Reg. Regn. Scot.* II., No. 454; *Abroath Liber.* I., No. 62)

Robert de London is known to have built Naughton Castle, which is not too far from the parish of Largo in Fife. He also lived for a while in Kellie Castle, Fife, as a tenant to his grandmother, Ada, countess of Kellie, mother of William the Lion. He held other lands in Fife, including those of

Couston, which sometime before 1199 he granted to Roger Frebern in return for military service (*Sale of Couston Castle 2004; Spalding Misc.*, V., 243).

Robert of London, witnessed many charters of his father. He appears being designed as *Roberto de Lundoun filio Regis; Roberto de Lundon filio meo; Rob. de London filio meo; Rob. de Lond' filio meo; Roberto de Lund' filio meo; Roberto de Londoniis filio meo; Roberto de London filio dominus regis;* (*Reg. Regn. Scot.* II., Nos. 209, 313, 452, 459, 460, 461, 462, 467, 468, 479, 483, 493, 498, 502, 503, 508). The earliest date of his witnessing his father's charters is sometime between 1178 and 1195; the latest 1211. He is a witness to the Charter granting the Barony of Allardice to Walter, son of Walter Scott, 16th October 1198.

In 1212, Robert of London was a religious delegate from King John (lackland) of England, being sent to see Khalif Muhammed El-Nasser. Around 1219 he writes to the English court to try and obtain payment for his services to King John.

> "Robert of London, brother of the King of Scotland, to Hubert de Burgo, Justiciar of England, earnestly begs (devote imploro) him for his love and above all his friends in the Kingdom of England, he more especially trusts him, to reply in writing advising him as to his arrears of service due by the King of England he [Hubert] well knowing that King John was wont each year to pay the writer 100*l* and 11(sic) and 14 schillings. That he would have come at present to England to speak with him on the matter, but is greatly hindered by infirmity and can no-wise leave Scotland. Asks him to signify his wishes and advice and good health, in writing, by the bearer."

(Calendar of Documents Relating to Scotland, I., 746)

Sir Robert de Londoniis, natural son of King William the lion, was granted by his father, by 1295, the Royal burgh of Inverkeithing in Fife. This reverted to the crown in 1235. Perhaps this dates Robert's death. He was certainly still alive in 1221, as on the 8th June of this year he witnesses his brother, Alexander King of Scotland, granting a charter to Johanna (spouse of Alexander), in dower, 1000*l* of land, Jedburgh, Hassendean, Lessudden and Kinghorn in Scotland (*Calendar of Documents Relating to Scotland*, I., 808).

PIERES DE LUNDY

Peires was married to a Lady Margaret, and was dead before 1296, as on August 28th 1296, Margaret, widow of "Pieres de Lundy del counte de Fife" signed the Ragman Roll (*Calendar of Documents relating to Scotland*, II., 210). It is hard to believe that he is the same 'Petro,' son of Walter Lord of Lundy, and Christina de Benne, but if this is a much younger wife, it cannot be impossible.

SIR WILLIAM DE LUNDY

In May 1297, William de Haselrig, who was the English appointed Sheriff of Clydesdale was holding a court at Lanark. At this court was William Wallace, the great Scottish Hero. Wallace became involved in an argument with some of the English there, which ultimately resulted in swords being un-sheathed. William, loosing the battle, managed to escape through the help of a Scots woman, some say Wallace's wife. For the assistance she gave Wallace, the woman was subsequently hanged. As a result, Wallace returned with a small group of men, set fire to the sheriff's quarters, killed Haselrig, and cut his body to pieces. It is this incident that triggered Wallace's fight with the English, and for which he was ultimately hung. It was not just the Sheriff who felt the wrath of Wallace and his compatriots. Sir Thomas de Grey of Helton; who had also been attacked by the band of men; was left for dead, stripped naked, lying between two burning houses. Sir Thomas survived this ordeal, and later imparted the details to his son, also Sir Thomas Grey, who recorded it all in "The Sacralonica of Sir Thomas Grey." This account states that Sir Thomas was kept alive through the cold night simply by his proximity to the burning houses. In the morning he was found by a William de Lundy; who rescued him from this state (*Sacralonica of Thomas Grey; The Dawn of the Constitution*).

SIR RICHARD DE LUNDY

Sir Richard is perhaps the most famous member of this family, due this his involvement with William Wallace and Scotland's fight for independence from Edward I of England. As read under the life of Sir William de Lundy, Wallace's campaign began in May 1297. Although his initial strikes, such as that made against Haselrig, were made within a group of outlaws, he was soon joined a few of the Scottish nobles, notably very shortly by Sir William Douglas, Lord of Douglas-dale. Upon Wallace's arrival in the west of Scotland, subsequent to his actions at Scone, he was joined by further members of the nobility such as the Stewart of Scotland and his brother, Sir Andrew Moray of Bothwell, Alexander de Lindsay, Wishart Bishop of Glasgow, and Sir Richard de Lundy (*Caledonia*). Sir Richard appears regularly in the account of Wallace given by Henry the Bard, or Blind Harry. It is hard to know how much of the details of this account are hard facts, and the truth is bent and merged in a number of places, but Sir Richards overall presence and involvement in the struggle is clear. He is credited by bringing to the aid of Wallace, during an encounter between him and Macfadzan, near Craigmore in Perth, 500 men. He and Sir John de Graham are also said to have fought a party of English together near Bothwell (*Metrical History of Wallace*, III., 42). He is said to have travelled with Wallace up until the treaty of Irvine. After Irvine, Sir Richard was so disgusted with the general attitude of the Scots nobility that he went over to the English side (not long after his departure other nobles such as Bruce and Stewart also left the Wallace camp to avoid forfeiture of lands). Come September 1297, and the Battle of Stirling Bridge, he was one of the leaders of the English army. He advised Sir Hugh Cressingham, Edward I's appointed Lord Treasurer of Scotland, that to cross Stirling Bridge itself would result in certain loss. He has been attributed with the following speech.

"My Lords if we go on to the bridge we are dead men; for we cannot cross it except two by two, and if the enemy are on our flank, and can come down on us as they will, all in one front. But there is a ford not far from here, where we can cross sixty at a time. Let me therefore have five hundred Knights and a small body of infantry, and we will get round the enemy on the rear and crush them"

(*Tales of a Grandfather*, Scott; *The Chronicle of Walter of Guisborough*).

Cressingham ignored the advice of the skilful soldier Sir Richard, and the battle was lost. After this Sir Richard is again thought to have fought with Wallace and is believed to have become a good friend. Sir Richard is listed as one of the Nobles of Scotland who appointed Sir William Wallace to the position of Governor of the Kingdom (*Life and Adventures of Sir William Wallace*). The sword of Sir Richard de Lundin, laird of Lundin, friend of Wallace, was taken to the ceremony of laying the foundation stone for the Wallace Monument (*Glasgow Herald*, 25/6/1861). Together with the swords of Sir William Wallace, King Robert the Bruce, John de Graham and the Black Douglas, it was displayed at the summit of Abbey Craig. This sword is now at Drummond Castle. The following extract comes from the Illustrated London News of the 6th of July 1881. A copy of the engraving of the five 'Swords of Scottish Heros' is shown after the extract. Note that the numbers and figure references in the extract refer to the picture of the swords that follows.

"On Monday week – the anniversary of the Battle of Bannockburn – the Duke of Athole, Most Worshipful Grand Master Mason of Scotland, laid the foundation-stone of the monument to be erected in remembrance of Sir William Wallace, on the summit of Abbey Craig, near Stirling. Towards the raising of this monument subscriptions have been sought and obtained in almost every quarter of the globe, and now, at the close of a five years' agitation, the fund amounts, after deducting expenses, to about £5500. The cost of the monument is an estimated £7000. There is thus a deficiency of £1500. The occasion of the laying of the foundation-stone brought together representatives of all parts of Scotland, and the ceremony was altogether of a most imposing character. The features in the procession, perhaps, which attracted the greatest curiosity were the various national relics. The first and the greatest of this was the "two-handed sword of Wallace," which was carried before the magistrates and Town Council of Dumbarton by the Master Gunner of Dumbarton Castle. Besides the sword of Wallace were "the sword of King Robert the Bruce," granted by the Earl of Elgin; "the sword of Sir John de Graeme," copatriot of Wallace, who fell at the battle of Falkirk; "the sword of Sir Richard Lundin," another friend of Wallace granted by Lady Willoughby de Eresby; and "the sword of the Black Douglas."

The day's proceedings were brought to a close with a grand banquet, at which Sir A. Alison presided. . . . .

DESCRIPTION OF THE SWORDS OF SCOTTISH HEROES EXHIBITED DURING THE PROCESSION.

1. The first of these national relics was the sword of Sir William Wallace, granted to the magistrates of Stirling by H.R.H. the Duke of Cambridge, Commanding-in-Chief, with the consent

of the Secretary of State for War. This interesting relic of ancient times has been retained in Dumbarton Castle since Wallace was sent to London to be executed. In 1505 James IV., when on a visit to the castle, according to the books of the Lord Treasurer, expended a sum of money in beautifying the sword called "Walis's Sword," and in procuring a new scabbard with accompanying belts. It is a two-handed weapon, measuring from point to point five feet and seven inches, and weighing 6lb. 7oz., forming indeed a "terrible thing" in such a hand as his. The handle is covered with blue velvet.

2. The sword of King Robert the Bruce, kindly sent by the Earl of Elgin and Kincardine, is an instrument which seems to have seen much service. It is also a two-handed weapon, and measures somewhere about five feet two or three inches. The noble Bruce seems not to have trusted much to the guard of his sword if we may compare it with that of fig.5, or even with that of Wallace.

3. This is a single-handed, double-edged sword of Wallace's copatriot and sincere friend, Sir John de Graeme, from the keeping of his Grace the Duke of Montrose. It is scarcely three feet and a half in length, but undoubtedly did many deeds of valour. Towards the hilt, and amongst the ornamentation of the blade, are inscribed the year 1406 and the initials S.F.G. Graeme was killed at the battle of Falkirk, to commemorate whose death Wallace himself erected a stone in the neighbouring churchyard:-

Sir John ye Grame verry vicht and wyse,
One of the Chiefes relievit Scotland thryse;
Fought vith ys Svord, and ner thout schame,
Commandit nane to Beir ir Bot his name

4. The Sword of the Laird of Lundin – also a friend of our hero – is supposed to have been used at the battle of Stirling, and, being two handed, is much the same length as that of Bruce. It is in the possession of Lady Willoughby d'Eresby, who kindly lent it for the occasion. The head part of the handle, which is on the one side open, is intended to be filled with lead, according as required by the bearer. The handle is covered with leather tightly bound with thick cord.

5. The sword of the "Black Douglas" is a most formidable weapon. Unlike those of Bruce and Lundin, the guards are most elaborate, and show a considerable deal of art and beauty. Its length is about five feet seven or eight inches, and belongs to W. Campbell, Esq., of Tillichewan. The handle is fringed and otherwise ornamented. But the chief peculiarity is its slender appearance, and the notched, sawlike blade, which only terminates a few inches from the point."

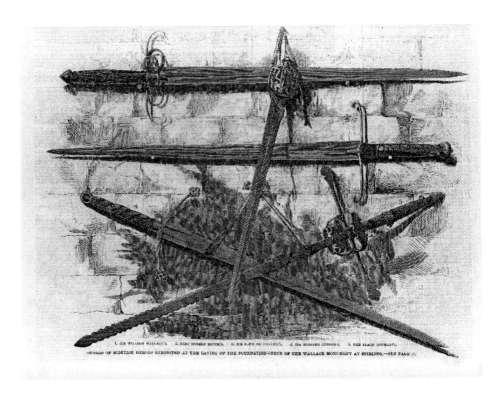

2 "The Swords of Scottish Heros," from the Illustrated London News of the 6th of July 1861. Showing the swords of (1) William Wallace: (2) King Robert The Bruce: (3) Sir John de Graeme: (4) Sir Richard de Lundin: (5) The Black Douglas.

It was mentioned previously that the exact details of the account of 'Blind Harry' must be taken with a pinch of salt. It is during his depictation of the battle of Stirling Bridge that Harry misses the fact that Sir Richard had at this time gone over to the English, and has him fighting side by side with Wallace, rather than opposing him.

> "The day of battle does approach at length,
> The English then advance with all their strength.
> And fifty thousand march in battle rank,
> Full six to one; yet Wallace never shrank.
> The rest they lay about the castle hill;
> Both field and castle thought to have at will.
> The worthy Scots together close did bide,
> In the plain field, upon the other side.
> Hugh Kirkingham (Cressingham), the vanguard on led he,
> With twenty thousand likely men to see;
> The Earl of Warren thirty thousand had;
> If all were good the number was not bad.
> Thus fifty thousand silly South'ron sots
> Proudly march up against nine thousand Scots.
> When Kirkingham his twenty thousand men
> Had past the bridge, quite to the other end,
> Some of the Scots in earnest, without scorn,
> Thought it high time to blow the warning horn;
> But Wallace he march'd stoutly through the plain,
> Led on his men, their number did disdain;
> Till Warren's host thick on the bridge did go,
> Then he from Jop did take the horn and blow:
> So loud and shrill, he warned good John Wright,
> Who soon struck out the roller with great slight.
> Then all went down, when the pin was got out;
> At which arose a fearful cry and shout.
> Both men and horse into the river fell,
> Honest John Wright did act his part so well.
> The hardy Scots with heavy strokes and sore,
> Attack the twenty thousand that came o'er.
> Wallace and Ramsay, **Lundie**, Boyd, and Graham,

With dreadful strokes made them retire - Fy, shame!
The South'rons front they fought all face to face,
Who to their ignominy and disgrace,
Did neither stand nor fairly foot the score,
But did retire five acre breadth and more.
Wallace on foot, with a great sharp sword goes,
Amongst the very thickest of his foes;
On Kirkingham there such a stroke he got,
In spite of all his armour and mailcoat,
That kill'd him dead; none durst him there rescue;
Then to that valiant captain bade adieu.
When Kirkingham dead on the spot to lie
The South'rons saw, then they began to fly:
Who, though they had fought it most bloody hot,
Ten thousand lost, and left dead on the spot;
The rest they fled, nor none durst stay behind;
Succour they sought, but none at all could they find.
Some east come west, and some fled to the north
Seven thousand flutter'd all at once in Forth,
Who from that river little mercy found;
For few escap'd, and most of all were drown'd.
On Wallace's side, no man was killed of note,
But Andrew Murray, a true hearted Scot.
When Warren's men saw all was lost and tint,
They fled as fast as fire does from a flint;
Ne'er look'd about, nor once a Scotsman fac'd,
But to Dunbar march'd in devilish haste."

Sir Richard is believed to have married Margaret de Dunbar, daughter of Patrick Dunbar, Earl of Dunbar and Marjorie Comyn, herself the daughter of Alexander Comyn, Earl of Buchan. He was succeeded by his son Walter, who married Euphemia Graham, daughter of Sir John de Graham (*East Neuk of Fife*).

SIR WALTER DE LUNDY

The son and successor of Sir Richard de Lundy; on 14th March 1295-6, Sir Walter de Lundy appears in a list of names of magnates and others who have performed homage to the King of England (*Calendar of Documents relating to Scotland*, II., 730). In 1305 Sir Walter de Lundy was a Juror at Perth, regarding a case concerning the rightful ownership of the barony of Crail (*Calendar of Documents relating to Scotland*, Bain, II. 1670)

> "May 31st 1305, Inquisition [under writ dated Westminster, 8th April previous] taken at the town of St John of Perthon the last day of May in the Kings 33rd Year before Sir John Earl of Athol, warden of Scotland beyond the forth, and Sir John de Sandale chamberlain of Scotland, and in the presence of Sirs.....Walter de Lundy knights."

It has been suggested in a few texts that the laird of Lundie fought at Bannockburn in 1314. Indeed, the book "Ancient Scottish Weapons," by James Drummond features a picture of the Sword of Lundin of that Ilk with the caption 'as used at the battle of Bannockburn.' However, unlike with Sir Richard and Stirling Bridge, I cannot as yet find a reference from around that time, to show a Lundie at Bannockburn. Some of the texts showing a Lundie at Bannockburn, ultimately reference the section of *The Chronicle of Walter of Guisborough*, that actually shows the speech of Sir Richard at Stirling.

The freedom of Scotland obtained at the aforementioned Bannockburn was short lived. Robert the Bruce died in 1329, and his heir was only four years old. Edward Baliol, son of King John Baliol, perceived this a good point to renew his family's claim to the throne. In early August 1332, he landed in Fife with strong English support. The Earl of Fife marched to oppose him, but was defeated. On the 12th of August 1332, Baliol defeated the Earl of Mar, Regent of the kingdom, at the Battle of Dupplin, and a day later he was in possession of Perth. After the battle of Dupplin, the Scots nobles seem to have capitulated for a while. The Earl of Fife, who six days prior to this battle had opposed Baliol and the English, marched to meet the new King and pledge allegiance, along with thirteen knights from Fife and Perth. One of these knights was Sir Walter de Lundie (*Chronicle of Lanercost; Medieval Scotland*).

Baliol, was crowned at Scone on the 24th of September, and began to form alliances with England, and submit to Edward III of England's power. He soon signed a treaty surrendering the independence of Scotland, and gave over Berwick to England. This treachery enacted the nobles to move. On the 25th of December, Archibald Douglas, later Earl of Douglas, the Earl of Murray, and 1000 horse, attacked Baliol at his castle in Annan. Edward Baliol escaped, but his brother Henry was killed. As a result, King Edward III resolved to invade Scotland.

The armies of England and Scotland met on the 19th of July 1333, at the Battle of Halidon Hill. The Scots army held five main bodies, the vanguard, commanded by Lord John Murray, and four divisions. Lord Archibald Douglas, who was also the commander in chief of the Scottish army, commanded the fourth body. His division featured the Earl of Lennox, the Earl of Carrick, John Campbell son of Lochow; Robert Sternlaw; William Vipont; Robert Lawder; John Lindsay; Alexander Graham; David Weems; Michael Scott; Thomas Bois; Roger Mortimer; William Umphraville; Thomas Vans; William Lundie; with 30 bachelors, 900 men at arms, and 10,000 commoners. Edward of England came to the field with many of his archers. This gave the English a huge advantage, and the Scots were totally routed. Around 15,000 persons, died on the field (*Family of Fraser*, 49).

The relationship between Sir Walter de Lundy, and William who fought at Halidon is not known. William Lundie at Halidon, is clearly distinguished as a noble and a man of rank. He may well be the son or brother of Sir Walter; or even Walter himself, with the name mistaken or corrupted with time.

Around this time (During the reign of David II., 1329-1371), the charter rolls of King David II show that the King granted the lands of Sheks, in the constabulary of Lithgow, Sheriffdom of Edinburgh, to Christian Lundy and her sister; that the lands of an Alice Lundie and Edward Lettam, had been granted by King David II to a Christian Anderson as a result of the lands being forfeit; and that the lands of Lethbertsheills, in the Sheriffdom of Stirling, which had been forfeit by a William Lundie, were granted by King David II to and Ade Argente (*Ind. Rec. Chart. 1309-1413*, 60, 61, 67).

SIR WILLIAM LUNDY OF THAT ILK

On the 31st of January 1360, William of Lundy is a witness to an inspection of a charter of John Campbell, Earl of Athol, to Roger Mortimer, of the lands of Ballandro in the sheriffdom of the Mearns; part of Peatie in the same; and a third of the demesne of Inverbervie in Forfar, (*Regestra Regnum Scottorum*, VI. 261). According to Johnston in his "A Short Memoir of James Young," a Sir William Lundy of that ilk died in either the battle of Otterburn (19th August, 1388), or Chevy Chase. His son, Sir John Lundy of that Ilk, who was alive in 1411, ultimately succeeded him.

At the aforementioned battle of Otterburn, was also a Richard Lundie, who was chaplain to Earl William Douglas. Popular history states that he was later to become Archdeacon of Aberdeen (*Minstrelsy of the Scottish Border*); and is also described by Scott in his *Tales of a grandfather*, as being 'of North Berwick.' Amongst many events, this battle is famous for the death of Earl Douglas. Richard Lundie is said to have fought by the Earl's side throughout the battle. When Douglas fell on the field, Richard, and Robert Harte, both who are believed to have been tutors to the Earl when younger, are said to have supported his dying body, with a makeshift stretcher of crossed pikes and a cloak (*Letters to Tatler and Spectator*, I., 278). When Sir James Lindsay arrived on the scene to find the Earl bleeding to death, he also found Richard Lundie bestriding the Earls body, protecting him from further injury with a battle-axe (*Great Historic Families of Scotland*).

The chaplain is most probably Richard Lundie, a monk of the Abbey of Melrose, who on the 26th of November 1435 was appointed to the position of Prior of the Abbey of Pluscarden in Moray. He was later, 5th of April 1440, appointed to the position of the Abbot of the Abbey of Melrose, an office which he held until the 4th of march 1444 (*Head Relig. Hous. Scot.*, p151, 179). He appears in the charters of the Abbey designed as Abbot and later 'Monachus' (*Liber. Melros.*, II. 504, 552). The attachment to religious houses in the Borders and North of Scotland may well explain the Aberdeen and Berwick commonplace connections.

Other than Sir John Lundy, nothing concrete is known about any other children of Sir William. From documents of the time, one can however hypothesis.

1   *Sir William de Lundy.* Sometime towards the end of the reign of King Robert III of Scotland (1390-1405), 'Willielmus de Lundin,

milites,' is a witness to a charter by Sir William Scot of Balweary to John Melville of Raith, of the lands of Pitscottie in Fife (*Douglas's Peerage*, p 470). On the 4th of August 1406, The Abbot and Convent of Cambuskenneth granted a charter in favour of William de Lundin of the lease of the lands of Balcormak in the barony of Lundin from the Abbey of Cambuskenneth. These lands had originally been granted to the abbey back in 1198, by Walter de Lundin, son of Phillip de Lundin (*NAS*, RH1/2/18/3). According to Sir James Balfour of Denmylne, a Sir William de Lundy was alive in 1408.

2   *Sir John Lundy*, of whom next.

3   *Thomas de Lundy*. On the 5th of October 1443 Thomas de Lundie was elected as almoner (abbot) of the Abbey of Newbattle. He held this post until the 20th of March 1458, and died before the 17th of October 1461 (*Head Relig. Hous. Scot.*, p 162). He is probably the same Thomas de Lundy who was Sheriff of Fife around 1450 (*East Neuk of Fife*).

Just to cloud the waters a bit more, it should be noted that on December 10th, 1395-6, there is a Crown charter of confirmation of a grant by Walter of Lundyn to Gilbert Grantseruyse of the lands of Stradherling. This however does not give the date of the grant by Walter, which could be much earlier (*NAS*, GD20/1/322).

Whether the relationship is as given, one cannot be sure, but the connection between these five Lundies must have been close.

SIR JOHN LUNDY OF THAT ILK

He succeeded his father, William de Lundy, by 1411. In 1428, John Lundy of that ilk received payment from the Customs of Cupar (*Exchequer rolls of Scotland*). Not much else is recorded of his life. He married Isobel Wemyss, relict of Sir Walter Ramsey of Pitcruvie. In 1496 Janet daughter and heiress of Walter Ramsey of Pitcruvie, spouse to David Lindsay 2nd Lord Lindsay of the Byres granted a charter to Thomas Fergusson chaplain of the parish of Largo and his successors of an annual rent of 5 merks of the lands of Scheithum and others for masses for the souls of Sir John Ramsey of Petcruvie, her grandfather, Walter Ramsey of Petcruvie, her father, Lady Elizabeth Wemyss, her mother, John Lundy of that Ilk, Andrew Lundy of

Pitlochy, her brothers, Sir John Lundy, now of that Ilk, and Robert Lundy of Balgony (*Scots Peerage*, V. 395).

He had issue:-

1　***Sir John Lundy of that Ilk***, who succeeded, and whose details follow.

2　***Andrew Lundy of Pitlochy.*** In 1452, 1455, 1456, 1468, 1471 the exchequer rolls of Scotland record him as Sheriff of Fife, (also *NAS*, GD430/169, GD45/28/33). Noting that Thomas de Lundy is said to have also been Sheriff of Fife around 1450 (*East Neuk of Fife*). The rolls also give us the information that in 1441, he received a payment from the state; in 1448, he received a remission of customs; in 1452 he was given shafts for making lances from; in 1454, he was given ward of Balgony; in 1455, the state purchased horses from him; in the same year he received a fee as part of the fines of chamberlain Ayre; in 1458, 1459 and 1460, he received annuity of the heirs of John Sibbald; and also in 1460 he was allowed the fermes of Petlochy (Pitlochy) from where he is styled. Pitlochy and the lands of Bannaty, both within the Parish of Strathmiglo, Fife, became hereditary within the family of Lundie of Balgonie. In later years the Lundies built a tower at Pitlochy. Andrew had at least one son:

i　*Robert Lundie of Balgonie (see Lundie of Balgonie).*

3　***Margaret***, married George Leslie 1st Earl of Rothes around 1435 (*Scots Peerage*, VII. 275). They had one child.

i　*Margaret.* She was contracted to marry William Leslie, son and heir apparent of Alexander Leslie of that Ilk around the 10th of July 1458. She was by 1488 married to Alexander Cumming of Earnside.

SIR JOHN LUNDY OF THAT ILK

As with many periods of Scottish history, Sir John's lairdship occurred at time of great political strife, with the bloody transition between the reigns of James III of Scotland and his son James IV of Scotland, in 1488. Sir John appears to have been well trusted by both monarchs and ruling parties, and the high offices he held prior to the murder of James III, do not seem to have been effected by the incoming of a new regime. Sir John appears to be a man of great influence and importance. He acted as ambassador for the King; was a governor of Stirling and Edinburgh castles; was keeper of Falkland Palace; chamberlain of Fife; sat in Parliament; and acquired many lands to add to his estate.

During the reign of James III (1460 – 1488)

King James III came to the throne upon the death of his father at the siege of Roxburgh castle in August 1460. At the time James was a minor. His government was thus the subject of the influence of his tutors and curators. He was first 'advised' by Bishop Kennedy, under whose guidance, the kingdom seems to have prospered. After the Bishop's death in 1466, King James came under the influence of the Boyd family who acquired the King's person on a riding trip out from his court at Linlithgow. This family, although initially receiving great honours from the King, were later to be tried for this action with Thomas Boyd, the Earl of Arran, and Sir Alexander Boyd, the brother of Lord Boyd being executed. Thus in charge of his own affairs, the King became suspicious of his two younger brothers, the Dukes of Albany and Mar. In 1479 he had his youngest brother, the Earl of Mar murdered, and would have put the Duke of Albany to the same fate, had he not then escaped the country. During this time, wars with the English were escalating, and in 1482, Edward IV of England planned an invasion of Scotland to recover the town of Berwick, and in this venture hoped to procure the assistance of the Duke of Albany who was then in France. The Scots forces marched to Lauder under King James III in order to combat this force, but when there, many of the Scots nobles held a secret meeting concerning the mis-government of Scotland and the mal-influence of King James's advisors. These advisors were killed, and King James taken prisoner. The English thus took possession of Berwick, and looked to ensue further into Scotland, but this was prevented by the movement of the Scottish forces from Lauder to Haddington. The Duke of Albany, mediated peace between the Scots and the English, and then between the Scots Nobility and the King, and was awarded custody of the King by those then holding his person.

A short period of peace between the English and Scottish Kingdoms ensued. As a consequence, in 1484, as part of a truce declared between England and Scotland, signed on the 21st of September that year, Sir John Lundy was named as one of the conservators of this peace (*Calendar of Documents relating to Scotland*, Bain, IV. 1505).

"Indenture between the Scottish ambassadors and the English commissioners, for a truce between the Kingdoms till 29th September 1487, the same not to include the Lordship of Lorne in Scotland nor the Island of Lundy in England; and the castle of Dunbar, then in the King of England's Hands, to be included in the truce for 6 months and thereafter till its conclusion unless the King of Scots within three weeks from its commencement shall intimate in writing to the King of England that he desires the protection of the castle to end within the 6 months. The conservators for Scotland to be David Earl of Crawford, Lord Lindsay, George Earl of Huntly, Lord Gordon and Badyenach, John Lord Dernley, John Lord Kennydy, Robert Lord Lile, Patrick Lord Halis, Laurence Lord Oliphant, William Lord Borthwick, Sirs John Ross of Halkhead, John Lundy of that Ilk, James Ogilvy of Airly......"

Around this time, King James III granted to Sir John the office of curator of James Barclay of Kippo. Sir John was later confirmed in this office by James IV, but renounced it in 1491, in favour of Andrew Murray, brother german of Sir William Murray of Tulibardine. It should be noted that the resignation was witnesses by among others an Andrew Lundy (*Protocol Book of J. Young*, 420).

During the later part of King James's reign, he built a great hall and royal chapel, in his castle of Stirling. In 1487, the exchequer rolls of Scotland record payment made to Sir John Lundy of that Ilk, for his position as governor of Stirling Castle. They also show he was governor of Edinburgh as well. These new buildings were in some way to provide the trigger for the end of King James's reign. To pay for these buildings, he annexed revenue from the Priory of Coldingham, in Berwickshire. This greatly angered the Homes and Hepburns, and they, along with many of the Nobels involved in killing the King's advisors at Lauder, rebelled against the King. There is no-evidence to show Sir John Lundy's involvement on either side, but as he was governor in 1487, was replaced by James Shaw of Fintrie before the battle of Sauchiburn, and then re-appointed as governor of Stirling after the said battle (*The History of Stirlingshire*), one must presume that he was involved with the party of James IV. His eldest son's alliance with the Hepburns would also go someway to suggest this.

During the reign of James IV (1488 – 1513)

The battle of Sauchieburn was on the 18th of June 1488. King James III was murdered off the battlefield, and his infant son, James IV. became King in his place. As stated above, Sir John was re-appointed governor of Stirling castle shortly after the battle of Sauchieburn. Sir John was still keeper of Stirling Castle in 1496, with records showing that Sir John and Lady Lundy (Elizabeth Forester) , keepers of Stirling castle had under their charge Margaret Drummond, daughter of Sir William, Master of Drummond, in 1496 (*Scot's Peerage*, VII., 44). In 1488 he sat in parliament (*General index to the acts of parliament of Scotland*); and the following year he was pardoned by parliament for his part in burning the town of Dunbertane (BLACK, *Surnames of Scotland; General index to the acts of parliament of Scotland*). As well as keeper of Stirling castle, the exchequer rolls of Scotland also show Sir John as keeper of Falkland Palace sometime between 1497 and 1507, and Chamberlain of Fife around the same time. They indicate that between 1488 and 1496 he was let the lands of Clachy and Thomastoun, which he proceeded to occupy sometime before 1501. Around this same time he also received the fermes of Roplouch and Aldpark.

In 1495 Sir John was sent to England by King James IV of Scotland to the court of King Henry VII of England (*Calendar of Documents relating to Scotland*, Bain, IV. 1612).

> "Safe conduct for six months for Andrew Bishop of Glasgow, John Lord of Drommond, Sir William of Knollis knight, Sir William of Murray of Tullybarne knight, Sir John of Lowndye knight, and master Richard Lawson, clerk, ambassadors of James King of Scots to England with 100 horsemen"

In 1507 Sir John was given Royal permission to undertake a pilgrimage along with the Earl of Arran, to the shrine of St. John of Amiens. For the duration of this trip, the King took Sir John's lands and bairns into his care (*East Neuk of Fife*, p 47).

Sir John is believed to have died around 1516. In this year, 6th June, there is a great seal charter, confirming a charter of mortmain, dated 12th November, 1510, by John Lundy of that Ilk, to the parish church of Largo, of the temple lands of Balcormo (*NAS*, GD160/293). The rent was to provide for a "chaplain to the altar in the new aisle contiguous to the parish church of Largo; for which he also mortified the templar lands of Balcormo, and the mansion thereof, with 6 roods of land lying on the south side of the parish church at the west, whereon was built a manse for the chaplain," (East Neuk of Fife, p 47). The Aisle mentioned here is most likely what is termed the 'Lundy Aisle,' and appears to have been the burial place of members of this family (*Lamont's Diary* p 140).

Land Deals
Benholm

The Barony of Benholm had come into the Lundie family through the marriage of Christian, daughter and heiress of Hugo de Benne, to Walter de Lundin, son of Phillip, the 1st Laird of Lundin. In 1469, William Lundy, son of Sir John, and his spouse Elizabeth Hepburn were given a crown charter of the Barony of Benholm. However, for unknown reasons, the situation changed, and on the 4th of January 1485 – 6, Sir John Lundy of that Ilk, knight, and Isabel Forester, his spouse, and the heirs male of their marriage, were granted a Charter by King James III, of the Barony of Benholm and Mains thereof, upon Sir John's resignation. This grant also included the lands of Tulloch, the Casteltoun, Carnenach, Mutehill and the Brewland, upon the resignation of William Lundy, son of Sir John by a previous marriage, and William's spouse. (*Reg. Mag. Sig.* II., 1631; *NAS*, GD4/8). Sir John was later to grant a Charter of the Barony of Benholm to his son by his spouse Isabel Forester, Robert Lundie, and more can be read on this subject in the chapter, '*Lundie of Benholm*.'

Drumden in Leslie.

In 1455, at the castle of Leslie, he resigned the lands of Drumden, in the Barony of Leslie, into the hands of George, Lord Leslie. He was asked at the time by Alexander Lumsden, rector of flisk, if he made this resignation willingly, notwithstanding that he was within the castle of Leslie at the time of its execution, Sir John is said to have replied that he came freely, and that it was not through force, fear, or being misguided, that he made the resignation (*East Neuk of Fife*, p 46)

Inchmeddan

The Lundy family at this time were superiors of the lands of Inchmeddan, which was held of the Lundies by the family of Inchmeddan of that Ilk. On 13ᵗʰ October, 1464, John of Inchmeddan of that Ilk agreed to resign half his lands of Inchmeddan, into the hands of John Lundy; note this could have been Sir John Lundy's father (*NAS*, GD4/46). On the 20ᵗʰ April 1483, Margaret Inchmeddan "lady portioner of that Ilk, in her pure virginity and in hope of a great tocher promised her towards her marriage", resigned her right to the third part of the half of the lands of Inchmeddan into the hands of her Superior, John Lundy of that Ilk, knight. The lands in question had fallen to her by the decease of John Inchmeddan her brother (*NAS*, GD4/48). On the 17ᵗʰ of December 1490, the resignation of half of the lands of Inchmeddan, which John Inchmeddan of that Ilk had previously agreed to resign into Sir John Lundy's hands, were registered as thus (*NAS*, GD4/51), and on this same day, Sir John Lundy, then granted these lands to his 'carnal' son, Robert Lundie (*NAS*, GD4/52). One wonders whether this illegitimate son, was not by a daughter of the family Inchmeddan of that Ilk. Seven years later, on the 1ˢᵗ July, 1497, Margaret Inchmeddan, now spouse of Duncan Stratton, resigned her sixth part of the lands of Inchmeddan into the hands of John Lundy of that Ilk knight; and appointed her husband her procurator to receive, from Sir John, 40 merks Scots in consideration of the said resignation (*NAS*, GD4/55).

Fossoway (Fossowquhy)

The lands of Fossoway were held by Robert Douglas of Lochleven. These lands were wadset to Sir John around 1490, redeemable for an unknown fee. On 21ˢᵗ December 1490, a precept was granted by Robert Douglas of Lochleven, charging Michael Balfour of Burle, George Dischington of Colennoquhy, Andrew Ayton, Florentine Auchmulty and Henry Thomson; his bailies in that part; to give sasine to Sir John Lundy of that Ilk and Isobel Forstar, his spouse, of the lands of Thornton of Fossowquhy (Fossoway), extending to eight pound lands, and a quarter of the lands of Kyrkton, in the barony of Errol and sheriffdom of Perth; following on a charter of the same date (*NAS*, GD1/87/1). These lands later passed to Sir John's son and heir William Lundy, and more can be read upon these transactions under his name

Sythrum (Schethum)

On the 3ʳᵈ October 1496, an instrument of Sasine was granted in favour of John Lundy of that Ilk, kt., of an annual rent of 5 merks from lands of Schethum (Sythrum), following on resignation of Patrick Lyndesay of Kyrkforthir. This was witnessed by John Dischintoune, son and apparent heir of John Dischintone of Ardros; Andrew Lundy, Sir Thomas Fergussone and Sir George Ferny, chaplains; and John Reyde (*NAS*, GD26/3/47). The relationship between Andrew Lundy, chaplain, and Sir John is not known.

Cullennochtis

On 2ⁿᵈ August, 1512, a great seal charter grants Sir John an annual rent of 12 merks, of the lands of the Nethirtoun of Cullennochtis pertaining to George Dischingtoun, lord of fee of lands and barony of Ardross, in sheriffdom of Kinross (*NAS*, GD160/281).

Family

From the descriptions in these charters it is clear that Sir John had at least two wives. His first wife is probably Elizabeth Lindsay, daughter of Sir John Lindsay 1ˢᵗ Lord of the Byres, to whom he was contracted to marry on the 21ˢᵗ of January 1434-5 (*NAS*, GD160/291). Elizabeth is believed the eldest of Lord Lindsay's children, but young when the contract was entered into (*Scots peerage*, V. 394). His second wife was Isabel Forrester, Sir John and Isabel being married by 1486. She was possibly related to Malcolm Forester of Torwood (*Protocol Book of J. Young*, 73). Sir James Balfour suggests that one Sir John Lundy of that Ilk (the generations being slightly merged in his account) around this time was married to Catherine Drummond, the daughter of John Drummond; so this could well be another wife (*East Neuk of Fife*, p 46). He had issue by at least two wives:-

Children by his first wife:

1   **Sir William Lundy of that Ilk**, who succeeded, and whose details follow.

2   **John Lundy**. On 25ᵗʰ October, 1495, John Lundy, the legitimate son of Sir John Lundy of that Ilk, resigned all claim that he might have to any moveable goods by the decease of his mother or of Mr. George

Lundy his brother-german. He is recorded as having sworn upon the Gospels that he would not to trouble his father or his father's then wife, and their children, in judgement or otherwise; and would desist from "sornyng of pure folk," especially in the parish of Largo. He also swore not to remain in Largo beyond one night or two at most, unless he was dwelling honestly with a master who has his residence there. He declared that he had made no assignation of his said rights, or if he had, at that moment revoked it; and in the event of his contravening the above, renounces the pension of 10 merks which his father had promised him in consideration thereof, (*NAS,* GD4/16). It is not clear what the circumstances behind this interesting occurrence were.

3   George Lundy

Children by Elizabeth Forrester:

1   Robert Lundie of Benholm, See Lundie of Benholm.

Legitimate children, by mother not determined:

1   Thomas Lundy. Thomas was Prebendary or Forlavin and Abirnethy (*Reg. Great Seal.* II. 3387; III. 78).

2   James Lundy. The accounts of the Lord High Treasurer of Scotland shows payment to James Lundy, son of the Laird of Lundy, for going to France, on the 22nd February, 1506, by the King's command. For this he received 20 French crowns. He is most probably the 'Captain Lundy' who features around the same time, in the same source, who rode to Rouen to buy streamers for the King's ships, and brought a Papingo for the King.

3   Andrew Lundy of Stratherlie, see *Lundie of Stratherlie.*

4   Christian Lundy, married John 6th Lord Forbes. On the 26th February 1509 they received a charter of the Barony of Fudes (*Reg. Mag. Sig.*). She died before 1513. They had issue (*Scots Peerage,* IV. 53) :-

i John Master of Forbes, executed at Edinburgh, in July, 1537, on an accusation of high treason, for and alleged desire to shoot King James V., as his Majesty passed through the town of Aberdeen.

ii William 7th Lord Forbes

iii Margaret, married Andrew Fraser of Muchalls.

iv Marjory, married Alexander Forbes of Brux

v Elizabeth, married first, Gilbert Keith of Troup; secondly Alexander Innes of Innes.

5 Isobel Lundy, married George Moncreiff of Tibbermella (*Reg. Sec. Sig.* I., 1229, 2623).

6 Janet Lundy, married John Allardice of Allardice. He succeeded his father in 1511, marrying Janet before then. In 1512, on the 21st of August, they had a crown charter in favour of themselves and heirs male, of the lands of Leys and the eastern half of the lands of Little Barras, in the Barony of Allardice. These lands were to be held in a free barony following on the resignation of John Allardice. (*NAS*, GD49/20). He died in 1523. Janet was still alive around 1540. On the 30th of March that year, an instrument of sasine in favour of John Allardice of Auchterless, son and heir of deceased John Allardice of that Ilk, of the lands and barony of Allirdes, included a reservation of a liferent to Janet Lundy (*NAS*, GD49/31). They had issue:-

i John, who succeeded. After his father's death Royal letters of tutory were given, 19th October, 1523, to Richard Lundy, burgess of Edinburgh, and Robert Allardice in Petty as tutors dative of John Allerdes, son and heir of deceased John Allerdes of that Ilk (*NAS*, 49/27).

ii James, who was killed at the battle of Pinkie 10th September 1547.

iii Janet

After the death of John Allardice, Janet married secondly to William Forbes of Ardmurdo (*Reg. Mag. Sig.* IV. 1308).

7 Elizabeth Lundy, married Sir Andrew Wood after 1483 and no later than 1487. Sir Andrew was Admiral to James II and James III. He became Baron of Largo.

8 Euphemia Lundy, married David Wemyss of Wemyss before 11th

May 1493. Note that the Scot's Peerage gives Euphemia as a daughter of John Lundy of that Ilk (VIII., 487); whereas, G.T. Welsh, in his *Lundins of Fife*, claims she is the daughter of Sir Thomas Lundin of Pratis. She died before 1508, he was killed at the Battle of Flodden, 9th September 1513. They had issue:-

i   *David Wemyss of Wemyss,* succeeded his father on the 9th of September 1513. He married twice; first to Katherine Sinclair, daughter of Henry Third Lord Sinclair; second to Mariota, daughter of Sir John Towers of Inverleith. He had issue:

a   *John Wemyss of Wemyss,* who succeeded

b   *James Wemyss of Caskieberran.*

c   *Captain David Wemyss.* He was a son of his father's second marriage. He was thrice married. His second wife, sometime around 1577, was Janet Beaton, the widow of James Lundie of Conland. She died on the 22nd of January 1578-79 (*Edin. Tests.*). His son James, who was married to a Helen Lundy, succeeded him (*Scots Peerage*, VIII. 489).

ii   *James Wemyss of Newton and Cameronmill*

iii   *Robert of Easter Lathrisk*

iv   *Elizabeth*

Natural Children

1   ***Robert of Inchmeddan,*** a natural (carnal) son. On 17th December 1490, Sir John Lundy of that Ilk, granted to Robert Lundie, his carnal son, half the lands of Inchmeddan, following the resignation of these lands by John Inchmeddan of that Ilk (*NAS*,GD4/52); these lands had been resigned by John Inchmeddan into the hands of Sir John Lundy, on that same day (*NAS*, GD4/51).

SIR WILLIAM LUNDIE OF THAT ILK

Married to Elizabeth Hepburn, daughter of Sir Patrick Hepburn 1st Lord Hailes (*Scots Peerage*, II. 148) ; he held the office of Sheriff of Fife, and the position of bailie of a Priory in St. Andrews. The office of Sheriff of Fife was held by William in 1491 (*Surnames of Scot.*). This indirectly followed on from his kinsman, Andrew Lundie of Pitlochy, who was sheriff of Fife regularly from 1452 to 1471, and who was a son of Sir John Lundy, William's grandfather. The office of Sheriff of Fife was to be held two years later by Robert Lundie of Balgonie, a cousin of William. The University of St. Andrews Muniments collection holds several records related to William, from 1484 up to 1513. He appears in their records designed "William Lundie (Lundy) of that Ilk, bailie of the priory, son and apparent heir of Dom. John L. of that Ilk kt."

On the 4th of January 1485, his father resigned the lands and Barony of Lundy in favour of William (*NAS*, GD160/292, No.7). Around the same time Sir John also resigned the lands of Hatton in favour of William. On the 5th of May 1486, Sir William was given sasine of the lands of Hatton; and on the 8th of May 1486, William was given sasine of the lands and Barony of Lundy, and the lands of Wester Pitcaple (*NAS*, GD160/292, Nos. 8,9).

There are a couple of interesting letters written by James Duke of Ross (the second son of King James III), in the year 1498, concerning William Lundie of that Ilk: One of these letters concerns property in St. Andrew's; the other the marriage of one of William's daughters. In the first, dated the 6th of April, 1498, the Duke of Ross grants to William Lundy, 'our lovit familiar squier', son and apparent heir of John Lundy of that Ilk, kt., a land and tenement with yard and pertinents in the city of St Andrews, located on the north part of north gate. These lands are described as being between the lands of Abbey of Scone on east; William's own lands on the west and north parts; and a common street on the south. This property had been in the King's hands by the decease of Christian Kennedy, who died without lawful heirs. The second letter is dated two days after the first. In this letter, the Duke of Ross grants 'eftir lang commonyng' to William Lundy of that Ilk, his squire, the ward of lands of Rerass and barony of Luquhiris Wemys in sheriffdom of Fife, pertaining to granter by the king's gift, in his hands by decease of Arthur Forbes, laird thereof, with profits of marriage of Arthur Forbes, son and heir of said Arthur, to Isabel, daughter of said William Lundy (*NAS*, GD160/293).

Land deals

As with his father, the records of the time show many details of the financial transactions of William and his spouse.

Benholm

On the 19th of March 1469, William and his spouse received a Royal Charter of the lands and Barony of Benholm (*NAS*, GD160). On the 19th of March 1485-6, Sir John Lundy, William's father, resigned 40 merklands of the Barony of Benholm, in favour of William (*NAS*, GD160/292). However, after William received the Barony of Benholm, it seems as if his father had a change of heart, and the Barony was to pass to William's younger brother Robert (a half-brother). Accordingly, on the 18th of February, 1484-85, William and Elizabeth resigned the lands of Benham, Tullo, Casteltoun, Carnenow, Mithil and Brewland, in favour of William's father, Sir John Lundy of that Ilk, and Isabel Forrester, then Sir John's spouse, and the heirs of their marriage, (*NAS*, GD4/4). On 6th January the following year these lands were resigned into the hands of the King, before being granted to William's brother Robert. William and Elizabeth received in return the lands of Halton of Balcormok and Nethyr Prateris, in Fife, which had been resigned by Sir John and Isabel Forrester (*NAS*, GD4/6). On 1st December 1488, William received a Charter under the Great Seal of Scotland of the lands of Kincrag in Fife, again upon the resignation of his father (*NAS*, GD160/292).

Newtoun of Reras, Burneshous

Sometime between 1488 and 1496 William and Elizabeth were let the lands of Newtoun of Reras and Burneshous (*Exchequer Rolls of Scotland*). About 20 years later (*circa* 1513-1522) the lands of Newtoun of Reras are to be found let to Richard Lundy, probably a son or grandson of William.

Strathairlie

The lands of Strathairlie (Stratherlie, Stratharly, Stratherly) were part of the Barony of Lundie; and one third of these lands were held of the Lundie's by Lindsay of the Byres. In October, 1498 John, Lord Lindesay (Lindsay) of the Byres; resigned into the hands of William Lundy, baron of the barony thereof, in favour of Patrick Lindesay of Byris, his brother (and later 4th Lord of the Byres); a third of the lands of Strathairlie. The next year, 8th May, William gave sasine of these lands in favour of Patrick, 4th Lord Lindesay of Byres, (*NAS*, GD20/1/323-324). When it came to passing these lands from Patrick Lord Lindsay to his son John, they were again resigned into the hands of William Lundy. On 1st February 1518 Patrick Lord Lindsay resigned Strathairlie into the hands of William, in favour of his son Sir John, master of Lindsay, of Petcrowie (*NAS*, GD20/1/325). William resigned on 12th March of that year, giving precept of sasine to John, master of Lindsay (*NAS*, GD20/1/328). John, Master of Lindsay received sasine of one third of Stratherlie on the 9th May, 1526 (*NAS*, GD20/1/328). William

Melvill of Carnbee held another one third of the lands of Strathairlie; the templar lands of Stratharlie, also known as Sandy Hillock. Upon William Melvill's death these lands passed to his daughter Janet Melvill, who married Sir William Lundy's brother Andrew. Andrew was the progenitor of the family of Lundie of Strathairlie, and his descendants ended up holding all the lands of Strathairlie; two-thirds with Lundie of that Ilk as superior, and one third with Lindsay of the Byres as superior. Further details of Lundie of that Ilk's dealings with the lands of Strathairlie, can be read under *Lundie of Strathairlie,* in section four.

Fossoway

William had a number of dealings with regards the Lands of Fossoway which he had received from his father in part compensation for resigning the Barony of Benholm. Sir John held these lands in Wadset from Robert Douglas of Lochleven. Robert Douglas would later redeem these lands from William.

On the 21st of June, 1496, William, his wife Elizabeth, and their son and heir, Thomas, discharged all claims that they may have had to the lands of Innerpeffray in Perthshire, and the lands and Barony of Benholm, in favour of Sir John Lundy of that Ilk, his spouse Isabel, and their son Robert. In return for this, they received 800 merks Scots, which included the lands of Fossoway as part security (*NAS,* GD4/17). One quarter of the lands of Fossoway were then passed to William towards the end of that year. On the 10th November 1496, an instrument of sasine stated that Henry Bikkirton, as bailie for John Lundy of that Ilk and Isabel Fostare, his spouse, should give sasine to Thomas Strang, as procurator for William Lundy, son and heir of said John Lundy, and Elizabeth Hebburn, his spouse, of a quarter of Kirkton of Fossoquhy (Fossoway) and of Thorntoun of Fossoquhy (*NAS,* GD150/252); this was confirmed by a charter dated 20th December of the same year (*NAS,* GD150/253).

On the 27th of February, 1508-9, William had to take legal action against his father, Robert Douglas of Lochleven and John Huston for wrongful occupation of Fossoway (*NAS,* GD150/1037); the decree by the Lords of the Council was given on this matter on the 4th July 1509 (*NAS,* GD150/10). On the 19th of March 1508, William Lundy of that Ilk and Elizabeth Hepburn granted to Mr. Thomas Dickson, Provost of Guthre; a charter of five merklands of Thorntoun of Fossoquhy, extending to a third and a twelfth part of the lands of Thorntoun of Fossoquhy. This was witnessed by amongst others a Mr. William Lundy, (*NAS*, GD150/1038). On 15th September, 1508, William Lundy of that Ilk and Elizabeth Hepburne, his spouse, granted a charter to Mr. Thomas Dicsoune, provost of Guthre, of a quarter of Kyrktoune of Fossoquhy and two merklands of Thorntoune of Fossoquhy, (*NAS*, GD150/1034). The 26th of the same month and year William Lundy of that Ilk and Elizabeth Hepburne, his spouse, granted another charter to Mr. Thomas Dicsoune, provost of Guthray, of five merklands of Thorntoune of Fossoquhy, occupied by John Betoune of Balfour, in warrandice of a quarter of Kyrktoune of Fossoquhy and two merklands of Thorntoune (*NAS*, GD150/1036). On the 2nd of April 1509, it is recorded that Elizabeth Hepburn, spouse to William Lundy of that Ilk gave her consent to the alienation of a quarter of Kyrktoun of Fossoquhy, extending to three merklands, two merklands of Thorntoun of Fossoquhy, five merklands of Thorntoun of Fossoquhy and five merklands of the same in warrandice. This consent is recorded as given in William Lundy's tenement in St. Andrews (*NAS*, GD150/1039). On the 12th of November 1509, Sir John Lundy of that Ilk and Henry Ramsay, procurator for William Lundy and Elizabeth Hepburn, resigned and renounced a quarter of the lands of Kyrktoun of Fossoquhy and the lands of Thorntoun of Fossoquhy, following on redemption by Robert Douglas of Lochleven. This action was carried out at the tolbooth of the burgh of Cupar (*NAS*, GD150/1041).

William died before 1528, when he was succeeded by his grandson, Walter Lundy of Pratis.

He had issue:-

1   **Sir Thomas Lundy of Pratis**, of whom next.

2   **Margaret**, who married Sir George Forbes 3rd of Rires around 1500. Sir George was the second son of Sir William Forbes of Rires and an Elizabeth Lundie (*East Neuk of Fife*, p 115). Sir George and Margaret had issue:

   i   *Arthur Forbes*, 4th of Rires
   ii *James Forbes*, died without issue
   iii *William Forbes*

3   **Anne**, who married John Melville of Carnbee. He received a charter of this land dated 14th August 1496. They had issue:

i John Melville of Carnbee, who succeeded. In memory of his mother he added a part of the Arms of Lundin to those of his own (*Scots Baronage*, 528, i).

4 *Isabel*, married an Arthur Forbes. She may well be the same Isobel Lundy, daughter of Lundy of that Ilk, who married David Lindsay, 8th Earl of Crawford. She was his third wife, and on the 28th September 1541, she was infeft for life in the Barony of Inverarity and the "Great House" in Dundee (*Scots Peerage*, III. 27). Shortly after this date, she is recorded as owning the lands of Rathullot (*Exchequer Rolls of Scotland*, XVIII. 19, 21). On the 13th of May 1539, Earl David granted to Walter Lundie of that Ilk, Isabel's nephew, ten pounds from the lands of Crawford (*NAS*, GD160/2825, No. 9). Isabel had issue by Earl David:-

i *John Lindsay of Earlscairnie*. He was given a charter of the barony of Ochtermonsy and lands of Carny, Tor and "le Mure" by his father and mother on the 18 December 1525, this was confirmed the following year by James, Archbishop of St Andrews (NAS, GD20/1/99).

ii *Isobel*, who married John Lord Borthwick, by whom she had issue. He died in 1566. She then married George Preston of Cameron, brother-german to Sir Simon Preston of that Ilk.

David Lindsay, Earl of Crawford died on the 28th November 1542 at Cairnie Castle. By April 1543 Isobel had remarried to George Leslie 4th Earl of Rothes. She was the 4th Wife of this Earl. On 10th April 1543 they were infeft as husband and wife in the lands of Fynmouth (*Scots Peerage*, VII. 285). Isobel died before 1549, as George Leslie Earl of Rothes attempted a fifth marriage on 22nd February 1549. She had no issue with the Earl of Rothes.

SIR THOMAS LUNDY OF PRATIS

Sir Robert Douglas in his 'Baronage' describes him as "head or chief of that ancient family," but in fact he predeceased his father, so never was Laird. He was twice married. His first wife was Isabella Boswell, daughter of the Laird of Balmuto. In the contract dated 4th July 1488, John, prior of St Andrews, on first part, William Lundy of that Ilk, on second part, and David Boswell of Balmuto, on third part, arranged that Thomas Lundy, sister son of the said prior, and apparent heir of said William, was to marry Isobel, daughter of the said David. William Lundy of that Ilk was then bound to pay David Boswell 1000 merks Scots as security, (*NAS*, GD160/292). An initial payment of 200 merks was made on the 6th July, 1488 (*NAS*, GD66/1/15). Sir Thomas' second wife was Christian Sutherland, daughter and heiress of Alexander Sutherland of Duffus, and relict of William Oliphant, son of 1st Lord Oliphant. This marriage took place sometime after 1508. With respect to this marriage Thomas is described as the grandson and heir apparent of Sir John Lundin of Lundin (*Scot's Peerage*, VI. 541).

On the 8th November, 1505, George, abbot of Arbroath, and the convent of Arbroath, granted to Sir Thomas of Lundyn, son and apparent heir of William of Lundyn of that Ilk, ward and nonentries of passage and ferry boat of Montrose. This was in the hands of the abbot and convent through the decease of William Bonar, cessioner of Saint Andrews. It was granted to Thomas until a rightful heir of William Bonar entered into this estate (*NAS*, GD160/280).

On the 28th of June 1508, William Lundy, fiar of that Ilk, signed an agreement whereby he would keep his heritage lands and annualrents undispersed and unsold, in favour of Thomas Lundy, his son and apparent heir, excepting a house in St Andrews to be given to William's spouse (*NAS*, GD160/280).

From 1504 to 1513 Thomas received an annuity as tenant of Thomastoun; Thomastoun, as may be recalled, being originally let by the crown to Sir John Lundy, Thomas's grandfather. Thomas died shortly after this date, and by 1522, Thomastoun was let to Walter Lundy of Pratis, Thomas's son and heir. Sir Thomas had issue:

1   ***Walter Lundy of Pratis later of that Ilk***, who succeeded his grandfather to Lundy, and whose details follow.

2   ***David Lundy of Breriehill***, brother-german to Walter. He married after 1525, Elizabeth Lundie, daughter of Sir Robert Lundie Lord High Treasurer of Scotland, relict of Sir John Lindsay of Pitcruvie, Master of Lindsay (*Scots Peerage*, V. 397). He later married Helen Stewart, daughter and Heiress of Adam Stewart of Breriehill. For further details see *Lundie of Breriehill*.

3   ***Richard Lundy, burgess of Edinburgh*** (probable son or brother of Sir Thomas). Sometime between 1513 and 1522, Richard was let

the lands of Newtoun of Reras and Burnshous, lands that had been let to Sir William Lundy of that Ilk around 1490 (*Exchequer Rolls of Scotland*). On the 19th of October 1523, following the death of John Allerdice of that Ilk, Royal letters of tutory were given to Richard Lundy, burgess of Edinburgh, and Robert Allardice in Petty as tutors dative of John Allerdes, son and heir of the deceased John Allerdes of that Ilk and his spouse Janet Lundy (*NAS*, 49/27). Richard had at least one son:

   i James Lundy, admitted Burgess and Guildsman of Edinburgh on the 4th of August 1542. whereupon he is designed as his father's heir apparent (*Roll Ed. Burgess*).

4   **Margaret Lundy.** She was the second wife of David Pringle of Smallholm and Gallashiels. In 1510, they had a charter to themselves, and the heirs of their marriage, of the lands of Redhead and Whytbank. They also had a charter of the barony of Manour, in Peeblesshire dated 16th June 1522. David was dead before 6th May 1539 (*NAS*, GD123/27); Margaret was still alive in 1555 (*NAS*, GD122/1/193). They had issue:

   i James Pringle of Woodhouse and Whytbank. He married Margaret Kerr of Linton, and had issue. Note that his grandson, James Pringle of Whytbank, married Christine or Christian Lundie, daughter of William Lundie of that Ilk (*Mem. Walter Pringle*, 118-9).

     a James Pringle of Woodhouse and Whytbank. He was twice married. His first wife was Marian Murray, daughter of Andrew Murray of Blackbony. They had one son.

       i James Pringle of Woodhouse and Whytbank. He married Christian Lundie, daughter of William Lundie of That ilk.

     b George Pringle

     c Robert Pringle

     d William Pringle

     e Marian Pringle, married in 1561, George Pringle of Blyndlee, and secondly, in 1568, William Home of Bassendean.

  ii Janet, married George Brown of Coalston

  iii daughter

5   **Janet Lundy**, married William Scott 8th of Balwearie, Lord of the articles of the barons, before 1496, as on that date they were granted the lands of Kilgour in Falkland Parish by James IV. In 1519, he gave a bond to Walter Lundy of that Ilk, his brother in Law (*NAS,* GD160/280, No. 19). He fought in Flodden with James IV, and was taken captive. He sold some of his lands in order to buy his freedom. Once freed, he was appointed to the position of Lord of the articles of the Barons, no-one else in the peerage attained this rank. He was nominated as first justice, but died soon after in 1532. They had issue.

   i Sir William Scott
   ii Sir Thomas Scott of Pitgormo, who succeeded to Balwearie.

6   Euphame Lundy. She appears in the *Sheriff court book of Fife (1515-1522),* with respect to her proposed marriage to David Moneypenny of Pitmillie. Her brother Walter had been given the gift of David's marriage by the King, and had proposed that David should marry Euphame. Records show he did not. An extract concerning this from the Sheriff Court Book of Fife can be read under her brother Walter's details.

WALTER LUNDIE OF THAT ILK

Born around 1490, he was the son of Sir Thomas Lundy of Pratis, and after hs father's death, became the heir of his grandfather Sir William Lundy of that Ilk. He married Elizabeth Lindsay, daughter of Sir John Lindsay of Pitcruvie, Master of Lindsay and Elizabeth Lundie, (who was herself a daughter of Robert Lundie of Balgonie).

He was given the gift of the marriage of David Moneypenny of Pitmillie, son and heir of William Moneypenny of Pitmillie in 1519 (*NAS,* GD160/280, No. 14). Walter proposed that David should marry Euphame Lundy, Walter's sister. David refused, and was finned one thousand two hundred merks Scots by the King. Details from the Sheriff Court Book of Fife concerning this matter follow:

> "James be the grace of God King of Scotland to our schiref of Fife and his deputis and to our louittus John Adamson, James Byssat messingeris oure shireffis in that part, coniunctlie and seueralie speciale constitut greeting Foresamekle as it is be the Lordis of our consale decreitit and deliuerit that Dauid Monipenny of Pitmulye sone and

aire of wmquhill William Monipenny of Pitmulye sall content and pay to Walter Lundy of Pratris, son and air of wmquhill Thomas Lundy of Pratris, knicht, the soume of ane thousand and two hundredth merkis usual money of our Realme for the single and double avale of his mariage as he the said Walter that hes the gyft of the sammyn of ws because the said Walter offerit to the said Dauid Eufam Lundy, his sister, in marriage, as an aggreable person to him and partii without disparissing, quhilk he refusit to do, and maryit wythtout the said Walteris lecens as ane actentik instrument of requisicione maid tharupone wnder the signe andsubscripcione manuale of maister Thomas Wemys notar publict schewin and producit before the saidis lordis proportit and bure of the dait At Sanctandrois the xxvj day of Februar, in the 3ere of god J^{m}V^c and xix 3^{eris}. As at more lyntht is contenit in an act and deceit gevin by the saidis lordis tharupone Our will is herefor and we charge zou straitly and comandis that incontinent thire our lettres sene zhe pas compell and distrenzhe the same Dauid Monipenny his landis and mak penny of his reddiest gudis and failzeing of his movable good that zhe apprisse his landis aftir the forme of our act of parliament to the avial of the said soume And mak the said Walter to be fullely contentint and apit tharof but delay and eftir the forme of the said decreit as zhe will answere to ws tharupon. The quhilk to do we commit to zou coniunctile and seueralie our full power to be thir our lettres. Deliuering thaim be zou deulie execute and indorsate agane the bevane gevin under our signet.

At Edinburgh, the 8th day of Aprile, 1522"

Walter was also given the ward and marriage of John Lord Innermeath, and a couple of interesting papers still exist in relation to this. On the 26th April 1531, privy seal letters granted to Walter the ward of the deceased Richard third Lord Innermeath, and the marriage of John 4th Lord Innermeath, Richards son and heir (*NAS*, GD160/284). On the 16th of June 1534 letters were written charging sheriffs to warn John, 4th Lord Innermeith, (whose gift of marriage was granted to Walter Lundy of that Ilk, and who cannot apprehend him personally,) either at his dwelling place or by open proclamation at market cross of head burgh of Forfar, 'to contract marriage with ane aggreabill party without disparage that the said Walter sall offer to him and mak intimatioun to him thairupoun at the hie mess in the parroche kirk quhair he duellis' (*NAS* GD160/280). It is not known if Lord John married a Lundy daughter. If he did, the bride must have died young as Lord John was contracted to marry Elizabeth Betoun, daughter of John Betoun of Creich, who had a gift of his marriage, on the 7th of January, 1536-7.

Walter succeeded to the Barony of Lundie, upon the death of his grandfather, Sir William Lundy of that Ilk. Walter was given sasine of the lands and Barony of Lundie in 1528 (*Exchequer Rolls of Scotland*). His inheritance of his lands appears to have not been straight forward. He recieved a new charter of infeftment of the lands and Barony of Lundie from King James V, on the 12th of July 1540 (NAS, GD160/280, No. 25). This charter was granted to him and his spouse and united the Lands of Haltoun and others into the barony of Lundie (*East Neuk of Fife*). However, from a charter of the 5th of April 1541, granted by Walter to James Sibbald of Rankelo (designed his franktenementer) of a third part of Strathairlie, it is stated that Walter had been summond to hear his lands declared in non-entry, despite this second charter of infeftment by the Monarch (*Laing Charters*, No. 454). He received a third charter of infeftment in the lands and Barony of Lundy on the 12th of July 1546 (*NAS*, GD160/285, No. 11), but his lands were again declared as being in non-entry in 1549:

> "At Edinburgh, 24th September 1549
> Ane Lettir maid to George Comendatour of Dunfermling, his airis and assignais, ane or ma – of the nonentries (etc) of all and hale the landis and barony underwrittin, thatis to say, the mainis of Lundy with the fortalice, manner place and mylne of the same, the landis of Haltoun, Balcormo and myln therof, the landis of Gilstoun, Bowsie, Muretoun and Prateris, Nethir Prateris, the Kame of Tewquhettis and half lands of Kincraig, with the superiorite of the landis of Stratherlie, with all thair annexis (etc), tennentis etc., advocation and donatioun (etc) lyand within the schirefdome of Fife, of all yeiris and terms bigane (etc) sen the deceis of umquhile William Lundy or ony uthir (etc), or by ressoun of recognitioun, forfaltour, purprusioun, or be

reductioun of retowris, sesingis, instrumentis, or any othir
maner of way, and als oft the saidis landis or any part thiarof
sall become in hir hienes handis be ony of the ressonis
forsaidis; and siklike of all yeris and termes tocum, etc"
(*Reg. Sec. Sig.* IV. 438)

By 1554, Walter had granted a charter of his lands and the Barony
of Lundie to his second son William (his eldest John dying before this date)
(*Reg. Mag. Sig.* IV. 977).

In 1531, following a disagreement between the Laird of Ardross
and the Prior of Pittenweem, a James Borthwick, John Anderson and John
Balzeat, were slaughtered. Amongst the party assigned guilty of involvment
in this slaughter were David Lundie, Walter's brother; Andrew Lundy,
brother of the Laird of Balgonie; John Lundy of Strathairlie, and his brother
James; William Dishington, fear of Ardross; James Sandilands of Cruvie;
William Lumisden of Airdrie and William Gourlay of Kincraig. Following
the judgement of their guilt, they were escheated, and the King made a gift
of their goods, both moveable and unmovable, to Walter Lundy of that Ilk
(*Reg. Sec. Sig. II. 1029*).

On July 22nd 1536, Walter and George Earl of Rothes were given a
Royal letter giving them special licence to "fulfil thar pilgrimage at sanct
Johnne of Amyss and do thar uthris lefull erandis and besynes quhar thair
ples in the parties beyond say" (*Reg. Sec. Sig.* II. 2018; *Acts Lords of Council
in Civil Caus.* 456).

On the 19th of October, 1541, Walter granted a charter of one third
of the lands of Stretharlye (Strathairlie) to John Lord Lindsay of the Byres
(*NAS*, GD20/1/329). Further details of dealings with Strathairlie can be read
under the details of that House. On the 28th of August, 1552, the lands of
Over Pratis; in the hands of Sir David Lindsay of the Mount, Lyon Herald,
and his spouse Janet Douglas; reverted back to Walter (*NAS*, GD160/281).
This was confirmed with a charter under the Privy Seal on the 16th of May
1562 (*Reg. Sec. Sig.* V. 1030). In relation to Walter's dealings with the
Lindsay family, in particular his father-in-law, he was escheated, and a gift
of his goods, "movable and unmovable, detis, takis obligationis, sowmes
of money, gold, silver, cunyeit and uncunyeit, actis, cotractis, jowellis and
uthiris gudis quhatsumevir" was made by Queen Mary to Walter's son George
Lundy. These goods were in the hands of the Queen "be reason of escheit,
throu being of the said Walter, or (etc) ordourlie denuncit rebel and at the

horne for non delivering of ane lettir of tak to Johnne, Lord Lindsay of the Byris, by virtew of lettiris in the foure formes past upoun ane decrete obtenit agains him be the same Lord" (*Reg. Sec. Sig.* IV. 2714). Shortly before this action was taken, on the 22nd of April 1550, Walter was given the gift of the non entry of all of Wemyss-shire, following the death of Sir John Wemyss of that Ilk.

Walter was one of the earliest and staunchest supporters of the Religious Reformation of Scotland. Some of Walter's contributions to this cause are summarised in the book "*A Short Memoir of James Young,*" by Alexander Johnston (1860). The following couple of extracts are taken from this text.

"In celebrating, in 1860, the Tercentenary of the Reformation of Religion in Scotland, considerable research seems to have been bestowed, by various individuals who took part in that Commemoration, in investigating the personal history of a few of those who shared in the transactions which, 300 years ago, excited public attention on the north side of the Tweed: of the existence of two gentlemen of Fifeshire, father and son – to be noticed in the sequel of this note, - the speakers and writers in 1860, on the subject of the Scottish Reformation, were apparently in ignorance; although by entries in "The Booke of the universall Kirk of Scotland," and other contemporary authorities, "the Lairds of Lundie" – Walter Lundie of that Ilk, in Fife, - and his son and heir – Mr. William Lundie of that Ilk, - are proved to have borne as much of the burden and heat of those Reforming days as did any two of their compeers:- the Lundies, however, had evidently not turned their religious zeal into such a profitable account as "the Lords that haud the guid caus in hand, wharof ane was hunting for fat kirk leiving, quhIlk gart them fecht fastar;" – as James Melville in his diary, - printed in 1842 for the Members of the Woodrow Society,- sarcastically observes – adding that "every Lord got a Bishopric, and sought and presented to the Kirk, sic a man as wald be content with least, and set them maist of fewes, takes, and pensiones" (feus, tacks, and pensions)."

"Walter Lundy of that Ilk, and his son Mr. William, were amongst the gentry of Scotland who first embraced the tenets of the Reformed Religion; nor, although each suffered in person, if not also in fortune, on that account, do they appear to have thereafter failed in avowing, and acting upon, their convictions. The following paragraphs, taken from the "Lives of the Lindsays," (Vol. I., p268), describe in graphic minuteness, the circumstances under which the zeal of the early reformers was aroused – a zeal which halted not until the ancient faith of the inhabitants was well nigh extirpated from Scotland. The Lairds of Lundie, referred to in the subjoined passage, were Walter and his son, Mr. William Lundy of that Ilk. Patrick, Master of Lindsay (of Byres) "one of the first of the Nobility who had joined the Reformers, and an enthusiast in their cause, with the Lairds of Lundie, elder and younger, and many gentlemen in Fife and Angus, convened at Perth in April, 1559, resolving to put their lives in peril for the gospel. Knox preached to them in the morning on the sin and abomination of idolatry, and in the afternoon, after they had dined, they returned to the Church, and heard a second sermon on the same subject. While the preacher had concluded, a monk opened a 'glorious tabernacle,' which stood at the high alter, filled with little images of the Saints, which he exhibited to their adoration; a boy, standing by, exclaimed that to worship them would be idolatry, - the friar struck him, and the boy retaliated by throwing a stone which broke one of the images; this served as a signal, - the rabble could no longer be restrained; images, alters, ornaments, all were broken with indiscriminate fury, and the building itself nearly destroyed. That same night they sacked the Convent of the Carthusians, and those of the Grey and Black Friars the next morning. 'Pull down the nests,' said John Knox, 'and the rooks will fly off.' – The rage for demolition spread like wildfire, and almost every Cathedral and religious house in Scotland fell a sacrifice to it, with the exception of the Cathedral of Glasgow, which was fortunately saved by the Provost, Patrick Lindsay, who affected to participate in the zeal of the iconoclasts, but recommended them, for their own sakes, to defer pulling it down till a new church should be built – an argument to their common sense which saved the building."

(It is greatly regretted today that, in those days, there were not Chief Magistrates of Royal Burghs – containing Cathedrals within their walls – possessed of the dexterous address of Provost Patrick Lindsay of Glasgow.)

In August, 1560, Walter Lundy of that Ilk was present, along with many other of the Barons, and not a few of the Nobles of Scotland, and Representatives from the Royal Burghs, at the Parliament held at Edinburgh, by which the Popish religion was abolished in that realm. – (*Scots Acts of Parliament*, 1560.) In reference to this proceeding it has been remarked – "On the morning of the 23rd of August, 1560, the Romish hierarchy was nominally in full existence; ere eve, it had become penal to perform its rites. In a Convention, or Parliament, assembled without Royal Authority, the Act, establishing the reformed polity, was passed as a trophy of victory over the beaten cause of the Catholics, and their head, the Queen Mother, Mary of Guise."

In John Knox's History of the Reformation in Scotland is given, *verbatim*, a speech of Walter Lundie of that Ilk, addressed to the General Assembly of the Kirk, which met at Edinburgh, on 26th June, 1564, - with the tenor of which oration, the Historian remarks – "The Courteouris at first semeit nocht a lyttill offendid, that thay sould be as it were suspectit of defectioun: yit, nevirtheles, upoun the morrow, thai joynit with the Assemblie, and come into it." The, - at least to those of whom it treated, - not very palatable address of the stout old Baron of Lundie, is thus introduced in John Knox's History:-

"The first day of the Generall Assemblie, the Courtoiuris nor the Lordis that dependid upoun the Court, presentit nocht thame selfis in the sessioun with thair Bretherin. Whairat monie wondering, ane anceyant and honourable man, the Laird of Lundie, said, 'Nay I wonder nocht of thair present absence; but I wonder that at our last Assemblie, thai drew, thame selfis, ane pairt, and joynit nocht with us, but drew from us some of our mynisteris, and wylleit thame to conclude sik thingis as were never proponit in the publick Assemblie, quhIlk apperis to me to be a thing verrie prejuciciall to the libertie of the Kirk. And, thairfoir, my judgement is, that thai salbe informit of this offence, quhIlk the whole Bretherin haif consaveit of thair former falt; humble requyring thame, that gif thai be Bretherin, thai will assist thair Bretherin with thair presence and counsall, for we had nevir grytter neid. And gif thai be myndit to fall back from us, it be better we knaw it now that afterward.' Thairto aggreyit the whole Assemblie, and gaif comissioun to certene Bretherin to signify the myndis of the Assemblie to the Lordis; quhIlk wes done that same day efter noon." (*The History of the Reformation in Scotland, by John Knox; edited by David Laing. Wodrow Society Edition*, 1848, Vol. II., pp. 422-23.)

In February, 1656, Walter Lundie of that Ilk, had the honour of receiving as a guest, within his Mansion of Lundie, Mary Queen of Scotland, on her Majesty's return from the City of St. Andrew's. This Royal visit took place on 12th February; and, on the following morning, the Queen left Lundie for Wemyss Castle; there, on 13th February, 1565, to meet, for the first time, at least on Scottish Ground, her youthful kinsman and future husband, Henry, Lord Darnley. Of this visit to Lundie, and the remarkable incident which occurred in the course of it, Miss Strickland (*Life of Mary Queen of Scots*, 1853, pages 109, 110), writes:- "The feelings with which the possibility of Mary's wedlock with a spouse of her own religion were met by the country gentry of her realm, are instanced in one of Randolf's letters, in an anecdote which he calls a 'lyttle hystorie.'" – (*State Paper Office, inedited MS., March 27, 1565, at Edninburgh, after ten at night, - Randolph to the Earl of Bedford; Scotch Correspondence.*):- "What mischief this mischievous mass worketh here amongst us your Lordship seeth, and hereby we may conjecture what will ensue if she match with a Popish Prince. At her coming to the Laird of Lundie's house in Fife, who is a grave and ancient man with white head and long beard, he kneeleth down unto her, and saith like words to these: "Madam, this is your own house, and the land belongeth to the same; and all my goods and gear is yours. These seven boys,' – which (quoth Randolph the writer of the letter) are as tall as any man hath in Scotland, and least the youngest of them, is 25 years of age, - 'and myself will wear our bodies in your Grace's service without your Majesty's charge, and we will serve you truly. But, Madam, one humble Petition I would make to your grace in recompense of this – that your Majesty will have no mass in this house so long as it pleaseth your Grace to tarry in it.' The Queen took well enough these words, but asked him 'Why?' He said, I know it to be worse than the 'mickle Devle,' with many other spiteful words against it." In september following, - some seven months after the date of the Queen's visit to Lundie, her majesty and her husband, Darnley, arrived at St. Andrew's: John Knox thus alludes to her Majesty's treatment of her former host, Walter Lundie of that Ilk –

"The second night after the Queen's coming to Saint Andrew's, she sent a band, or troop of horsemen, and another of foot, to Lundie, and at midnight took out the Laird, being a man of eighty years old; then passed to Fawside, and took likewise Thomas Scot, and brought him to Saint Andrew's; where they, with the Laird of Bavard, and some others, were commanded to prison. This manner of handling and usage being onkend and strange, were heavily spoken of, and a great terrour to others, who though themselves warned of greater severity to come." –

(*The History of the Reformation in Scotland*, Vol. II., p. 503.)

At page 139 of Volume I. of Kennedy's "Annals of Aberdeen," it is noticed that, *anno*, 1565, Sir Patrick Lermond of Dersy, Andrew Wood of Largo, Andrew Wood, Younger, Alexander Trail of Blabo, Andrew Murray of Baward, William Lunday, son and heir of – Lunday of that Ilk, surrendered themselves, in the lodgings of David Marr, Bailie in Aberdeen, as prisoners, interms of the King and Queens letters.

In the parliament called by the Regent Moray, assembled at Edinburgh in December, 1567, it was agreed that, in place of Walter Lundy of that Ilk, the House should receive and admit amongst them, Mr. William Lundy, his son and apparent heir, and some others, including Mr. John Spottiswood, John Knox, Mr. John Craig, Mr. John Row, and Mr David Lindsay, Ministers, in debating, treating and reasoning of the matters to be proponed concerning the Estate of the Kirk. At this meeting of the House, on 6th December, 1567, "Lundy, Zoungar," appeared; and, having taken the oaths, was admitted a member of the Convention. "Walterus Lundy de eodem" is mentioned as having, along with many other barons, been present at the meeting at the Parliament, at Edinburgh, 24th November, 1572, - by which period laird Walter must have attained an advanced age. At this meeting James, Earl of Morton, was elected Regent of Scotland, in succession to John Earl of Mar, deceased.

Adding to this extract, John Knox, is known to have stayed at Lundie House as Walter's guest around the 23rd of August 1559. On this date he wrote a letter from the house of Lundie to Sir James Crofts, the governor and warden of the East marches, entreating that a safe conduct might be given to his wife to come and nurse him, as he was lying ill of an ague fever (*East Neuk of Fife*, p 49).

Walter died before the 2nd of May, 1569 (*Edin. Tests.*). His will is held in the Lundin Writs (*NAS*, GD160/280, No. 73). His spouse Elizabeth Lindsay predeceased him, passing away before 1544 (*Reg. Mag. Sig.* IV. 295). Walter had issue:-

1   **John Lundie**, married Elizabeth Hepburn, daughter of Sir Alexander Hepburn of Whitsome (Quhilfon) by Elene Sinclair (*Scots Peerage*, II. 145); an antenatal contract for this marriage dates from 29th March 1543 (*NAS*, GD160/284). On 23rd March 1543, he was granted a Crown Charter of Confirmation of the lands of Bonnytown and Auchterhouse, in Angus. On the 16th of August 1544, John's father granted to John and his spouse, the lands of Haltoun, in the Barony of Lundy, that were previously held by Walter and his late spouse Elizabeth Lindasy. A Crown Charter of confirmation of this grant was made on the 12th of February 1548-9 (*Reg. Mag. Sig.* IV. 295; *Reg. Sec. Sig.* IV. 113). John was also granted by his uncle, William Scott of Balwearie, an annual annuity of 12 Merks out of the lands of Demperston in Fifeshire (*East Neuk of Fife; Scots Baronage*). John predeceased his father, dying before March 1554. Towards the end of that year, Walter granted a charter of the lands and barony of Lundie to his second son William (*Reg. Mag. Sig.* IV. 977). On the 12th of March 1556, Elizabeth Hepburn, designed as relict of John Lundie of that Ilk, gave letters of reversion to her father-in-law, Walter Lundie of that Ilk, of part of the lands of Balcormo (*NAS*, GD160/ 280, No.68). John had issue:

   i   *William*, died before his father, with no issue (*Lundins of Fife*).

2   **William Lundie of that Ilk**, who succeeded and whose details follow.

3   **Andrew Lundie, portioner of Lamylethame**, brother German to William and John. He married Elizabeth Kerr, daughter of Sir Andrew Kerr of Fernihurst around 1560 (*Scots Peerage*, V. 62). She died around 1594 with the reading of her testament being on 26th July of that year (*Edin. Tests.*). He died around 1597, with the reading of his testament being on 15th of July of that year (*Edin. Tests.*). They had no issue.

4   **James Lundie**, named as provisional heir to his brother Andrew on April 9th 1600 in an annual rent of 80 merks from the lands and

barony of Ardross (*Inq. Spec. Ret. Fife*, No. 83). He married and had issue.

    i   *James*, (assumed), see Lundin of Baldastard,

    ii *Patrick* (*East Neuk of Fife*)

5   *George Lundie,* On the 8th of April, 1554, George was given the gift of his father's goods, following his father being declared a rebel. "At Hamilton, 8 April 1554

Ane Letir maid to George Lundy, sone to Walter Lundy of that Ilk, his aris and assignais – of the gift of all gudis, movable and unmovable, detis, takis obligationis, sowmes of money, gold, silver, cunyeit and uncunyeit, actis, cotractis, jowellis and uthiris gudis quhatsumevir, quhilkis pertenit to the said Walter Lundy of that Ilk, and now pertaining, or (etc) to oure soverane lady be reason of escheit, throu being of the said Walter, or (etc) ordourlie denuncit rebel and at the horne for non delivering of ane lettir of tak to Johnne, Lord Lindsay of the Byris, by virtew of lettiris in the foure formes past upoun ane decrete obtenit agains him be the same Lord."

(*Reg. Sec. Sig.* IV. 2714).

6   *David Lundie of Bonnyton,* married Margaret Johnstone. He had a charter of the lands of Bonnyton and Auchterhouse in Angus, in May 1569 (*Mem. James Young*). On the 23rd of November 1570, David Lundie, brother german of Mr. William Lundie of that Ilk, made Robert Douglas of Lochleven his assignee in a tack of the teind of sheaves of the Parish of Portmoak (*NAS*, GD150/1761). He died in 1610 (*East Neuk of Fife*). David had issue:-

    i *John Lundie* (*East Neuk of Fife*)

7   *Paul Lundie.* On the 21st of July, 1576, Dame Margaret Home, Prioress of the Abbey of North Berwick gave tack to Paul Lundye, brother of Mr William Lundye of that Ilk, of the teinds of the lands of Baldastart, in the Parish of Largo, for 19 years (*NAS*, GD/57/477). On the 10th November, 1583, Robert and Andrew Lundy, sons of Paul Lundy, brother of Mr. William Lundy of that Ilk, were granted a pension of annual rent in the Lordship of Rescobie, by Patrick, Archbishop of St. Andrews (*NAS*, GD/45/16/2205). Paul is witness to three charters dated 1564, 1583 and 1588, (*Univ. St. And. Muni.* SM110B13.11; SM110B14.2; SM110B14.2). Paul had at least two sons:

    i *Robert Lundie*

    ii *Andrew Lundie*

8 *Elizabeth Lundie,* married John Haldane of Gleneagles. Between the 7th and 16th of December, 1563, John Haldane of Gleneagles resigned, into the hands of the Queen, at Holyrood, the lands of Rusky; Lanerk; and Over and Nether Auchreg in the barony of Haldane; in favour of his spouse, Elizabeth Lundy; for her infeftment in annual rent (*NAS*, GD198/131-6, *Reg. Mag. Sig.* IV. 1489). John died in shortly afterwards, and was succeeded by their son George. Elizabeth was still alive in 1587, as she appears twice that year in the Register of the Privy Council, named in letters raised by her son David against Robert Forrester of Boquhanne, Provost of Stirling (*Reg. Privy Council.* Series I. IV. 153, 179). John and Elizabeth had issue:

i	*George Haldane of Glenealges*
ii	*John Haldane of Glenagles*
iii	*James Haldane*
iv	*Joseph Haldane of Briglands*
v	*David Haldane*
vi	*Archibald Haldane,* constable of Stirling Castle
vii	*Margaret Haldane*
viii	*Isobel Haldane*
ix	*Elizabeth Haldane*
x	*Beatrix Haldane*
xi	*Jean Haldane*

9 *Catherine Lundie,* born 1523; she married Paul Dishington, Lord of Ardross. They were proclaimed as married 14th and 18th June, 1543, by Andrew Hunter, Vicar of Kilconquhar, and John Chalmers, Vicar of Largo (*NAS*, GD160/285). The marriage may well have been arranged well before then, as several agreements exist between Walter Lundie of that Ilk, and William Dishington of Ardross dated around 1537 (*NAS*, GD160/285, No. 22). Paul Dishington died sometime before 1553-4. On the 8th of May 1553-4 Catherine was granted the gift of the non-entry of all of the lands of Carmwry, following the death of her husband (*Reg. Sec. Sig.* IV. 2494). They had issue (*East Neuk of Fife*):

i Margaret Dishington, married James Hamilton of Rouchbank.

ii Jean Dishington, married Gavin Hamilton of Raploch

After the death of her first husband she married David Moneypenny

(*Ind. Cal. Deeds*, I. 62, 368) . She died before the 28th of March 1565 (*Edin. Tests.*).

10   *Martha Lundie*, married Archibald Moneypenny of Pitmilly (*Reg. Mag. Sig.* V. 552). Archibald died before 18th August 1607. They had issue:-

   i   Patrick Moneypenny of Pilrig, heir to his father.

11   *Cecilia Lundie*, married George Kerr of Fawdenside. On the 2nd of March 1576, a Privy Seal Charter confirmed a charter by Andrew Ker of Fawdenside to his son and apparent heir George, and Geroge's future spouse, Sicilia Lundy, granting them and the survior of them both "seven husbandlands which the said Andrew holds in capite of the King of his lands of Ferrygait and Leichislandis, with houses, buildings and gardens with a third of the rabbit-warrens thereof, in the barony of Dirltoun and constabulary of Haddinggton" (Reg. Sec. Sig. VII. 934). Cecilia died on the 25th of August 1593. Her testament being proved on the 27th of November 1594 (*Edin. Tests.*).

12   *Margaret Lundie*, married Sir Patrick Hepburn of Waughton, contract dated 31st March, 1565. Sir Patrick granted a charter in favour of Margaret on the 7th of April that year, in accordance with the marriage contract, of life rent of the lands of Brotherton (*NAS*, GD70/19). Margaret died before the 31st of January 1593; as on that date her testament is proved (*Edin. Tests.*). In it she is described as 'ane honorabil woman.'

   i   Isabel Hepburn, married; (1) George Halket of Pitfirran (*Scots Baronage*, 285); (2) Colonel William Stewart, Commendator of Pittenweem. She had issue by her second husband, Frederick Stewart, Lord Pittenweem.

13   *Isobel Lundie*, who married John Melville, 5th of Raith, contract dated 30th March 1563 (*Scots Peerage*, VI. 102). She died before 1570. They had issue:-

   i   John Melville 6th of Raith, who succeeded to Raith, and was the father of the 3rd Lord Melville

   ii   Margaret Melville, married James Wemyss of Bogie, with issue.

   iii Isobel Melville, married George Auchinleck, younger of Balmanno.

14   *daughter*, possibly contracted married to John Lord Innermeath with no issue (*NAS* GD160/280).

WILLIAM LUNDIE OF THAT ILK

Born around 1522; on the 27th of December 1554, he was granted a charter of the lands and Barony of Lundie by his father (*NAS* GD160/280, No. 66). This was confirmed under the great seal on the 5th of January the following year (*Reg. Mag. Sig.* IV. 977; *Reg. Sec. Sig.* IV. 2888). The charter to William by his father was witnessed by among others a Richard Lundy. On the 27th of May 1574, John Arnot of – resigned the lands of over Pratis into the hands of William (*NAS*, GD160/281, No. 14). On the 3rd of August 1582, William was given a charter of the lands of Baldastard by the Abbot of Dunfermline (*NAS*, GD160/280, No. 74).

Shortly after William's father's imprisonment by Mary Queen of Scots, as a result of Walter's religious beliefs and his request for Mary not perform Mass in his house, William, along with Andrew Murray of Balviard; Patrick Lermonth of Daisy; Andrew Wood, younger of Largo; Thomas Scott of Abbotshall; and Alexander Traill of Blebo; were all ordered by the King and Queen into ward, north of the river Dee:

"At Edinburgh, 15th November 1565

The King and Quenis Majesteis ordains Andro Murray of Balvard, Patrick Lermonth of Darst, Maister William Lundy youngar of that Ilk, Andro Wod youngar of Largo, Thomas Scot of Abbotishall, and Alexander Traill of Blabo, to find souertie that thai sall entir thair personis in ward in quhat place or places is sall pleis thair Hienessis, quhen thai sal be requirit, upon sex dayis warning, undir the pane following; that is to say, ilkand of the saidis Andro Murray, Patrick Lermonth, Maister Williame Lundy, Andro Wod, and Thomas Scot undir the pane of twa thowsand pundis; and the said Alexander Traill undir the pane of ane thowsand pundis; and the said sourtie being fundin be the said personis, the Kings and Quenis Majesties relevis thame of thair present wardis, and grantis thamc licence and libertie to pas hame to thair dwelling places, and utherwyise at thair plesour, without ony cryme, skayth, or danger, to be incurrit be thame or thair souerteis fund be thame for hair remaining in Ward be north the wattir of Dee and within Stratherne respective."

(*Reg. Privy Council.* Series I. I. 404).

William's entry into ward occurred shortly before the abdication of Queen Mary in June of 1567. This was in favour of her infant son James VI of Scotland. As James was only an infant at this time, Scotland was ruled by Regents in his place. Four Regents took control of the country during James's infancy. First was James Stewart, Earl of Moray, Mary's half brother. He was assassinated in 1570, and the Earl of Lennox was appointed Regent. The Earl of Lennox was also killed, and was succeeded in the post by the Earl of Mar. The Earl of Mar died in 1572, and the Earl of Morton became the last Regent before James VI took power for himself. With Scotland ruled by the protestant party, the Lundie family, having long professed these religious beliefs again gained favour with the ruling party. William was to be appointed to several high offices, and perform important duties, especially in relation to the religious reformation.

In 1573, William was himself a member of the Privy Council, along with the Regent Morton, Lord Glamis, Lord Boyd, the Bishop of Orkney, the Commendator of Dunfermline, Douglas of Wittinghame, John Erskine of Dun, and Sir John Wishart of Pitarrow (*Reg. Privy Council*, Series I. II. 346). Shortly afterwards, William appears in the Register of the Privy Seal as a result of being excused from the need to attend inquests. In 1574, William was excused from the need to attend musters and service at inquests, and in 1578 he was again excused from attending inquests, with this second entry showing that around this time William was one of the Senators of the College of Justice:

> 16th of August 1578 at the Castle of Stirling
>
> "Ane lettir maid makand mentioun that foasmekill as Maister Williame Lundyn of that Ilk not only hes at all tymes sen the inaugurating of our soverane lord in his kingdome gevin his debtful obedience to his hienes bot als jeopardy his body, warit, expendit and bestowit his substance in the commoun cause for preservation of our said soverane lord and his auctotitie, swa that his hienes mycht enjoy in tranquilitie his croun agains the mynd and willis of sic as opponit thame thairto, the said Mr Williame in maist dangerous tyme acceptit the office of ane fo the Senators of the College of justice upon him and servit, thairfoir with avise of all the lordis of his hienes Secret Counsall examand the said Mr William fra oistis . . . and fra all compearing and passing upon inquestis or assyissis."
>
> (*Reg. Sec. Sig.* VII. 30, 1619)

As alluded to above, like his father, William was a strong supporter of the Reformation. Again, Alexander Johnston in his *"Memoirs of James Young,"* describes this well.

"From the great age of Walter Lundy of that Ilk, he could not have long survived 1572. His successor in the family estate, Mr. William Lundy, or Lundie, of that Ilk, was born, *circa*, 1522. The fact of the word "Master" being uniformly found prefixed to his name, evidences that this baron had graduated, as Master of Arts, at one of the Universities – probably St. Andrew's – which ancient seat of learning is at no great distance from the Lundie estate in Fife. In his early days, Mr. William had, adopted the law as his profession;- as the name of "the Laird of Lundy, Younger," is to be found in Mr. Pitcairn's Collection of Criminal Trials in Scotland, as one of the prolocutors, or Counsel, for the pannel, or accused, on the trial, on 9th May, 1562, of John Sibbald, for the slaughter in September, 1560, of Archibald Ballinghall; on that occasion, the prisoner found as sureties, Robert Lundy of Balgony; Mr. William Lundy fiar of that Ilk; and David Sibbet (Sibbald) of Lethonie [note that his David Sibbald was married to a Margaret Lundie; he predeceased her, and she died before the 23rd of May 1581 (*Edin. Tests.*)].

From various notices occurring in "the Booke of the Universall Kirk of Scotland," from 1567 downwards, - by which date Walter of Lundy had, in all likelihood, through the infirmities of age, become disabled from bearing so active a share as formerly in the proceedings of the Reformers, - it is evidenced that Mr. William Lundie of that Ilk, or the Laird of Lundie, - as he is frequently styled, - had borne no undistinguished share in the proceedings of John Knox and his ecclesiastical coadjutors; the influential position of the Laird of Lundie in those transactions, and the estimation in which he was held by his contemporaries, may be judged of from the fact of his name being generally nominated the first specified amongst the laymen, or elders, who were nominated by members of Committees, &c.

So high stood the character of Mr. William Lundie of that Ilk, at the Court of King James VI., that, in 1580, he was nominated to represent his Majesty at the meetings of the General Assembly of the Church of Scotland, held at the town of Dundee, in July that year, in conjunction with the Prior of Pittenweem. That dignitary (no Ecclesiastic, but one who took the style in question from the fact of his having obtained a grant of the temporalities of the Priory) – did not make his appearance at the Dundee Assembly, - of which Mr. James Lowsone was chosen Moderator; - the Laird of Lundie accordingly was, at the meetings of that Venerable Assembly, the sole representative of his Sovereign. To Mr. John Craig, Minister of Aberdeen, "ane of the Ministers of the King's House," – or one of his Majesty's Chaplains, according to the phrase of the present day, - had been entrusted King James's missive, or commission, referred to; it is chronicled, that at Session Third of the Dundee Assembly –

"Mr. Johne Craig, ane of the Ministers of the King's House, presentit his Hienes missive (directed to the Assemblie) quhIlk was opinly red in face of the haill brether, with all humilitie; and God praised in his Hienes good zeale. The tenor of which missive (followeth): 'Trustie and welbelovit freinds, We greit zou weill; We have directed toward zou, our trest freinds, the Pryour of Pettinweime, and the Laird of Lundie, instructit with our power to that effect, for assisting zou with thair presence and counsell in all things that they may, tending to the glorie of God, and preservation of Vs and our Estate; desyrand zou heartlie accept them, and our good will committit to them, for the present in good part. So we commend zou, to God's blessed protectioun. From our Palace at Falkland, the 12 of July 1580. Sic subscribitur. James Rex.'" – (*The Booke of the Universall Kirk of Scotland; Bannatyne Club Edition*, 1839. *John Row's History of the Kirk of Scotland; Wodrow Society Edition*, 1842, pp. 69, 69.)

"Lundy of that Ilk subscribed, at St. Andrew's, penult. July 1580, the "Band anent the true religioun;" and "Lundy" was present at the Convention of the Estates of Scotland, held at Holyrood, on 12th June, 1590, when King James VI. was personally present."

In 1580, Andrew Melville, the new leader of the Scottish Church after the death of John Knox, came to Lundie House on his way to St. Andrews, where he was to be installed as Principal of the New College and deliver his inaugural lecture. He was accompanied by Mr. James Lawson and Mr. John Durie, ministers of Edinburgh, and the Lairds of Braid and Faldonside.

William conducted the whole party to St. Andrews for the ceremony (*East Neuk of Fife*).

In 1585, William appears in the Register of the Privy Council, along with Robert Durie of that Ilk, and other tenants and feuars of the Regality of Dunfermline, complaining against William Commendator of Dunfermline. The Commendator had requested payment of all the crop duties for 1584, and if not received in the immediate future, would put William, Robert and others at the horn for non-payment. The Lords of Council sided with the Commendator in this instance, and ordered immediate payment of the crop duties in order for the bailies of Dunfermline to be paid (*Reg. Privy Council*, Series I. III. 754).

On the 15th of April 1589, William was admitted as a Burgess of Dundee (*Roll of Eminent Burgesses of Dundee*).

William was twice married. His first wife was the Honourable Christian Ruthven, seventh and youngest daughter of William Second Lord Ruthven by his wife the heiress of Dirleton. It is suggested that they were married around 1550. Christians father died 16th December 1552. Fourteen years later, her brother, Patrick Lord Ruthven and Dirleton, was deeply involved in the murder of Rizzo, and afterwards fled to England, where he died. This act also involved an Andrew Lundy, who was later given remission for his participation in 1566 (*Reg. Sec. Sig.* V. 2925). As part of the contract for the marriage between Christian and William, Christian came with a marriage tocher of 2500 merks, which was still being paid to William in 1556 (*NAS*, GD160/285, No. 3). On the 14th of December 1562, a Privy Seal Charter confirms an earlier charter of William's father Walter, granting to William and his wife Christian, the lands of Nether Pratis, Tewquhetts, and Bowsie (*Reg. Sec. Sig.* V. 1163). On the 31st of August 1568, a charter under the Privy Seal confirms a charter made by William himself, granting to Christian the lands of Over Pratis, Haltoun and Balcormobank, in liferent (*Reg. Sec. Sig.* VI. 465). Christian died before the 17th of July 1575, the date of her testament, as recorded in the Edinburgh Commissariat register of Testaments. By 1577, William had re-married to Elizabeth (or Elspeth) Lundie, a daughter of Robert Lundie 5th of Balgonie (*NAS*, GD160/284, No. 23). On 14th February, 1580-81, Mr. William Lundy of that Ilk, and Elizabeth Lundy his spouse, had a Crown Charter of confirmation of the lands of Lathalland, in Fifeshire. Elizabeth died before the 10th June 1601. William died on the 13th April 1600; his testament proved on the 22nd of

August 1600 (*Edin. Tests.*).

He had issue by both wives.

By Christian Ruthven:-

1   *John Lundie of that Ilk*, who succeeded.

2   *Sir James Lundie of that Ilk*, was twice married. His first spouse was Christian Ruthven, daughter of Sir William Ruthven of Ballendean, third Lord Ruthven. They were married on the 1st of March 1602. The arrangement of this marriage was testified by an act of Parliament in 1600 (*East Neuk*). Christian died before 1634 (*Scots Peerage*, IV. 102). After the death of his first wife, he married secondly Christina Balneavie (Balneaves), she survived Sir James, and was later married to Lieutenant-Colonel George Heriot. It would appear that for some reason, after Sir James's death, Christian was due a yearly payment of around 2000 merks, from Lord Durie. What ever the reason for this arrangement, Lord Durie reneged upon it – "1652, Sept. 1 – In the afternoon, the Lord Durie in Fyfe, was taken away violently from Leuin to Edenbroughe, by an English officer of arms, at Kirsten Banavees instance, relict to wmq" Sʳ Jn. Lunde, he having paid hir litell or nothin ever since hir husbands deathe; where as he had obliged himself to pay hir yearlie about 2000 or 2500 marks yeirlie" (*Lamont's Diary*, p 46). Christian died in February 1666, at her husband's house. She was interred in Musselbrough on the 24th of February that year.

In 1595 Sir James had a charter of one twelfth of Kincaple, and in 1596 of a house in St. Andrews (*East Neuk*). It is highly possible that Sir James held the title of H.M. Carver. On the 12th April 1596, privy seal letters grant to James Lundie, H.M. Carver, the escheat of Thomas Wilson, portitioner of Drone (*NAS*, GD160/281). Thomas was a denounced rebel for his part in the slaughter of a Peter Grey in St. Andrew's. In 1600 James had 500 merks of annual rent disponed to him from lands annexed by the crown, until a total of 5000 merks were paid to him by the King (*General index to the acts of parliament of Scotland*). In 1601, James Lundie, brother of John Lundie of that Ilk, gave discharge to Andrew Henderson, chamberlain of Huntingtower, of 250 merks annual rent for the mill and Haugh of Huntingtower (*NAS*, RH9/1/9). In 1623 he was given a charter of the Temple

Lands of Lundin (*East Neuk*). On the 21st of July 1634, Sir James granted a Precept of Clare Constat in favour of John Lord Lindsay, as heir to his uncle, John Lord Lindsay, of one third of the lands of Stratherlie (*NAS*, GD20/1/331). The Laird of Lundie had in previous generations carried out grants of this type. Although Sir James was at this time uncle of the rightful Laird of Lundie, he was however assuming and holding this role, and had done for almost thirty years. Upon the death of his elder brother, John Lundie of that Ilk, in 1605, Sir James attempted to defraud his nephews one by one from their rightful inheritance, and take the Lairdship of Lundie for himself. He had his eldest nephew, James Lundie declared unfit to be head of the house of Lundie; had him sign over Lundie to himself; and eventually sent him to Sweden whereupon he died shortly after. Two of his younger nephews, William Lundie of that Ilk and John Lundie of that Ilk, were also sent off to foreign countries as mercenaries. The third youngest of Sir James Lundie's nephews, John Lundie of that Ilk, was still trying to get control of his estates in 1634, when the case came before the Lords of the Privy Council of Scotland. Further details of this affair may be read under the life of Sir James's nephew, John Lundie of that Ilk.

Sir James appears in the Register of the Privy Council of Scotland again in 1637, where he issues a complaint, along with his servant, George Henderson, against a John Lundie in Langraw and other parties, for assaulting the said George Henderson. Further details may be read on this matter under Lundie of Langraw.

In 1640 the Scottish Parliament cites Sir James Lundie as an 'incendiary' (*General index to the acts of Parliaments of Scotland*); and in 1641, he is mentioned on the roll of delinquents (*Register of the Privy Council of Scotland*, Series II. VII., 512). These two actions are most probably related to his actions with regard his nephews. Letters from Anne of Denmark to Sir Thomas Hamilton of Byres, HM Advocate, indicate that Sir James had at some time been of service to the court of Denmark (*NAS*, GD249/2/1). As well as holding the Lundie lands in Fife, Sir James held lands in East Reston and Eymouth (*Register of the Privy Council of Scotland*, Series II. IV., 643).

Sir James died in 1652, in St. Andrews, and would appear to have left no issue (*East Neuk*, p 52).

3   *Elizabeth or Elspeth Lundie*. She was twice married. Her first husband was Alexander Fairlie, younger of Braid, son of Robert Fairlie of Braid. As part of their marriage contract, in February 1573, she and Alexander were granted a charter of joint infeftment, of the lands of Over Braid, within the barony of Braid, Sheriffdom of Edinburgh. This was confirmed under the Great Seal on the 15th of March 1573-4 (*Reg. Mag. Sig.* IV. 2204). The charter was witnessed by Andrew Lundyn, brother german to William Lundyn of that Ilk, and several others. Her second spouse was Andrew Wood of Largo, to whom she was married on the 13th of October 1580 (*NAS*, GD160/284).

4   *Christian or Christine Lundie*, married James, eldest son and heir apparent of James Pringle of Whytbank (*NAS*, GD160/285). She died 19th July 1602 and lies interred in Melrose Abbey. Her tomb has the following inscription, "Here lies ane honorable woman Christine Lundie, spouse to James Hoppringle of Whytbank. She deceased 19th July 1602. Syn and still thou murn, for to the grave thou turn."

  i James Pringle, who succeeded his grandfather to Whytebank in 1622 (*Mem. Walter Pringle*, 119).

  ii George Pringle of Balmungo, whose descendants became the present family of Whytbank.

  iii Thomas Pringle

  iii Catherine Pringle, married the Rev. William Penman of Hagbrae, minister of Crichton.

5   *Katherine Lundie*, married, in 1597, John Johnston of Caskieben (of that Ilk), son of George Johnston of that Ilk by Christian Forbes, daughter of William 7th Lord Forbes, grand-daughter of Christian Lundie and John 6th Lord Forbes. John was born in 1565. Katherine was John's second wife (*Scots Baronage*, 37 i). As part of their marriage contract, after their marriage, John granted a charter to Katherine on the 5th of November 1597 (*NAS*, GD160/285, No. 5); following this she was given sasine of the lands of Overtoun and M-toun in the Barony of Johnston (*NAS*, GD160/285, No. 23). They had issue:

  i Thomas of Craig, ancestor of Johnstons of Hilton and of that Ilk. By 1616, both of his parents were dead, and Thomas was still in minority. Sir James Lundy, Knight, Sir Robert Farlie of Braid, Knight, Patrick Monypenny of Pilrig, James Lundie of Balcormie mill, and Umphra Lundie at Lundie mill, were appointed as his curators, or Guardians, by a decreet, or judgement, of the Lords of

Council and Session (*Lundins of Fife*)
ii *Gilbert*
iii *Margaret*
6   **Isobel Lundie**, married James Sibbald in Scoonie (*PRS Fife and Kinross, Vol. 1*)
7   **Jean Lundie**, married William Myrton, son of Thomas Myrton of Cambo and Catherine Lindsay. She is supposed the youngest of his daughters by his first marriage (*East Neuk of Fife*). She died in 1597.

By Elizabeth Lundie:-
8   **Robert Lundie of Newhall**. Although designed of Newhall, Robert was effectively the first Lundie Laird of Auchtermairnie, and further details of his life can be read under the history of that particular house. He died in October 1602, without issue, and was succeeded to his estates by his brother german David.
9   **Andrew Lundie**. Andrew died before 1594, as on the 29th of January that year his brother Robert Lundie was served as heir "*ratione conquestus*" in an annual rent of 500 merks from the lands of Barnis; and an annual rent of 200 merks from the land of Cambo; both in the Parish of Crail (*Inq. Spec. Ret. Fife*, No. 1520).
10   **David Lundie of Newhall and Auchtermairnie**. See the history of the House of Auchtermairnie for further details of his life and descendants.
11   **Margaret Lundie**, described in her marriage contract as the eldest daughter of William and Elizabeth, she married Michael Balfour, 1st Lord Balfour, contract dated the 12th of July 1591 (*NAS*, GD160/285, No. 24). She died in 1625, at Kilmanie in Fife, her testament being confirmed on the 10th of June 1626 (*Scots Peerage*, I. 542). They only had one child, a daughter,
   i *Margaret Balfour*, the heiress of Lord Balfour. She married in 1606, Robert Arnot the eldest son and heir of Robert Arnot. Prior to the marriage Robert had assumed the name Balfour, and upon the death of his father-in-law, became the 2nd Lord Balfour. They had five children including John, the 3rd Lord Balfour (*Scots Peerage*, I. 542-4)
12   **Agnes Lundie**, married George Johnston, younger brother of the

fore mentioned John Johnston of that Ilk. She also married Andrew Ayton 1st Laird of Ayton in Fife, 4th of Dunmuir. He had Dunmuir and other lands erected into a Barony of Ayton in 1617, by King James VI. He died in 1624. Sir Robert Douglas, in his Baronage suggests that the Agnes who married George Johnston was daughter of the Laird of Conland (*Scots Baronage*, 36 ii).

13   **Helen Lundie**, married John Creichtone of Strathord, the son of Patrick Creichtone of Strathord. Her mother is not certain (*PRS Fife, PRS Perth 1601-9*).

14   **Elizabeth Lundie**, married Andrew Ayton of Logie. He was the son of Andrew Ayton, the third son of Andrew Ayton, 2nd Laird of Dunmuir. They were married before 1614, as on the 14th of November, Elizabeth, designed the spouse of Andrew Ayton, granted a charter of annual rent to her brother Sir James (*NAS*, GD160/282, No. 3). On the 12th of March, 1631, Elizabeth and Andrew received a charter of the lands and Barony of Myrecairnie, the lands of Cruvie Wester, and the lands of Brighous of Logie (*NAS*, 122/1/648). She is supposed the youngest daughter of William Lundie's second marriage (*East Neuk of Fife*).

JOHN LUNDIE OF THAT ILK

He inherited the barony of Lundie in Fife from his father William in 1600, being served as heir in the land and Barony of Lundie and half of the lands of Kincraig on the 6th of May 1600 (*Inq. Spec. Ret. Fife*, No. 84). Prior to John succeeding to Lundie, in 1592-3, on the 15th of January, he is shown, along with Andrew Balfour, apparent of Monquhanny, as providing £10,000 caution for Sir Michael Balfour of Burlie, who had just been released from ward within Edinburgh Castle, and the £10,000 was to ensure his ward within the City of Edinburgh, until freed by the King. Sir Michael was John's brother-in-law (*Reg. Privy Council*. Series I. V. 1,11, 37)

During the period that John was Laird a feud ensued between the Lundies and the Murrays, that in 1600 and 1602, was presented before the Privy Council and King James VI, in order to prevent further slaughter and bloodshed, and to submit the feud for arbitration. During this feud, David Lundie, the brother of George Lundie of Gorthie had slaughtered one John Murray, and had later himself been killed by Sir Andrew Murray of Balviard (*Scots Peerage*, VIII. 190; *Reg. Privy Council*, Series I. VI. 83, 467). Full details of this can be read under the history of the House of Gorthy.

Also in 1602, the Laird of Lundie was ordered by James VI, to deliver to the Laird of Fordell, the 'sparhaulk' which he had taken besides Walter Leslie's house; "quhIlk we suppone is the haulk (hawk) of Fordell of quhais kynd we have gottin one haulk this yeir." (*NAS*, GD172/254); and on the 13th of June that year he was given sasine of an annual rent of 500 merks, payable form the Easter and Wester Haugh and Miln of Ruthven, which followed on a charter granted to him by his brother James. The charter was witnessed by among others his brother David Lundie of Newhall. Robert Lundie, son of George Lundie of Gorthie acted as the attorney (*Sec. Reg. Sasines. Perth.* II fo. 280). In 1603, on the 5th of July, John, as principal, with Sir Duncan Campbel of Glenurquhy, Andrew Lundie of Conland, Andrew Ayton of Denmure, George Lundie of Gorthie, William Graham of Claverhouse and David Sibbald of Lethame, acted as sureties for £20,000, that he would keep in company with his brother David Lundie of Newhall, and would produce him whenever required, before the Lords of the Privy Council, or the Justice General (*Reg. Privy Council*, Series I. VI. 794). In 1604, on the 20th of June, a David Lundie in Largo, as bailie there, on behalf of 'a noble man' John Lundie of that Ilk, gave sasine to William Lundie of Faufield, of an annual rent of eighty merks out of the lands and barony of Lundie (*Fife sasines*, II fo. 123; *NAS*, GD50/185/57).

John married Margaret Durie, second daughter of David Durie of Durie and Catherine Douglas (sister of Sir George Douglas of Lochleven), before 1577. On the 11th of July 1577, Elizabeth Lundy, John's step mother granted an instrument of redemption in favour of Margaret Durie, spouse of John Lundie, apparent of that Ilk (*NAS*, GD160/284, No. 23). Margaret died before June 1605. John died on the 7th of October 1605.

They had issue:-

1   *James Lundie of that Ilk*, who succeeded.

2   *William Lundie of that Ilk*, who succeeded his brother James.

3   *John Lundie of that Ilk*. On April 6th 1625 John Lundie, apparent of that Ilk, brother german to William Lundie of that Ilk, is recorded as trying to establish a claim to be served as heir to his brother William Lundie of that Ilk. In 1634 he is referred to with this designation when fighting in the courts with his uncle, Sir James Lundie, for his inheritance. He ultimately succeeded his brother

William.

4 *George Lundie in Saltgrein.* He married Margaret Lundie, daughter of Robert Lundie 8th of Balgonie. Note that Saltgrein is now known as Methil. He died before 1599. They had issue, and further details can be read under *Lundie of Clatto*.

5 *Andrew Lundie of Falfield.* He is know to have been alive in 1627 (*Lundins of Fife*)

6 *Margaret Lundie*, married Patrick Lindsay of Wolmerton around 1615. The had issue (*Scots Peerage*, V. 413; *Scots Baronage*, 258 i):

  i John, served heir to his father 1640

  ii Robert, charged with his father and brother to keep the peace, 31st December, 1634.

  iii Catherine, married Dr. John Douglas, minister of Crail

  iv Alison, married Joseph Douglas of Edrington

7 *Agnes Lundie* (*PRS Fife; Reg. Mag. Sig.* VII., 1811). She married, after 1627, Sir John Prestoun of Aidrie. Sometime prior to 1618 she had been granted an annual rent of 400 merks out of part of the barony of Lundie (*Reg. Mag. Sig.* VII. 1811). On the 4th of April 1632 her signature was registered for a charter granted to her under the great seal, of the Barony of Airdrie, in liferent (*Register of Signatures* 2iii, fo.27; *NAS*, GD50/185/75). In April 1646, her consent was required for a contract between Sir John, their son John, fiar of Airdrie, and the Countess of Eglintoun (*NAS*, GD18/140, GD18/142). They had issue:

  i   *John Preston*

  ii   *James Preston*, died without issue 1662.

  iii   *William Preston*

  iv   *David Preston*

  v   *Thomas Preston*

  vi   *Ann Preston*

  vii   *Elizabeth Preston*

8 *Catherine Lundie*, married to a William Lundie (*PRS Fife*)

JAMES LUNDIE OF THAT ILK

James succeeded his father in 1605, On the 8th of October 1605 he was infeft in the barony of Lundie (*NAS*, GD160/282, No. 9). The next day he married Catherine Lindsay, daughter of James 7th Lord Lindsay of the Byres by Euphemia Leslie, daughter of Andrew 5th Earl of Rothes (*Scots Peerage*, V. 401). The wedding was two days before his father's death, and the marriage was carried out without proclamation and issuing of ward. This was later to provide financial difficulties for James, and presented an opportunity for his uncle Sir James Lundie to take control of Lundie. James was served as heir to his father on the 9th of November 1605 in the land and barony of Lundie comprising the land of Haltoun, the land of Balcormo, the land of Over and Nether Prateris, the Land of Tewquheittis, the land of Kenie, the lands of Gilstoun, the land of Bowsie and the lands of Stratherlie; also half of the lands of Kincraig (*Inq. Spec. Ret. Fife*, No. 161). On the 6th of November 1606 James was confirmed as his father's hier. This confirmation was witnessed by among others, Robert Lundy of Balgonie, Andrew Lundy of Conland, and Lundin in Largo (*NAS*, GD160/282, No. 16). It is suggested that he was a 'simple' man, and he was declared unfit by his uncle, Sir James, to be head of the house. Due to the nature of his marriage, he was required to pay £1000 to the Treasurer, to account for ward. However, upon the advise of his uncle, Sir James Lundie, he tried to avoid payment of this sum and eventually ended up signing over the lands of Lundie to the said Sir James. From this act stems a number of improprieties concerning the actions of Sir James, of which more can be read under the life of James's brother John. It would be fair to say Sir James took a great advantage of his nephew's simplicity. On the 24th of July 1607, James Lundie of that Ilk, granted to his uncle Sir James Lundie, tack of the whole of Lundin (*NAS*, GD160/282, No. 8; *Reg. Mag. Sig.* VI. 1972). The original charter was granted on the 31st of May, and was witnessed by James's brothers William and John; also Umphra Lundie in Lundie Mill. This charter was confirmed under the Great Seal on the 21st of September 1607.

There were two feuds involving the Lundies during the time James was Laird. One anent the Laird of Largo, James's uncle, the other with the family of Learmonth. In 1606, he, along with Sir James Lundie, Robert Lundie of Balgonie, David Lundy of Newhall, Andrew Lundy of Conland, George Lundie, younger of Gorthie, and others related to the Lundie family, were summoned along with those of the Learmonth party, in order to stop the feud.

"Edinburgh 29th May 1606
Forasmekil as it is understand to the Lords of Secret

Councill that the variance and controversie quhilk fell out betuixt James Lundy of that Ilk, Sir James Lundy, his brother, Robert Lundy of Balgonie, David Lundy of Newhall, Andrew Lundy of Conland, George Lundy, younger of Gorthie, Andro Aytoun of Dunmure, and Mr John Aytoun of Kynnaber, on the ane part, and William Leamonth of Dersy, William Learmonth, apparand of Dersy, Mr Robert, John and Patrick Learmonthis, sons to the said William Learmonth, elder, Sir John Learmonth of Balcomie, Mr William Learmonth his brother, David Learmonth, son to umquhile Robert Learmonth in St. Andrews, Sir Robert Foster of Buquhane, knicht, and Mr James Martein, apperand of Cordon, on the uther pairt, yit remaines unremovit or tane away, swa that baith the pairties awaitis the commoditie to prosequute thair private revenge against uthers, to the trouble and disturbance of the peace of the country, and bringing on furder inconvenients, without remeid be provydit: thairfoire ordains letters to be direct to command and charge baith the saids parties to compeir personally before the saids Lords of Secret Councill upon the … day of . . ., to underlie sic order as salbe tane with thaim twitching the observation of his Majesties peace and keeping the guide rule and quietness in the cuntrey, under pain of rebellion, etc, with certification etc."

(*Reg. Privy Council.* Series I. VII. 212)

Another summons was issued against James Lundye of that Ilk, along with Sir James Lundye, and George and David Lundye in 1609 (*NAS*, GD20/8138) This may well have been as a result of the second feud, that between the Lundies and the Laird of Largo. The origins of this feud seems to have resulted from the errection of a seat and desk in the Kirk of Largo by Umpha (Humphey) Lundy in Lundy Mill. The laird of Largo appears to have objected to this, and evidently destroyed the said seat and desk. There are many references to this disagreement in the Register of the Privy Seal, in particular Series One, Volume VIII. An extract from one such reference is given below. Here a number of the Lundies, including James Lundie of that Ilk, are accused by the Laird of Largo with coming to his property, and threatening his son:

"Edinburgh, 10th August 1609.
Complaint by the King's advocate for his Majesty's interest,

and by Andro Wood of Largo, Andro Wod, his son and apparent heir, and Henry Makiesoun, their servitor, that, on 16th February last, James Lundy of that Ilk, Sir James Lundy, his uncle, with Andro Luny, Umphra Lundy at Lundy Mill, James Lundy at Bacormo Mill, James Edisoun and Thomas Playfier, servants to the Laird of Lundy, and others, all armed with hagbuts and pistolets and other weapons, came "undir a pretendit colorit maner of hunting," to the place of Largo, and there offered great occasion of offence to the complainers; also that on 17th February, the said defenders, accompanied with Manypenny of Pilrig, came riding on horseback to the place of Largo, and there fiercely "brak at" the Laird of Largo, younger, and Makiesoun, running at them "with all the speid of thair horsis and the points of thair lances andspeiris," Playfeir and James Lundy at Balcormo-mill running Makiesoun "in at the oxter" and striking "him to the eird." Both parties appearing, with the exeption of Playfeir, the Lords ordain the Lundy of that Ilk and James Lundy at Balcormok-mill to be committed to ward in the castle of Edinburgh, because they have confessed that on 16th February one of their number had a pistolet. They assoilzie Sir James Lundy, on his oath of innocence."

(*Reg. Privy Council.* Series I. VIII. 350)

The feud between the Lundies and the Laird of Largo, over Largo Kirk, ran for many years. In 1618, Sir James Lundie wrote to the King over this matter:

"Edinburgh, the 8 of Aprile 1618
To his most excellent Maiestie
Most Gracious Soverane,

It may pleas your most excellent Maiestie, vmquhile King Williame, of worthie momorie, for the lufe wiche he caryit towardis his sone naturall, my predicessour, callit Sir Robert, thairefter callit Sir Robert of Lundy be King Alexander the Second, gaue all and haill the barony of Lundy, of whome the Lairdis of Lundy hes linialie discendit, as our charteris and evidentis dois record; and evir since the dayis of King Williame, be the space of foure hundreth fyftie and fyve yeiris, we haue bene in peciable possessioun of our awin tendis, quhill now laitlie, that the Laird of Largo hes procurit the kirk of Largo, erectit in ane laick patronage, quha intendis most regorouslie to leid our teindis: albeit that I have causit deall with him thir sevin yeiris bigane for ane new tak of oure awin teindis, qhairunto he will nawayis condicend be ony persuasioun offer: bot hes intentit actioun agains ws for spliatioun thairof, whairintill be the rigour of law he is liklie to prevale. The haill Senatouris of your Maisties Colledge of Justice thinkis it aggreable with reason and conscience that we suld still continue in possessioun of our awin teindis, seing we ar fa lang kyndlie takismen and possessouris thairof; and I am fullie resolvit that thair is no mean hold me in possessioun of the saidis teindis, but that it wald pleas your most excellent Maiestie to direct ane letter to the Lordis of your Hienes Colledge of Justice, to caus ws both submitt that mater to thame, anent quhat takis the Laird of Largo sall giue of our awin teindis, and quhat sall be given thairfoir. This I am most willing to do. It is weill knowin to your Maiestie quhat querrellis and deidlie feidis hes followit vpoun rigourous teinding within your Hienes kingdome fo Scotland, whiche hes bene the ruine of monie houses thairof. Most humlie thairfoir beseiking your gracious Maiestie to prevent ws, be your Heines letter to the Lordis of your Maiesties College of Justice. Thus in all humilitie expeciting your Maiesties most gracious will and intercessioun in this point, I most humlie tak my leve, kissing, will all reverence and humilitie, your most gracious hand.

Your Maiesties most humle and obedient

subject and servitour

S^R James Lundie"

(*"Original Letters relating to Eclesiastical affairs"*, No. 557)

In the same year as Sir James wrote the letter above, Sir James granted a charter of the lands and barony of Lundie, back to his nephew, James Lundie of that Ilk. This charter from Sir James to James was granted on the 2nd of April 1618, and confirmed under the Great Seal the same day. It reserved the liferent that had been granted out of the barony to James's spouse Katherine Lindsay; the liferent of 600 merks granted to Sir James's spouse Christian Ruthven, from the lands and town of Bowsie; and the annual rent of 400 merks granted out of Lundie to Agnes Lundie, legitimate daughter of the late John Lundie of that Ilk. The charter also specified the succession to Lundie, failing heirs male of James Lundie of that Ilk. Following such an event, the barony was to pass to his brother german William. Failing heirs male legitimately begotten from his body, it would pass to his brother John. Failing heirs male legitimately begotten from his body, it would pass to his brother George. Failing heirs male legitimately begotten from his body, it would pass to his brother Andrew. Failing heirs male legitimately begotten from his body, it would pass back to Sir James and to any legitimate issue of his body. This is important to note, as shall be seen shortly, the succession did not follow this progression (*Reg. Mag. Sig.* VII. 1811).

In 1620, James Lundie of that Ilk's wife Katherine Lindsay died. Six months later, Sir James sent his nephew James to Sweden, where he died one month later. His brother William Lundie succeeded him:

WILLIAM LUNDIE OF THAT ILK

At the time of his succession was a Captain in Sweden. He married Anna Wardlaw, daughter of Sir Henry Wardlaw 1st Bart of Pitreavie and Balamle, contract dated 16th June 1623. (*Reg. Mag. Sig.* VIII. 464, 490, 647)His succession to Lundie was also hampered by the actions of his uncle, of which details can be read under the life of John Lundie of that Ilk, his brother, who ultimately succeeded him. William died in 1623 shortly after his marriage. His uncle Sir James Lundie had himself served as his provisional heir in the land and barony of Lundie that same year *Inq. Spec. Ret. Fife*, No. 1561). His brother John established himself as general heir in 1625 (*Gen. Retour,* No. 1189).

It should be noted that James Balfour Paul in his *Scot's Peerage* (IV. 105), states that he married Elspeth Ruthven, a daughter of Patrick Ruthven, Earl of Forth and Brentford. Elspeth is said to have survived him, and subsequently married George Pringle of Balmungo. It also states that Elspet has issue by both. This however seems to be fairly impossible.

JOHN LUNDIE OF THAT ILK

Upon the death of his brother William, John was rightful heir to the lands and Barony of Lundie, however, as has been briefly touched on under the details of his brothers' lives and that of his uncle, Sir James Lundie, Sir James was in possession of these lands, and was clearly not wanting to yield them up. On the 6th June 1634, the case of John Lundie of that Ilk against his uncle Sir James Lundie was brought before the Lords of the Privy Council of Scotland. Some details of this case from the Register of the Privy Council of Scotland are included below. (*Reg. Privy Council Scot.*, Series II, V., 628)

"At Edinburgh 26 of Junij, the yeere of God jᵐvjᶜxxxiiij yeeres, the Lords of Secret Counsell ordains a maisser to pas and warne Sir James Lundie, knicht, to compeir personallie before the said Lords upon Tuesday nixt, the first of July, to ansuer to the petition given in to the Kings Majestie agains him be John Lundie of that Ilk, of the quhilk petition ordanis a copie to be delyvered to the said Sir James and to heere and see suche order tane thairanent as apperteines, under the paine of rebellion and putting of the said Sir James to the horne with certification to him and he failyie letters sall be direct simpliciter to put him thairto.

Primo July 1634. Parties personalie. The Lords ordanis Sir James Lundie to make ane ansuer in writt to the Laird of Lundeis articles upon the Thursday nixt.

1st July, 1634. Parteis personallie. Sir James gave his ansuer in writt conteaning a declinatour of the Counsell as incompetent Judges, quherunto it wes ansuered be Mʳ John Gilmor, proloquutor for Lundie, that they wer not insisting for a definitive sentence upon anie point of right bot onelie for a precognitioun and tryell of the fraude and circumventioun committed be Sir James in the matter compleanned upon.

The Lords find thameselffes nowayes judges to the validitie or invaliditie of Sir James Lundie his infefrmentis or other rights quhatsomever, nor yitt judges to the tryall of quhatsomever fraud or circumventioun alledget used by the said . . . may infer or be used for infringeing or annull . . . feftments and rights. Bot the Lords for obedience . . . letter declares that thay will proceede to the tryall . . . said Sir James his dwtie and behaviour . . . others his procedingis towardis his three nepheus . . . decease of the Laird of Lundye his brother and after tryall . . . mak report theirof to his Majestie accordinglie."

"Ansueirs for the pairt of Sir James Lundin to the Articles given agains him be John Lundin of that Ilk, quhairunto the Lordis of his Majesteis Secreit Counsall hath ordaned the said Sir James to ansueir.

The said Sir James maketh this generall ansueir to all the saids Articles that the samye beiring a progress of the tymes and circumstances when and how the said Sir James came to the richt and possessioun of the lands and leving of Lundie ar mere civile and aucht properly to be discussit be the Lords of Sessioun, and (without offence be it said) the Lords of his Majesteis Secreit Counsell ar not nor cannot be competent judges in suche causes, nor use they to determine in maters of that kynd, as is notour to thair Lordships selves, for gif his richts and infeftments of the said lands wer nocht gude and valide from the begining and sua his possessioun un lauchfull and vitious, which is not, he shall answeir thairto as accords of the law whensoevir he beis persewit befoir the said ordinar and civile judge, and whilks infeftments, rights and possessioun, the said Sir James being convened, as said is, shall schaw and evince to be the most valide and effectuall, and to have bene so frome the begining, and that the saids haill articles given in agains him ar nothing bot groundles informationes and wrong and calumnious suggestiones."

"Ane nott of Sir James Lundy his haill proceidar how he come to the trust of the leving of Lundye.

Wmquhile Johne Lundie of that Ilk, brother germane to the said Sir James Lundie, deceissit in anno 1605, at the quhilk tyme vmquhile James Lundie, eldest sone and air to the said vmquile Johne, was be advyse of freindis mariet upone Katherine Lindesay, sister to Johne, Lord Lindesay, tua dayis befoir his fatheris deceis without proclaimatioun for eschewing of the ward and mariag, and at the same tyme the said vmquhile John Lundie of that Ilk, be his letter will and testament, maid and constituit Williame and Johne Lundeis, his sones, his onlie executoris and intromittouris with his guidis and geir, quhilk extendit to the sowme of 30 thousand merkis and abone.

Now, efter the deceis of the said umquhile John Lundie of

that Ilk, the freindis of the hous, finding the said vmquhile James Lundie, eldest sone [and] air to the said vmquhile John, vnhable to govern his awin estait and so minor in understanding thocht nocht in yeiris, the said freindis maid choise of the said Sir James, his uncle, to quhome thay committit in trust the government of the haill estait and bairnes with this conditioun that within sewin yeiris thairefter he suld releive the landis og the haill dettis and provyd the haill bairnes, quhilk the said Sir James promeissit to do in the presence of famous witnesses *omni exeeptione majorie*.

Now, at his first entrie to the government of the estaitt he makis the haill dettis licht upone the plenisching, quhilk wes left, as said is, to Williame and Johne Lundies, and par thame both furth of the cuntrie to fecht for thair leiving. Thairefter umquile James Lundie, his marriag nocht being ordourlie done, was challengit be the Thesaurar for the tyme, for the quhilk Johne, Lord Lyndesay, componit with the Thesaurar for ane thousand punds, and thairefter desyrit the said vmquhile James Lundie, his brother in law, to pay the said sowme to the Thesaurair to the end that he mycht tak the gift of the waird in his name, quhilk the said vmquhile James, be advyse of the said Sir James, his uncle, refuissit to do, quhairupone my Lord Lyndesay did tak the gift of waird in his awin persone and so refuissit to pay ony tocher at all. Wpone the quhilk refuissal Sir James did steir his awin tyme and so to circumveine the simpill man cumes to the said James and schew him how uncorteouslie his gudbrother, my Lord Lyndessay, did use him in taking of his waird of marriage, and that seing the said Lord Lyndesay did refuis to pay ony tocher it was na resone to infeft Katherine Lyndesay, his Lordships sister, in any cunjuctfie, quhilk the said vmquhile James Lundie, hir spous, was obleist to do be contract of mariage and schew him that the onlie way to eschew that infeftment wes to resigne the haill landis in his mejesties handis in favours of the said Sir James and so having no land . . . . infeft his vyfe in conjuctfie. The simple man upone . . . . . promeis to repone him in his awin place agane quhensoever he . . . . so, and so the said Sir James wes infeft in the haill landis . . . . . ony bak band and so remanit in possessioun of the saidis . . . . of auchtene yeiris applying the hail rent theirof to his awin use . .

. . . fiyve scoir chalderis victuall yeirlie (exeptand onlie intertenem . . . . and the land nocht havand ane servand to attend thame. So the . . . . . said Sir James miscariage to thame both the lady deceissit the . . . . . in anno 1620, quhilk wes fyftein yeirs efter the said Sir James . . . . . nement of the said estaitt and within the space of sex monethis . . . . . deceis he did send the Laird himself being liiij yeiris of age . . . . cuntrie to seik his fortoun at the weiris with his uthar tua brether, William and Johne, and within the space of ane moneth efter his landin in Suadin he deceissit.

Than, efter the deceis of the said James, vmquhile William Lundie, his brother, his narrest and lauchfull air, being for the tyme ane capitane in Suadin, heiring of his brotheris death come hame to succeid to his brotheris estaitt, bot far by his expectatioun finds that Sir James, making use of his brotheris simplicitie, had intrudit himself in the land and so wes standing infeft and, befoir he wald denud himself of the land quhairin he wes onlie intrustit, first he takis his hail tocher gud frome him extending to the sowme of thretie thousand merkis (albiet he was forced to give the same back againe becaus the said William died within the yeir efter his mariage) for payment of his fatheris dettis, for paying of the quhilk dettis Sir james had befoir, as said is, takin frome the said William and Johne thair fatheris haill guidis and geir, extending to the said sowme of fourtie thousand merkis; as also he takis him bund for the payment of tuelf thousand merkis for the plenisching on the Maynes of Lundie quhilk wes ane part of that same geir left to him be his said vmquhile father. So that, he takis his bairnes parte of geir frome him to pay his fatheris dettis, Secundlie, he takis his tocher gude frome him to pay that same dett *de novo* (albeit he repayed it agane), Thirdlie, he causis him by his awin geir bak agane, Fourthlie, for his gud offices done to the house be his dispositioun to Williame of the landis he reservis his awin lyffrent from the Maynes of Lundie, and forces the said William to tak ane tak bac agane fra him of the said maynes for yeirlie payment to the said Sir James of tua thousand merkis yeirlie during his lyftyme, quhairby the said Sir James acknawledges in effect that he wes onlie put in trust of the saidis landis, yit nochtwithstanding be his dispositioun maid to

Williame the said Sir James provydis himself air of tailyie failyeing airis maill of the said Williames awin bodie, and efter the said Williames deceis nochtwithstanding of the said trust Sir James maid use of the said tailyie and obtenit himself infeft *de novo* in the landis and intromettit with his haill guidis and gear, quhilk wes worth tuentie ane thousand pundis and abone.

And thairefter Johne Lundie, now of that Ilk, brother and narrest and lauchfull air to the said umqhile William, having delt with the said Sir James both be himself and be his honorable freindis as being trew air, to quhais behuive he wes onlie intrustit, to denud himself of the estait in his favouris he forcit the said Johne, he having nather wreitt nor legallobleisment quhilk culd compell him thairto to yeild to sic conditiounes as he craivit, quhilk wes so rigorus as gif the said Johne had bene ane stranger to haif maid conqueis of the landis he culd hardlie bene burdanit with moir strait conditiounes; nochtwithstanding the said Sir James in presence of famous witnesses *omni exceptione majore* had ever profest himself to haif bene ane persone quha in respect of his proximitie of band to the hous had tane doing upone him in trust to the behoive of the trew airis and profest that in effect he wes and wald be ever bot a chalmerlane to the house of Lundie, and yit wald never quhitt his richt committit to him in trust bot upone the rigeorous conditiouns following:-

Firt he tuik frome the said Johne the sowme of tuentie thousand merkis for payment of his fatheris dettis quhilk dettis suld haif bene payit with the [plen]isching takin be him fra the saidis Williame and Johne, as said is, nixt . . . . . the said Johne obleist to provyd his haill brether and sisteris extend[ing] amangis them to the sowme of tuentie four thousand merkis, quhilk wes Sir James pairt till haif done first, conforme to his promeis to the freindis of the hous, as said is, at his first entrie in trust to govern the estait nixt as universall intromettour with the said wmquhile Williames guidis and geir quhilk belangit to his saidis brether and sisteris as executouris to him; than he takis the said Johne obleist to pay the said Williames hail dettis, extending to the sowme of swein thousand merkis; moir he forces the said John to by the plenisching of Lundie, quhilk belangit to himself first as executour with the said Williame to his father and nixt as onlie executour to the said Williame, seing he provydit the rest of the bairnes to the sowme abonewrittin. And last of allhe takis him obleist to warrand him at the handis of all persones quhatsomever havand entres or may challenge him for quhatsumever thing as being ane Laird of Lundie or intromettour with his father and brether thair guidis and geir. And nochtwithstanding of this intromissioun with the said vmquhile Williames guidis and geir he hes nocht nor will nocht confirme the said Williames testament, and is respect of his refuissall the procurator fiscall of the Commissariat of Sanct Androis hes disponit his guidis and geir to ane stranger and brocht the saids Jhon in that inconvenient to pay the hail sowmnes contenit in the said testament because Sir James hes him obleist to warrand and kelp him skaithles thairof at all handis, lyk as he hes mais intimatioun to him under forme of instrument to warrand him thairof according to his band. And mairour in the dispositioun made be him to the said Johnne of the landis he reservit his awin lyffrent of the Maynes of Lundie and hes set the said Maynes to the said Jhone in tak for yeirlie payment to him of tua thousand merkis during his lyftyme. All the forsaidis obleismentis the said Johne was forcit to grant to behoir the said James wald denud himself of the landis quharin he wes put in trust. Quhilk trus and professioun and confessioun of the samyn the said Johne offerit him to preive, as said is, quhilk being provin it followis necessar of the law that all forsaid strait conditiounes and obleismentis man be presumit to have bene extortit out of the said John *in debite et sine causa* seing the said Sir James can not condescend upone nor qualifie ony trew caus of the granting thairof for the quhilk the said Johne was dettour to him *alliunde* bot onlie to mak him denud himself of the said estait quhilk was dew unto him and quhilk he was obleist to do without ony gratitud or gud deid.

And farder the said Sir James forced the said Johne Lundie to undertake the payment upon him of thretteine thowsand merkis for byrun spuilyies of the teyndis of Lundy quherwith he intometted himselff."

(signed at the foot) JA. Gallouay

In 1628 he signed a submission by the Lords, of an erection to the King anent teinds, and was on a committee of war of Fife in the years 1643, 1644, 1646, and 1648 (*General index to the acts of parliament of Scotland*). He was appointed Justice of the Peace for Fife and Kinross sometime between 1635 and 1637 (*Register of the Privy Council of Scotland*, Series II. VI., 131). In June 1629 he granted to David Brown of Finmount and his son James (legitimately begotten between him and his late wife, Margaret Murray) and the heirs of his body in fee, of an annual rent out of the land of Lundin, in liferent. A crown charter confirmed this on the 23rd of August 1629 (*Browns of Fordell*, p52).

He married Katherine Lindsay, one of two daughters of Alexander Lindsay, Bishop of Dunkeld, with the contract dated the 4th of October 1627 (*NAS*, GD160/282, No. 44, 45). Alexander was a younger brother of Lindsay of Evlick. In Sir James Balfour Paul's "*Scots Peerage*", he is described as the last Laird. He is the last of the male line of the Lundies to hold the barony of Lundie. He died in 1647, when his only daughter Margaret succeeded him to Lundin. On his death he is styled R. H., which would imply he was connected with the Royal Court (*East Neuk of Fife*, p 51-2).

DAME MARGARET LUNDIE OF THAT ILK

Following her father's death, Margaret was served as his heir, on the 25th of April 1648, in the lands and barony of Lundin (*Inq. Spec. Ret. Fife*, No. 753; see also, *Gen. Retours*, No. 3444). She married, in 1643, Robert Maitland the second son of John Maitland, 2nd Lord Thirlestane, Viscount Lauderdale, Earl of Lauderdale, Viscount Maitland, Lord Bolton (*East Neuk*, p 52). An agreement was made upon the marriage of Margaret to Robert Maitland whereupon George Lundin in Saltgreen, the younger brother of John Lundin of that Ilk, consented to Robert Maitland becoming Laird of Lundin on the death of the said John Lundin of that Ilk (*Lundins of Fife*). Her husband took part in the "engagement," and had to make a public repentance in his own seat in Largo Church on 13th January 1650. On the 14th of April 1651 Robert, designed Sir Robert Lundie of Lundie, was chosen by the Parliament held at St. Johnston, to sit as one of the Barons on the Committie of Estates. The committee was made up of 25 nobles, 25 Barons, and 23 'Burrows.' The nobles were The Duke of Hamilton, The Marques of

Douglas, The Marques of Argyle; Earls Crawford, Marschall, Errol, Atholl, Rothes, Dunfermline, Casellis, Lauderdale, Lothian, Lithgow, Glencairn, Eglinton, Galaway, Kelly, Dalhowsie, Roxburgh, Balclouch; Lords Newburg, Spince, and Belcaris. The Barons comprised Wachob of Nidin, Sir Alexander Hepburn of Humby, Robert Hepburn of Roch, Keinton of Lamerton, Ker of Cavers, Sir Alexander Bellatin of Toff, Walter Scot of Whithis, Straghan of Thomton, Beaton of Criech, Sir Robert Lundie of Lundie, Lockhart of Leis, Sir James Murray of Stirling, Sir Alexander Gibson of Durie, King of Darough, Sir William Scot of Husden, Sir Patrick Hamilton of Preston, Sir William Scot of Ardross, Innis younger, Sir James Aront of Fernie, Sir Elliot of Stobs, Sir James Fowler of Colington, Douglas of Colwood, Weaver of Bogie, Colram of Leist, and Hepburn of Ormiston. The twenty three persons, termed Burrows, included Sir James Smith and Sir Alexander Wederburn (*General index to the acts of parliament of Scotland; Colect. Orig. Pap. Let. Concern. Eng.*, 457-8). Shortly after this appointment, he took part in the battle of Worcester, 3rd of September, 1651, on the side of the King, and was taken prisoner. In 1654 he was fined £1000 under Cromwell's Act of Grace and Pardon. He died of consumption in Lundin on 15th December 1658 (*Scots Peerage*, V. 303). In 1680, a Robert Maitland, one assumes a close relation of Robert Maitland of Lundie, renounced an annual rent of 2880 merks from the Barony of Lundie (*NAS*, GD160/283, No. 17).

The civil war took a great strain on the Scottish estates. It is estimated that on average, from 1651 to the restoration, in the county of Fife and Kinross, a cess of £26 in every £100 of rental was levied by the English. On top of this problem, the estates of those persons who took up arms in support of the King were to be sequestrated. On the 3rd of April 1652, a Mr. Butler and Mr. Coinyers, who were two of the English sequestrators, came to Lundin, and took and inventory of everything in the house, the farm stock, and tenants rental. An extract is given below:

> "suits of hangings, standing beds, a pair of virginals in the children's chamber, carpets, and, in my lady's closet, a cabinet containing a whole series of small items including 2 bracelets of amber, a silver case for a toothpick, 2 small bracelets of pearl, a little sugar spoon tipped with silver, a silver box with 31 sixpences in it, a gold box with a necklace of pearl in it, 2 jewels of worth, the laird's portraiture enamelled in gold, a purse with an account

of the laird's debts, a pair of bodies with silver lace and divers papers; also a cabinet with divers writs, another cabinet containing other curiosities including a psalmbook with tortoiseshell cover, a great tortoiseshell comb, three pairs of broidered gloves one with pearls; and a trunk containing clothing; linen in the upper and lower wardrobes; embroidered hangings and needlework hangings; kitchen furnishings and farm animals (*NAS*, GD160/285).

To obtain the best deal on the fees levied on the Lundin estate by the new government, Dame Margaret Lundin and her mother travelled to Edinburgh. It was the first time that the elder Lady Lundin had crossed the Forth. This trip was apparently quite a success. All the plenishings in and out of the house, were declared the property of the elder Lady Lundin, along with the jointure left to her by her husband, the late John Lundin of that Ilk. Although the lands were sequested, Dame Margaret obtained a tack of them, paying £145 per year, which is thought to be one fifth of the rental (*East Neuk of Fife*). A document relating to this issue is held as part of the Lundin Writs, recorded in April 1652. It states that Katherine Lindsay, wife of the late John Lundin of Lundin, as part of their marriage contract was infeft in the lands of Hattwne, neither prattowes, Balcormo and the lands of Bosie in Fife. This infeftment took place in 1627. It also states that in 1645, she was also infeft in the house and yard of Lundie, and as she owned these lands, they shoud avoid sequestration (*NAS*, GD160/283, No. 34).

As well as the problems with sequestration, the family suffered greatly due to the money that needed to be sent to Dame Margaret's husband during his imprisonment in London. In total he was sent £288 on top of the £1000 fine already mentioned.

> "1652 – Sept. 13 – The Laird of Lundy (being prisoner of warre), came down post from London. He had libertie to stay att home for 3 monthes, in a passe from Ge. Cromuell; the time was from the 30 of August to the last of Nouemb; there was money sent to him whille he was att London, 3 severall tymes, by bill of exchange, 50 lib. sterl. a time; in all 150 lib. sterl. More, 50 lib. stirl. also, after he came home, was sent to London for his vse. Obs. When thir forsaid months were out, he got libertie for ane other monthe; he tooke post from Edenb. to London the 24 Dec.

he galt alonge with him, and upon bill of exchange, another 50 lib. sterl.; June 14 ther was sent to him 33 lib. sterl." (*Lamont's Diary*, p 46)

There have been several extracts already from Mr Lamont's diary, and there will be more to follow. It is worth commenting that this is a contemporary account, and his diary features quite a few accounts of the Lundies. During the writing of this diary, Lamont was a factor for the family of Lundie of that Ilk (*Univ. St. And. Arch.* MSDA880.F412 [Ms797, Ms798]).

In 1671, Dame Margaret was given a charter of the links of Balcormo (*NAS*, GD160/283, No. 26)

Dame Margaret and Robert Maitland had issue:-

1   *John Lundin of that Ilk*. He dropped the name of Maitland and took his mothers name of Lundin. On the 17th of February, 1659 he commenced study at the School of Humantie in St. Leonard's College, and studied at the University up to his third year:

"1659, Feb. 17 – Johne Lundy, son to the deceased Robert Maitlande of Lundy, apparet aire of the lands of Lundy in Fife, wen in to the St. Leonards colledge, to the Humanitie school ther, Mr. James Allane then being master of Humanitie. He was about 14 years of age when he went to St Androus. Mr. Thomas Kinninmount waited upon him and Robert Bruce, James Bruce son, in Largo, was his boy. (Kincragie elder, and Straerly younger, went into St Androus with this younge gentleman.) May, 1660, he entered into bujan (1st year) with Mr Ja Weyms, maior regent there. he staid his semy yeire with him, and the nixt yeir being his 3 yeir, the 9 of June, 1662, he left colledge, and came home, being sick, and did not returne at all againe. Oct. 16, 1663, he took jowrney from Lundy to Edinb. with a purpose to go to London with the Er. of Ladedaile, one Mungo Grahame, Bawchapells brother waiting upon him" (*Lamont's Diary*, p 113).

He was appointed a Justice of the Peace in 1663 (*General index to the acts of parliament of Scotland*); and died unmarried on 25th November 1664 at Lundin at the age of 20. His funeral was on the 5th of January 1665, and he was interred in Largo Church. An account of the funeral proceedings is given in *The Domestic Annals of Scotland*, by Robert Chalmers, adapted from the account given by Lamont in his *Diary*.

"It was attended by many of the nobility and gentry both of Fife, Lothian, and Carse, viz. Earls Crawford, Athol, Kelly, Wemyss, Tweedale, Balcarres; Lord Burleigh, Lord Lyon, Lord Elphinstone, Lord Newark, etc., who all dined before the corpse was lifted. He was carried to the church in that sam coach that the Earl of Leven was carried in, with that same pale upon it, with four chains of white iron above it, with his eight branches upon it. The four chains with two loosen arms were placed after in the aisle, with one upon the gate of Lundie. Three trumpeters and four heralds went before the coffin."

'The heralds and painter got, for their pains, about 800 merks; the poor ten dollars; the coachmen seven dollars; the trumpeteers forty-eight dollars; the baxter, James Weiland, seven dollars; George Wan, master of the household . . . ; the cooks, . . . ; Mr Walters, that dressed the coach, seven dollars; . . . some men that served . . .; the Kirkcaldy man, for the coffin, 40 lib.; John Gourlay, apothecary, for drogs, attendance, and bowelling of him, . . . ; James Thomson, in Kirkcaldy, for mournings, 412 lib. or therby; at Edinburgh, for mournings, 600 lib. or thereby; Gid. Sword for drogs, 16 lib. or thereby; to the writer at Edinburgh for paper and the burial letters, 12 lib.; at Edinburgh, for Claret wine, 200 merks; for seck, 100 lib.; at Edinburgh, two divers times, for spices, about 100 lib.; for sugar . . . R. Dobie, for tobacco, seven lib.; R. Clydesdale, for ware, 54 lib., 11s.; Will. Fogo, for beef, 84 lib., 12s.; Capper, at Scoonie, for capps, 6s. ster.; An. Brebner, smith, for the chimlay and work, near ane 100 lib. or thereby; Robert Bonaly, for dyeing to the servants, 21 lib., 62. 8d.; Glover in the Wemyss, for servants' gloves, 4 lib.'. – Lam."

2   *Robert Lundin*, born 17th April 1651, died 3rd December 1651

3   *Sophia Lundin*, succeeded to Lundin.

4   *Elizabeth Lundin*, born 24th July 1653, died April 24th 1655 – "1653, July 24, being the Sabath – The Lady Lundie, younger, was brought to bed of a daughter, called Elizabeth. She was baptized att Largo Church by Mr James Magill, Jul. 25; the Laird of Aytoune did present hir to be baptized, because hir father, the Laird of Lundie, att this time, was att London prisoner of warr: witnesses, Ardross, Auchmouthie, Kincragie, Fenges Weymes, James Preston, Doctor Mairtin, etc. This child was put foorth to be nursed by Margaret Spence in Londie Mylle. She departed out of this life at Lundie, Apr. 24 about 11 at night, 1655" (*Lamont's Diary*, p 58)

5   **Anna Lundin**, married James Carnegie of Finhaven, second son of David second Earl of Northesk in 1674. She died 3rd September 1694. They had issue (*Scots Peerage*, VI. 498):-

i   Charles, who was palised and died without issue in 1712

ii   James Carnegie of Finhaven, who succeeded his father. He killed the Earl of Strathmore in a fight in Forfar, and died himself in 1765. He married Margaret, daughter of Sir William Bennet of Grubbet, by whom he had two daughters; and secondly Violet, daughter of Sir James Nasmith of Posso, Bart., by whom he had a son and three daughters.

a   James Carnegie of Finhaven, who died at Lisbon in 1777, unmarried

b   Margaret, married to John Foulis of Woodhall, and Charles Lewis

c   Barbara, who succeeded her brother James in Finhaven. She married Sir Robert Douglas of Glenbervie, Bart., author of the Peerage and Baronage of Scotland.

SOPHIA LUNDIN OF THAT ILK

Upon the death of her brother John, she became the heiress of the Lundin estates. She married, on the 30th of April 1670, John Drummond, the second son of James Drummond 3rd Earl of Perth. He would later become the Viscount of Melfort, Earl of Melfort, Viscount of Forth, and Lord Drummond of Riccartoun, Castlemains and Gilestoun. In 1679, he was present at the battle of Bothwell Brig, and is said to have left the field by 10 o'clock, at which time victory was assured, and the troops were in pursuit of the defeated Covenanters (*East Neuk*, p 54). From around 1679 to 1681, he was governor of the garrison in Edinburgh Castle; in 1681 he was master general of H.M ordinance; from 1682 to 1684, he was deputy treasurer of Scotland (the Treasurer being the Marquis of Queensbury); and in 1684, he held the office of secretary of State for Scotland. Sophia Lundin passed away sometime before 1686, at which time John Drummond had re-married to Euphemia, a daughter of Sir Thomas Wallace of Cragie, the Lord Justice-Clerk. In this same year he was created Earl of Melfort and Viscount Forth. John Drummond was a staunch Catholic, and he was so disappointed in the protestant upbringing of his children by Sophia Lundin and her family, that both of his patents of Peerage (Earl and later Duke of Melfort) state that the succession went first to the heirs male of his body by his second marriage, whom failing to the heirs male whatsoever of his body. This fact would later protect his children by Sophia Lundin against incurring penalties as a result of their father's support of King James VII. under the government King William and Queen Mary. The Earl attended James VII. in Ireland in 1690, whereupon he was created the Duke of Melfort. James VII. was defeated by the armies of William of Orange; James and his court moved in exile to France; and many of the supporters of the King James suffered grave consequences, loosing their lands and titles. Accordingly, a court of justiciary outlawed John Drummond, Duke of Melfort, on the 23rd of July 1694, and he had his titles attained on the 2nd of July 1694 by an act of parliament. There was however a clause that provided his forfeiture should in no way affect or taint the blood of the children procreated betwixt him and Sophia Lundin and so Sophia's heirs could carry on holding Lundin (*Scots Peerage*, IV. 67-8). John Drummond died in 1714; he and Sophia had the following issue:-

1   *John Lundin*, born 31st October 1673, died young.

2   *James Lundin of that Ilk.* Born in 1674. He took his mothers name and succeeded in her estates. Further details follow.

3   *Robert Lundin of that Ilk*, married Anne Inglis, eldest daughter of Sir James Inglis of Cramond. he succeeded his brother James to Lundin, and further details of his life follow.

4   *Charles Lundin*

5   *Anne*, born 3rd March 1671, married Sir John Houston of Houston with issue.

6   *Elizabeth*, born 22nd July 1672, married William 2nd Viscount Strathallan with issue.

7   *Mary*, baptised 13th August 1677. She married first Gideon Scott of Highchester. The antinuptial contract for this was dated the 28th of February, 1700 (*NAS*, GD157/1574). Secondly, she

married Sir James Sharp of Scotscraig. Bart. She had issue by both husbands.

JAMES LUNDIN OF THAT ILK

Second son of Sophia Lundin and John Drummond, he was born in 1674, and succeeded his mother to the estates of Lundin. On the 8th of December, 1689, whilst still in his minority, he petitioned the Lords of the Privy Council for assistance with the running of the Lundin estate, as due the circumstances of the time, it was beginning to enter a state of ruin.

Decreta June 1689 – December 1691, folio 86i,
folio 87a.
8th December, 1689

"Petition by James Lundin of that Ilk for himself and his brothers and sisters, narrating that "the lands and estait of Lundine, being obnoxious to many inconveniences by reasone their is no persone will take upon him to maintein and oversee the affairs therof, whereby the business of that familie is exposed to much dissorded and confusione, the rents ly in the tennents hands unuplifted, which in a short tyme will desperat to the Master, as hes been often experienced in such caises, the moveables belonging to the familie are scattered and lost, the debts are increasing, their being non to take course with the annual rents, the lands are quartered upon for bygone cess and publict burdeane, and, quhich is yet more hard, the petitioner and remanent children are depryved of the benefeit of their necessary mentinence and education," and some remedy needs to be applied for preventin their utter ruin. He therefore humbly proposes "that some of the nearest freinds and relationes of the familie being authorized by their Lordships to mannadge the affairs of the samen by uplifting the rents and applying therof towards the necessary ends and uses abovewritten, and having pouer to dispose upon the moveables belonging to the familie, and also having accesss to the charter chist to the effect that any papers neidful for persuit or defence relative to the estait may be the more easilie fund out as occasione should require and that the writts themselves may be inventared, this might tend to preserve the forsaid familie"; otherwise "the petitioner and remanent orphanes" will be exposed to a very sad and ruinous condition. The Lords nominate and appoint the Earl of Leven, the Master of Melville, the Master of Burleigh, Mr Archibald Hope of Rankeilor, Senator of the College of Justice, Sir John Aytoun of that ilk, the Laird of Houston, younger of that Ilk, the Laird of Cassingray, the Laird of Megginch, the Laird of Auchtermairnie, and James Craufurd of Montwhannie, or any three of them, to inspect, manage and oversee the children and their estates, "not only in the particulars abovementionit bot also in all other things that may concerne the familie, that so every thing that in necessary and expedient for the preservatione therof may be done and performed, the saids persones abovenamed being always comptable for what they shall intromett with of the petitioners fortoun and estait. And the saids Lords recalls the former act and warrand granted be them in favours of the pettitioners."

(*Register of the Privy Council of Scotland*, Series III, XIV., 483)

James was a student of St. Leonard's College St. Andrews in 1692 and 1693; during which years he is recorded as paying board, and owing the University diet money (*Univ. St. And. Monim*). James died unmarried in 1698, and was succeeded by his brother Robert.

ROBERT LUNDIN OF THAT ILK

Born around 1675, he married Anne Inglis, the eldest daughter of Sir James Inglis, Bt., of Cramond on 20th January 1704 (*Scots Peerage*, VII. 57). That same year he is shown in the acts of the Scottish Parliament as a commissioner of Supply (*General index to the acts of parliament of Scotland*). He succeeded to the estates of Lundin on the death of his elder brother James Lundin of Lundin, being served as heir male on 29th April 1699 (*Inq. Spec. Ret. Fife*, No. 1426; *Gen. Retours*, No. 8095). He granted Andrew Cornfoot younger, the mill master of Lundin Miln, tack of the corn miln known as Lundin Miln on the 4th of August 1719. This tack was previously possessed by Andrew's father, Andrew Cornfoot elder, in Over Drummochy (SC20/

33/9). As a slight aside, Andrew Cornfoot younger (later feuar in Over Largo) was married to an Elizabeth Lundin, who later, on the 25th of January 1750, married David Fernie, feuar & maltster in Colinsburgh (SC20/36/9, SC20/36/10, SC20/36/13).

Robert died in December 1716. He had issue:-

1   *John Lundin of that ilk*, succeeded his father, and whose details follow.

2   *William Lundin*, born September 10th 1705, died young

3   *Anne Lundin*, born 9th October 1706. She died prior to January 1737, whereupon Sophia is styled eldest daughter.

4   *James Lundin of that ilk*, succeeded his brother, of more later.

5   *Robert Lundin*, baptised, October 31st 1709, died young

6   *Patrick Lundin*, born 1710. On the 29th of March 1725, he was registered as an apprentice to an Alexander Arbuthnot, merchant in Edinburgh (*Reg. Appren. Edin.*) On the 8th August 1726, he was admitted to the company of Archers (*NAS*, GD160/288).

7   *Sophia Lundin*, born 1710, married Robert Lumsden of Innergellie on January 27th 1738. She was given sasine of life rent of 200 merks to be uplifted from Lundin (*NAS*, GD160/293, No. 13)

8   *Margaret Lundin*, baptised November 22nd 1711

9   *Robert Lundin*, baptised May 21st 1713

10   *Archibald Lundin*, baptised 4th May 1715

11   *Henrietta Lundin*, twin sister of Archibald, baptised 4th May 1715. She married (probably) John Drummond, merchant in Drummochy (SC20/33/14).

JOHN LUNDIN OF THAT ILK

He was born on the 10th of November 1704 (*Scots Peerage*, VII. 57). He succeeded to Lundin upon the death of his father. On the 7th April 1727 (recorded 6 years later on the 3rd of November 1733) he was served as heir of Tail. and Provision Special of his grandmother Sophia Lundin, in Lundin and other lands (*Retours*). He died on the 9th of October 1735 without issue. A deed registered with the Sheriff Court of Fife shows that James may have designed himself as the 'Earl of Lundin.' The deed in question, dated 13th March 1722, shows that a George Johnstoune, tenant in Cladcoats, was granted tack of the town and lands of Teuchats, by Mr. David Lundin, advocate, and Factor for the EARL OF LUNDIN (SC20/33/10).

JAMES LUNDIN OF THAT ILK

James was married to Rachel Bruce, the third daughter of Thomas Bruce 7th Earl of Kincardine. He succeeded to Lundin upon the death of his brother John. On the 16th August 1737, he was served as heir special to his brother in the Barony of Lundin, including Haltoun, Balcormie, Stratherlie, one half of Kincraig, and others (*Retours*). He was given a Commission by Captain James Baillie of Parbroath, on the 3rd of November 1756 (SC20/36/9-12). On 30th June 1760, after the death of James Drummond the 6th titular Duke of Perth, he was served heir male and of provision to him, and nearest male heir of James 4th Earl of Perth. James assumed the later title. The title of Earl of Perth had however been attained, otherwise James would have been 10th Earl of Perth. He died at Stobhall 18 July 1781. His Wife died in Lundin on 29th June 1769 (*East Neuk*, p 55). James put up the Lundin estates for sale, and sold them in 1755; it is supposed that this was to help with the costs of attending the prosecution of the Perth peerage case, to gain hold of the lands and titles he was entitled to as heir male of the Earls of Perth, but did not possess due to the previous holder's forfeiture and attachment to the Stewart Cause. Associated with this sale is an action taken by John Abercromby, a Surgeon in Dysart, against James. James Lundin sold to the said James Abercromby the lands of Nether Pratis on the 2nd of June 1748, for £16900 Scots. When the Lundin estates were put up for sale in 1755, it would appear as if James was trying to sell Nether Pratis twice, as it appeared listed as part of the 1755 sale (*NAS*, GD50/185/57). James Lundin of that Ilk and his wife Rachel had issue:-

1   *Robert,* born 1741, died un-married in Lundin 10th May 1758
2   *Thomas, styled Lord Drummond.* He was baptised at Largo on the 24th of July 1742. He went to America in 1768. He died in the Bermudas in 1780.
3   *Rachel Drummond*, died unmarried at Cardross on the 24th May 1798 (*Scots Peerage*, VII. 58).
4   *James Drummond, Lord Perth Baron Drummond*; whose details follow.

JAMES DRUMMOND, LORD PERTH, BARRON DRUMMOND, FORMERLY LUNDIN

Born in Lundin on the 12th of February 1744; he would, apart from the attainer, have been the 11th Earl of Perth. On the 26th of October 1797, he was created Baron Drummond of Stobhall and Lord Perth. These titles were to go to the heirs male of his body. Prior to this he had unsuccessfully tried to petition the crown for the restoration of the title of Earl of Perth. He married Clementina, daughter of Charles 10th Lord Elphinstone in Edinburgh 31st March 1785. He died on the 2nd of July 1800 without male issue. His estates were passed to his daughter, Clementina Sarah Drummond and heirs of her body. The claim to the Earldom of Perth passed to a James Louis Drummond, forth-titular Duke of Melfort (the Earldom of Perth has now passed to the Strathallan Drummonds). He had issue:-

1   *James Drummond*, born on the 16th of October 1791, and died on the 11th of August 1799.

2   *Clementina Sarah Drummond*, who succeeded to her fathers estates.

3   *Jemima Rachel Drummond*, Born in Edinburgh on the 1st of May 1787, and died at Drummond Castle on the 28th of April 1788.

CLEMENTINA SARAH DRUMMOND.

Born in Edinburgh on the 5th of May 1786; she married the Hon. Peter Robert Burrell, eldest son of Peter 1st Lord Gwydyr and Priscilla Baroness Willoughby de Eresby, on the 20th of October 1807. She succeeded to the estates of Perth on the death of her Father. Her husband succeeded his father as 2nd Lord Gwydyr and his mother as Lord Willoughby de Eresby. Ultimately, their estates and titles passed to their daughter Clementina. They had three children:

1   *Alberci Burrell-Drummond*, born on the 25th of December 1821, and died on the 26th August 1870

2   *Clementina Elizabeth Burrell-Drummond*, of whom next.

3   *Charlotte Augustus Annabella Burrell-Drummond*, born on the 3rd of November 1815. She married on the 10th of August 1840, Robert John Carrington of Upton. She died on the 26th of July 1879,

Robert on the 17th March 1768. They had issue.

4   *Elizabeth Susancha Burrell-Drummond*. She died a spinster on the 10th of October 1853.

CLEMENTINA ELIZABETH BURREL-DRUMMOND.

Born on the 2nd of September 1809, in Piccadilly, London; and christened on the 15th of September 1809, St. Georges Square, London. She married Sir Gilbert John Heathcote, Bart., on the 8th of October 1827, at Drummond Castle. He died in 1867. In 1871 the barony of Willoughby de Eresby, then in abeyance, was revived in favour of Clementina. She died 13th November 1888. They had issue:-

1   *Gilbert Henry Heathcote-Drummond Willoughby*.
2   *Mary Heathcote-Drummond Willoughby*, married 15th Earl of Dalhousie.

GILBERT HENRY HEATHCOTE-DRUMMOND WILLOUGHBY

Born on the 1st of October 1830; he was the 23rd Baron Willoughby de Eresby; joint hereditary Lord Chamberlain; and was created Earl of Ancaster in 1898. He married Evelyn Elizabeth Gordon on the 14th of July 1863. They had issue:-

GILBERT HENRY HEATHCOTE-DRUMMOND WILLOUGHBY, 2ND EARL OF ANCASTER

He married Eloise Laurence Breeze. They had issue:-

1   *James   Heathcote-Drummond   Willoughby*, 3rd Earl of Ancaster
2   *Pricilla   Heathcote-Drummond   Willoughby*, married John Renton Muir

JAMES HEATHCOTE-DRUMMOND WILLOUGHBY, 3RD EARL OF ANCASTER

Baron Willoughby de Erseby. He married the Right Hon. Nancy Astor, and was succeeded in the barony of Willoughby de Eresby by his only daughter:

LADY JANE HEATHCOTE-DRUMMOND WILLOUGHBY

The Right Hon. The Baroness Willoughby de Eresby, joint hereditary Lord Great Chamberlain of England, was born 1st December 1934. She succeeded as Baroness on the death of her father, on the 29th of March 1983. She was one of the maids of honour at the wedding of H.M. Queen Elizabeth II. Lady Jane is unmarried. She is the senior representative of Lundin of that Ilk.

Lundin Tower and Lundin House

3   *Lundin Tower*

Very little now remains of Lundin tower and house, and it is suggested that what does remain, although dating back to the 16th or early 17th century, was altered a great deal, long after the Lundie family had left the estate. The origins of a castle at Lundin would certainly date from the time Phillip the Chamberlain was granted the barony by King Malcolm IV. Here he would have had to build a fortress as part of the feudal law governing his grant. This would not have been a stone castle, but the typical Norman type, of a motte with wooden bailey. It is generally suggested that his castle would have occupied the same site as the remains of the tower.

However, Eunson and Band, in their *Largo, An Illustrated history*, suggest another possible site for the first castle. Their interpretations of the Gaelic word Lundie/Lundin comes from Linn and Dun, meaning fort of the pool. They go on to interpret this further, stating that the Linn component does not just mean any type of water feature, but more specifically a waterfall, or pool besides a waterfall. This term would then not apply to the Loch that used to surround the present site of the castle (drained in the 18th century to provide arable lands), but may well apply to a site a mile or so from the current remains, opposite to Lundin Links Post Office. Here there is what appears to be a mound of a motte style, which is pretty close to a waterfall, the waterfall that also used to power Lundin Mill.

The stone castle that stood at Lundin was believed to be of the traditional Tower House type; the same as Balgonie and Benhom Castles, both of which survive. Sadly no remnants of the original tower at Lundin now remain. Lamont in his *Diary*, records details of several alterations and additions made to Lundin around 1660. He mentions that a chimney was fitted in to the hall of Lundie; two chambers, the Doctors chamber and blue chamber, were laid with floor boards; The low gallery, back house and tower head were slated in 1660, and the high gallery in 1661. The document also shows evidence of a dovecot, ox house, and storage for coal and salt. In 1671, a new bake house and brew house were added, and the hall was hung with green cloth hangings with leather between each piece. This is evidently the first time the hall was hung with such material.

Lundin Tower was greatly changed when in the possession of Sir William Erskine, and a number of gothic style features added and created. Although the Royal Commission for Architecture and historic Monuments in Scotland, suggests that the remaining tower is from the 16th or early 17th century, it has many of these gothic alterations made by William Erskine.

From a picture drawn in 1838, showing a front view of the mansion, the building appears to have comprised four sections. The first, the main house, was four stories high (including attic rooms), and in the centre, at the front, was a half octagonal bay rising from the ground to the top of the building. The second section was central and at the back of the main house. This is now almost all that remains, the so called 'stair tower.' This stood around 1 ½ stories higher than the main building, and was about a quarter of the width. The third and forth sections were to the side of the main house. To the right hand side was another four-story section, perhaps of a different age, but around a third the size of the main building. To the right was a one-story building with a very high roof, rising up to the third floor of the main house. These four sections were contiguous.

This main Mansion House of Lundin was demolished in 1876, by Sir John Gilmour of Lundin, then owner of the estate, and the only part he left was the old stair tower, and an adjoining part of the more modern mansion, which was kept as a lunchroom. The stair tower would have once been attached to the older tower house, and contains a small room at the top. Legend says that this is the room where Mary Queen of Scots spent the night while at Lundin. This cannot be proved, and many believe that the tower might be too new to have been around when she visited. Another Legend states that the bottom two steps of the tower were once stained with blood, "which the curious went to see." These steps were broken off "to remove the last traces of a tragedy" supposedly connected with "a love affair and attempted flight." It is even suggested that this tragedy is connected with the Green Lady of Lundin who is said to have haunted the tower (Bygone Fife, p 159)

For a long time the tower stood as a folly on the Lundin estate, but has recently been incorporated into a house. Lundin Tower is now very much a private residence, and the current owners, who themselves built the house now adjoining the old tower, request it made clear that the Tower is not open to the public.

Heraldry.

Before entering an in depth discussion concerning the heraldry of the Lundie family, it might be wise to introduce various basic concepts of heraldry in general so as to make the heraldic details of the family more understandable.

Colours

There are a limited number of colours (tinctures) and metals used in heraldic design. The metals comprise *Argent* (which is Silver or White); and *Or* (which is Gold or yellow). The number of tinctures used may vary slightly from source to source, but one can say it is roughly nine: *Gules* (red); *Azure* (blue); *Sable* (black); *Vert* (green); *Purpure* (Purple); *Sanguine* (Blood Red); *Tenne* (orange); *Marron* (brown); and *Fer* (grey).

Elements of Heraldry.

There are many different heraldic elements that can be used to make up a shield. Here we shall only consider elements that feature on Lundie armorials. For those interested to know more than the brief description given here, the book "A system of heraldry. Speculative and practical." in two volumes, by Alexander Nisbet, usually refered to in this text simply as Heraldry, is an invaluable source of information. As heraldry is a visual 'science,' the best and easiest was to explain the different design features relevant to the different Lundie arms is in a figure. The figure that follows illustrates an explaination of the following terms/elements, all of which elements are present in the different Lundie armorials; the bend; the palet; paly of *x*; the cushion; the mascle, the cross Moline; shield quartering; and the bordure indented.

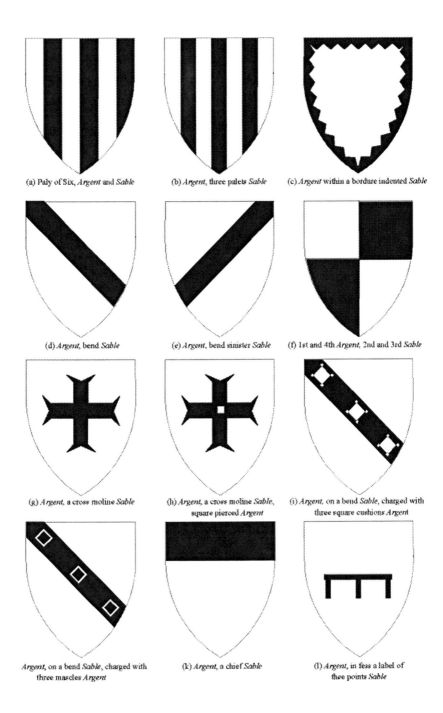

(a) Paly of Six, *Argent* and *Sable*

(b) *Argent*, three palets *Sable*

(c) *Argent* within a bordure indented *Sable*

(d) *Argent*, bend *Sable*

(e) *Argent*, bend sinister *Sable*

(f) 1st and 4th *Argent*, 2nd and 3rd *Sable*

(g) *Argent*, a cross moline *Sable*

(h) *Argent*, a cross moline *Sable*, square pierced *Argent*

(i) *Argent*, on a bend *Sable*, charged with three square cushions *Argent*

Argent, on a bend *Sable*, charged with three mascles *Argent*

(k) *Argent*, a chief *Sable*

(l) *Argent*, in fess a label of thee points *Sable*

4 Elements of Heraldry

The ancient arms of Lundy of that Ilk

The earliest arms on record are those used by Walter de London sometime prior to 1289. Record of these arms comes from a drawing of a seal made by Sir James Balfour. From the date, and nature of the arms, it is most likely that they are those born by Sir Walter de Lundy, the son of Sir Richard de Lundy.

The seal shows arms of two piles issuing from a chief charged with three pallets, over all in fess a label of three points (*Scottish Arms*, Stoddart, II, 233). The label of three points is a mark of cadency commonly added by the first son to his paternal coat of arms to difference it during the lifetime of his father. The arms of the family would have therefore just been two piles issuing from a chief charged with three pallets.

Heraldic texts state that the armorial motif in chief is more important than that in the remainder of the shield, and the subsequent arms on record are based upon a design of three palets over the whole shield. It is these subsequent arms that are commonly referred to as the ancient arms of Lundie of that Ilk, as after 1679, the family changed their shield to a completely new design.

These ancient arms appear in several of the ancient Scottish armorials. The Lindsay Armorial of 1542 (held at the NLS) records the arms of *Lundy of yat Ilk* being paly of six, *Gules* and *Argent*, on a bend *Azure* three tasselled cushions *Argent*. This can also be seen in plate 67 of the 1885 reproduction "Emblazoned". The Slains Armorial (held by the Earl of Errol) of 1565 records the arms of *Lundy of that Ilk* as paly of six *Gules* and *Argent*, on a bend *Azure* three cushions *Argent*. The Seton Armorial of 1591 (owned by Sir David Ogilvy Bt.) records the arms of *Lunde of that Ilk* as *Or*, three pales *Gules* surmounted by a bend *Azure* charged with three cushions *Argent*. The second Lindsay Armorial of 1599 (owned by the Earl of Crawford and Balacarres) shows the arms of *Lundie of that Ilk* as *Gules* five palets *Or* overall on a bend *Azure*, three cushions *Argent*. The Gentlemans Arms MS, which dates from around 1640 and is held in the Lion Office in Edinburgh, depicts the arms of *Lundye of that Ilk* as *Or*, three cushions pendant *Azure*.

A very early book on Heraldry in Scotland, 'Scotland's Herauldrie' by George Mackenzie of Roschaugh, which was published in 1680, gives the arms of *Lundie of that Ilk* as paly of six *Gules* and *Argent*, on a bend *Azure*, three cushions *Or*. The arms also appear in the Workmans Armorial held at the Lion Office. Nisbet in his *Heraldry* describes the ancient arms as a "paly of six pieces, *argent* and *gules*, surmounted on a bend *azure*, charged with three cushions *or*," and it is this description that is commonly used to describe the armorial. It is believed that the addition of the cushions to the arms was to signify the holding of an important government office by one of the family members, most likely Chamberlain.

The ancient arms also form part of the arms of Lundie of Balgonie, Lundin of Auchtermairnie, Lundin of Baldaster and Lundin of Drums. The arms of Balgonie also appear in many of the ancient Scottish armorials, and show the same slight variation in description from armorial to armorial as for the arms of Lundie of that Ilk. A full description of these arms will be given in the chapter concerning this family. The first record of the arms of Auchtermairnie is in the Lion Register, between 1672 and 1680. They bare the ancient arms of Lundie within a bordure indented *Azure*. For this entry the ancient arms are described as paly of six *Argent* and *Gules* on a bend *Azure* three cushions *Or*. As with the arms of Auchtermairnie, those of Baldaster first appear in the Lion register, but a few years later, 1698. Here the ancient arms of Lundie are quartered with those of the new arms (to be discussed shortly), within a bordure *Azure*. In this matriculation, the description of the ancient arms differs from Auchtermairnie, in that the Baldaster arms have the three cushions *Argent*, rather than *Or*. Looking through the earlier descriptions of the Lundie arms from the 16th century armorials, the cushions appear as both *Or* and *Argent*.

There is one final coat of arms to take note of that incorporate the ancient arms; that is the arms recorded in the Lion Register by a Mr Robert Lundin around the same time those of 'Lunden of Auchtermernie' were recorded. The arms are described as paly of six *Argent* and *Gules*, on a bend *Azure*, three cushions *Argent*, differenced in chief with a rose *Gules*: Motto, E Spinis Surgit Rosa. The rose in chief is usually added as a mark of cadency to difference the paternal arms for a seventh son; armed with such information it is still not possible to fully identify this Robert Lundin. The most obvious candidate for these arms is Mr Robert Lundie (Lundin) minister of Dysart and Leuchars, son of James Lundie 7th of Strathairlie; but he was only the 3rd son. However, as a minister in those times, Robert would be able to bear his paternal or chief arms without difference; which is illustrated for the case of James Lundie, minister of North Leith. This would imply the arms described would be those of Strathairlie; the rose in chief being a result of

Andrew Lundie, 1st of Strathairlie being the 7th legitimate son of Sir John Lundie of that Ilk. This of course is simply supposition, but the only Mr. Robert Lundie/Lundin on record around this time, of an age to register arms, is the said minister of Dysart and Leuchars.

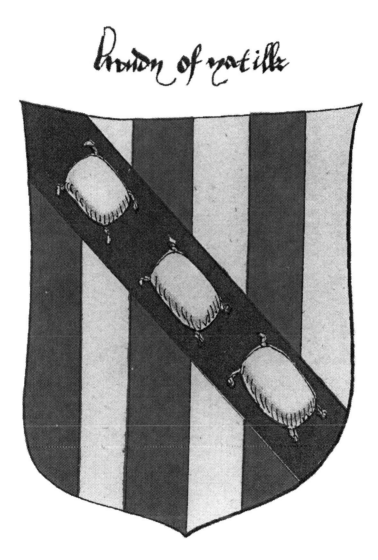

5. *Lundy of yat Ilk, from plate 67 of the 1885 reproduction "Emblazoned," of the 1542 Armorial produced by Sir David Lindsay of the Mount .*

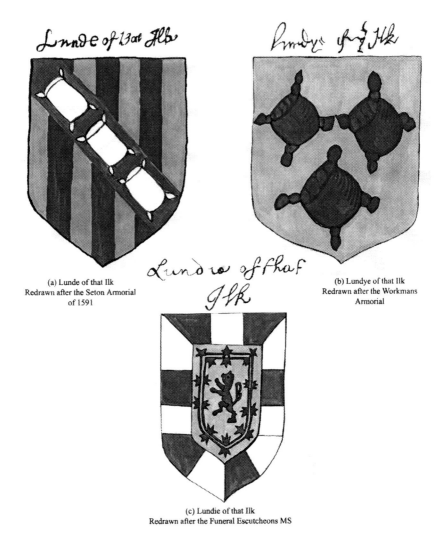

(a) Lunde of that Ilk
Redrawn after the Seton Armorial
of 1591

(b) Lundye of that Ilk
Redrawn after the Workmans
Armorial

(c) Lundie of that Ilk
Redrawn after the Funeral Escutcheons MS

*6. (a) Lunde of that Ilk redrawn from the Seton Armorial of 1591;
(b) Arms of Lundye of that Ilk reproduced from the Workmans Armorial
MS; (c) Arms of Lundie of that Ilk, reproduced from the Funeral Suctions
MS.Escutcheons MS*

One can also see examples of the family heraldry in seals that have survived on old charters. There are two examples of different seals of Sir John Lundy of that ilk. From the Dupplin Charters, 12th May, 1467, Sir John's seal is described as "Three pallets surmounted on a bend charged with as many mascles." His second seal is seen on several of the Benholm charters, dated between 1485 – 1495. It is described as a shield of arms: Paly of six, on a bend three square cushions. The seal of William Lundie of that ilk, Sir John's son, survives on several charters, that all date from a period when Sir John was still alive (Ch., 28 Oct. 1492, *per* J. J. Boswell, Leeds – Cast; 1 Mar. 1493-4, *per* do. – Cast. St. Andrews, L.P. 59 (1) Ch., 25 May 1483 – Cast; L.P. 62 Ch., 16 April 1495 – Cast; L.P. 76 (1) Ch., 24 May 1510 – Cast). The arms are described as three pallets surmounted of a bend charged with as many mascles. This is identical to the seal of Sir John from 1467. The arms of Margaret Lundie, wife of David Pringle of Smailholm, daughter of Sir Thomas Lundie of Pratis, are preserved on charter dating from the 8th of May 1539. They are also described as three pallets surmounted of a bend charged with as many mascles. The seal of Andrew Lundie, Portioner of Lambinethame, husband of Elizabeth Kerr, son of Walter Lundie of that Ilk, shows a variation on the 'three pallets surmounted of a bend charged with as many mascles.' A seal of his surviving on the Glamis Charters, from 1575 shows a shield of arms: Three pallets surmounted of a bend sinister charged with a crescent between two stars of six points; with a background semé of gouttes or leaves (*Scottish Heraldic Seals,* II.). This is very similar to the seal of William Lundie, one of the bailies of St. Andrews. His seal from a charter of St. Leonards College in 1520, shows three pallets surmounted of a bend sinister charged with a three stars of six points.

A seal of the so-called 'last laird,' John Lundie of that ilk, dated from 1634, survives in the Crawford Priory Chartularies. It is described as 'a shield of arms: On a bend three square cushions with foliage at top and sides of shield.'

Further details of seals showing the ancient arms can be read at the end of this chapter in the section on the Lundin Writs, where parts of seals of the Lundie family also remain.

Walter de London (*ante* 1289)

Sir John Lundie of that Ilk, Kt.
(1485, 1490, 1495)

Sir John Lundie of that Ilk (1489)
Sir William Lundie of that Ilk
(1483, 1495, 1510)
Margaret Lundie (1539)

Andrew Lundie,
portioner of Lambinethame
(1575)

William Lundie,
bailie of St. Andrews (1520)

7. Representations of the arms from several seals of the Lundie family

New arms

In 1669, the family of Lundin of that Ilk laid aside the ancient armorials, as discussed above, in favour of a new honour bestowed upon them by the King. They were warranted by the crown, (King Charles II) to carry the arms of Scotland upon their shield to show and account for descent from a natural son of King William the Lion of Scotland.

"Charles Rex,

Whereas by a declaration, under the hand of our Lyon-Depute, in our ancient Kingdom of Scotland, bearing date the 2d of September last, it doth appear to us, that it is sufficiently instructed, by original charters and other ancient documents, that the ancient family of Lundin (London), in our said Kingdom, is lineally descended of Robert of London, natural son of William the Lion King of Scotland, and brother to King Alexander II. and in that regard of this descent, it may be proper (if Wee be pleased to allow ye same) for the Laird of Lundin to bear ye Royal armes of Scotland, within a bordure componed (or gobonated) Argent & Azure: and for ye Crest a Lyon Gules Issuant of an open (or antiquz) Crowne Or; And for Supporters two Lyons Guardant Gules, each having a Collar Or, charged with three thistles Vert with this Motto Dei donno sum, quod sum. And we being graciously desirous (upon all fitt occasions) to give Testimony of the Esteem Wee have of that antient and honourable Family, Doe by these Presents Give full power, Warrant and Authority to the present laird of Lundin, and his lawful successors of the name Lundin, and descending from that family, to bear the Royal armes of Scotland, within a bordure componed (or gobonated) Argent and Azure: And for the crest a Lyon Gules issuant forth of an open (or anticz) Crowne Or : And for supporters two Lyons Guardant Gules each having a collar Or charged with three thistles Vert, with this Motto: Dei dono sum, quod sum. for doing whereof This Shall be to him (and our Lyon King at armes, in that Our Kingdom now, or ye time being for extending and giving out ye said armes in due forme) a sufficient Warrant, which Wee doe hereby appoint to be recorded in the Bookes or Registers of Our

Lyon Office, and this Originall Warrant remaine in the Custodie
of the said Laird of Lundin and his Successors aforesaid. Given
under the Royal hand and Signet at Our Court at Whitehall the
27ᵗʰ Day of October 1679. And of our Reigne ye 31 th year.

By His Majts. command Sic Subsc.
(signed) Lauderdale

The description of the arms is slightly different in Burkes General
Armoury. It gives a much more specific description of the crest, perhaps
slight additions were made after the initial grant: *"Or,* a lion rampant *gules*
within the royal tressure flory and counter flory of the last, all within a
bourdure gorbonated *azure* and *argent*; Crest – Out of an antique crown *Or,*
a lion issuing affrontee gules, holding in the dexter paw a sword errect, and
in the sinister a thistle slipped all proper; Supporters, - Two lions guardant
gules having collars *or,* charged with three thistles *vert.* Motto – Del dono
sum quod sum." The motto translates, as, 'by the bounty of God, I am
what I am.' The new arms of Lundin of that Ilk are recorded in the armorial
entitled "Funeral Escutcheons." They can be seen as part (c) in the figure
6 (redrawn after the Funeral Eschutcheons MS), and in the figure opposite
(taken from Nisbet's *Heraldry*).

John Drummond, who was initially granted these new arms by King
Charles when simply the Laird of Lundin, adopted a slightly differenced
version as Earl of Melfort. These arms appear in the great hall of Edinburgh
Castle and are those of the new arms of Lundin of that Ilk, quartered with
those for Drummond: Quarterly 1ˢᵗ and 4ᵗʰ *Or,* three bars wavy *Gules:* 2ⁿᵈ
and 3ʳᵈ *Or,* a lion rampant within a double tressure flory counter flory *Gules:*
all within a bordure compony *Argent* and *Azure.*

Three seals of John Lundin of that ilk, dated sometime in the
seventeenth century, show the Royal arms rather than the Paly of six ancient
arms. The first must date from before the new grant of 1679, as it features
a different motto. 1) To the sinister, in plate armour, sword in the sinister
hand, scabbard at the side, sash over the shoulder. Horse pacing on a mount
by the sea. In the background over the horse on the sinister side a carved
shield of arms bearing the Royal arms of Scotland within a bordure gobony.
Motto: AB ORIGINE SACRA. (2) A shield of arms bearing the Royal arms
of Scotland within a bordure gobony. *Crest:* On a helmet an mantling, out of
an antique coronet a lion issuing affronté in the dexter paw a sword erect,

8. The Arms of Lundin of that Ilk, as adopted in 1679; taken from 'Nisbet's Heraldry'.

in the sinister a thistle slipped. *Supporters:* Two lions collared. Motto, on a scroll in base: DEI . DONO . SVM . QVOD . SVM. (3) A lion sejuant guardant, a sword in the dexter paw erect, and in from an ornamental escutcheon charged with a cypher, D.I.L.S., above is the *Motto:* DEI DONO SVM QUOD SVM, (*Scottish Heraldic Seals*).

The Lundin Writs.

As can be gleamed from many of the references in this last chapter, and in those that follow, the National Archives of Scotland hold many papers, which make reference to the Lundie family. These papers and references come from many many different collections. However there is one particular collection that should be discussed as an entity itself, rather than just referred to by number. The collection is gifts and donations (GD) one hundred and sixty. These are the papers of the Drummond Family, coming from the charter chests of Drummond Castle. As the main line of the Lundie family was to succeed to the Earldom of Perth, and as their heir of line still holds the property of Drummond Castle, it should not be surprising to note that this collection of documents also includes the writs and charters of Lundie of that Ilk.

The Drummond papers in this collection are fairly well inventoried, with a copy of a description of the various papers held on the bookshelves of the NAS historical reading rooms. The Lundin writs are in a much poorer state. I had the privilege of reading through some of these old family papers, and many were in a very sorry state. There is currently no detailed inventory of these writs. It appears that at one point, many years ago, the writs were inventoried, but this is no longer in existence. Many of the papers bear a number (different to the current catalogue), and a brief description. However on many, even this more modern description on the back of the papers is now illegible, with ink fading and many documents beginning to show signs of great age, perhaps as a result of their life before being acquired by the NAS. Whilst examining these papers, many were even withheld, as they are now too fragile to be handled.

The earliest writ in the collection is said to date from around 1150, and is an agreement between Geoffrey de Malville and Robert Hutlaga. The next in age is from around 1166-1171, and is the charter by King William the Lion, re-grating Lundin to Walter, son of Phillip the chamberlain, that was transcribed earlier in this chapter. There are two other writs of a similar date, and they are concerned with Robert de London, son of King William the Lion. Both of these charters concern the Forrest of Ueth, and have again been described earlier in this chapter. These four charters are held together under the reference, GD160/269, and with three transcriptions of charters, consist the contents of the 'bundle.' Following these, the next writ chronologically dates from around 1435, and is the marriage contract of Sir John Lundie and Elizabeth Lindsay, daughter of Lord Lindsay of the Byres. This shows a gap of around 250 years in the family writs, and it is not known what happened to these documents, why or when they went missing; but it is this lack of documentation in the Lundie family's own archives that does not help one to determine the precise succession of the Barony from Thomas de Lundin (around 1251), to Sir John Lundy of Lundy, in 1430. It would appear that all of these charters were extant in the early 17th century. Under the details of James Lundie of that Ilk, written earlier in this section, is included a transcription of a letter written by Sir James Lundie to the King. In this letter he states that he can trace his lineage back to Robert de London through the family charters. To make such a claim now would be impossible. Nisbet in his *Heraldry* also alludes to the fact that family charters can prove the claim of descent from Robert de London, and thus the entitlement to the Royal Arms.

From 1430 onwards, the rest of the family's occupation is fairly well represented in the writs, but far more papers survive for Drummond of Lundin, than do Lundin of Lundin. The bundles of writs directly concerning Lundin of Lundin range from GD160/269 to 160/293. Many of the subsequent catalogue numbers contain papers concerning the Drummond of Lundin claim on the Earldom of Perth. These writs would have at one time been adorned with a great many seals of the family, but the seals as well as the writs themselves have suffered with time. In the collection, there are very few remnants of seals, and those that do remain, show little detail; however, there are few examples still worth noting:

GD160/280, writ number 69, is a charter by William Lundy of that Ilk. This particular charter shows the most complete seal in the collection, and shows a shield of arms, three palets surmounted of a bend. Above the shield is decorated with some foliage. One can make out the lettering "...I LVDYDE ODEM."

GD160/281, writ no 28, which is a Precept of Clare Constat by Lundie of Balgonie from 1523, shows a shield of arms, quartered, all surmounted of a bend sinister charged with three cushions; with 1st and 4th, a bend sinister; 2nd and 3rd, details cannot be made out.

GD 160/284, writ no. 13, which concerns Walter Lundy of that Ilk, and his son Andrew from around 1550, has Walter's seal on a tag. The seal shows a shield of arms three palets surmounted of a bend. Above the shield appears to be a small crown. This particular writ also shows a very good example of Walter's signature; a representation of which can be seen in a figure to follow.

GD 160/284, writ no. 24, again shows the arms of Walter. Part of the seal survives, where the lettering "ATERI," presumably Walteri, can be made out. The clearest picture of the arms comes from the impression made by the seal on the opposing page. Here one sees a shield surmounted of a bend with three cushions.

GD 160/284, writ no 37, which is a charter by Walter's son William, from the 24th of May 1591, shows about a third of the seal remaining. The lettering "WI – LLMI LV-DI," presumably Willellmi Lvndi, can be read, and the shield shows signs of the three palets or paly of six, and a bend.

GD 160/285, writ no 8, a discharge by David Lundy to Walter Lundy in 1532, shows a very small fragment of the seal of David. Only the lettering "DVD" can be made out. The far left side of the shield remains. One can make out the remains of the bend, and enough still exists to show clearly one cushion. One palet, of what one assumes is three, is also visible. Above the shield is some flowering foliage.

GD 160/285, writ no. 35, letters of reversion for redeeming Pratis, 15th January 1519, shows a full seal of Walter Lundy of that Ilk, but it is very worn, and much detail has been lost. Lettering is visible, but now illegible. The shield of arms has remnants of palets, surmounted of a bend with three cushions.

As well as having these few remnants of the seals, the writs show many of the signatures of the family. Those of Walter Lundy of that Ilk, John Lundie of that Ilk, and Margaret Lundin of that Ilk, can be seen in the figure that follows.

Walter Lundy of that Ilk, 1545

John Lundie of that Ilk, 1632

Margaret Lundie of that Ilk, 1676

9. Signatures from the Lundin Writs.

Section Three

Other Baronial Branches

The History of the Houses of Balgonie, Benholm, Drums (formerly Conland), & Gorthie

The House of Balgonie

The Barony of Balgonie is situated within the parish of Markinch, due east of Glenrothes, in the Sheriffdom of Fife. The barony was first associated with the family of Sibbald, and the castle of Balgonie was built for Sir Thomas Sibbald. The tower that Sir Thomas built is now the oldest still standing in Fife. It is regarded as one of the finest 14th century towers in Scotland. The castle and Barony came into the possession of the Lundie family through marriage.

SIR ROBERT LUNDY, 1ST OF THAT NAME OF BALGONIE

The Lord High Treasurer of Scotland, he was the son of Andrew Lundy of Pitlochie, a brother to Sir John Lundy of that Ilk. Robert is commonly presented as the son of Sir John Lundy of that Ilk himself, but there is no evidence to show this, and as shall be seen, the passing of Balgonie, Pitlochie and Bannaty from Andrew to Robert, along with the office of Sheriff of Fife, notwithstanding the naming of Sir Robert's first son, would far more indicate Sir Robert as Andrew's son, than Sir John's. He married Elizabeth Sibbald, daughter and heiress of Sir John Sibbald of Balgonie, Sheriff of Fife. The Sibbalds are said to descend from Sybaldi, who flourished in the middle of the 12th century. Sir Duncan Sibbald was living in Balgonie before 1246 (mentioned in a Papal Bull of 1250); and Sir Thomas Sibbald of Balgonie, who built the original tower, was the King's Treasurer around 1360.

Elizabeth's grandfather, also a John Sibbald of Balgonie, had been Treasurer of Scotland. For a long time, Sibbald the Treasurer only had one daughter to succeed him, Elizabeth. She was given in marriage to Archibald Douglas 5th Earl of Angus, with a wedding portion of 3000 merks. It is thought that the marriage was upon the supposition that Elizabeth, as John the treasurer's only heir, would succeed to Balgonie, and thus Angus and his descendants by Elizabeth, would hold the lands and barony. However, sometime after the marriage, Sibbald the treasurer's first wife died. He remarried, and his second wife bore him sons. Thus with a male heir to Sibbald the treasurer, Angus found the estate no longer settled upon him. Instead, the treasurer's son John suceeded to Balgonie, and in turn was succeeded by his only daughter Elizabeth, and thus the estate was settled upon her and her spouse, Robert Lundy. Sir Robert Lundy and a descendant of the marriage between Angus and Elizabeth Sibbald, George, master of Angus, are said to have interacted on a case in 1489, whereupon they both agreed upon a general remission for Ewsdale, Eskdale and Liddisdale, upon payment of £1000 (*History of the House and Race of Douglas and Angus*, II. 11-13; 61). It is interesting to note that another descendant of the marriage between Angus and Elizabeth Sibbald was Lord Darnley, the second husband of Mary Queen of Scots. Queen Mary spent the night at Balgonie before travelling to Wemyss Castle, where it was she met her future husband for the first time.

The Lundie family association with Balgony seems to date from 1454, when Andrew Lundy of Pitlochy, Sheriff of Fife, was given ward of Balgony, and received payments on behalf of the heirs of John Sibbald of Balgony (*Exchequer Rolls of Scotland*, V. 640; VI. 406, 511, 597; VII. 437). Robert Lundy, Andrew's son, first appears on record associated with Balgonie in 1471, where the Exchequer Rolls of Scotland show him receiving payment, for the fermes of Crail, on behalf of his wife 'the Lady of Balgony'. The records show him receiving these payments each year until his death, upon which his son Andrew receives the annuity (*Exchequer Rolls of Scotland*, VIII. 109, 204, 263, 397, 473, 556, 636; IX. 87, 230, 295, 348, 454, 553; X. 70, 148, 241, 309, 368, 393, 467, 540, 620; XI. 56, 128, 237, 280; XII. 380, 476, 603). Elizabeth Sibbald was alive by 1483, but predeceased her husband, as Nisbet in his Heraldry, states that Sir Robert was also married to Jean Lindsay, a daughter of one of the Lords of the Byres.

Sir Robert features frequently in the Exchequer Rolls of Scotland. They tell us that sometime between 1480 and 1487 Robert claimed that the lands of Bannochty and Petlochty with mill and Bordland were fued to him;

and that between 1488 and 1496 he occupied them. He was later asked to prove his claim to these lands, which must have been done as they are found to be in the possession of his grandson, James Lundy of Balgony, many years later. Also between 1488 and 1496 the Exchequer Rolls show that he was paid a fee by the state for the position of 'usher'. Between 1497 and 1501 they indicate that he received fees from the state as first usher of the King's chamber; he received a fee from Kinclevin; he received a fee from the state for the position of Lord High Treasurer of Scotland (to which he was appointed in 1494 and held until his death in 1501); he received fees and furniture as Comptroller; he received payment from the state for him and his servant in Edinburgh; he was let the lands of Innerallone, Lupnoch and Lessintrule; he was let several 'crown' lands; he was shown to be chamberlain of Galloway, Stratherne, Pety, Brauchly, Menteith, and Ballincreif; and was paid fee for his custody of Stirling Castle (*Exchequer Rolls of Scotland*, X. 484, 577, 589, 591, 595; XI. 27, 216, 217, 237, 246, 255, 261, 277, 278, 292, 314, 339, 343, 352, 377, 396, 406, 411, 424, 428, 432, 434, 437; XVII. 725).

There are a great many charters in existence where Sir Robert is a witness, most probably due to his high position in the Scottish Court. One particular charter of which he is a witness is of note to mention, mainly due to one of the other names presented as a witness. On 30th of December, 1495, a Mr Andrew Wood, as procurator of John Comry of that Ilk, resigned into the King's hands, the lands of Comry, Kingartht, Litill Keplandy, Glemayke, Sclouchmonawze, Sclouchnatoy, a quarter of Megour and the office of mair of fee in the stewartry of Strathearn, in favour of John Comry, younger. This charter was witnessed, at Linlithgow; by the most excellent Richard Plantagenet, `as he asserts', son of the serene Prince Edward illustrious King of England; Robert Lundy of Balgony; Peter Crechtoune; William Spishous and James Jaklene. Notary: Andrew McBrek priest of the diocese of Dunkeld (*NAS*, GD279/9). Another couple of charters, not involving Robert directly, but containing his name are of importance to note as they give us the information that Robert held the office of Sheriff of Fife in the year 1493 (*NAS*, GD82/30, GD82/32). These two charters involve: (1) John Sibbald, mair of the north quarter of the water of eding and depute of Robert Lundy of Balgonie, Sheriff of Fife; 2nd March, 1493: (2) Andrew Hatton, depute of Robert Lundie of Balgonie, Sheriff of Fife; 16th April, 1493. It was noted in the previous section that Andrew Lundie of Pitlochry is known to have held this office in 1452, 1455, 1456, 1468 and 1471; and

William Lundy of that Ilk held it in 1491. Upon Robert's death his son Andrew was to hold this office. It does seem that for a while, this office, at least in some part, was hereditary in the Lundie family.

As well as there being many charters with Robert Lundy as witness, there are many still in existence either granted by Robert, or granted to Robert. As well as the general historic interest involving the transactions of this family, these charters help to show us that Robert Lundy of Balgonie was knighted sometime between February and March 1497.

1487

On the 10th February, Sir Robert was granted two charters by Andrew Schethum of that Ilk; the first grants to Robert a mill, whose name cannot now be determined (*NAS*, GD26/3/10); the second grants Robert a sixth part of the lands of Schethum, south of the river Leven (*NAS*, GD26/3/9). On the 10th of November of that year, Robert was granted a charter of an annual rent of 4 merks out of the lands of Schethum by Thomas Schethum (*NAS*, DG26/3/16). Before the year was out, on the 31st of December, Robert was granted a charter by Andrew Schethum of an annual rent of 4 merks from half lands of Schethum (*NAS*, GD26/3/21).

1488

On the 17th April, George, Earl of Rothes granted a charter to Robert of the lands of Balcely, within the Barony of Leslie and Sheriffdom of Fife (*NAS*, GD241/200). On the 22nd of December, Andrew Schethum, portioner of that Ilk, granted a charter in favour of Robert of half the lands of Schethum, on the south side of the River Leven (*NAS*, GD26/3/23)

1489

On the 24th January Thomas Schethum of that Ilk, granted a charter in favour of Robert Lundy of Balgony of half lands of Schethum, south of the river Leven (*NAS*, GD GD26/3/27). The next day Robert recorded an instrument of resignation of these lands (*NAS*, GD 26/3/30); and Thomas Schethum of that Ilk declared that he had granted no writs to the half lands of Schethum that would be prejudicial to Robert Lundie's possession (*NAS*, 26/3/29).

1491

On the 17th of April, Robert Lundy granted a charter in favour of Thomas Schethum of that Ilk, of an annualrent of 13 merks out of lands of Schethum south of the River Leven. Amongst others, this charter was witnessed by an Andrew Lundy of Demperstoun (*NAS*, GD26/3/32). On

20th April, Thomas Schethum of that Ilk granted a charter in favour of Robert Lundy of Balgony of a third part of half lands of Schethum, south of the River Leven (*NAS*, GD26/3/34). On the same date Thomas Schethum of that Ilk granted a charter in favour of Robert Lundy of 'Balgowny' of half the lands of Schethum on the south of the River Leven (*NAS*, GD26/3/36). The 21st April Robert gave to Thomas Schethum of that Ilk; a bond of reversion to a of third part of half lands of Schethum, south of the River Leven, on payment of £40 Scots (*NAS*, GD26/3/38); and a bond not to disturb the tenants of third part of half lands of Schethum in the peaceable possession thereof (*NAS*, GD26/3/39). On the 19th May there is record of an arbitral decreed between Robert Lundy of Balgony and Thomas Schethum of that Ilk, regarding the marches between the east and west halves of the lands of Schethum belonging to said Robert and Thomas respectively (*NAS*, GD26/3/40). On the 25th of that month there is also record of an indenture between Robert Lundy of Balgony and Thomas Schethum of that Ilk, regarding the marches of their respective halves of the lands of Schethum (*NAS*, GD26/3/41). On the 13th of August, Thomas Schethum of that Ilk gave an assignation to Robert Lundy of Balgonie of the right of redemption of an annual rent of 5 merks out of lands of Schethum, redeemable on payment of £40 Scots (*NAS*, GD26/3/45).

1493

Letters dated February 5th, addressed to the King, by William Lewingstoun of Drumry with consent of Robert Lewingstoune, his son and apparent heir, resigned into the King's hands the lands of barony of Hassendene in sheriffdom of Roxburgh, held in chief, containing procuratory in favour of Robert Lundy of Balgony, Patrick Home of Polwarth, Adam Creichtoun of Kippandavy and Thomas Blair (*NAS*, GD224/918/26)

1495

On the 10th of August a notarial instrument narrates a Decreet Arbitral, by Andrew, protonotary apostolic and prior of Petynweme and Robert Lundy of Balgony, arbiters for Archibald, Earl of Argyll, on the one part, and Patrick Blakader of Tuleallane, on the other part, whereby it was decreed that Patrick, having been granted a Tack of bailiary of Culross for 19 years, resigned the same into the hands of the abbot of Culross in favour of the Earl, in return for which the Earl of Argyll granted to aid Patrick the right to be deputy in Culross, to be able hold courts and draw profits from them. This right was to be for him and his successors for 19 years (*NAS*,

GD15/153)

1496

Although the Sibbald family built the tower of Balgonie Castle, the North Range was built in 1496 for Sir Robert Lundie of Balgonie. This date is so precise as King James IV visited on the 20th of August 1496. He was so impressed by the mason's work that he gave them a gift of 20 shillings. A drawing of the North Range, and Hall House of Balgonie as it is today can be seen at the end of the details of Sir Robert's life.

1497

Robert Lundy of Balgony was granted a Charter under the great seal of lands of Schethum and Caldhame on the north and south sides of the River Leven, following on the resignation of Thomas Schethum (*Reg. Mag. Sig.* II, 2343; *NAS*, GD26/3/49).

1498

In the summer of 1498, Sir Robert Lundy, accompanied King James IV to Kintyre, along with Elphinstone, the Lord Privy Seal, Master Richard Murehede, the Secretary, and Master Walter Drummond, Clerk of Rolls, Register, and Council, (*Reg. Mag. Sig.*, II., No. 2436.)

1499

Sir Robert Lundy of Balgony was granted a charter, by John Cockburn of Treaton, of lands of Tretone Myre (The Mires) with Dalginch Myre and Myltoune of Balgony (*NAS*, GD26/3/52).

In this year Sir Robert also travelled to England to arrange the marriage of King James of Scotland to Lady Margaret Tudor, daughter of King Henry VII of England.

> "June 28 1499. The King of Scots having received from his counsellor 'Doctour Hatton' the King of Scots 'wryting' that he is in brief time about to send an 'honourable ambassade,' viz. the Archbishop of Glasgow, Patrick Earl of Bothwell, the Reverend Father [Andrew Forman] the prothonotary of Scotland, and Sir Robert Lundy knight, his treasurer, to treat for the marriage with the Lady Margaret, orders a safe conduct for them and 'an hundred horses' by the bearer."
>
> (*Calendar of Documents relating to Scotland, Bain*; IV. 1505)

Sir Robert died before May 1501 while still holding the Lord Treasurers office. This is the date his son, Sir Andrew Lundie, was given sasine of his late father's property. Shortly before this it is known that he was also the governor of Stirling castle. It is not known how long he had held this office previous to this, remembering that Sir John Lundy of that Ilk was appointed governor in 1488, and was in office in 1496. Sir Robert had issue:-

1 ***Sir Andrew Lundie, 2ⁿᵈ of Balgonie***, who succeeded, and whose details follow.

2 ***Euphemia Lundie***, married William Melville of Raith before 1490 (*Scots Peerage*, IV. 84-6). William is believed to have died before the 29th of October 1502, as on that date his grandson was retoured as heir of his father in the Melville estates. After William's death, Euphemia appears in record in 1506 with regards property disagreements between Janet Bonar, relict of her eldest son, and her other sons. Euphemia and William had issue:-

   i John Melville, younger of Raith. He married Janet Bonar, daughter of *William Bonar of Rossie*. He died before his father. They had issue.

      a   *Sir John Melville*, 4th of Raith. He had a great many children. His second son and successor, John Melville 5th of Raith, married Isobel Lundie, daughter of Walter Lundie of that Ilk, the contract dated the 30th of March 1563 (*Scots Peerage*, VI. 102; *Reg. Deeds*, VI. f.147). His third son, Robert, born around 1527, was created 1st Lord Melville.

      b   *David*, burgess of Edinburgh.

   ii William, who held the lands of Pitscottie and Dura.

   iii Andrew

   iv David

   v Elizabeth, who married John Gourlay, younger of Lamathlan

   vi Margaret, who married James Bonar of Rossie

   vii   *Gelis*, married Henry Pitcairn of Drongy.

3 ***Elizabeth Lundie***, married Sir John Lindsay of Pitcruvie, Master of Lindsay, eldest son of Patrick Lindsay 4th Lord Lindsay of the Byres (*Scots Peerage*, V. 397; note that the *Scots Compendium* of 1756 gives her as the daughter of Andrew Lundie of Balgonie, p154). Elizabeth and Sir John received a crown charter of the lands of Pitcruvie,

Montschele and Edindowny, following the resignation of Patrick 4th Lord Lindsay, on the 14th of June 1498 (*NAS*, GD20/1/61). On the 28th of August, 1521, they both were granted a charter of a third of the lands of Balmane, by James Kincragye, provost of the Church of the Virgin Mary de Rupe in St Andrews (*NAS*, GD20/1/71). Sir John died in 1525. Lady Elizabeth re-married David Lundie, brother-german to Walter Lundie of that Ilk. Elizabeth and Sir John had issue:

i   Sir John Lindsay, 5th Lord Lindsay of the Byres. Granted the Sheriffship of Fife in 1541. He had nine children, including Patrick, Sixth Lord Lindsay of the Byres, and Norman Lindsay of Kilquhis. Norman requires mentioning, as his first wife was an Isobel Lundie. Although the connection is not fully known, she must have been very closely related to the family of Lundie of that Ilk, as their eldest son was receiving an annuity of 100 merks from Lundie, for which his son in turn was served as heir on the 2nd October 1617. Isabel Lundie died on the 9th of September, 1574 (*Scots Peerage*, V. 402-3); and had her testament proved on the 16th of November that year (*Edin. Tests.*).

ii   Patrick Lindsay of Kirkfothar, who died at Flodden 19th May 1514.

iii   David Lindsay of Kirkfothar.

iv   Elizabeth Lindsay, who married Walter Lundin of that Ilk.

v   Janet Lindsay

vi   Alison Lindsay

SIR ANDREW LUNDIE, 2ND OF BALGONIE

Sir Andrew, as son and apparent heir of Robert Lundy of Balgony and his spouse Elizabeth Sibbald, received a charter under the great seal of the lands and barony of Balgonie on the 7th March 1483. The charter of these lands followed on the resignation of Sir Andrew's mother Elizabeth Sibbald (*NAS*, GD26/3/4). As heir of his father he received sasine of the lands of Tretoun Myre on the 27th May 1501; this followed on a precept by John Cockburn of Treatoun granted the previous day (*NAS*, GD26/3/55). In 1506, upon the payment of 140 merks Scots, Sir Andrew gave letters of reversion to John Cockburn of Treatoun, of the lands of the Myre of Treatoun

10. *Hall House and North range of Balgonie Castle.*

(*NAS*, GD15/707). On the 6th March, 1510, the lands of the Spittal, reverted back to the possession of the Laird of Balgonie, from the hands of Alan Coutts of the Spittale. This reversion also included an annual rent of 12 merks from the lands of Schethum, due to a chaplainry and chaplain in the Parish Kirk of Markinch, for the soul of the deceased Andrew Wemyss. The reversion occurred upon payment of £160 Scots (*NAS*, GD26/3/56). Sir Andrew, now designed Knight, Sheriff of Fife, granted a precept of two seventh parts of the lands of Fordell, in favour of Robert Drummond, son and heir of Robert Drummond of Armor. Sasine of these lands was given on the 8th of February 1510-11 (*NAS*, GD172/8). Sometime between 1502 and 1507, Andrew was given sasine of the Barony of Mundynes in Kincardineshire (Mondynes) (*Exchequer Rolls of Scotland*, XII, 714).

In 1511, Sir Andrew expanded the Barony of Balgonie by annexing other lands in his possession to it. On the 30th of April 1511, Sir Andrew resigned into the hands of the King, the lands of Under Balgony, Nethir Balgony, Myltoun, Byris, Inverlochty alias Spittale, and Schethum, all in the sheriffdom of Fife; the lands of Nether Carnbo, three quarters of the lands of Under Carnbo, the lands of Brachte, and Gowlane, in sheriffdom of Perth and Stewartry of Straitherne (Strathearn). That same day Sir Andrew was granted a charter under the Great Seal incorporating the fore mentioned lands in to a free Barony of Balgonie (*NAS*, GD26/3/56-7)

It appears that Sir Andrew was threatened with excommunication around 1512. The reason for this is not know, but it appears to be at the instance of his sister Elizabeth and her Husband John Lyndsay of Pitcruvie, Master of Lindsay. He was however absolved of whatever charge was made on the 11th August, 1512, the reason given was so that he could carry out his duties as Sheriff of Fife, and hear cause between David Kinnear of that Ilk, and John and Andrew Kynneir, his sons, on one part, and Alexander Ramsay of Brachmontht and John Gourlay of Souththeld, on the other (*NAS*, GD82/53).

Sir Andrew appears to have also had a disagreement with Robert Douglas of Lochleven. There is record of need, in 1512, for arbitration between Sir Andrew, and Robert Douglas of Lochleven, tenant of the lands of Fossoway, concerning the perambulation between the common of Fossoway and the lands of Carnbo, part of the Barony of Balgonie (*NAS*, GD150/1044).

He was granted the office of Sheriff of Fife from 1497 to 1513, and in

1513 he was granted the office for another five years, but he died sometime before April 1518. It is in this year that his son and heir, James Lundie, is given sasine to the lands of his late father. Andrew was twice married, firstly to Katherine Seton (*Reg. Mag. Sig.* II) and secondly Janet Dishington (*Sheriff Court Book of Fife*). Sir Andrew had issue:-

1　*James Lundie, 3rd of Balgonie*
2　*Andrew Lundie, 4th of Balgonie*
3　*Robert Lundie, 5th of Balgonie*
4　*Alexander Lundie.* He appears in the local records of Dysart in December 1545, designed as brother german to James Lundie of Balgonie. He probably had a son Alexander, who can be seen in the charter of Conland, granted to his cousin Robert, as a witness designed as Alexander Lundie Junior.
5　*Margaret Lundie*, later Lady Colluthie, spouse of David Ramsay of Colluthie. (*Reg. Mag. Sig.* II., 3311.) She had as one of her servants in 1569, one John Lundie (*Calendar of Laing Charters*, 849). They had issue:

　i Henry Ramsay. In 1539, Margaret Lundie and David Ramsay conferred upon their son Henry "one half of the lands of Cruvy, with the tower, fortalice, and rights to fishing in the water of Motray." He died at the battle of Pinkie, leaving an only daughter, who married Mr David Carnegie of Panbride, who by his second wife was the father of the first Earl of Southesk and Northesk.

JAMES LUNDIE, 3RD OF BALGONIE

On the 15th April, 1518, James Lundy of Balgonie was served as son and heir of his late father, Andrew Lundy of Balgonie, in the lands of Lochtoune and Wilkestoun, in the barony of Kippo and sheriffdom of Fife (*NAS*, GD26/3/914). On the 8th of May that year he was given Sasine propriis manibus, by David Cockburn of Treatoun, of the lands of Treatoun Mire (*NAS*, GD26/3/61). On the 17th February 1522, David Cockburn of Treatoun renounced to James Lundy of Balgonie, the possibility of reversion of the lands of Treatoun Myre (*NAS*, GD26/3/62).

In 1524, James tried to obtain for himself the office of Sheriff of Fife, which had been held by John Lindsay, Master of Pitcruvie, under a Privy Seal grant from the 30th of May 1524. On the 16th of September 1524, James made faith to the Lords of Council that "he sall leley and trewly minister in the office of scherefshcip of Fiff in all punctis eftir the forme and tenoure of the commissioun grauntit and gevin thairupone," and sought instrument. He obtained letters and a Great Seal writ appointing him to this office, but the Lords of Council, on the 10th of March 1525, suspended the letters he purchased declaring them as "past unordourelie and without cognitioun in the caus," and on the 14th of July 1525, at the instance of the crown and Patrick Lord Lindsay, annulled the Great Seal writ, stating that the office could not be granted to James, as it was held by James Lindsay of Pitcruvie (*Acts Lords of Council in Civil Caus.* 211, 213, 225).

Sometime between the dates of 1523 and 1529, according to the Exchequer Rolls of Scotland, James was given sasine of the lands of Drumman and Petcarle; was given the office of keeper of the Lord Governor's horses; and was let the lands and mill of Thomastoun, land previously associated with Lundie of that Ilk. The same source shows James as holding the lands and mill of Pitlochry and Bannachty, and each year as Laird, receiving annuity from the fermes of Crail (*Exchequer Rolls of Scotland*, XV. 78, 124, 134, 190, 235, 279, 355, 369, 447, 523, 558, 595).

Towards the end of 1526, Murray of Kippo and Murray of Tulibardine requested that James appear before the Lords of Council, but the King, describing James as "our lovit James Lundy of Balgouny," postponed his summons until a later date. It is not known if James did appear at a later date, or what the summons concerned.

15th December 1526

"Rex. My Lordis of sessioune, forsamekle as we have undirstand that schir Androw Murray of Kippo and his spous and William Murray of Tullybardyn hes rasit ane sommondis apone our lovit James Lundy of Balgouny to be callit in this present sessione, and we have considerate that the matter of the said summondis is gret and wechty, and requires ane gret set of our lordis, herfore and divers utheris consideraciouns just and ressonable moving us tharto oure will is ans we desir the said summondis to be continewit unto the xxti day of Yole nixt hereftir, lyke as we be tennour herof continewis the samyn be our autorite: Subsrcibvit with our hand at Edinburgh the xii Day of December the yer of god imvcxxvi yeris." "James Rex"

(*Acts Lords of Council in Civil Caus.* 255).

In 1527 James attended King James V in his efforts to settle the borders. On his way home, along with the Laird of Raith, and David Wemyss of that Ilk, he was attacked by the Moutrays of Seafield (*Melville Book*, III. 71; *Scots Peerage*, VIII. 488). In 1528, Andrew Lumisden, son of Thomas Lumisden of Conland, granted a deed of the lands of Wester Conland, to and in favours of James Lundie of Balgonie (*Heraldry*). On the 18th of June 1545, following the death of Lady Isobel Balfour, herior of the lands of Carraldstoun in Fife, James was made a gift of the ward and non-entries of this land by the Monarch (*Reg. Sec. Sig.* III. 1212). In 1547, there is a record of and instrument of discharge by James Lundy of Balgony to Mr. David Cockburn of Tretoun, for sums paid by James for marriage portion of David, and for redemption of lands of Tretoun in name of David; also for rents and duties for half lands of Schethum and 2 quarters of lands of Tretoun. This record is dated the 14th of January, 1547 (*NAS*, GD26/3/64). James died at the battle of Pinkie that same year, 10th September, 1547 (*Inq. Spec. Ret. Forfar*, No.3). Shortly before his death James is described in a letter excusing him from attending the Royal Court, as being infirm and continually sick. The same letter also excuses his brother Robert, stating that Robert has a deadly wound. This wound must not have been as deadly as thought, as Robert lived a good many years more (*Reg. Sec. Sig.* III. 1651). James was succeded to Balgonie by his brother Andrew. James's spouse is not known, but around this period one of the Lundies of Balgonie married the 6th (of 16) daughter of Sir Alexander Stewart of Gairlies (*Douglas's Peerage of Scotland*, 266).

He had issue:-

1 **Alison Lundie**, who married Robert Ayton, 1st Laird of Inchdairnie, in 1521. The arms of Alison Lundie of Balgonie and Robert Ayton of Inchdairnie were carved in stone together to commemorate this wedding, and were placed on Inchdairnie House. This House was latterly demolished, but the stone with the arms on now form a part of a wall at St. Paul's Primary School, Glenrothes. These are shown in the figure overleaf.

2 **Katherine Lundie**, a bastard daughter of James, she was legitimised after the death of her father, on the 6th of May 1550 (*Reg.*

11. *The arms of Alison Lundie of Balgonie and Robert Ayton of Inchdairnie, carved to commemorate their wedding in 1521.*

Sec. Sig. IV. 714). Katherine married Henry Wardlaw, heir apparent of John Wardlaw of Torry Their marriage contract was dated the 9th of January 1546. The contract, between John Wardlaw of Torry, baron of Inchegall and his spouse Elizabeth Bethune on the one part; and James Lundy of Balgonie and his daughter Katherine on the other part; stated that "Katherine in her pure virginity was infeft for life in the lands of Corsehill, Balbegy, with granary and the loch of Inchegall, the land of Tempilland, Brewland and Smiddeland, all withing the Barony of Inchegall". This on the condition that hey were married before 20th December 1546. This was confirmed under the great seal on the 15th of January 1547 (*Reg. Mag. Sig.* IV. 47). Note that Robert Ayton in Inchdairne was one of the witnesses to the original contract. On the 24th of March 1561-2, under the contract of marriage between Andrew Wardlaw fiar of the west part of the lands and Barony of Lochquhareschire, son of Henry Wardlaw of Torry, and Janet Durie, daughter of Henry Durie of that Ilk, Katherine was given a life rent of the tower and Loch of Inchegall (*NAS*, GD15/673; GD15/821).

SIR ANDREW LUNDIE, 4TH OF BALGONIE

Before Andrew's succession to Balgonie, he is listed as one of a number of persons, found guilty of involvement in the slaughter of James Borthwick, John Anderson and John Balzeat. He was escheated, and a gift of his goods, moveable and unmovable, was made by the King to Walter Lundy of that Ilk (*Reg. Sec. Sig.* II. 1029). He succeeded his brother James to Balgonie, being served as his brothers heir in the lands of Wester Gogy, in the regality of Keremure (Kiriemuir), on the 4th March, 1458 (*Inq. Spec. Ret. Forfar*, No.3); and as his heir in the lands and Barony of Balgony, the lands of Pitlochie, Bannachtye, Greenside, Muir of Tretoun and Caldicottis on the 13th April, 1548 (*NAS*, GD26/3/65). He was given sasine of these lands on the 29th of April that year (*NAS*, GD26/3/66). On the 14th and 15th of February, 1549, Andrew was given sasine propriis manibus, by Alexander Cockburn of Tretoun, of the lands of Tretoun Myre, and two quarters of the town and lands of Treatoun (*NAS*, GD26/3/67-8). On the 10th of November 1550, Andrew was made a gift of the escheat of all the goods of Thomas Wobster Elder, Sir John Wobster; Thomas Wobstar, younger; Mathew Wobstar alias Gregsoniis; and John Colzear (*Reg. Sec. Sig.* IV. 962). On the 16th May,

1551, Andrew redeemed a fourth part of the lands of Schethum, from David Marshall, burgess of Dysart, and Grizel Auchmuty, his spouse, for the cost of 215 merks (*NAS*, GD26/3/70)

There appears to have been a disagreement between Andrew and William, Lord Sinclair, over who owned the mills lying upon the Water of Ore, beneath the Brig of Ore. It is stated that at one point Andrew Lundy prevented Sinclair's servants from repairing a dam that was broken in a flood. The Sheriff of Fife was called in, 14th March 1550, to solve the problem, the outcome is not known (*NAS*, GD164/3). Andrew died in April 1559, and was succeeded by his bother Robert (Sir Andrew's testament is however not registered until 1575-6 (*Edin. Tests.*)).

Andrew was twice married. His first wife was Janet Sibbald, to who he was married to by 1549. On the 21st of October 1549, Andrew Lundy of Balgony, and Janet Sibbald, his spouse, had a Crown Charter of the Barony of Mondynes, following Andrew's resignation (*Reg, Mag. Sig.* IV. 385; *Reg. Sec. Sig.* IV. 456). He was later to marry Janet Lindsay of Dowhill. On the 5th of October 1577, they were given a charter under the Great Seal, of the lands of Pitlochry (with the fortalice) and Bannachty, also following Andrew's resignation (*Reg, Mag. Sig.* IV. 1210; *Reg. Sec. Sig.* V. 215). She had previously been married to Sir George Douglas of Helenhill, and after her marriage to Sir Andrew Lundie, married Sir William Scott of Balwearie (after 1568). Janet Lindsay of Dowhill appears in 1560, designed as relict of Andrew Lundy of Balgonie, when William Douglas of Lochleven issues a caution to Henry Wardlaw of Torry, on her behalf (*NAS*, GD150/331).

ROBERT LUNDIE FIRST OF THAT NAME OF CONLAND AND 5TH BALGONIE

Robert married Margaret Lumisden, the heiress of Thomas Lumisden of Conland. According to Nisbet's account of this family in his Heraldry, there is a sasine in favour of Robert Lundie, of the lands of Conland dated 1544; and in 1564, Thomas Lumisden renounced the lands of Wester Conland in favour of an honourable lady, Margaret Lumisden, spouse to Robert Lundie of Balgonie. He was thus designed as 'of Conland,' upon his marriage.

He succeeded his brother Andrew by 1560, thus becoming Robert Lundie of both Conland and Balgonie, holding one of the greatest estates in Fife.

"At Edinburgh Castell, 2 Maii (1560) ane Lettir made to Robert Lundie, brother and air to umpqhile Andro Lundie of Balgonie, his aris and assignais, of the gift of nonentres (etc.) of all and haill the landis and barony of balgonye with the castell, tour, fortalice, mylne, fichein, tannantis (etc) and thair pertinentis, liand within the shirefdome of Fiffe, and of uthiris landis quhatsumever quhilkis pertenit to the said umpqhile Andro Lundye of Balgonye, haldin be him immediatlie of our soveranis, ay sen his deceis, quha deceissit laitlie in the month of April last bipast, and siclike of all yeiris and termes to cum ay and quhill (etc.) with the releif thair of quhen it said happin: Providing always that the said Robert enter to the for saidis landis within the space of the terms nixt eftir the date heir of. With the power etc [composito] gratis. Per Signaturum." (*Reg. Sec. Sig.* V. 789)

He was served as his brother's heir on the 21st May, 1560; designated as Robert Lundy of Condland, brother and heir of deceased Andrew Lundy of Balgony; in the lands and Barony of Balgony, the lands of Greeside, Muir of Tretoun, and Balsillie (*NAS*, GD26/3/71). He was given sasine of these lands on the 6th June, 1560 (*NAS*, GD26/3/72). As his brothers heir he was given sasine propriis manibus by Andrew Cockburn of Tretoun, of lands of Tretoun Muir, on the 23rd of July, 1563. In this document he is now designed Robert Lundy of Balgony (*NAS*, GD26/3/73). On the 1st of May, 1567, Robert, as superior of the lands of Easter and Wester Dovan, was charged to infeft David Balfour of Balledmund in these lands, with the mill, milltown and mill lands. These lands had previously been taken from David Balfour for non-payment of a debt of £2133 6s 8d (*NAS*, GD66/1/26). On the 13th of October, 1572, Robert granted a precept of Clare Constat in favour of George Mowtraye, as son and heir of the deceased John Mowtraye of Markinche, of the lands and mill of Cadham (*NAS*, GD26/3/74).

Both Robert and his spouse Margaret Lumisden were still alive in 1578. Robert died by 1581, his testament being recorded 5th August of that month (*Edin. Tests.*).

Robert had the following children:-

1   *David Lundie, 6th of Balgonie*, of whom later.

2   *James Lundie, 2nd of Conland*, second legitimate son of Robert Lundie of Conland, and later of Balgonie, and his spouse Margaret Lumisden. On the 15th of April 1564 he was given sasine of the Barony of Conland by his parents. Failing heirs of his body, this barony was to pass to his brother german, Robert Lundie (*Reg. Mag. Sig.* IV. 1523; *Reg. Sec. Sig* V. 1668). He was twice married. His first spouse was Christian Betoun (Bethune) (*NAS* RD XV. 389). His second spouse was Janet Betoun, daughter of John Betoun of Auchmithie by Helen Melville (*Scot's Peerage*, VIII. 488). James died before 1569, and was succeeded to Conland by his brother Robert. Janet Beaton, afterwards married Captain David Wemyss, son of David Wemyss of that Ilk, around 1577 (*Scot's Peerage*, VIII. 488).

3   *Robert Lundie, 3rd of Conland*, brother german to James Lundie 2nd of Conland, he was given sasine of Conland by his parents in 1568 (*Exchequer Rolls of Scotland*, XX. 390), and had a charter of Condland (Condlane) confirmed under the Great Seal in 1659 (*Reg. Mag. Sig.* IV. 1851). The original charter was dated at Condland in April that year, and was witnessed amongst others by an Alexander Lundie Jr. Robert married Janet Bethune, 3rd and youngest daughter of John Bethune of Balfour (*East Neuk of Fife*, p 372). Robert died before the 5th of May 1575 (*Edin Tests*).

4   *Andrew Lundie, 4th of Conland*. According to Nisbet there is a sasine of the lands of Conland by Robert Lundie of Balgonie; Margaret Lumisden his wife, in favour of Andrew Lundie their son, in 1578. He was certainly in possession of Conland by 1585 as on the 30th of March 1585, Andro Lundy of Condolane is a witness to an obligation by John Douglas in Kennestoun to Sir John Brown of Fordell (*Browns of Fordell*, p100). Andrew married Elizabeth Broun, daughter of Sir John Broun of Fordell and Katherine Boswell, herself the daughter of David Boswell of Glasmont and Balmuto (*Heraldry; Browns of Fordell, p20*). On 22nd December 1591, they were given a charter of Conland under the great Seal of Scotland. For further details read 'Lundie / Lundin of Drums, formerly of Conland'

5   *William Lundie in Crail*, living in 1594 (*Lundins of Fife*).

6   *Elizabeth Lundie*, married firstly Patrick Halket of Pitferran, and secondly, William Lundie of that Ilk.

7   *Agnes Lundie*, married Sir William Graham of Claverhouse (*Scot's Peerage*, III. 321-22). Agnes died in November 1613. Sir William died around 1642. With Agnes he had issue:-

i William, who died before 13th August 1619
ii George, who succeeded. His Grandson became John Graham, 1st Viscount of Dundee, Lord Graham of Claverhouse.
iii Walter
iv Margaret
v Mariot
vi Helen, married George Lundie of Wester Denhead on 22nd November 1616.

8   *Janet Lundie* (*Index Cal. Deeds*, XXV., 277).

DAVID LUNDIE, 6TH OF BALGONIE

On the 19th of April 1561, he married Lillias Oliphant, the daughter of Laurence 3rd Lord Oliphant. On the 26th of October 1565, designed as younger of Balgonie, David was given the gift of the goods of Robert Duncan in Craigheir, within the barony of Carnele (*Reg. Sec. Sig.* V. 2395). On the 1st of January 1577-8, a Privy Seal Charter confirmed a grant by David, with the consent of his spouse Lillias, to James Richardson of Smetoun, younger, his heirs and assignees, of an annual rent of £100 from the lands of Schethum in the Barony of Balgonie (*Reg. Sec. Sig.* VII. 1371). This was later redeemed by David through payment of 1600 merks to James, on the 28th of May, 1583 (*NAS*, GD26/3/78).

He succeeded his father to Balgonie in 1581. On the 29th April 1581, he was given sasine to Mondyne (*Exchequer Rolls of Scotland*, XXI. 451, 452). On the 11th of May, 1581, he was given sasine, as son and heir of Robert Lundy of Balgony, of the lands and Barony of Balgony (*NAS*, GD26/3/75). On the 30th of October 1582, he granted sasine in favour of Robert Stobbs in Scotlandwell, and his spouse Katherine Boswell, of an annual rent of 90 merks from the lands of Balgonie; David Lundy's son and heir, Robert Lundy of Balgony, later redeemed this on the 29th May, 1585 (*NAS*, GD26/3/76). In 1583, David was granted sasine propriis manibus, as heir to his father, by Mr. Thomas Lumisden, rector of Kinketell, tutor testamentary of Andrew Cockburn of Tretoun, of the lands of Tretoun Myre (*NAS*, GD26/3/77). There is an instrument of redemption dated the 4th of June, 1584, whereby

Catharine Forestar, relict of David Arnot of that Ilk, and Mr. George Arnot, her son, paid 400 merks to David Lundy of Balgony, to redeem an annualrent of 40 merks from lands of Schethum (*NAS*, GD26/3/79).

David died before May 1585. His testament dated 29th June of 1586 (*Edin. Tests.*). His wife Lillias died before 1588 (*Edin. Tests.*). They had issue of five sons and eight daughters:-

1 *Robert Lundie, 7th of Balgonie*, who succeeded his father, and whose details follow.

2 *James Lundie*

3 *David Lundie*, he died before 1611, his brother William was one of his executors (*NAS*, GD26/3/113).

4 *Richard Lundie of Inverlochtie* (*see that family*)

5 *Margaret Lundie*

6 *Lillias Lundie*

7 *Elspeth Lundie*

8 *William Lundie*. On the 16th of December 1611, William, designed as 'brother of deceased Robert Lundie of Balgony, and one of executors of deceased David Lundie, his brother;' renounced to his nephew, Robert Lundie 8th of Balgony, claim of mill and mill lands of Sythrum (*NAS*, GD26/3/113). On the 31st of December 1616, a Decreet of Apprising was issued at instance of William, against Henry Multray of Seyfeild, of the north half lands of Seyfield, lands of Viccarris Grange, Over and Nethir Tyrie, lands and barony of Markinch, and others, for a debt of 2180 merks (*NAS*, GD26/3/825). Following on this Decreet, William was given a Precept of Sasine 'of lands called the Law of Markinch and Walke Mylne of Markinch,' by his nephew Robert Lundie 8th of Balgonie (*NAS*, GD26/3/826). This obviously did not settle the matter, as that same year, letters of horning were initiated at the instance of William Lundie, against William, Earl of Mortoun; Mr. Patrick Wardlaw of Torrie; and Robert Lundie of Balgonie; for infeftment in the lands of Seyfield, Tyrie, Viccarris Grange, and lands and barony of Markinch. These letters were issued with executions dated 30th January, 18th March, 11th July, 12th and 29th September, 1617 (*NAS*, GD26/4/707, GD26/4/709). His is most probably the same William Lundie, brother of Robert Lundie of Balgonie, who was married to a Janet Scot (*PRS Fife and Kinross*).

9   *Agnes Lundie,* The national archives of Scotland, GD26/3/90, records an instrument of redemption by Robert Lundy of Balgony from Agnes Lundy, his sister, of an annual rent of £100 Scots from the mill of Balgony, on payment of £1000 Scots. This is dated the 26th May 1595.

10   *Katherine Lundie*

11   *Isobel Lundie*

12   *Helen Lundie*

13   *Marion Lundie.* Marion is listed, along with her siblings, when her mother gave up the testament of her father in 1585. She is most probably the same Marion Lundie, daughter of a Lundie of Balgonie, who married Andrew Ayton, 2nd Laird of Kinaldie. Andrew Ayton died in 1589.

ROBERT LUNDIE, 7TH OF BALGONIE

In 1578, Robert was denounced a rebel, at the instance of Allan Coutts of the Grange, and the Lords of the Privy Council ordained that he should be detained and entered into ward, at his own expense, within the castle of Blackness:

> "8th December 1578
>
> Complaint by Allane Cowtis of the grange against Robert Lundy of Balgony as follows: Lundy, "for non-fullfilling of letters in the foure formes rasit at the said Allanes instance agains him, chairging him to warrand, acquyet, and defend the said Allane, his tennentis and occupyaris of the landis of Spittell, at the handis of George Dowglas, broder-german to Williame Dowglas of lochlevin, pensionar of the teindschevis of the saidis landis, of the cropis and yeiris of God j^mv^clxxii, lxxiiii, and lxxv, yeiris, and in tyme cuming, for paymcnt of the sowme of ten merks yeirlie," had, on the 2nd of September last, been "denunceit rebel and put to the horne." He had remained at the horn ever since "takand na regaird theirof, bot hantis, frequentis, and repairis, in all patent and publict places of this realme, siclyk and als frelie as if he wer our Soverane Lordis frie lege, in hie contemptioun of his Hienes auctorite and lawes." Accordingly summons in due form

had been sent to Lundy to appear before the King and Council, "to have hard and sene utheris letters direct, chairging him to pass and enter his persoun in ward within the castle of Blacknes, thairin to remain upoun his awin expenses, ay quill he hed fulfilit the command of the sadis letters of horning, and obtene himself relaxit therefra, within aucht dayis efter the charge, under the pane of tressoun, or ellis to have schawin ane ressonabil caus quhy the same sould not have bene done." And now, " the said Allane Cowtis compeirand be James Oiswald, his procuratour, and the said Robert Lundy, being oftymes callit and not compeirand," the Lords ordain letters to pass punctually to the threatened effect, and requiring Lundy to "cum to the Secretar or his deputes and resave utheris letters for his ressait in ward within the said castell."

(*Reg. Privy Council*. Series I. III. 54).

By 1585 Robert had succeeded his father to Balgonie, and was served as son and heir of his father, 'the deceased David Lundie of Balgony,' in the lands and Barony of Balgony, the lands of Muir of Treatoun, and the lands of Innerlevin, alias Caldcottis on the 19th of May that year (*NAS*, GD26/3/80). Robert was given sasine of these lands on the same day (*NAS*, GD26/3/81). He was served as heir to his father in the land and barony of Mondynes in the Sheriffdom of Kincardine, on the 20th of May 1585 (*Inq. Spec. Ret. Kincardine*, No. 3). In this same year there are also several instruments of redemption recorded in favour of Robert. The first was on the 28th of May 1585, from Arthur Sinclair of Aythe to Robert Lundy of Balgony, of an annual rent of £20 Scots from the Manes of Balgony, upon payment of 300 merks: the second was on the 30th of May 1585, from Duncan Wemis of the Kirkland Wemis, and Bessie Wemys, his spouse, to Robert Lundy, of an annualrent of £40 Scots from lands of Spittall, upon payment of 600 merks: and the third was on the 30th of May 1585, from John Lumisdene, burgess of Dysert, to Robert Lundie, of annualrent of 40 merks from Manes of Balgonie, upon payment of 400 merks (*NAS*, GD26/3/79). In the following year, on the 20th of January, Robert was given Sasine Propriis Manibus by Mr. Thomas Lumisdain, rector of Kinketel, tutor testamentary to Andrew Cockburn, 'as heir of deceased David Lundy of Balgony,' of the lands of Tretoun Myre (*NAS*, GD26/3/82).

In May 1587, Robert appears in a bond of caution on the behalf of

John Boswell of Balmuto, such that John would not harm Johnne Kirkaldy and Petir Sandielandis, who were both bailies of Kinghorn; and a Robert Cunynghame; also these persons wives, children, tenants and servants. The caution was later deleted by the King and his chancellor in July of 1588 (*Reg. Privy Council*, Series I. IV. 182). In September of 1587 Robert granted a charter to Margaret Broun, daughter of the deceased John Broun, mariner burgess of Dysart, an annual rent of 22 bolls and 2 firlots of bier, from the Mains of Balgony. This was under reversion of 1000 merks. Robert also granted the same to Margaret's brother, John Broun (*NAS*, GD26/3/83-4).

The following year, 1588, in a contract of Wadset dated the 15th July, Robert disponed to Mathew Andersoun, burgess of Kirkcaldy, and Alison Ramsay, his spouse, and survivor, an annualrent of £40 Scots from lands and Mains of Balgony, under reversion of 600 merks (*NAS*, GD26/3/85-6). This is the first of two or three contracts of wadset found during Roberts and his son's lairdships, and the family appears to have been building up a large amount of debt. This becomes far clearer in his son and grandson's lairdships, whereupon the barony was eventually sold.

In 1589 there is evidence of a disagreement between Robert, and both David Reid of Aikinhead and Robert Bruce of Blairhall. This disagreement concerned the marches of Brauchtie and Craigheid on one part, and the tenandry of Carnbo on the other (*NAS*, GD150/1957). The details of this are not known.

Robert was married to Margaret Boswell. On the 5th of May 1592, a charter was granted by Robert Lundy of Balgony and Margaret Boswell, his spouse; in favour of George Broun, burgess of Kirkcaldie, and Margaret Bosuell, his spouse, and the survivor; of annualrent of 70 merks from Mains of Balgony (*NAS*, GD26/3/88). On the 30th of June that same year, Robert granted an instrument of Sasine propriis manibus to John Christesoun, burgess of Dysart, of annualrent of 40 merks from Mains of Balgony. This was redeemed on payment of 500 merks on the 17th of July 1595 (*NAS*, GD26/3/89). On 20th May 1595, Robert and his spouse Margaret Boswell were granted a charter under the great seal of the lands of Pitlochy and Bannachty. Robert died on the 1st of November 1597; his testament being read 19th July 1598 (*Edin. Tests.*). He had issue:-

1   ***Robert Lundie, 8th of Balgonie***, who succeeded, and whose details follow.

2   ***John Lundie***.

3   **David Lundie**, died June 1603.

4   **James Lundie of Skeddoway** (Skathowie, Skeddowie, Skeduy). The lands of Skeddoway, located just south of Glenrothes, were held around 1610 by Allardice (Alledes) of Skedoway. This family appears to have owed James various sums of money, which they were unable, or unwilling to pay. James had George Allerdice of Skeddoway, Robert Allerdice, Henry Allardice and Andrew Allardice, declared as rebels. The said Robert then fled the country to Flanders, but then returned and is said to have tried to kill James, a number of his brothers also tried to harm James's servants, who were at the time in Skeddoway. These actions are well chronicled in the Register of the Privy Council. Note that George Allardice of Skedoway was married to one Elizabeth Lundie (*P.R.S. Fife and Kinross*, XIII 236).

> "Edinburgh, 18th of December 1617
> Compaint by James Lundy, brother german of Robert Lundy of Balgony, that George Allerdes of Skathowie, and Robert Allerdes, his son and heir, remain unrelaxed from a horning of the 26th August last for not paying 900 merks of principal and 100 merks expenses. Pursuer appearing by Mr Johnne Rollock, and defenders not appearing, the Lords give the order as above"
> (*Reg. Privy Council.* Series I. XI. 283)

> "Holyrood House, 30th of September 1618
> Complaint by James Lundy, brother German of Robert Lundy of Balgonie, that George Allerdyse of Skeddowie, Robert, Henry and Andro Allerdyse, his sons, remain un relaxed from a horning of 28th July last for not finding caution and lawburrows for the indemnity of pursuers tenants and servants, the said George in 1000 merks, and each of his sons in 400 merks. Pursuer appearing by Mr Johnne Rollock, and the defenders not appearing, the Lords give the order to the Captain of the guard."
> (*Reg. Privy Council.* Series I. XI. 451)

> "Holyrood 7th of march 1620
> Complaint by Andrew Gib and William Broun, servitors to James Lundy of Skeddowy, as follows:- On 10th February instant,

Henry, Andrew, George and David Allerdes, sons of George Allerdes, some time of Skeddowy, and Roger Auchmowtie, son to the late David Auchmowtie of Bitchie, came by night, armed to the place of Skeddowy, where complainers were for the time, and "first treasounablie and awfullie cryit for fyre to have brynt the saidis compleanairis in the said place," then came to the hall door thereof "and with swerdis and lang staulffis strak in at the said complenairis a long time." Finally, "thay enterit in the said place, and cruellie and unmercifullie invadit and persewit the saidis complenairis of thair lyveis, hurte and woundit the said William Broun in the head and left hand, and the said Andro Gib in the face," and gave them "mony bauch and bla straikis upoun divers utheris pairtis of thair bodyis," with intent to kill them had they not made thair escape by a back door. – James Lundy of Skeddowy appearing for the complainers, and the defenders not appearing, the Lords order defenders to be denounced rebels."
(*Reg. Privy Council.* Series I. XII. 225-6)

Edinburgh 6th of July 1621
Complaint by James Lundie, brother to the laird of Balgony, as follows:- He had formerly petitioned the Lords showing that Robert Allerdes, who had been denounced rebel at his instance, and had escaped out of the country to the wars of Flanders, was now returned, and had come to the complainers house with the intent to slay him, but, missing him, had shot with pistols at his servants, and being followed to the town of Falkland, had been seized by the bailies there on letters of caption and warded in their tolbooth. In terms of this petition the Lords had sent up two of the King's guard to Falkland to charge the bailies to deliver up Allerdes to be warded in the tolbooth of Edinburgh; but, before the guard arrived, the bailies had of their own accord set him at liberty. – Charges had been given to Hector Arnot, James Haitlie, and George Paterson, bailies of Falkland, to produce the rebel; and now, the pursuer appearing personally, and the defenders neither appearing, nor having produced Allerdes, the Lords order them to be denounced rebels."
(*Reg. Privy Council.* Series I. XII. 522)

526

"Edinburgh 10th of July 1621

This day in the presence of the Lords appear personally Hecotr Arnot, James Haitlie and George patersoun, bailies of Falkland, and in obedience to the charge executed against them by Andrew Stewart, messenger, at the instance of james Lundy, brother to the Laird of Balgonie (ante p522) presented before the Lords Robert Allerdes, son to the Laird of Skeduy. They affirm that they were charged to do so on the 10th day of july, and in evidence produce a copy of the charge written and signed by Andrew Stewart to the effect. James Lundy having produced the original letters, showing that Andrew Stewart had charged the bailies to appear on 5th of July, on which day they were denounced rebels for not appearing, the Lords fin that the bailies had been ill used in this point, and they suspend the letters of horning against them. The Lords also order Robert Allerdes to find caution to appear on the "the sevintene [sic] day of July instant" to answer james Lundy's complaint against him, while Lundy is also charged to appear "upon thetwentie sevin [sic] day of Julij" to pursue his complaint."

(*Reg. Privy Council*. Series I. XII. 526)

550-1

"Edinburgh 25th July 1621

This day Mr George Flescheour, advocate, as procurator for the cautioners, registers a bond of caution in 400 merks by James Wemeis of Caskieberrane, james Wymis, his eldest lawful son and apparent heir, Daniel Alledes, burgess of Falkland, and Henry Thomesoun *alias* Baill, maltman in Frewchie, for Robert Allerdes, eldest lawful son to George Allerdes of Skedowie, not to molest James Lundie, brother german to the deceased Robert Lundie of Balgonie, or his family. With clause of relief by Robert Allerdes to all his cautioners, and by each of them *pro rata* to one another. – The bond, which is written by John Aitkyne, servitor to James Prymrois, Clerk of Council, is dated at Falkland and Blairrothis, the 20th and 21st July 1621, and witnessed by Andro law, burgess of Falkland, Andro Sibbald, burgess there, Johnne

Weymis, son to the late James Wemyis of Caskieberran, and Thomas Boiswall, "myservitor." David Allerdes and Thomesone alias Baill are unable to write, and sign by Johnne Nicoll and Alexander Merschell, notaries."

(*Reg. Privy Council.* Series I. XII. 550-1)

Through these actions and debts, James obtained control of the lands of Skeddoway. He held them until 1637, when he resigned them into the hands of Lord James Sinclair. James Lundie, then designed sometime of Skaddowie, died before 11th April 1640 (*St. Andrews. Comm. Court*).

5   *Margaret Lundie*
6   *Isobel Lundie*
7   *Andrew Lundie*
8   *Katherine Lundie*
9   *George Lundie*, who is listed as apprentice to a merchant, Gilbert Atchison, 26th July 1615 (*Reg. Appren. Edin.*).

ROBERT LUNDIE, 8TH OF BALGONIE

Robert was in minority upon the death of his father, and in 1598, £1000 was charged for the ward of his marriage (*Exchequer Rolls of Scotland*, XXII. 195). Several papers relating to his ward and marriage are held at the National Archives of Scotland (*NAS*, GD66/1/113). Robert was served as heir to his father on 20th April 1603 in the lands and Barony of Balgonie, comprising the lands of Over Balgony, Nether Balgony, the Milltown, Byris and Innerlochtie *alias* Spittal; the land of Dowane, which comprised Over Dowan, Nether Dowan, Myldamis; the Lands of Scherthum (Schethum), comprising Scherthum, Blaukfauldis and Cowdame; the lands of Pitlochie and Bannachtie; the lands of Denekery in the Barony of Kirkcaldie; the lands of Drumdeill in the Barony of Pitgornow; the land of Innerleven (alias Couldcottis) in the Barony of Methill; and the land of Tietone with Myltone of Balgony and Dalginsche, all in the Sheriffdom of Fife (*Inq. Spec. Ret. Fife*, No. 129). He was also served as heir to his grandfather, David Lundie of Balgony in an annual rent of 5 *lib.* from the town of Crail (*Inq. Spec. Ret. Fife*, No. 130). On the same date, in the Sheriffdom of Kincardine, he was served as heir to his father in the land and Barony of Mondynes (*Inq. Spec. Ret. Kincardine,* No. 10); and in the Sheriffdom of Perth, he was served as heir to his father in the land of Nether Combo (*Inq. Spec. Ret. Perth*, No 113). On the 9th of June 1603, Robert issued papers requiring Andrew Cockburn of Tretone to infeft him in lands of Tretone Myre, as heir to his father (*NAS*, GD26/3/91).

Robert was the penultimate Lundie of Balgonie, but in most aspects could be effectively considered the last. Although he had sons to succeed him, the amount of debt on the estate meant that as soon as his eldest son was served as heir and had been given sasine of the lands of Balgonie, he resigned them for payment of 10,000 merks and payment of the debts.

1603

Following a payment of 1000 merks by Robert, John Broun, the eldest son and heir of the deceased John Broun, a mariner burgess of Dysert, renounced to Robert, an annualrent of 22 bolls 2 firlots beir from the town, lands and Mains of Balgony (*NAS*, GD26/3/93). This was done on the 12th December that year.

1604

In a Contract of Wadset, written in 1604, registered on the 14th of November 1621, Robert disponed to George Philpe, an indweller in Caldcottis, and Helen Symsoun, his spouse, and the survivor of them both, an annualrent of 100 merks in liferent. In the same contract, Robert disponed to David Philpe, son of the aforementioned George and Helen, in fee, an annualrent of £46 Scots; and to Marjory Philpe, daughter of George and Helen, in fee, an annualrent of £20 Scots. The annual rent was to be uplifted from the lands and Maynis of Balgony, under reversion of 1000 merks (*NAS*, GD26/3/94). A few years later, on the 9th of December 1619, George and his children disponed and assigned the annual rent to Mr. Robert Aytoune of Inchedernye (*NAS*, GD26/3/126).

1605

On the 15th of June 1605, Robert issued a Precept of Clare Constat in favour of Henry Multray, as the son and heir of the deceased George Multray of Seafield, of the lands of Calden in the barony of Balgonye (*NAS*, GD26/3/97).

On the 29th of October 1605, following payment of 1300 merks by Robert; James Wemyss of Balquhairge, eldest son and heir of the deceased David Wemyss of Dron, renounced to Robert an annualrent of £48 and £30 from lands and Mains of Balgony, (*NAS*, GD26/3/98).

1606

On the 29th of May 1606, Robert was summond by the Lords of

the Privy Council, along with James Lundie of that Ilk, Sir James Lundie, Robert Lundie of Balgonie, David Lundie of Newhall, Andrew Lundie of Conland and George Lundie younger of Gorthie, in order to quell a feud between the Lundies and the family of Learmonth (*Reg. Privy Council.* Series I. VII. 212).

On the 18th of August 1606, in a contract of Wadset, Robert Lundy of Balgony disponed to Mathew Andersone, a baker burgess of Kirkcaldie, and Alison Ramsay, his spouse, and the survivor of the two, an annualrent of £40 Scots from lands and Manis of Balgony. This was granted under reversion of 600 merks, and Robert issued a Charter accordingly on the same day (*NAS*, GD26/3/99; GD26/3/100).

In a contract written around this time, Martin Balfour, portioner of Lalathen, and Sir Andrew Balfour of Monquhany, had agreed to dispone to Robert, the lands of Dovend Mill, upon payment of 10,000 merks, which according to the contract should have been divided between Martin and Andrew. It would appear that Martin required the permission of 'John Balfour of Doving, heir served and retoured to the deceased Jonet Pitcairn; Sir Andrew Balfour of Monquhany, knight, and Henry Pitcairn of Forther,' in order to carry out this transaction. In 1606, Martin Balfour is recorded as appearing before these three persons, but John and Sir Andrew Balfour did not give their consent. Record exists showing Martin Balfour attempting to establish that John Balfour of Doving, and Sir Andrew Balfour of Monquhany, should pay the penalty in the contract (*NAS*, GD66/1/143). Robert had given these lands; Over and Nether Dovene, mill and mill-lands; to Sir George Boswell of Balgonie (perhaps one of Robert's Curators). In 1608 Sir George was taking action against 'John Balfour, son and apparent heir to the deceased Jonet Pitcairne of Dovein and deceased Robert Balfour, her spouse; and Mairtene Balfour, portioner of Lalethen,' with regards these lands. A Decreet issued as part of that action shows various details (*NAS*, GD66/1/146).

1607

On the 22nd of June 1607, following on a Precept by the Chancery, sasine was given in favour of 'Robert Lundy, now of Balgony, as son and heir of deceased Robert Lundy of Balgony,' of the lands and barony of Balgony. This was registered in the Secretary's Register for Fife, on the 1st of July 1607, (*NAS*, GD26/3/102-3).

On the 22nd of November 1607, Robert acted as a cautioner, along with John Bosuall of Balmouto, knight; and Walter Arnot of that Ilk; for David Bosuall of Admoir, in a bond granted to David by Robert Arnot, the brother to the deceased David Arnot of that Ilk. Two years later, on the 31st of August 1609, letters of horning were issed by Robert Arnot, against Robert Lundy of Balgony; John Bosuall of Balmouto, knight; Walter Arnot of that Ilk; and David Bosuall of Admoir; for non-payment of 500 merks and 3000 merks, contained within the bonds. In dorso executions of the letters of Horning are dated the 2nd and 19th of September 1609 (*NAS*, GD66/1/149).

1608

On the 20th of April 1608 Robert was served as heir to his father in the land of Wester Gaigill (Gaige or Gogie) in the regality of Keremure (*Inq. Spec. Ret. Forfar,* No 34).

1610

On the 10th of January 1610, after payment of £220; Euphame Coutts, relict of John Melville, burgess of Kirkcaldy; and Mawsie Coutts, relict of James Melville, burgess there; renounced to Robert Lundy of Balgony, an annualrent of 12 merks from lands and mill of Schethum, (*NAS*, GD26/3/105).

On the 3rd of July 1610, following payment of 300 merks; David Landellis of Coull and Henry Landellis, his son; renounced to Robert Lundy of Balgony, an annualrent of £20 Scots from lands and Maynes of Balgony (*NAS*, GD26/3/108).

1611

On the 7th of March 1611, following payment of 600 merks, George Bosuall of the West Mylnes of Kirkcaldy, son and heir of deceased Mr. Andrew Bosuall of the West Mylnes of Kirkcaldy, resigned to Robert Lundie of Balgonie, an annualrent of £40 from lands and Maines of Balgonie, mill and mill-lands (*NAS*, GD26/3/109).

On the 20th of November 1611, a contract was written between Robert Lundie of Balgony and Andrew Law in Eister Pitteuchar, whereby for the sum of 1000 merks, Robert would infeft Andrew in an annualrent of 100 merks from lands of Sythrum in barony of Balgony. This was under reversion of 1000 merks. A charter of the annual rent was given by Robert to Andrew on the same date *NAS*, GD26/3/110-11).

On the 16th of December 1611, Robert's uncle, William Lundie, designed as 'brother of deceased Robert Lundie of Balgony, and one of executors of deceased David Lundie, his brother;' renounced to Robert Lundie claim on the mill and mill lands of Sythrum (*NAS*, GD26/3/113).

1612

On the 28th of November 1612, Robert was served as heir to his grandmother, Lillias Oliphant of Balgonie (*Gen. Retours*, No. 8494).

1613

On the 26th of March 1613, Robert Lundie of Balgony gave a heritable bond of 40 merks; from Mylnetoun of Balgony; to Margaret Lambert, the relict of David Wright, son of James Wright in the Mylnetoun of Balgony; and Margaret Wright, her daughter. This was granted under reversion of 400 merks (*NAS*, GD26/3/114).

1615

A contract dated the 12th of September 1615, between Robert Lundie of Balgony and his cautioners, on the one part, and George Hew alias Thomesone, tailor in Kennoquhie, and Margaret Durie, his spouse, on the other, stated that George and Margaret were to be infeft in annualrent of 90 merks from lands and Maynes of Balgony. This was agreed, under a reversion of 900 merks. Robert granted a charter accordingly on the 19th of September 1615 (*NAS*, GD26/3/116-7).

On the 14th of September 1615 Duncan Wemyss of Pitkeny, Duncan and James Wemyss, his sons, renounced to Robert Lundy of Balgony, an annualrent of 200 merks from the lands, Manes and barony of Balgony; this follwed a payment of 2000 merks. It was registered on the 6th of June 1616 in the Books of Council (*NAS*, GD26/3/119).

1616

The lands of Innerlochtie (Inverlochtie) alias Spittal, in the Barony of Balgonie, had on the 12th of June 1610, been alienated to Robert's uncle, Richard Lundie, and Richards spouse Sara Wemyss; upon payment of 6000 merks (*NAS*, GD23/6/106). On the 15th of June 1616, Robert and his second spouse, Eupham Durie, were contracted, after payment of a further 4000 merks, to ratify the previous alienation of Inverlochtie; renounce the clause of reversion; and infeft Sara and Richard anew. Robert granted a charter in favour of Richard and Sara on that same date (*NAS*, GD26/3/121-22).

On the 15th of June 1616, after paymet of 2000 merks, David Symsoun, elder of Smetoun, renounced to Robert Lundie of Balgonie, an annnualrent of 200 merks from the barony and Maynes of Balgonie (*NAS*,

GD26/3/120).

1617

Several dealings between Robert and his uncle William in this year and others can be read under William's details.

1618

Robert was admitted as a Burgess of Glasgow (*Surnames of Scotland*).

1619

On the 7th of May 1619, Robert Lundy of Balgonie, with Sir John Boswall of Balmuto, kt., Mr. John Aytoun of Kynnaldie and James Boswall of Lochgellie as cautioners, gave a bond for £1000 Scots, to Mr. Andrew Pitcarne, younger of Innernethie. It was registered in the Books of Council on the 24th of November 1619 (*NAS*, GD26/4/12). Robert had not paid this bond by November, and as a result on the 24th of November this year, Robert Pitcairn, a tailor burgess of the Canongate, issued letters of horning against Robert and his cautioners for payment of the bond. Executions of the letters were dated the 20th and 27th of February 1621 (*NAS*, GD26/4/710).

On the 12th of June 1619, Robert Lundy of Balgony, with Mr. John Ayttone of Kynnaldie and James Bosuell of Eister Lochgelly as his cautioners; gave bond to William Bruce of Earlshall, for 4400 merks. It was stated that if William Bruce permited the 4400 merks to remain in Robert's hands after the term of repayment, Robert bound himself to infeft William in an annualrent of 440 merks from his lands. This was registered in the books of Council on the 2nd of February 1621 (*NAS*, GD26/3/124).

Family

Robert was twice married. His first wife was Jane Lindsay, daughter of James 7th Lord Lindsay of the Byres by Euphemia Leslie, herself the daughter of Andrew Leslie 4th Earl of Rothes. They married sometime between 1598 and 1600; note that her sister Catherine married James Lundie of that Ilk, 9th October 1605 (*Scots Peerage*, V. 400). Robert secondly married Euphame Durie, daughter of Robert Durie of that Ilk; in a contract dated the 6th of February 1606 (*NAS*, GD26/4/706). Robert appears to have reneged upon part of this marriage contract, as on the 5th of November 1616, letters of inhibition were issued against Robert, by 'Robert Durie of that Ilk and Euphame Durie, his daughter, now Lady Balgony,' for fulfilment of their marriage contract. Executions of these letters are dated the 11th and 17th January 1617, and a copy was registered in the Books of Council on the 14th of February 1617 (*NAS*, GD26/4/706).

Robert Lundie, 8th of Balgonie, died sometime before July 1621. He was succeeded by his son Robert, whom he had by his first marriage. It would also appear that John Lundie, the eldest son by his second marriage inherited a large proportion of the lands from his father.

Robert had issue by both marriages:-

Children by Janet Lindsay:

1   *Robert Lundie, 9th of Balgonie*

2   *Euphame Lundie*, eldest daughter (*NAS*, GD26/3/177), contracted to marry John Moncrief of Balcaskie on the 5th of February, 1635 (*Reg. Mag. Sig.* IX. 463).

Children by Euphame Durie:

1   *John Lundie of Easter Conland*, eldest son of Robert Lundie, by Euphame Durie. Details of John's associations with the lands of Balgonie can be read in the details of his half-brother Robert's Life. He married Janet Wemyss, daughter of Sir James Wemyss of Bogie (second son of Sir David Wemyss of Wemyss) on 31st December 1630. He died in April 1641 without issue. Janet sold Easter Conland to her brother Henry Wemyss (*Scots Peerage*, VIII. 494). Their brother, George Wemyss, Principal of St. Leonard's College, St. Andrews married a Magdalene Lundie. They had a charter of Wester Pitcaple on the 1st of March 1648. Magdalene Lundie died 4th March 1666. Magdalene might therefore be a sister of John Lundie. Janet Wemyss, Lady Condland died 20th April 1653. She died at her mother's house in Bannochie, and was interred in the church of Kirkcaldie on the 24th of May (*Lamont's Diary*, p 55).

2   *David Lundie of Wester Condland*, listed as an apprentice in Edinburgh to a merchant, John Fairholm, 26th May 1630 1615 (*Reg. Appren. Edin.*). He later purchased Wester Condland, from where he takes his designation (*East Neuk of Fife*, p 52). In 1663, he disponed this estate to Walter Law – "This tyme, Dauid Lundy of Condland Wester, disponed heretably the lands of Condland to Walter Law, Bruntons yowngest son; the said Walter ingageing for his debt, especially undertaking for 6500 markes that he was due to one Johne Kinnairde; as also, the said Walter undertaking to pay yeirly to the said Dauid 73 lib. 6s. 8d. Scots, out of the said lands, during all the dayes of the said Dauid his life" (*Lamont's Diary*, p 165). He and his

brother James are named as two of the seven curators of their nephew and nieces, (the children of their sister Margaret and George Lundie in Saltgrein), between 1659 and 1665 (*Lamont's Diary*, p 86).

3   *Lt. Col. James Lundy in Saltgrein*. (*Index Reg. Deeds*, Mack. IV. 263). He was one of the curators of his nephews and nieces, between 1659 and 1665, (*Lamont's Diary*, p 86). He died in 1664 – "1664, Aug. 12 – Att night, James Lundy in Salt-grine, depairted out of this life att his dwelling house ther, and was interred att the church of Scony the 15 of Aug. in the evening. He dyed of a cancer in his throat as was supposed; for about 3 monthes before his death, he could eate no bread because of the straitness of the passage in his craige. Aug. 11, Euphame Lundy, his sister daughter, who depairted out of this life at Ardrosse in Fife, was interred at Crail the said day; she died of the Cruells in hir knee, which issue did run some yeirs before hir death" (*Lamont's Diary*, p 171). He had at least one daughter.

   i   *Janet Lundie*, (*Index Reg. Deeds*, Dur. LVII. 8).

4   *Margaret Lundie*, married George Lundie of Saltgrein, fifth son of John Lundie of that Ilk. For their issue, see *Lundie of Clato*.

5   *Magdalene Lundie* (probably). She was married to George Wemyss, Principal of St. Leonard's College, St. Andrews, and later Provost of the Old College in St. Andrews. George was the brother of Janet Wemyss, spouse of John Lundie of Easter Condland. He was also named as one of the curators of the children of the late George Lundie in Saltgrein, and Margaret Lundie. This would imply a strong relationship between himself and this generation of Lundie of Balgonie, which lends one to surmise his spouse was the daughter of Robert Lundie of Balgonie. Magdalene died on the 4th of March 1666, and was interred in St. Andrews (*Lamont's Diary*, p 185).

6   *Laurence Lundie*, a captain in the Army by 1648. Captain Laurence was given command of Fencibles in Nairn, Elgin and Inverness in 1649. He was given £1479 a month for the pay of his 60 men (*General index to the acts of parliament of Scotland*).

ROBERT LUNDIE, 9TH AND LAST OF BALGONIE

The eldest son of Robert Lundie of Balgonie, and his first Spouse, Janet Lindsay; he appears to have inherited the barony of Balgonie in a great state of debt, and as a result was forced to sell his family seat and lands. On the

26th July, 1621, a summons was issued, and executed, against Robert Lundie of Balgonie, as son and heir to the deceased Robert Lundie of Balgonie, by Mathew Anderson, Burgess of Kirkcaldy, and Alison Ramsay, his spouse, for not fulfilling a contact of wadset given by his father on the 18th August 1606 (*NAS*, GD26/3/85; GD/26/3/99-100; GD26/3/129).

In 1622, Robert seems to have suffered the consequences of the marriage contract between his father and step-mother, Euphame Durie. On the 23rd July, 1622, a decreet of apprising was issued the at instance of John Lundye, son and heir of deceased Robert Lundye of Balgony and Euphame Durie, his spouse, against Robert Lundy now of Balgony, of lands and Maynes of Balgony and lands of Caldcoittis, for a sum of 28,000 merks contained in the marriage contract, between the deceased Robert and Euphame (*NAS*, GD26/4/718); John was granted a charter under the great seal on the 18th September that year; of the towns and lands of Maynis of Balgonie; Bankheid, Lochtisyde and Milntoun of Balgonie; Spittell; Trettounmyre; Sythrum; and Dovin; in barony of Balgonie (*NAS*, GD26/3/131). Robert was served as heir to his grandfather in the lands of Drumdaill in the barony of Pitgorno on June the 8th 1624 (*Inq. Spec. Ret. Fife*, No. 341).

With all the debts building up on the estate, it seems to have driven Robert to some extreme measures in order to avoid payment, and preserve his freedom; as the following extract from the Register of the Privy Council will illustrate:

"Edinburgh, 29th January 1624

Complaint by Sir William Oliphant, Kings advocate, John Lanyng, messanger and Gilbert Atchesoun, merchant burgess of Edinburgh, as follows:- Robert Lundie of Balgonie was indebted in various sums to the said Gilbert; who, becoming exasperated by delay in payment raised a horning and then a caption against Lundie. John Layng, as messenger, was employed to apprehend Lundie, and on the 14th . . . went to the place "callit the . . . myris in Fyff" where the rebel was. When Lundie and [William Downy] his servant, saw the messenger approaching, they seized hagbuts and pistols, and avowed to God that, if the messenger and his men laid hands on Lundie, they would have their lives. The messenger having then in due form charged the rebel "thrie several tymes" to surrender, he not only refused obedience, but "avowit with many horibill oaths that befoir he wer tane with any messenger he haid rather be hangit and headit at the croce of Edinburgh," all the while presenting "his chargit hagbut" at the messenger and witnesses, so that the messenger, for fear of his life, dared not lay hands on him. Lundie and his servant afterwards went to Markinch, whither also the the messenger and witness proceeded. There, finding the rebel and his servant "standing in the kirkyaird with thair charged and bendit hagbutssis and pistollettis in thair handis," the messenger again charged the rebel to give obedience, but he refused to acknowledge the King's authority. The messenger then, in the King's name, charged James Clerk, elder of Balbirny, a Justice of the Peace, . . . Clerk, younger of Balbirny, Mr . . . Law, son of the Archbishop of Glasgow, and Robert Mowbray of Seyfield, heritable proprietors of the lands of markinch, and other gentlemen present, to concur with him in apprehending the rebel. These gentlemen "persaveing the said rebel and his servandis foirsaidis in suche ane desperat resolutioun," declared that "thay wald most willinglie concure with the said messenger, bot thay wald not proceid so violentlie agains the said rebel for apprehending of him as might irriat him to tak thair lyves with the saidis hagbuttis and pistollettis." The justices of the peace, therefore, with the messenger and the others, united in commanding Lundie to surrender and give obedience to the law, but his still refused, and threatened to shoot at any one trying to lay hands on him, so that the messenger was forced to break his wand of office and withdraw. – Charge had been given to the said Robert Lundie, and William Downey, his servant; and now the pursuers appearing personally, as also William Downey, while Lundie does not appear, the Lords find Lundie guilty, and order him to be charged to enter ward on the Tolbooth of Edinburgh within six days. They assoilzie the other defender."

(*Reg. Privy Council.* Series I. XIII. 412)

By 1626 the debts were too great, and Balgonie passed from the Lundies to the Boswells. On the 29th September, 1626, Robert Lundie, designed as eldest son and heir of deceased Robert Lundie of Balgonie, contracted, for a sum of 10,000 merks and payment of debts, to dispone to

James Boswell of Loachgellie and David Boswell of Craigincate, the barony, lands and mains of Balgonie comprising mill and mill-lands of Balgonie, the Bankhead, Byris Lon, Lochtyside, the Coaltown, lands of Sythrum, mill and mill-lands thereof, town called Mylntown of Balgonie, lands of Dovan, and lands of Cauldcoittis with coal and coal-heuchs thereof (*NAS*, GD26/3/138). On the 24th of March 1627, he was served as heir to his father, in the lands and Barony of Balgonie; the lands of Dovaine, comprising Over and Nether Dovaine, and Mylndamis; the lands of Schethum, with the lands of Schethume, Blackfaldis and Cowdam; and the lands of 'marresie de Treatton' (*Inq. Spec. Ret. Fife*, No. 384). On the 3rd of February, 1627, Robert was bound to the contract with the Boswell's (*NAS*, GD26/3/140) and issued a charter accordingly (*NAS*, GD26/3/139). Robert was given sasine of the lands and Barony of Balgony on the 15th February, 1627 (*NAS*, 26/3/141). On the same day, according to the contract with the Boswell's, he resigned the same (*NAS*, 26/3/140). On March the 24th 1627 he was served as heir to his father, in the lands of Donykier, in the regality of Dunfermline (*Inq. Spec. Ret. Fife*, No. 388). It is not known what happened to these lands. As yet I have seen no record of Robert beign served as heir to his father in the land and Barony of Mondynes, and what directly happened to these lands is also unknown; however, by 1649 it was in possession of the family of Sibbald of Keirs, as on the 16th of November that year James Sibbald of Keir was served as heir to his father, David Sibbald of Keir, in the lands and Barony of Mondynes (*Inq. Spec. Ret. Kincardine*, No. 84).

On the 14th April, 1628, Robert Lundie, now not designed as of Balgonie, just as the son and heir of Robert Lundie of Balgonie, ratified his previous bonds and contracts with the Boswells. That same day he granted charters in favour of James Boswell of Loachgellie and David Boswell of Craigincate, of the lands of Tretoun Myre (*NAS*, GD26/3/150-1). This seems to be the end of Robert's association with these lands, and he died soon after. On the 23rd May, 1629, his half brother, John Lundie, appears designed as the 'eldest son of the deceased Robert Lundie of Balgonie,' when he renounced to James Boswell of Lochgellie and David Boswell of Craigincatt his claim on lands and barony of Balgony. This was upon payment of a reversion sum of 30,000 merks and 3000 merks as 1 year's tack duty (*NAS*, GD26/3/159). John then received a Bond by Sir George Boswell of Balgonie, kt., with David Boswell of Craigincat as cautioner, for 1000 merks, dated 29th November, 1631 (*NAS*, GD26/4/43). It would appear that this bond was not paid when it was supposed to be as on the 5th May, 1632 letters of inhibition were issued at the instance of John Lundie, son of deceased Robert Lundie of Balgonie, against Sir George Boswell of Balgonie, kt., and David Boswell of Cragincat, his cautioner, for payment of the1,000 merks contained in the bond dated 29 November 1631 (*NAS*, GD26/4/733). The national archives of Scotland also record the Renunciation by Euphame Lundie, eldest daughter of deceased Robert Lundie of Balgonie and Jean Lindsay, his first spouse, to James Boswell of Balgonie and David Boswell of Craigincat, of an annualrent of 300 merks from lands and Maynes of Balgonie, on payment of 3000 merks. Registered in Secretary's register for Fife, 10 December, (*NAS*, GD26/3/177). In 1634 a charter of confirmation, under the great seal, to Michael Balfour of Denmyle, of the lands and town of Drumdeill in Fife, which were described as previously pertaining to John Lundie and Euphame Lundie, described John as "heir masculine of his brother the late Robert Lundie of Balgonie, his father, the late Robert Lundie of Balgonie, his grandfather, Robert Lundie of Balgonie, and his greatgrandfather, David Lundie of Balgonie;" and Euphame as heir of Line of her late brother Robert (*Reg. Mag. Sig.* IX. 33).

It would appear that the Boswells did not retain Balgony for long. A Contract dated the 19th of September 1634, between John Leslie, Earl of Rothes, on one part, and Sir John Boswell of Balmuto, kt., David Boswell, fiar thereof, his eldest son, Sir George Boswell of Littill Balgonie, kt., James Boswell of Balgonie, David Boswell of Lochgellie, John Lundie, son and heir of deceased Robert Lundie of Balgonie, and George Boswell of Wastmylne of Kirkcaldy, on the other; states that for a sum of 102,000 merks, which includes 95,250 merks for disburdening the lands and wadsets, the Earl of Rothes is disponed the lands and barony of Balgonie and lands of Tretoun Myre. This was registered in the books of Council on the 9th of July 1635 (*NAS*, GD26/3/206, GD66/1/181). Thus ended the family of Lundie of Balgonie. The arms of Balgonie were later to be born by the family of Lundie, or Lundin, of Drums, who descended from the family of Lundie of Conland, who descended from and became the representatives of this House.

Balgonie Castle

Of the castles held by the Lundie family, Balgonie is by far in the best condition. It is currently owned by the family of Morris of Balgonie, who purchased it around twenty years ago. Although at this time it was in a state of disrepair, it has now undergone a great deal of renovation. The main tower is again habitable, and is lived in by the Laird of Balgonie, Lady Balgonie, and their son, Mr. Stuart Morris, Younger of Balgonie. The lower level of the Hall-House constructed by Sir Robert Lundie of Balgonie is also in use as a chapel, and is a popular venue for weddings. Much work has been already carried out on the restoration, but the family have further plans to completely restore this castle to its former glory. The large estate of Balgonie is no longer associated with the castle.

Balgonie castle in the statistical accounts of Scotland

As with a number of the buildings associated with this family, a good description is given in the 1791-99 and 1845 statistical accounts of Scotland.

"Balgonie castle, one of the seats of the Earl of Leven, is a fabric of great antiquity, and considerable strength. The time when it was built cannot be ascertained; but from the best information that can be got, it appears to be of the same age with the cathedral of St. Andrew's, which was built in the 12th century. This castle is pleasantly situated on the S. bank of the Leven, elevated about 36 feet above the bed of the river. It is of a quadrangular form, and stands upon an area of 135 feet by 105. The open court within, is 108 feet by 65. The tower*, which stands on the N. side, and near the N. W. angle is 45 feet by 36 over the walls, and 80 feet high. The top is surrounded with battlements, projecting about a foot beyond the walls. The roof, which appears to have been repeatedly repaired since it was first built, is rafted in the middle, and between that and the battlements is flat, and covered with stones. The walls of the two lower stories, both of which are vaulted, are 8 ½ feet thick: but above that, they are only 7 feet thick. There is an apartment in it called the Chapel, and, in the wall on the opposite side of the court, the ruins of a room are still to be seen, which was called the Chaplain's room. The architecture of this tower is still very perfect and entire, and the third story hath been lately repaired by the present Lord Balgonie.

*Connected with the tower is a house of three stories built by General Sir Alexander Leslie, extending to the N. E. corner; and on the E. side of the court of another house of the same height, built by the present Earl of Leven's grandfather. From the vaults under these new buildings, and the thickness of the walls in the lower story, it appears probable that the old buildings had been equally quite extensive, and that the new houses had been raised on the foundations of the old. On the S. and W. sides of the court, there is a strong wall, which appears to be coeval with the tower: and without the wall there has been a large fosse, the remains of which are still to be seen. The gateway is on the W. side, beside which, and under the wall, there is a pit. There is also a dungeon, or dark cell in the bottom of the tower. This castle stands in the middle of an oblong square, inclusive of 300 acres, fenced by a stone and lime wall. Near it there is a garden of about 7 acres, enclosed by a wall of 2 feet high, and a great deal of fine old trees around."

Rev. Mr John Thomson, statistical accounts 1791-99

"Westward from Balfour, and on a steep bank overhanging the Leven, stands the ancient baronial castle of Balgonie. The most ancient part of this venerable structure consists of a *donjon* or keep, 80 feet in height, and 45 feet by 36 over walls. The basement story, dimly lighted by a single narrow slit in the massive thickness of the walls, seems to have served as a prison. It is vaulted, as well as the storey above. The summit is surrounded by slightly projecting battlements, with circular *tourelles* at the angles. The roof is flat, and paved with square slabs of freestone. On the terrace thus formed, and several feet within the external battlements, on three sides is erected a lodge of an oblong form, with chimneys and a sloping roof, serving probably in former times as a *corps de garde* for the garrison."

The Rev. J. Sieveright, statistical accounts of Scotland 1845

12. *The main Tower of Balgonie Castle*

Heraldry

The arms of Balgonie are those of the ancient family of Sibbald of Balgonie (Argent a cross moline Gules, square pierced Argent), quartered with those of the ancient arms of Lundie of that Ilk. The Lindsay Armorial of 1542 (National Library of Scotland) records the arms of *Lundy of Balgonie* as Quarterly first and fourth paly of six *Gules* and *Argent*, on a bend *Azure* three cushions *Argent*; second and third, *Argent*, a cross moline *Gules*. Queen Mary's Roll of 1562 (National Library of Scotland) records the arms of *Lundey of Balgonie* as quarterly: first and fourth *Argent* three pales *Gules* on a bend *Azure* charged with three lozenges *Argent*, second and third *Argent*, a cross moline *Gules*. The Forman Armorial of 1563 (National Library of Scotland), records the arms of *Lvndy of Balgony* as, quarterly: first and fourth *Gules*, four pales *Argent*, on a bend *Azure* charged with three cushions *Argent*; second and third *Argent*, a cross moline *Gules*. The Slains Armorial of 1565 (held by the Earl of Errol) depicts the arms of *Lundy of Balgony* as: quarterly: first and fourth, paly of six *Gules* and *Argent*, on a bend *Azure* three cushions *Argent*; second and third *Argent*, a cross potent *Gules*. The Dunvegan Armorial of 1582, held by McLeod of Mcleod, shows 1st and 4th paly of eight *Gules* and *Argent*, on a bend *Azure* three tasselled cushions *Argent*: 2nd and 3rd *Argent*, a cross moline *Gules*. The Seton Armorial of 1591 (held by Sir David Ogilvy Bt.) shows the arms of *Lunde of Balgonie*: Quarterly: first and fourth *Or*, two pales *Gules*, on a bend *Azure* three cushions *Argent*; second and third *Argent*, a cross moline *Sable* square pierced *Argent*. The second Lindsay armorial of 1591 (held by the Earl of Crawford and Balcarres) shows *Lundie of Balgonie* as quarterly first and fourth *Argent* a cross moline (horns inverted) *Gules*, second and third *Gules* four pales *Or* on a bend *Azure* three cushions *Argent*. The Balgonie arms are also included in the Workmans Armorial held in the Lion office.

As described previously, the family of Lundie of Balgonie went on to be represented by the family of Lundie/Lundin of Drums (formerly of Conland), and a further account of their arms can be read there. The description Nisbet in his Heraldry gives of the arms of Drums, as representatives of Balgonie as "quarterly first and fourth argent, a cross Moline *gules*, by the surname of Sibbald; second and third, *argent* and *gules*, in place of six *argents* and *gules*, on a bend of the last three escutcheons of the first; crest a cross Moline *gules*: motto, *Justitia*." This puts the quartering of the Sibbald and Lundie arms the same as that given in the second Lindsay armorial, but at odds with all of the others which give Lundie in the first and fourth, and Sibbald in the second and third quarters.

13. *Lundy of Balgony from the 1885 reproduction "Emblazoned,"*
of the 1542 Armorial produced by Sir David Lindsay of the Mount .

Lr̂ndey of Balgornie L.

LVNDY OF BALGONY

(a) Lundey of Balgonie
Redrawn after Queen Mary's Roll
of 1562

(b) Lvndy of Balgony
Redrawn after the Forman Armorial
of 1563

(b) Lundie of Balgonie
Redrawn after the Seton Armorial
of 1591

14. (a) Lundie of Balgonie re-drawn from Queen Mary's Roll of 1562
(b) Lundy of Balgony re-drawn from the Forman Armorial of 1563
(b)Lundie of Balgonie re-drawn from the from the Seton Armorial of
1591

Seals.

A seal of Sir Andrew Lundie, 2nd of Balgonie, and Sheriff of Fife, survives on a charter dated the 24th of May 1512. The arms on his seal are given simply to be a cross moline; that of Sibbald of Balgonie (*Scottish Heraldic Seals*).

James Lundie, 3rd of Balgonie has a seal surviving in the Lundin Writs at the National Archives of Scotland (*NAS*, GD160/281, writ no 28). The seal shows a shield of arms, quartered, all surmounted of a bend sinister charged with three cushions; with 1st and 4th, a bend sinister; the details in the 2nd and 3rd, quarters cannot be made out, one asumes that they would have shown a moline.

From a document in the Balmuto charters, dated the 1st of May 1595, the seal of Robert Lundie, 7th of Balgonie can be seen. Here the arms on the seal are described as a shield much defaced, bearing arms: Quarterly, 1st and 4th: Three pallets surmounted of a bend charged with as many mascles. 2nd and 3rd: A lion rampant (or an eagle), (*Scottish Heraldic Seals*).

The House of Benholm

Introduction

The lands of Benholm (Benne, Benhame, Benholme) were first granted to Hugo de Benne in 1145, the family of de Benne taking their name from this land. During the reign of King William the Lion, these lands were then granted to his son, Hugo, by a Charter dated the 20th of August, 1201, at Kincardine.

"William by the grace of God King of Scots to all good men of his whole land clerks and laymen greeting. Know men present and future that I have restored and granted and by this my charter confirmed to Hugo son of Hugo de Benne, Benne by its right marches and with all its just pertinents: To be held &c. Doing therefor to me and my heirs half' a knight's service, as the charter of the foresaid Hugo his father witnesses."

The witnesses to this charter were, Reginald, bishop of Ross; William & Walter, chaplains of the King; Earl Duncan of Fife; Philip de Valoniis, chamberlain; Robert de Quincy; Alan son of Rolland the constable; William Comyn; John de Hasting; William de Hay; Ranulph de Soules; William de Vipont; Humphrey de Berkeley; David de Hay; Ivo de Vipont; Roger de la Kerneille; and Malcolm de Lascelles (*NAS*, GD4/2).

In the thirteenth century, the lands and barony then passed from the de Benne family to the Lundies, through the marriage of Christian de Benne, the daughter and heiress of Hugo de Benne, to Walter de Lundy (*NAS*, GD4).

On the 5th of January 1390, at Perth King Robert II of Scotland granted a Royal charter confirming a charter granted by Christian, daughter of Hugo de Benne, of parts of the lands of Benholme to Allan Lundy, who was noted as a kinsman of Thomas de Lundy.

On the 16th of October, 1445, John Lundie of that Ilk was granted sasine of the barony of Benham; following on a Precept from Chancery. Sasine was given at the 'Castell-wallis of Benham' (*NAS*, GD4/3).

On the 4th of May 1469, William Lundie, son and heir of Sir John Lundy of that Ilk (see that line) had a Royal charter of Benholm to him and his spouse (*NAS*, GD160).

Around 1474, the 'Mainlandis' (Mains) of Benholm were wadset by the Lundies to the family of Bonnar of Rossie. There is a narrative dated the 13th of May, 1474, stating that Sir John Lundy of that Ilk, in obedience to the King's decreet, offered to William Bonar of Rossie a Charter and Precept of Sasine of 24 merklands of the Mains of Benham. It also stated that William Bonar wished to take time to satisfy himself as to the security of the title (*NAS*, GD4/33). Five days later there are letters of revision by William Bonar of Rossie, granting that Sir John of Lundy of that Ilk, or his heirs, might redeem the Maynelandis of Benham and the principal "chymis" thereof by payment of 500 merks Scots upon the altar of St. Michael in St. Andrews parish kirk, or half thereof by payment of half the money (*NAS*, GD4/34). It appears that Sir John wished to redeem these lands eight years later, but that James Bonar of Rossie, the heir of William Bonar of Rossie, was reluctant to keep his father's agreement.

In 1482, Sir John paid to James Bonar of Rossie the 250 merks for the redemption of half of the Mains of Benholm. Sir John visited James Bonar at his house in St. Andrews on the 25th May, 1482, where there lay upon a counter the 250 merks of Scots money, and £38 which Sir John had sent to James Bonar. This £38 was to be used to make good any 'bad' money delivered with the 250 merks. The redemption process was to take place in the sight of two Bailies of St. Andrew's and Sir John Lundy's Chaplain. Sir John's chaplain was also there in case the £38 proved insufficient (*NAS*, GD4/36).

It appears that James Bonar did not complete his side of the bargain, as on the 24th of February 1484-5, James Bonar, whilst in Edinburgh at Russell's Tavern, for the purposes of 'playing and drinking,' was confronted by Sir John Lundy, Sir John requiring James Bonar to resign half the lands of Bennum and the "chemys" thereof, as then redeemed from him, and conform to a Decreet of the Lords of Council (*NAS*, GD4/37). After this James Bonar must have resigned half of the lands back to Sir John as per the agreement. However, in November of that year, Sir John tried to redeem the second half of these lands, and again there seems to have been a problem on the part of James Bonar of Rossie. On the 5th of November, 1484, Sir John Lundy placed 250 merks on St. Michael's altar in St. Andrews parish kirk, and offered this money to James Bonar for the redemption of the last half of the Mains of Benham. He apparently waited until sundown, but the money was not taken. Sir John solemnly protested that he had done exact diligence anent the redemption, and ought to have free regress to the lands (NAS, GD4/39). On the 17th November, 1487, James Bonar of Rossie finally resigned the half of the lands of Mains of Benholm, into the hands of Sir John Lundy of that Ilk, Knight, Lord superior thereof (*NAS*, GD4/40).

ROBERT LUNDIE, 1ST OF BENHOLM

Since the barony of Benholm had been obtained by the family of Lundie of that Ilk, through Walter de Lundy's marriage to Christian de Benne, it would appear that the Lairds of Lundie held the lands and Barony as part of their paternal estate. This all changed in 1491, when Sir John Lundy of that Ilk granted Benholm one of his younger son's, founding the House of Benholm.

Robert was a son of Sir John Lundy of that Ilk and Isabel Forrester; Isabel being Sir John's second spouse. On the 4th of January 1485-6 a charter was granted by King James III to Sir John Lundy of that Ilk, knight, and Isabel Forstare, his spouse, and the heirs male of their marriage, of the barony of Benholme and Mains thereof (on Sir John's resignation); also the land's of Tulloch, the Casteltoun, Carnenach, Mutehill and the Brewland (on the resignation of William Lundy and his spouse). (*NAS* GD/8. *Reg. Mag. Sig.* II 1631.). William Lundy was a half brother to Robert, and succeeded Sir John as Laird of Lundy. William Lundy, having originally being granted a Royal charter of the barony of Benholm to himself and his spouse, in 1469, had resigned the lands of Benham, Tullo, Casteltoun, Carnenow, Mithil and Brewland, on the 18th of February 1484-85, in favour of his father, Sir John, and Isabel, then his father's spouse, and the heirs of their marriage. Following the charter by King James III, a Charter was granted by John Lundy of that Ilk, and Isabel his spouse, to Robert Lundy, their son, of the lands and barony of Benhame, viz. the Manis, Casteltoune and Tulloch, with the mill. This was to be held of the King, reserving the granters' life rent. This charter was dated at Lundy, on the 24th of March 1491-92 (*NAS*, GD/10).

Around 1495, negotiations were underway for the marriage of Robert Lundie of Benholm to Elizabeth Erskine, a daughter of John Erskine of Dun. On contemplation of this marriage, Robert granted (on the 22nd of July, 1495) a precept of sasine in favour of Elizabeth Erskine, of the lands of Tullowcht of Benhame (*NAS*, GD4/15). On the 21st June 1496, dated a Stirling, a contract was produced whereby William Lundy, the fore mentioned brother of Robert Lundie of Benholm; Elizabeth Hepburn, the spouse of William Lundy; and, Thomas Lundy, son and heir of William, all resigned any claims to the Barony of Benholm. This was in exchange for 800 merks, (500 merks in instalments, and the lands of Fossoway as security for the remaining 300 merks) (*NAS*, GD4/17,18). The contract was fulfilled by the 12th of November of the following year (*NAS*, GD4/19). By 1498 Robert had married Elizabeth Erskine. On the 14th October of that year a Great Seal Charter by King James IV of Scotland granted the lands of Tullow of Benhame (Tully of Benholm) to Robert Lundy of Benhame and Elizabeth Erskine, his spouse, upon Elizabeth's resignation. (*Reg. Mag. Sig.* II. 2460; *NAS*, GD4/21).

Sometime before 1497, Robert Menzies of Enoch had promised to the King, to present to Robert Lundie of Benholm, the parsonage of Weyme, in the Diocese of Dunkeld. On the 12th of November, 1497, Robert Menzies offered to seal with his own seal a presentation of the this parsonage, at the instance of the King, and deliver this presentation to Robert. This offer was however provided that Robert fulfilled a yet unknown promise made to Robert Menzies. It is not known of Robert ever received this gift (*Protocol Book of J. Young*, 974)

Robert died around 1519. He had issue:-

1 *Andrew Lundie of Benholm*, who succeeded his father in the Barony of Benholm

2 *John Lundie*, brother-german to Andrew. He was given sasine by his brother Andrew of the shadow half of the lands of Tollow in the barony of Benhom on the 26th of February 1525 (*NAS*, GD4/26). In 1533 he was appointed along with his brother Andrew, in the service of the crown, to accompany Sir Thomas Erskine of Brechin to foreign parts (*Acts Lords of Council in Civil Caus.* 420).

3 *Marion Lundie*, married firstly Alexander Keith of Pittendrum, forth son of William Keith, 3rd Earl Marischal by Elizabeth Gordon daughter of George 2nd Earl of Huntly (*Scots Peerage*, I, 284). They had one son:-

   i *John Keith of Pittendrum.*

Alexander Keith died before 1515 as she married secondly Robert Arbuthnott of Banff, second son of Robert Arbuthnott by Marjorie

Scrymgeour, on 22nd September 1515 (*Scots Peerage*, VI. 44).
4   **Margaret Lundie**, (*Reg. Mag. Sig.* IV. 549).

ANDREW LUNDIE, 2ND OF BENHOLM

In 1523, whilst still in his minority, at the Kings dispensation, Andrew, as heir to his father, was given sasine of the lands of Inchmeddan, Tulloch of Benhome and Kyrktone of Benholme, with the mill thereof; which had been in nonentry for four years (*Exchequer Rolls of Scotland*, XV. 605, 608; *NAS*, GD4/21). On the 20th of May 1524 he was given sasine of the 'Manis of Benholme', which had been in the King's hands for five years by reason of ward (*Exchequer Rolls of Scotland,* XV. 620; *NAS*, GD4/25). Soon after he was given a commission of Justiciary (*Exchequer Rolls of Scotland*, XV. 653). On the 26th of February 1525-6 he granted a precept of sasine in favour of his brother-german John Lundie, of the shadow half lands of Tollow within the Barony of Benholm (*NAS*, GD4/26). In 1533, on the 13th of March, Andrew, his brother John, with a number of others, including a Richard Lundy of whom no more is known than his name, were appointed by the King to accompany Sir Thomas Erskine of Brechin, in the service of "parties beyond sey for maters concerning us and the common weil of our realme" (*Acts Lords of Council in Civil Caus.* 420).

Andrew was married to Margaret Scrymgeour. They had a charter under the great seal dated 30th June 1542. According to documents at the National archives of Scotland, Andrew died at the battle of Pinkie (a.k.a Falside), on the 10th of September 1547 (*NAS*, GD4/27; *Exchequer Rolls of Scotland*, XVIII. 434). He had issue:-

1   **William Lundie (alias Robert Lundie) 3rd of Benholm**, who succeeded, and whose details follow.
2   **John Lundie in Lumgair.** (See Lundie of Lungar)
3   **other sons x 6**
4   **Janet Lundie**, married by the 15th of July, 1545, James Bruce of Fingask. On this date he infeft her for life in his lands of Rait (*Fingask Papers, Perth Archives*). They had issue.
5   **Second daughter**

WILLIAM LUNDIE, 3ᴿᴰ OF BENHOLM

William (alias Robert) succeeded to Benholm after the death of his father. There is a sasine to William as heir of his father Andrew dated the 2ⁿᵈ of July, 1548, of the Manis of Benholme, the lands of Inchmeddan, Tullo of Benholme, and Kirktoun of Benholme, with mill thereof (*NAS*, GD4/27). On the 25ᵗʰ of June 1551, William Lundie of Benholm and his wife Helen Carnegie, daughter of Sir Robert Carnegie, 5ᵗʰ of Kinnaird, by Margaret Guthrie, received as spouses a Crown charter of the lands of Tullo and Inchmeddan in Kincardineshire upon William's resignation (*Scots Peerage*, VIII. 56). On the 18ᵗʰ of November 1551, William was given a gift from the Monarch of the nonenty of the lands of Lumgar, within the sheriffdom of Kincardine, which were in the King's hands following the death of Sir Thomas Erskine of Brechin (*Reg. Sec. Sig.* IV. 1419). William's brother and nephew are later to be found designed as 'of Lumgar.'

William died shortly after his marriage, before 1553. He left only one child, Elizabeth Lundie. It is not certain whether she was the daughter of Helen Carnegie or not, but as Helen's father was given the gift of ward of William's daughter by the King, it is most probable. Helen Carnegie remarried after the death of William, to William Turring of Foveran (*Crawford's Scots Peerage*, 447).

ELIZABETH LUNDIE, 4ᵀᴴ, AND LAST OF THAT NAME, OF BENHOLM.

After the death of her father a gift of the ward and non-entry of the his lands was made by Queen Mary to Robert Carnegie of Kinnard, Robert being the father of William's widow Helen, on the 16ᵗʰ of August, 1553 (*NAS*, GD4/29). Elizabeth must have been in minority at this time. A gift of her marriage was also made to Sir Robert. Seven years later, on the 6ᵗʰ of February 1559-60, Sir Robert had arranged the marriage between Elizabeth Lundie and Sir Robert Keith, the second son of William, Fourth Earl Marischal. An assignation was made of the ward of entry of all the lands of the late William Lundie of Benholm, and the marriage of his daughter and heir, Elizabeth, to the said Robert Keith. Failing Robert, this would pass to William Keith, again son of William, Fourth Earl Marischal, failing him, to George Keith, eldest son of Earl Marishcal, and failing him to any other person the Earl or his heirs should name (*NAS*, GD4/30). The actual marriage contract predates this arrangement by four years, being dated the 24th of May, 1556. It would appear that at this point Elizabeth was still in minority as she did not obtain her fathers lands in her own right until 1565. On the 10th of May of this year she had sasine, following a precept of Clare Constat dated 11th April that year, of the Manis of Benholme, the lands of Inchmeddan, Tullo of Benholme, and Kirktoun of Benholme, with mill thereof (*NAS*, GD4/31).

Robert Keith, husband of Elizabeth, was a man of power an influence, extending from his own person, and that of the Marischal family itself. He was born circa 1540, the second son of William Keith Fourth Earl Marischal, by Margaret, eldest daughter of William Keith, younger of Inverugie. By 1555, although only around 15, he was appointed Commendator of the Abbey of Deer, succeeding his uncle Robert Keith, brother to William Fourth Earl Marischal, to that post. After the abolition of Catholasism in Scotland, Robert resigned all the lands belonging to the Abbey into the hands of King James VI. These were then granted back to Robert under a charter dated 29th July, 1587, errecting this property into a temporal Lordship, giving Robert the title of Lord Altrie.

On the 13th of June, 1566, Elizabeth, with consent of Robert Keith and her curators, resigned the lands and Manis of Benholme, with the tower and fortalice thereof, Over and Nether Knox, Inchmadan, Tulloch of Benholme, Kyrktoun of Benholme, with the mill, and the lands and barony of Benholme, into the hands of Queen Mary, in favour of her spouse and herself in conjunct fee (*NAS*, GD4/61). The next month, 2nd July, these lands were granted under a Charter of the Great Seal, by Henry and Mary, King and Queen of Scots, erecting the fore mentioned lands into one free Barony of Benholm, and granting it to Robert Keith and Elizabeth Lundy (*NAS*, GD4/65). In 1587, on the 28th June, the lands were again resigned to the Monarch, this time King James VI (*NAS*, GD4/69). Upon regranting the lands from to Robert and Elizabeth, 30th July of the same year, they had annexed the patronage of the kirk of Benholme, parsonage and vicarage, to the Barony of Benholm. (*Reg. Mag. Sig.* V. 1324; *NAS*, GD4/71). In that same year, on the 27th of June, they were granted a charter by George, Earl Marischall, Lord Keith, of a third part of the lands of Arbirnie. There were given sasine the next day (*NAS*, GD70/25). Twenty years later both a John and James Lundie are found to be living in Arbirnie, with John later moving to Montrose (*Reg. Privy Council*, Series I. VII. 594; IX. 128; X. 457, 470).

Both Robert Keith, Lord Altrie, and Elizabeth Lundie, Lady Beholm, died before the 8th June, 1597, as there is a Retour in favour of Isobel Keith, lady Dalgety; and Margaret Keith, lady Dun as heirs in general of Robert Lord of Altrie and Dame Isobel Lundye, lady of Benholme their father and mother, dated at Cowie, and recorded before the sheriff depute of Kincardine (*NAS*, GD4/89). The property, lands and Barony of Benholm thus passed into the family of Keith Marischal. Further details of this can be read under the 'House of Lungar,' and details of other probable desendants of this house can be read in section six 'in Benholm.' Robert and Elizabeth had issue:-

1   ***Elizabeth Keith***, married Alexander Hay of Dalgaty, on 4th December 1584.

2   ***Margaret Keith***, married first, before 28th August 1588, John Erskine, son and heir apparent of John Erskine of Logy and later Dun. By this marriage she had John Erskine who succeeded to Dun on 5th November 1603. Secondly she married Sir John Lindsay of Ballincho, third son of David Lindsay 9th Earl of Crawford, on 26th May 1599.

Benholm Castle

Benholm Castle is located in the Parish of Benholm in Kincardineshire. Subsequent to the 17th Century, the ancient barony of Benholm was divided into the estates of Benholm, Brotherton, Nether Benholm and Knox. Benholm castle is an ancient building associated with the Lundie family since it's conception, until it's passing to the Keith Marischal family at the end of the 16th Century. Up until recently the square Tower House of Benholm Castle was still standing. Sadly it would appear that recently whilst the owners of Benholm Castle were discussing with relevant authorities the restoration of the Tower, it collapsed. The tower at the time was complete to the parapets, but had a two large cracks down each side. Attached to the side of the tower was a derelict Georgian mansion. When the mansion was constructed, the ground around the tower had been lowered, thus causing some instability in the castle foundations, and the eventual cracking of the Tower. In order to prevent these cracks from further development, it was proposed to support the tower with a concrete raft, but this would have involved removing the more modern derelict house attached. This idea was not approved by the authorities as they wished to maintain both the castle and house attached. When discussions were taking place, half of the tower collapsed, destroying the mansion anyway.

Benholm castle in the statistical accounts of Scotland

One can find an account of Benholm Castle in the 1790-99 and 1845 statistical accounts of Scotland. Both of these accounts give a good description of the tower and mansion when still intact.

> "The only ancient building now remaining in the parish is the tower of Benholm. This at one time had been a place of considerable strength. It is a high and massive square building of sandstone, still in a state of complete preservation. It seems at one time to have stood on a peninsula, formed by one of the streams above-mentioned on the east and south sides, and be a deep trench or moat on the west. A passage was formed over this moat by the late proprietor, G. R. Scott, Esq., in opening a new approach to the mansion-house."
>
> *Rev. Mr. James Scott, Statistical accounts of Scotland, 1791-99*

"Among the few antiquities in this parish, may be mentioned a square tower, which was the ancient residence of the family of Benholm, and is still kept in repair, though not inhabited. From its peninsular situation, thickness of walls, and battlements on the roof; this building seems to have been originally intended for a place of strength; and before the use of artillery, was probably not ill calculated to resist the sudden attack of an enemy. When this strong hold was built is uncertain."

Rev. James Glen, Statistical accounts of Scotland, 1845

15. Benholm Castle

Heraldry

The arms of Lundie of Benholm, do not seem to have been included in any of the ancient armorials, however, from a seal of Robert Lundie of Benholm, son of Sir John Lundy of that Ilk, we can get an idea of the arms. The seal is from one of the Benholm charters, dated the 22nd of July 1495. The shield of arms is described as Paly of six, the fourth charged with a saltire couped in chief, on a bend three square cushions. The shield was on a background of diagonal crossing lines.

16. Representation of the Arms of Lundie of Benholm, from the seal of Robert Lundie of Benholm in 1495

The House of Drums, formerly Conland

History

The Lundie family took possession of the Barony of Conland (Condland, Condlene, Condlane) after the marriage of Robert Lundie, son of Andrew Lundie 2nd of Balgonie, to Margaret Lumisden, the heiress of Conland. Their eldest son David succeeded to Balgonie, and Conland was settled first upon their second son James; later their third son Robert, and last their forth son Andrew. Andrew was to loose much of the lands through debt, and left his eldest surviving son David with the lands of Drums, from where the family then took their designation. Parts of Conland were later to be purchased by descendants of Andrew's elder brother David Lundie of Balgonie, viz. John Lundie of Easter Conland, and his brother David Lundie of Wester Conland. The Balgonie line however failed, and the heir male of this family became the Lundin's of Drum (Drums, Drummes, Drumes). There were no lands for them to inherit, as the Barony of Balgonie had been sold by 1640, so the designation as 'of Drums' was maintained. However the Lundie's of Drums (becoming Lundin of Drums) carried the Arms of the Lundie family of Balgonie.

JAMES LUNDIE, 2ND OF CONLAND

The second legitimate son of Robert Lundie of Conland, and Balgonie, and his spouse Margaret Lumisden; James was given sasine of the Barony of Conland by his parents in 1564. Failing heirs of his body, this barony was to pass to his brother german, Robert Lundie (*Reg. Mag. Sig.* IV. 1523; *Reg. Sec. Sig.* V. 1668). He was twice married. His first spouse was Christian Betoun (Bethune) (*NAS* RD XV. 389). His second spouse was Janet Betoun, daughter of John Betoun of Auchmithie by Helen Melville (*Scot's Peerage*, VIII. 488). James died before the 28th of April 1569, and was succeeded to Conland by his brother Robert. Janet Beaton, afterwards married Captain David Wemyss, son of David Wemyss of that Ilk, around 1577 (*Scot's Peerage*, VIII. 488).

ROBERT LUNDIE, 3RD OF CONLAND

The brother german to James Lundie 2nd of Conland, he has a charter of Condland (Condlane) confirmed under the Great Seal in 1659 (*Reg. Mag. Sig.* IV. 1851). The original charter was dated at Condland in April that year, and witnessed amongst others by an Alexander Lundie Jr. Robert married Janet Bethune, 3rd and youngest daughter of John Bethune of Balfour (*East Neuk of Fife*, p 372). Robert died before the 5th of May 1575.

ANDREW LUNDIE, 4TH OF CONLAND

The fourth son of Robert Lundie and Margaret Lumisden; according to Nisbet in his *Heraldry* there is a sasine of the lands of Conland by Robert Lundie of Balgonie and Margaret Lumisden his wife, in favour of Andrew Lundie their son, in 1578. Andrew was certainly in possession of Conland by 1585, as on the 30th of March that year, Andro Lundy of Condolane is a witness to an obligation by John Douglas in Kennestoun to Sir John Brown of Fordell (*Browns of Fordell*, p100). Andrew married Elizabeth Broun, daughter of Sir John Broun of Fordell and Katherine Boswell, herself the daughter of David Boswell of Glasmont and Balmuto (*Heraldry; Browns of Fordell, p20*). On 22nd December 1591, they were given a charter of Conland under the great Seal of Scotland.

> "Charter in favour of Andrew Lundie of Condland and Elizabeth Brown, his spouse, and their heirs, etc., of the lands of Condland, Drum, Wester Condland, etc., in the shire of Fife, and Midlairis in the shire of Aberdeen, by annexation in Fife, all united into the barony of Condland; held of the Crown for the usual services. At Holyrood, 22d December 1591. – *Reg. Mag. Sig.* (from Nisbet's *Heraldy*)" (*Browns of Fordell*, p 101)

At Conland, on the 24th of May 1599, Andro Lundie of Condlane and Elizabeth Brown, his spouse, and David Brown of Fynmonth (Andrew's Brother-in-law), gave a bond to George Scott, burgess of Dysert, for 6400 merks, as the price of the lands of Drimey (Drums) Over and Nether (*Browns of Fordell*, p 155). After the death of the said Geroge Scott, Walter Scott, his son and heir, renounced all claims he had against David Broun of Fynmonth, as cautioner in the aforementioned contract. The renunciation was dated at Falkland 13th December 1613 (*Reg. Deeds; Browns of Fordell*, p 162-3).

In 1601 Andrew appears as a member of the assize in an action between Patrick Commendator of Lindores and Henry Bonar of Lumquhat Mill in 1601 (*Univ. St. And. Arch.* Ms36929 Box2/15). On the 18th of May 1611, at Falkland, Harry Boswell, a burgess of Kinghorn, acting as cautioner for Andrew Lundie of Condlane, gave an obligation to Mr Robert Broun of Pitkenny, for 630 merks (*Reg. Deeds* 4th Jul 1615; *Browns of Fordell*, p110). That same year, on the 2nd of October, at Kirkcaldy, Andro Lundy of Condland, gave an obligation to his 'beloved brother-in-law' David Broun of Finmonth, for 500 merks (*Reg. Deeds* 19th November 1630; *Browns of Fordell*, p 161).

During the time Andrew was laird, the interaction between the House of Conland and various other Lundie houses seems to have been fairly strong. In 1593, Andrew appears in the register of the Privy Council in a bond of caution, giving surety for George Lundie, apparent of Gorthie, for the sum of 1000 merks, for George not to harm many members of the Drummond family (*Reg. Privy Council*, Series I. V. 590-591). In 1603, Andrew was named along with Sir Duncan Campbell of Glenurquhy, Andrew Ayton of Denmure, George Lundie of Gorthie, William Grahame of Claverhouse, and David Sibbald of Lethame, as sureties for £20,000, for John Lundie of that Ilk to keep in company with his brother David Lundy of Newhall, and to produce him whenever required before either the Lords of Privy Council or the Justice general (*Reg. Privy Council.* Series I. VI. 794). In 1606, Andrew was summond by the Lords of the Privy Council, along with James Lundie of that Ilk, Sir James Lundie, Robert Lundie of Balgonie, David Lundie of Newhall, and George Lundie younger of Gorthie, in order to quell a feud between the Lundies and the family of Learmonth (*Reg. Privy Council.* Series I. VII. 212).

Andrew was said to have been in good favour with King James VI of Scotland (I of England), and so he went to England with King James when he succeeded to the Crown of England upon the decease of Queen Elizabeth, *anno* 1603. Here he spent most of his estate, as well as what he had by the King's bounty. As a result of the expense of being at the Royal Court based now in England, the barony of Conland was apprised from Andrew by Sir Michael Arnot of that Ilk (*Heraldry*). He died sometime between 1647 and 1648 (*Univ. St. And. Arch.* Ms36220/708 + Ms36929 Box4/348). Andrew and Elizabeth had issue:-

1   ***Robert Lundie, fear of Conland***. He appears twice in the register of the Privy Council in 1606 alongside his father in bonds of caution:

> "Edinburgh 21st July 1606
> Mr William Adamsone of Graycruke for Androw Lundy of Conland £1000, and for Robert Lundy, his son and apparent heir, 1000 merks, not to harm Johne Burrel, wester, Johnne Burrell, easter, Androw Burrel, elder and younger, Thomas Burrell, William Cowpar, or Androw Ged, portioner of Frequhy."
> (*Reg. Privy Council*, Series I. VII. 645)

> "Edinburgh, 29th July 1606
> William Cowper and Andrew Burrell, younger, portioners of Frewquhy, for Johne Burrel, called Wester Johne, Johne Burrell, called Easter Johne, Andrew Burrell elder, Thomas Burrell and Androw Ged, portioners of Frewquhy, et vice versa, 500 merks, not to harm Androw Lundy of Condland, or Robert Lundy, his eldest son and apparent heir."
> (*Reg. Privy Council*, Series I. VII. 646).

He appears designed as 'feodatarius of condland' when a witness in 1608 (*Reg. Mag Sig.* VI. 2139). He predeceased his father, and must have died before 1632, as by that time his brother David is designed as eldest son (*Browns of Fordell*, p167)

2   ***David Lundie, 1ˢᵗ of Drums***, whose details will follow.

3   ***Andrew Lundie of Carrie and The Provost Maynes of Abernethie***.   He married Jean Broun, his cousin, and daughter of David Broun of Finmonth (*Browns of Fordell*, p179) on the 17ᵗʰ of November, 1647. Most details of his life are intertwined with the affairs of his mother and wife's family, the Brown's of Fordell.

In 1648 he is witness to the marriage contract between his kinsman, Sir John Brown of Fordell kt; and on the other part Sir James Scott of Rossie and his spouse Dame Antonia Willobie, on behalf of their daughter, Mary (*Univ. St. And. Arch.* MS36929 Box4/348; *Browns of Fordell*, p220). Here he appears designed as Andrew Lundie, son to the deceased Andrew Lundy of Condland. On the 19ᵗʰ of March the following year, he appears designed as of 'The Provost Mainis of Abernethie,' when he received a discharge by Mr Archibald Moncreiff, on behalf of Sir John Browne of Fordell (designed as Heritor of Colfargie, Carie and Fargis Miln), for 50 merks as part of a stipend. Archibald Moncreiff gave a discharge of the same content to Andrew on the 12th of November, at Abernethie, that same year (*Univ. St. And. Arch. Ms*36220/517 + 520). On the 24th of May that year, again designed of the Provost Mainis of Abernethie he received a discharge from a John Brown, on the behalf of Sir John Brown of Fordell, for £151, as a years annual rent (*Univ. St. And. Arch. Ms*36220/516). In 1644 he also appears in the records of parliament (*General index to the acts of parliament of Scotland,* VI. ii. 191a).

Towards the end of 1649, and early 1650, Andrew went about purchasing the lands of Easter and Wester Carrie, in the Parish of Abernethy, from Sir John Brown of Fordell. The contract of alienation of these lands by Sir John, to Andrew is dated the 19th of December 1649, and 28th of June 1650. He was given a disposition of these lands on the 8th of July 1650, and sasine on the 24th of July 1650. The description of both the contract and disposition is included below (*Browns of Fordell,* p140).

"Contract of Alienation between Sir John Brown of Fordell, knight, heritable proprietor of the lands aftermentioned, with consent of Dame Mary Scott, his spouse, and Andrew Lundie of Provostmains, whereby, in consideration of a certain sum of money having been paid, the said Sir John sells and dispones to the said Andrew Lundie, his heirs and assignees whatsoever heritably and irredeemably, all and sundry the lands of Easter and Wester Carrie, Hiltoun, etc., lying in the Parish and barony of Abernethy and sheriffdom of Perth. Dated and subscribed at Edinburgh and Rossie, 19th December 1649, and 28th June 1650 respectively, and recorded 7th August 1677. The witnesses to the subscription of the said Sir John Brown and Andrew Lundie are; William Oliphant of Balgonie; James Brown, weaver in Edinburgh; and John Muir, servitor to Alexander Douglas, W.S.; and to that of the said Dame Mary Scott were; Sir James Scott of Rossie, knight, her father; John Seaton of Lawtrick; and John

Crichton, servitor to the said Sir James. – Reg. of Deeds, Mack. office, vol. 222 p 236."

"Disposition dated at Rosie 8th July 1650, by Sir John Browne of Fordell, and Marie Scott, his spouse, of the lands of Easter and Wester Caries, in the Parish of Abernethy, in favour of Andrew Lundie of Provostmaines of Abernethy; he had sasine 24th of same month."

On the 17th of July 1650, Andrew Lundie of Carye is witness to a bond by Sir John Brown of Fordell, to Sir James Arnot of Ferny Kt, for 28,826 merks (*Univ. St. And. Arch.* Ms36220/713). On the 19th of May the following year he is recorded as receiving a receipt from Sir John Brown for two bonds granted two years previous (*Univ. St. And. Arch. Ms36220/ 714*). On the 24th May, 1652, George Oliphant, son of William Oliphant of Balgouny, granted a charter in favour of Andrew Lundy of Carthes, of the lands of Turflindy alias Earlsmure in the parish of Abernethie and sheriffdom of Perth. He was given sasine the next day; registered P.R.S. Perth, 22 June, 1652, which was confirmed by a charter of Archibald, Earl of Angus, on the 2nd of June 1652. In the charter of confirmation he is designed of Caryis (*NAS*, GD62/124-125). On the 12th of December 1655, Andrew; along with John Oliphant, son of William Oliphant of Balgonye; David Brown of Fynmoth; and John Browne of Vicars Grange; granted a bond to Patrick Campbell of Innergeldie and Bathia Moray, his spouse, for 3010 merks. (*NAS*, GD26/4/120; GD26/4/126; GD26/5/301).

Sir John Brown of Fordell, Andrew's cousin, died on the 1st of September 1651. He left two children, John and Antonia, both in minority. Andrew, along with David Brown of Finmonth and Sir James Scott of Rossie were nominated as Tutors of the heirs of Sir John. The position of tutor involved Andrew deeply in the business of Sir John's estate, and involved him in much legal action from the estate's creditors (ironically of which he was also one). Andrew was one of the witnesses to the inquisition that named David Brown of Finmonth as nearest heir male to the aforementioned John and Antonia Brown, in 1654 (*Browns of Fordell*, p178-9).

"1st August 1654. Tutela, xxi. 336
This inquisition wes done in ane Shreff-court of the

Sherifdome of Fyffe, holden within the Tolbuith of the burghe of Cupar, befor Mr. Dauid Weymes of Balfarge, Shereff of Fyffe, the first day of August j^mjvj^c fiftie four yeirs, be dispensatione anent the tyme of vacance be thir good and faithfull me of this nation underwritten, to writ, James MckGill of Nether Rankeilour; Gawine Weymes of Unthank; David Weymes of Fudie, David Beattoune, fiar of Bondoie; Mr. John Weymes, brother to the Laird of Fingask; George Orme, portioner of Newbarne; William Schaw of Lethangie; Andro Lundie of Carie; Mr David Methven of Craigtoun; Alexander Luiklow, burgess of Cupar; Andrew Greg, thair; John Geddie, wryter thair; William Clephane, thair; James Luiklow, thair; and Richard Mylne in Balmedie: quah being sworn, declair that David Broune of Finmonth is neirest agnett, that is to say neirest of kine on the father syde to Jon Broune, lawful sone to the deceast Sir Jon Broune of Fordell, knight, and that he is ane provinent manager of his own affairs, and able to advert to the due administration of other men's affaires; and that he is past the age of twentie fyve yeris compleit, and that the said David Broune is not neirest to succeed to the said Jon. Broune in caise of his decease, in respect Antonia Broune, his sister, will succeid to him in cais of his deceis: In faith and treuth of the quhilkis the severall sealls of the maist part of the forseads persones of inquest with the said breiff inclosit are here appendit, and subscrywit be James Litilljon, Shereff-clerk of the said Shereffdome, day, yeir, place and month above wryttin. Subsct. thus – John Littiljohne, notter publict and Shrff-clerk of Fyffe."

In 1655 he appears along with William Oliphant of Balgonie, named as one of the cautioners for debts due to Sir David Carmichaell of Balmedie by the late Sir John Brown of Fordell (*Browns of Fordell*, p140).

"7th Feb. 1655. The inventarie and testament dative *ad hunc effectum* of the goodis, gear, and debtis of umquhile Sir John Brown of Fordell, within the parochin therof and sherefdome of Fyff, the tyme of his deceis, quilk wes vpone the first day of September 1651 yeares, ffaithfulie made and given vp be Johne Oliphant, resident in Dysart, executor dative *ad hunc effectum,* surrogat to the said defunct in the place of Alexander Ingles, procuratour-fiscall of the commissariat of Fyff for the tyme, eftir dew citatioun, etc. In swa far as the said defunct, the tym of his deceiss foirsaid, restit awan to Sir David Carmichaell of Balmedie, knicht, the sowme of thrie thousand threi hundreth threttie-thrie pundis vj s. viij d. money Scotis, as principall, with the sowme of ij^c lib. for ane yeiris annualrent therof, and ij^c lib. of penaltie, contenit in and band grantit be the said defunct as principall, and William Oliphant of Balgonie and Andro Lundie of Provost Maines of Abernethie, as cautionaris for him, of the dait the twelff and fourtein dayes of Junij 1650 yeiris, registrat in the Shereff bookis of Perth, and ane decreit of the Shereffes thairof interponed therto vpone the first day of October 1652 yearis; in and to the quhilk band, sowmes of money, principall, annualrentis, and liquidat expenssis abone writtin, therin contenit respective, and decreit of registration foirsaid, the said Sir David Carmichaell of Balmeddie, be his lettres of assignatioun subsribit with his hand of the dait the sextein day of August 1653 yeiris, for the caussis therein specifeit, made, and constitute the said Johne Oliphant his assignay, extending the said sowmes to iij^{m}vij^{c}xxiij lib. vj s. viij d., and for peyment and satisfactioun to the said executour of the expenssis of this present confirmatioun, in swa far as the samen will extend to be decreit of the Shereffes and Commissaris of Fyff, of the dait the etc. day of December 1654 yeiris,-"

When Sir John died, his estate was in a great deal of debt. Sir John's only son John had died after his father's death, leaving Antonia Brown as his sole heir. In 1661, Antonia Brown, along with Andrew Lundie, and her other tutors presented a petition to the Estates of Parliament with regard to the settlement of her father's affairs (*Browns of Fordell*, p45):

"To the commissioner's grace and honorable Estaits of Parliament the humble petitione of Antonia Browne, only daughter and heir surveit ant retourit to Sir John Browne of Fordall, Knight, and Sir James Scott of Rossie, Knight, David Browne of Finmonthe and Andrew Lundy of Carrie, Tutors testementars to heir for hir entress;

"*Sheweth -*

"That wher the said Sir John Browne having deceist in his Majesties service, and considerable debts and burdenings equivalent to his estait, and the petitioners therupon having meanet themselves to the lait Judges craving that they might be authorized and warranted to dispone upon the said Sr John his lands and estait for defraying and paying his debts and burdenings, they thereupon granted commissione to the Shirreffe of Fyff for the tyme, impowring him to congnosce and tak up Inventar of the said Sir John his debts, togither with a rentall of his estait; and what they sould find therin, to report to the said Judges; which was accordingly reported, as the said commissione and report radie to be producit will testifie: But be the stopping of the courts of Justice the said report was not taken in nor approven, nor any furder procedor maid therin: And since be the delay the minor will be heavilie prejudged and hir estait lyklie to ruin, the debts still increasing by rening on of annual rents.

"May it therefor please the Commissioner's grace and your lordships to ratify and approve the said Report, And to grant power and warrant to the saids tutors, to sell and dispone upon the said Sir John, his lands and estait, to any persone or persons for payment and defraying of the saidis debtis and burdings, and according to the worth and valew of the saidis lands alreadie cognosceit by an Inquest in persuance of the said commissione: And that your grace and honors wold interpone your authoritie to all the dispositions and sales that sall be maid of the saidis landis for payment of the saidis debts in tyme coming, and the petitioner sall ever pray."

"Edr. 18 Apryll 1661.
"The Lord Commissioner and Lords of the Articles having heard the petition abovewrittin, It is their opinion That the Estaits may grant the desyre of the Bill."

"Edr. 19 Apryll 1661.
"The Lord Commissioner and Estaits of Parliament doe

heirby give Warrand and Commission to the tutors abovespecifiet, to sell and dispone such lands as they shall find necessar for payment of the petitioners debts, and remitts & recommends to the Lords of the session to aprove the said sale and dispositions, and interpone their auctoritie theirto.

GLENCAIRNE CANllrius.

I.P.D., Par."

Following this judgement, much the estate of the late Sir John Brown was apprised. The barony of Weddersbie adjoining Rossie, and comprehending the lands of Weddersbie, Pitlair, Pitlochie, Woodhead, Bowhouse, &c., in the parishes of Collessie and Strathmiglo, was apprised by James Arnot of Ferny, Sir Robert Montgomery, John Brown of Kirkcaldy, and others.

In 1668, William Hamilton of Wishaw, writer in Edinburgh took action against Antonia Brown and her husband Dunlop for 28,165 merks. William Hamilton took further action the following year for 30,688 merks; both actions at the instance of Alexander Crawfurd, son of John Crawfurd, elder of Crawfurdland. William acquired the rights to these aprisings against the Fordell estate, and had the Crown Charter of Fordell, which had been given to the late Sir John Brown, ratified in his own favour in December of 1669. William was then engaged in a legal battle with Andrew Lundie concerning rents uplifted by Andrew when tutor to John and Antonia Brown. It was William's insistence that the rents collected on the deceased Sir John Brown's estate should be used to pay the creditors of the late Sir John, it was Andrew's position that these monies were not part of Sir John's estate, but that of his children. The actions between the two parties ran from 1669 until after Andrew had died, when the actions were carried out between Wishaw and Andrew's children.

In 1669, a record was made of debts owing by Andrew to the late Sir John Brown of Fordell, to which William Hamilton was said to have right to by adjudication (*Univ. St. And. Arch.* Ms36220/556), and around 1673 legal processes seem to have begun between the two parties. In January 1679, Sir Robert Montgomery of Skelmorlie gave concurrence that the rents uplifted by Andrew Lundie from Fordell and Blayrstrulie be applied to paying what was due to him from the deceased Sir John Broun of Fordell (*Univ. St. And. Arch.* Ms36220/257). On the same date Sir Robert Montgomery wrote to William Hamilton of Wishaw regarding Andrew Lundie and the affairs of Fordell (*Univ. St. And. Arch.* Ms36220/258). The '*Browns of Fordell*' includes extracts of a couple of actions involving Andrew Lundie and William Hamilton of Wishaw in the year 1684.

"1684, Jan. – Wishaw against Andrew Lundie. Andrew Lundie, tutor and creditor to Sir John Brown's children, having comprised his pupil's lands, the prior apprizers of the estate raised a declaration of extinction of Lundie's apprizing, upon this ground that the apprizing was led, and the debt apprized for acquired *durante tutela*; and consequently presumed to have been acquired by the pupil's money, till the contrary appear by the tutor's counting for intromissions and omissions.

Answered for Lundie, that his omissions are discharged by Dunlop, younger, the husband of Antonia, the apparent heir, to whom they belonged *jure mariti*; secondly, a tutor's obligement for omissions and accumulations of annualrents are personal to the pupil, and are not communicable to the father's creditors by diligence; especially in the case in this case where the pupil has renounced to be heir to her father; Thirdly, Esto she had not renounced, yet a tutor's personal obligement *ex quassi*, contracted with the heir, cannot fall under the diligence of the defuncts creditors affecting the *hæreditatem jacentem*, seeing it was never *in bonis* of the defunct, but resulted after his decease to the pupil as creditor.

Reply – rights in person of debtor, transmissible to heirs; John did not renounce; Antonia, although she did, must purge all deeds done by herself or husband to the prejudice of the tutor. There was also an incident reduction upon minority, and lesion at the Dunlops' instance, of a contract between them and Wishaw. The Lords recommended the parties to agree.

1684, Feb. 27. – Dunlop against Lundie. In the action of reduction pursued by Dunlop younger and his lady Antonia Brown, of a discharge granted to Andrew Lundie by the said Dunlop of his omissions as tutor to the said Antonia; the Lords found that Wishaw having comprised from John Brown as lawfully charged to enter heir to Sir John Brown his father, for payment of a debt due by the said Sir John had good interest to allege that Lundie's comprising was extinct by omissions as tutor to John Brown; and that by the decreet obtained against John as lawfully charged to enter heir to Sir John, the debt became John's debt, and he became personally liable therefor, and so Wishaw might propone compensation upon the omissions which were due by the tutor to the pupil. But the Lords found that Wishaw having comprised or adjudged from Antonia Brown as heir to her father Sir John (after the death of the said John, her brother), and she having reduced the service upon minority and lesion, whereby the comprising was of the nature of adjudications upon a decreet *cognitionis causa* – wherefore Wishaw could not compense the sums contained in the tutor's comprising by the tutor's omissions, during the time of Antonia's tutory, in regard they found the privilege of making the tutor liable for these omissions was personal to the pupil and to her assignees, and so sustained the discharge granted by Dunlop of the said omissions, and found that the adjudgers could not quarrel the same."

1684, March. – In the case of Wishaw against the children of Andrew Lundie, the Lords found that the tutor, having been in possession after his apprizing, must hold count for the rents, and be liable for ought and should as other comprizers.

George, Earl of Melville, was also embroiled in the actions between Lundie and Wishaw, as part of the Lundie party. The National Archives of Scotland record several papers in actions regarding the lands belonging to the deceased Sir John Brown of Fordell, between Andrew Lundie and George, Earl of Melville, on the one part, and William Hamilton of Wishaw on the other (*NAS*, GD26/4/790). The National Archives of Scotland also lists several bonds granted by Andrew to Lord Melville, and Alexander master of Melville (*NAS* GD26/4/922; GD26/4/148-50; GD26/4/152; GD26/4/154-5; GD26/4/159 GD26/4/161 GD26/4/163 GD26/4/170 GD26/4/175 GD26/4/178; GD26/4/182; GD26/4/185-9). On the 16th of January 1694, the Lords of Council and Session record a decision in an action by the Earl of Melville, and Andrew Lundie's children against William Hamilton of Wishaw:

"Eodem die. The Earl of Melville and the Children of Andrew Lundie *contra* William Hamilton of Wishaw. The Lords thought, that it being Andrew Lundie's alledgeance, that he could not intromit with the rents of Sir John Brown of Fordell's lands, crop 1653, &c. and so was not accountable as Tutor to Antonia Brown, his daughter, he ought to prove there was a sequestration; but that having been done, that it was only presumed to be general over the whole estate, unless Wishaw proved it only to be particular." (*Dec. L.O.C & S. 1678-1712*, I. 609)

With regards to Andrew's own estate, by 1669 he was no longer holding Carrie, and was living in St. Andrews (*Univ. St. And. Arch. Ms*36220/556). He is described as a resident of Edinburgh in 1670; St. Andrews from 1670 to 1677; Edinburgh again in 1677-1679; and St. Andrews in 1679. He died before 1688; with, as previously stated, the legal action continuing between his children and widow; and William Hamilton. The matter was still unsolved in 1699.

Andrew had issue:

i Antonia Lundie, married Mr. James Young, minister, in 1684. On the 10th of July 1699, there is record of a bond between Antonia Lundine, daughter of deceased Andrew Lundine of Carrie, with consent of Mr. James Young, minister, her spouse, to George, Earl of Melville, for £10,000 Scots (*NAS*, GD26/4/285). They had issue:

   a   *James*, born 1684
   b   *Margaret*, born 1686
   c   *Elizabeth*, born 1688

ii Robert Lundie, Provost of Perth. He married, on the 8th of February 1670, at Edinburgh, Katherine Reid. Robert died before the 22nd of March, 1688, and Katherine died before 29th December 1693. They had issue

   a   *Robert Lundie*, christened on the 29th of March 1671, at Perth
   b   *Margaret Lundie*, christened on the 10th of June 1672, at Perth.
   c   *Thomas Lundie*, christened on the 1st of July 1673, at Perth.

d   *Agnes Lundie,* christened on the 25th of August 1674, at Perth.

e   *John Lundie,* christened on the 25th of August 1674, at Perth.

f   *Katherine Lundie,* christened on the 5th of February 1676, at Perth.

g   *Robert Lundie,* christened on the 19th of March 1678, at Perth.

h   *Andrew Lundie,* christened on the 12th of May 1680, at Perth. He appears in the burgh register of Perth (folio 255) on the 14th of October 1693.

4   **Patrick Lundie.** (*Index Reg. Deeds*, Dal. III. 550).

DAVID LUNDIE, 1ST OF DRUMES

"He went into the army in the time of the civil war, and being a gentleman of courage, prudence and industry, he rose to be a captain; and withal, being a frugal man, he redeemed the lands of Over and Nether Drums, a part of the estate that his father had wadset and mortgaged; and upon that he took the title and designation of Lundie of Drum," (*Heraldry*).

Recalling from details of his father's life, in 1599, a bond had been given by Andrew Lundie of Condlane, Elizabeth Brown his spouse, and David Brown of Fynmonth, to George Scott, burgess of Dysart, for 6400 merks, as the price of the lands of Over and Nether Drum (Drimey). In 1632, David, designed as his father's eldest son; and his uncle, David Brown of Fynmonth; made a contract whereby David Brown assigned to David Lundie his mother's (Elizabeth Brown) reversion over the lands of 'Drumme' (*Browns of Fordell*, p167). As a result of this, David was able to redeem Drums, as referred to in the extract in the previous paragraph.

On 1st September 1648, David was given Sasine; in terms of Charter; by Andrew Birrell, portioner of Freuchie, Thomas Birrell, son and heir of the deceased John Birrell portioner there, and Mr. David Wemys of Balfarg; selling to him a 1/32 part of the town and lands of Freuchie, sometime belonging to the deceased John Cowpar alias John abone the gait (*NAS*, GD1/344/3). He purchased other portions of the said town and lands, eventually cumulating to a fourth part of the lands of Freuchie. He obtained a considerable estate in and about Falkland, by marriage to Elizabeth, daughter and heir of George Paterson, a grandson of the House of

Dunmore in Fife. In 1649 he appears in an act of the Scottish parliament as being on a committee of War for Fife (*General index to the acts of parliament of Scotland*). In 1662 he was given commission to try witches (*Register of the Privy Council of Scotland,* Series III. I., 142). He died on March the 10th 1666, at his house in Falkland, and was interred at the family burial place on the 14th of March (*Lamont's Diary*, p 185).

By Elizabeth Paterson he had issue:-

1   *George Lundie, 2nd of Drumes*, whose details follow.

2   *Colonel Robert Lundie*. First a captain in the Earl of Dumbarton's regiment, after serving in such places as Tangier he reached the rank of Lt. Col. in the regiment of William Stuart, Viscount Montjoy. In 1688, he and the regiment were sent to Londonderry. Soon after their arrival, the Viscount Montjoy left, and Robert took command of the garrison. In 1689 he signed a declaration stating that he would stand by the new government, that of King William III and Queen Mary II, upon the pain of being considered as a coward and a traitor. A commission from William and Mary then confirmed him as governor of Londonderry; an office that he had unofficially carried out since the Viscount Montjoy had left. On the 16th of April, 1689, he led a force of 7,000 to 10,000 protestant men at the river crossings of Lifford and Clady, near Strabane, into an encounter with the forces of King James VII, which were under Richard Hamilton. Robert's force was heavily defeated and he had to retreat back to the City of Londonderry. During this command he fell under some suspicion as favouring giving the town to King James VII. while his army lay before it. On the 18th of April, Robert was confined to his quarters, supposed for his own safety, but escaped and fled the city. There are a couple of stories that relate to his escape. The first is that he climbed down a pear tree that grew close to the walls of the city. This pear tree stood until 1844, when a gale blew it down. The second is that he escaped with a bag of matchwood strapped to his back to protect him from musket fire. He returned to Scotland; was captured by Protestant Forces; and taken to the Tower of London to face charges of treason. Later in 1689, the House of Parliament were considering sending Col. Lundie to Ireland to face the charges of Treason there. Col. Lundie then petitioned the House that he might receive his trial in England rather than Ireland, and also specifically in Parliament. This was

following the fact that Col. Lundie was one several persons accused of treason in the change of government from James VII to William III, who were excluded from the King's Bill of Indemnity (*Proc. Hous. Comm. Frm.* 1660, II, 349, 355, 383). After being held briefly at the Tower of London, he had his conduct approved by the English Parliament, and was released. Although the English Parliament ruled against treacherous behaviour, the Protestants of Londonderry burn an effigy of Robert each year in their city celebrations. In the reign of Queen Anne, he was a commissary-general in the army, and was at the battle of Almanza in Spain. He became an Adjunct General and Brigadier with the Army of the King of Portugal. Robert married Martha Davies, daughter of the Very Rev. Richard Davies, Dean of Ross, and later Dean of Cork. She was a descendant of the Davies of Richard's Castle. Robert died sometime before 1711, his testament being proved the 12th of January of that year.

"In the Name of God Amen,
I Collonell Robert Lundie of the Parish of St James in the County of Middlesex being in perfect bodily heath and of perfect mind and memory thanks be given unto God but talling to mind the uncertainty of this life and knowing that it is appointed for all inon ours to dye … and ordain this my last will and testament in manner and form in following (that is to say) I give my soul into the hands of God who gave it me and for my body from – it to the earth to be buried in the Christian and … manner not doubting but att tho generall resurrection I shall rersive the same again by the mighty power of God and astourhing such wouldly estate whouswith it hath pleased God to bles me in this life I give devise bequeath and dispose the same in manner and form following … I will that my just debts logaries and funeral charges be first paid and discharged Hon. I give and bequeath unto my dear an beloved wife Martha Lundie all such sum and sums of money as shall be due to me for my pay or salary as one of the Brigadiors to the King of Portugall's Army and all such other sum and sums of money as shall be due and owing to me at the time of my decease. And I also give and bequeath unto my said dear beloved Wife all such plate, Jewells, household goods and furniture and all other my goods … and personall estate that I shall be possessed of at the

time of my decease but my mind and will is that my said dear Wife does hold possess and enjoy the same for her life only and after her decease that the same doe go and be to the only … and … of my well beloved daughter Aramintha Lundie her heirs and assigns for ever but in case my said daughter doo marry during the lifetime of my said Wife that then and in such case my said dear Wife do raise such sum … as to how shall seem meet to be given with her in marriage and what shall be remaining in my wifes hands after such sum paid as aforesaid the same to go to my said daughter Aramintha her heirs and assigns for ever as aforesaid . . . I will that my said dear wife do give unto my wellbeloved son Robert Lundie thirty pounds to buy him mourning and of this my last will and testament I make and ordain my said dear beloved wife sole exorutrix but my mind and will is that she does not exceed twenty pounds for my funeral charges and I doe hereby utterly disallow revoke and annul all and every other fourmor wills and testaments heretofore by me made … Confirming this to be my last will and testament in witness whereof I have hereunto this my last will and testament being contained in one sheet of paper sett my hand and seal this fourteenth of October One thousand and seven hundred and declared by the said Robert Lundie as his last will and Testament in the prescence of George Hume, Ja: Innes, Geo: Jennings.

After his death, his wife Martha appears in trouble with the law with regards causing wilful damage to the property of one Robert Petre. The reasons for these actions is not know, but details of the crimes she was accused of, are contained in details of Bail for the case:

"*Middlesex.* The Sheriff was commanded, that he should take *Martha Lundie*, late of *Westminster*, in your County, Widow, is she could have been found in your Bailiwick; and that he should have kept her safely, so that he might have had her Body at this Day, (that is to say) *on the Morrow of All-Souls*, to answer *Robert Petre* of a Plea, wherefore she broke the Close of the said Robert, with Force and Arms, and did other Wrongs to the said *Robert*, to his great Damage, and against the Peace of our Sovereign Lord the King; and also in a Plea of *Trespass upon the Case*, on Promises unperform'd, to the Damage of the said Robert, thirty Pounds. And now here at this Day, *Joseph Summers* of *Yorkstreet* in *Covent-Garden*, in the said County, Gentleman, and *Alicia Arthur* of *St James's-street*, in the said County, *Spinster*, come in their Persons before Sir *Robert Eyre*, Knight, and his Companions Justices of this Court of *Common-Bench*: And they and each of them acknowledge themselves to owe the said *Robert* the Sum of thirty Pounds: which said Sum they the said *Joseph* and *Alicia* do, and each of them doth, will and grant, for them and their Heirs, to be made and levied of their, and each of their Lands and Chattels, to the Use and Behoof of the said *Robert*; and also at the same Day, the said *Martha* comes in her proper Person before the said Justices, and acknowledges to owe the said *Robert* the sum of sixty Pounds; which said sum of sixty Pounds the said *Martha*, for herself and her Heirs, doth will and grant for herself and her Heirs, to be made and levied of her Lands and Chattels, to the Use and Behoof of the said *Robert*, subject to this Condition, that if Judgment should happen to be given in the same Court here, for the said *Robert*, against the Said *Martha*, in a certain Plea of *Trespass upon the Case*; then the said *Martha* shall make Satisfaction to the said *Robert*, for all such Damages which shall be awarded to the said *Robert* in the same Court here agains the said *Martha*, or will render her Body, in execution of the said Judgment, to the Prison of the Fleet, *and so forth*." (*Attourney's Pocket Companion*. Pt II, p 20-21)

Robert and Martha had issue:
i Robert Lundie, who according to Nisbet had achieved the Rank of Captain at the time of publication of his works (Nisbet died in 1725).
ii Aramintha Lundie, christened on the 17th of May, 1686, at Derry Cathedral Templemore, Londonderry, Ireland. Her grandfather, the Very Rev. Roland Davies, died on the 11th December, 1721. In his will, he left a large amount of his personal effects to Aramintha.

" . . . he bequeaths to his granddaughter Araminta, the daughter of Captain Robert Lundy, for the services of her mother, &c. the great damask bed and the small field bed which stand in the room over the parlour in his house at Dawstown, with the bedsteads and bedclothes belonging to them, as also the chest of drawers of olive wood, the black looking-glass, chairs, and other furniture in the said chamber; two beds likewise with bedsteads and bedclothes proper for servants to lie in, six pair of sheets, such as he usually lies in himself, with as many pillow-cases and pillows as are usually employed in those beds, and four pair of handle cloth a sheets for servants; two of his oval tables, with all the new diaper table cloths which he lately bought, and were made up for her; six bullrushed-bottomed chairs, six pewter dishes, a dozen pewter plates, six case knives, two iron spits, two iron pots of different size, two barrels and four half-barrels for beer, six in-calf cows and eight garrons or working-horses, his own pad called Lourre, also his great silver tankard, and six new silver spoons, &c."

(*Journal of the Very Rev. Rowland Davies*)

GEORGE LUNDIE, 2ND OF DRUMES

On the 4th of July 1688, George Lundie of Drummes was served heir to his father, David Lundie of Drummes (*Gen. Retours*, No. 5161). He, himself, died in May 1704 (*Index Retours*); although his testament was not proved until the 19th of November 1729 (*St Andrews Comm. Court*). He married Isabel Arnot, daughter of Sir Michael Arnot of that Ilk, baronet, and had issue by her:-

1   John Lundie, born around 1660, "his eldest son, who, after he passed the course of studies at the university of St. Andrews, went into the army, and had a commission in the Earl of Dumbarton's regiment, and was slain at Sedgemoor in the engagement against the Duke of Monmouth; a very hopeful as well as rising young man, but was snatched away in his twenty-fifth year, universally regretted by all who knew him, or heard his character," (*Heraldry*). The battle of Sedgemoor refered to in the extract from Nisbet's Heraldry above, was fought on the 6th of July 1685, the Duke of Monmouth invading England on behalf of the deposed King James VII of Scotland.

2   Michael Lundie, 3rd of Drumes, who succeeded

3   *David Lundie*, "who was a captain in the war in Ireland, died with the character of a very brave man," (*Heraldry*).

4   *Anna Lundie.* She married Mr William Grant, minister of Newburgh. By 1695, Mr Grant had been deprived of his stipend, and George Lundie of Drums can be seen acting on behalf of his daughter Anna, in an action of the heritors of the parish against Anna (*Univ. St. And. Arch. Ms*36220/153). George took action against Lord Lindores in this respect, a decision in the case being taken by the Lords of Council and Session on the 20th of July 1699:

> "*Eodem die*. I reported Lundie of Drums against the Lord Lindores. The stipend of Newburgh, for the year 1694, being gifted by the Privy-Council to Anna Lundy and her children, yet' tis made payable to Lundy of Drums, her father, for the use and behoof foresaid, in regard Mr. William Grant her husband was not so frugal as was alleged. Drums having charged Lindores for his proportion of that stipend, he suspends on this reason, that he had made the payment to the said Anna and he husband, and recovered their discharge.
>
> *Answered*, This payment is unwarrantable, for they had no the *jus exigendi*, but that was expressly stated in Drums as the channel and hand to convey to his daughter and grand children, and debar their father. The Lords thought him but a factor, and real payment being made to his constituents, for whom he was entrusted, it were hard to make them pay over again; but allowed them to be heard if the payment was simulate or collusive." (*Dec. L.O.C & S. 1678-1712*, II. 62)

William Grant died before 1723, at which time Anna as his relict is in possession of 'two roods' in Newburgh (*Univ. St. And. Arch. Ms*36220/1213).

5   *Margaret Lundie.* She married James Balcaquall of that Ilk, from the Parish of Strathmiglo. On the 29th of June 1707, she and James gave up their names for proclamation, and were subsequently married on the 15th of July that year. Her surname appears in the register as *Lunday*, the same as for her brother Michael at his wedding (*Falkland Reg.*; *NAS*, GD50/185/57).

MICHAEL LUNIDIE, 3RD OF DRUMES

He succeeded his father to Drumes, being served as heir special in portions of Fruchy on the 24th April 1707 (*Index Retours*). He soon after married Sophia, daughter and co-heiress of James Lundin of Drumeldrie (who was the brother of John Lundie 8th of Strathairlie), with their names give up for proclamation on the 22nd of November 1707 (*Falkland Reg.*; *NAS*, GD50/185/57). In 1704, he appears in an act of the Scottish parliament as a commissioner of supply for Fife (*General index to the acts of parliament of Scotland*). On the 19th of August 1724 he granted a 4 year tack to David Briggs, tenant in Conland, of the West side of Drums (*NAS* SC20/33/10). On the 9th of July 1725, he granted a 13-year tack of Nether Drum to John Dall, son of John Dall tenant in Nether Drum (*NAS* SC20/33/10). Along with Andrew Lundin of Strathairlie, Michael granted a bond to Margaret Leitch, relict of Hugh Grandistone on the 10th of August 1731. This was registered with the sheriff Court of Fife on the 21st of October 1740 (*NAS* SC20/36/7). On the 18th April 1734, he gave tack to James Gibb, tenant in Pitlour, of the lands of Over Drumms (*NAS* SC20/36/6).

Michael had issue:-

1 *James Lundin*, his only son and apparent heir, whose details follow.

JAMES LUNDIN, 4TH OF DRUMS

He was educated at the University of St. Andrews, boarding at St. Leonard's College 1726/1727 (*Univ. St. And. Munim.*) Twice married, his first wife would appear to be Ann Douglas, daughter of John Douglas of Strathendry, by his first marriage. On the 12th of July 1742, James was involved in legal action for payment of 2,400 merks in right of his wife, the aforementioned Ann Douglas, following her father's second marriage (*NAS*, GD446/30). His second wife was Katherine Lindsay, the second and youngest daughter of John Lindsay 8th of Kirkforthar, and Katherine Seton (eldest daughter of Christopher Seton of Careston) (*NAS* SC20/36/11, SC20/36/12); who was born on the 14th of March 1716, christened on the 20th of March that year. Katherine's nephew, Sergeant David Lindsay, son of her brother John Lindsay, became; upon the death of George sixth Earl of Lindsay, twenty-second Earl of Crawford, in 1808; the seventh, *de jure*,

Earl of Lindsay. David Earl of Lindsay died without issue in 1809, and the Earldom passed to Patrick Lindsay of Eaglescairny, a distant kinsman of David. The descendants of Katherine's four brothers; Christopher Lindsay 9th of Kirkforthar (whose only son died without issue), David (who died young), George Lindsay 10th of Kirkforthar, and John Lindsay (father of David 7th Earl of Lindsay) all failed. The estate of Kirkforthar was entailed and subsequently settled; by Georgina Lindsay 11th of Kirkforthar, daughter of George 10th Lindsay of Kirkforthar afore mentioned; first upon George Johnstone of Kedlock, whose heirs failing, upon Col. Patrick Lindsay (later 8th Earl of Lindsay). George Johnstone, was the son of Helen Lindsay and George Johnstone; Helen being Katherine's eldest sister, and who's heirs would of course be the rightful heirs of Kirkforthar. However, with the next in line being Col. Patrick Lindsay, the settlement omitted the issue of Katherine Lindsay and James Lundin of Drumms, and for that reason appears quite strange.

In 1733, James, designed as the *only* son of Michael Lundin of Drums, was given factorie by his father (*NAS* SC20/36/5). In 1738, James, designed 'James Lundy younger of Drums' was witness to a discharge of a bond by James Cheape of Rossie, to Robert Ross, a 'chirugeon apothecary' in Falkland (*Univ. St. And. Arch.* Ms36929 Box7/573). On the 6th of June 1739, James Lundin, jr. of Drums granted a 15-year tack of part of the east part of the lands of Upper Drums to John Inglis in Carslogie and Alexander Grigg (*NAS* SC20/36/6). A deed recorded on the 10th of December 1756 shows that he was granted an 11 year tack of the manor place, yard and Gleib of Nuthill, from William Thomson of Nuthill (*NAS* B21/5/1 fol 238-39).

James was dead by 1790, and left issue.

1   *Michael Lundin, 5th of Drums*, whose details follow.

2   *Richard Lundin*. Attended the 'college of Physik,' finishing his course in 1779. On the 24th of February that year his father wrote to Wemyss to try to enroll Richard as a surgeon's assistant in his regiment (*NAS, GD50/185/57*):

> 24th Feb 1779
> Ja Lundin at Drums
> Honourable Sir,
>   I hope you will pardon the trouble of which this is to beg the favour of surgeons mate in your son's regiment for my son

Richard who will finish his course at the college of Physik in a few weeks. I have the honour to be related to the family of Wemyss, who shall always find me and my sons well disposed to serve them: Lord Perth would certainly apply if he knew I warrented this. I have wrote both to Weymss hous and – in case of delays by accident, which freedom I hope you will excuse.

From

Honourable sir, your most obedient noble servant

Ja. Lundin

3   *Katherine Lundin.* A disposition and Assignation in favour of Katherine is registered with the Sheriff Court of Fife, 20th of September 1769. This was granted by Katherine Seton; relict of John Lindsay of Kirkforthar; in favour of her eldest daughter, Helen Lindsay, and her grandchild, Katharine Lundin, the eldest daughter of James Lundin of Drums; (*NAS* SC20/36/12).

4   *Isobel Lundin.* On the 17th of April, 1790, Isabel, daughter of the late James Lundin of Drums, married James Cooper, a saddler in College Kirk Parish. They had issue:

i *James Lundin Cooper.* He was a writer in Kirkcaldy. Initially working on his own (1816-1825), he became a senior partner in the firm of Cooper and Pearson (1825-35). In 1835 he went bankrupt, and his assets were sold off by creditors. On the 28th of May 1816 he married Sarah Brown, a daughter of Robert Brown, merchant in Kirkcaldy. James died on the 2nd of August 1838. Sarah on the 30th of January 1878, at the age of 78. They had issue. (*Univ. St. And. Archives: Fife Shopkeepers + Traders*).

a   *Sarah Brown Cooper*, christened on the 18th of April 1817, at Kirkcaldy, Fife.

b   *Michael Lundin (Lunden) Cooper*, christened on the 11th of December 1818, at Kirkcaldy, Fife. He must have died young.

c   *Elizabeth Kinnear Cooper*, christened on the 2nd of October 1820 at Kirkcaldy, Fife. She must have died young.

d   *James Lundin Cooper*, born on the 14th of September 1824, at Kirkcaldy, Fife.

e   *Elizabeth Kinnear Cooper*, christened on the 14th of July 1825 at Kirkcaldy, Fife.

f   *Michael Lundin Cooper*, christened on the 19th of June 1828, at Kirkcaldy, Fife.

g   *Mary Stark Cooper*. Christened on the 11th of July 1832 at Kirkcaldy, Fife.

MICHAEL LUNDIN 5TH OF DRUMS

Born around 1745; it would appear that around 1803, Michael was having financial difficulties, and may have even sold Drums prior to this date. In a letter dated at Falkland, the 10th of September 1803, Michael Lundin, not designed of Drums, writes to a William Berry to reassure him of his intention to pay at Martinmass, despite difficulties with banks in Cupar and Perth (*Univ. St. And. Arch.* MsDA817.B4 Ms4970). Michael again writes to William Berry from Falkland, on the 2nd of September 1811 with regards financial payments (*Univ. St. And. Arch.* MsDA817.B4 Ms4971). By the time of writing of this second letter, Drums was in the hands of Captain Arthur Law of Pittilock and his wife Penelope Newell Law, who were distant relations of this William Berry. The Laws also appear to have had financial troubles and were trying at this time to sell Drums themselves in order to settle their debts. On the 10th of December 1825, 'Michael Lundin of Drumms' died at the age of 80 in Falkland. He was buried on the 18th of that month (*Pittenweem Church records*). By 1845, the statistical account of Scotland records a Mrs. Jamison as the proprietor of the estate of Drums.

Heraldry

The armorial bearing of the family of Lundie of Drum, as representing the Lundies of Balgonie as heir male, and the ancient family of Sibbald of Balgonie as heir of line, is that of Lundie of Balgonie. These arms have been discussed in detail under that family. The arms specifically shown as being for the family of Lundin of Conland, rather than for Balgonie, are shown in the 'Memorials of the Browns of Fordell, Finmount and Vicarsgrange.' by Robert Riddle Stodart, 1887. Here they are depicted as "Quarterly, First and Fourth, Pale of six gules and argent, on a bend azure three Cushions of the second, for Lundin; Second and Third, argent, a Cross Moline gules square pierced, for Sibbald" and are taken from the version of the Balgonie arms in the Illuminated MS. of Sir David Lindsay, Lyon King of Arms of

1542. Nisbet's Heraldry also includes a description of the arms as being for Lundin of Drums, "quarterly first and fourth argent, a cross Moline *gules*, by the surname of Sibbald; second and third, *argent* and *gules*, in place of six *argents* and *gules*, on a bend of the last three escutcheons of the first; crest a cross Moline *gules*: motto, *Justitia*." A copy of the armorial from Nisbet's "Heraldry," is shown below.

17. *The arms of Lundin of Drums, formerly of Conland, from Nisbet's Heraldry*

The House of Gorthie

The Barony of Gorthie is located in the Parish of Fowlis Wester, in Perthshire. It had been held by the family of Gorthie of that Ilk for many years, and came into the Lundie family by marriage of the heiress of Gorthie to a Mr George Lundie in the latter half of the sixteenth century.

GEORGE LUNDIE, FIRST OF THAT NAME OF GORTHIE

On the 16th of June 1591, Andrew Lundie, son of William Lundie of that Ilk, issued a charge against George Halket of Pitferran, for payment of a bond of 1000 merks Scots. Seven years later, on the 5th of July 1598, George Lundie of Gorthie was retoured as heir to his brother Andrew, and the following year George assigned a bond of 1000 merks due to him by the laird of Pitferran to his son, a Humphery Murray (*NAS, Halket of Pitferran Papers*). This information would strongly suggest that George was the son of William Lundie of that Ilk. However, chronologically, due to the date of his marriage (prior to 1564); and also because in 1594 Robert Lundie of Newhall had been retoured as heir to Andrew Lundie, son of William Lundie of that Ilk; one would think George more likely the son of Walter Lundie of that Ilk than William. Walter's son Andrew Lundie, portioner of Lamylethame, had his testament proved on the 15th of July 1597 (*Edin. Tests.*), so he could well be the brother George Lundie of Gorthie was retoured heir to in 1598.

George married Catherine Gorthie of that Ilk, daughter and heiress of Tristram Gorthie of that Ilk. George Lundie thus became designated as 'of Gorthie'. George Lundie and Catherine Gorthie were married by the 12th of March 1564-5, on which date they received letters of reversion of lands previously held by the late George Gorthie of that Ilk, Katherine's grandfather, and Tristram Gorthie of that Ilk Katherine's father (*Reg. Sec. Sig.* V. 1960, 1961). The year prior to that, Catherine had resigned her rights to the lands of Easter Broughty in favour of John Arbuthnott (*Reg. Mag. Sig.* VI. 1337). In July 1566, George was excused from attending functions of the Royal Court (for example inquisitions) as he was "vexit with divers infirmities and siknesis swa that he may nocht guidlie indure travel without danger of his lyfe and incressing of his sikness." This was provided that "Maister George send ane man for him to oure saidis soceranis oistis, raids and weiris sufficientlie bodin and furnist as efferis for serving of thair hienes thairin" (*Reg. Sec. Sig.* V. 2939).

On the 15th of September 1574 there is an instrument of Redemption by John Melville of Raith from Mr. George Lundy of Gorthie, of annualrent of 100 merks from lands of Raith, by payment of 1000 merks (*NAS*, GD26/ 3/304). On the 24th of May 1576, both George Lundie and Catherine Gorthie were given a Crown charter of confirmation of the lands and barony of Gorthie, and lands of Dalpatrick under the great seal. The charter determined that the lands were to be held jointly by the spouses, and by their heirs and assignees (*Reg. Mag. Sig.* IV. 2573).

Around the year 1593, George is mentioned a couple of times in bonds of caution, where surety is provided for various persons, in order to compel them to not harm George:

> "Edinburgh, 17th of May 1593.
> George Musshett of Tolgath, and Mr Moreis Drummond, tutor of Bordland, for James, Commendator of Incheffray, 5000 merks, and the said sureties and principal for William Drummond of Pitcairnis, William Drummond of Belliclone, Johnne Drummond of Pitallony and George Drummond of Balloch, 2000 merks each, not to harm George Lundy of Gorthie."
> (*Reg. Privy Council, Series* I. V. 589)

> "Edinburgh 29th of June 1593
> Thomas Drummond of Corscaple, as principal, and Richard Abircrumby of Poltoun, as surety for him, £500, not to harm Mr George Lundy of Gorthie."
> (*Reg. Privy Council, Series* I. V. 595)

He also appears several times in bonds where surety is provided for himself and his sons, to leave others unharmed. Further details of these can be read under his sons lives.

As may well be surmised by George's son, Humphrey Murray, there was a clear connection between him and the Murray family. The relationship between the two families was however very hostile, and on two occasions George Lundy of Gorthy, and Andrew Murray of Balviard, were required to appear before the Privy Council in order to stop the slaughter and bloodshed that was occurring as a result of the feud between the two families. On the first occasion, John Lundy of that Ilk was also summoned.

"Edinburgh, 21ˢᵗ Feb 1600

Johnne Lundy of that Ilk, and Mr. George Lundy of Gorthie, on the one part, and Andro Murray of Balviard, on the other part, appearing before the King and Council as charged, submit all feuds standing between them, with the assythement and satisfaction which shall be made for "slachteris and bluidis hic inde," and also for actions and causes with either has to propone against the other, to Sir Michael Balfour of Burlie,. . . . Boswell of Balmuto, Arthor Forbes of Rires, and David Kynnynmonth of Craighall, or any three of them, as arbiters chosed for the lairds of Lundy and Gorthy, and to Sir Johnne Murray of Tullibardin, . . . Murray of Blakbarony, . . . Balfour of Montquhany, and Sir David Murray of Gospartie, comptroller, or any three of them, as arbiters chosen for the Laird of Balviard, "to be amicable composit, agreit, and packit up" by the said judges as they shall think expedient: said arbiters, if they cannot agree among themselves, to have power to choose an overman. The said parties are to cause their said judges to meet at Couper upon 27ᵗʰ instant, and shall there give in to them their "clames and grieffis"; and also they become bound to fulfil whatever the said judges pronounce as their judgement."

(*Reg. Privy Council, Series* I. VI. 83)

The arbiters selected for each party as given in the exctract above, did not come to a descision, so a couple of years later, King James VI was appointed the "overman," and the fued submitted before him.

"Falkland 16ᵗʰ September 1602

His majesty as judge arbiter and amicable compositor chosen by the parties underwritten according to the submission following, having pronounced his decreet arbital thereanent, commands both the submission and decreet to be registered in the Books of Secret Council. The tenor of the submission is the following effect. "This blank within contenit" subscribed by Johne Murray of Tullybardin, and William Murray, his son and apparent heir, for themselves and the whole of the Murrays within Stratherne, and others whom they "may stop or latt," and by Murray of Balviard for himself and his friends, on the one side, and by George Lundy, apparent of Gorthie, and for himself and for Mr George Lundy of Gorthie, his father, as having warrant from his said father to that effect, and for all others their kin, friends and dependers, is to be filled up by his majesty, as the only judge arbiter chosen by the said parties, to whom they submit the present feud standing between them for the slaughter of the late Johne Murray, commited by the late David Lundy, brother of the said George, and for the slaughter of the said David Lundy by the said Laird of Balviard together with the assythment to be made for the said slaughters *hinc inde*, and also all other actions and quarrels between the said parties, to be amicably settled and "pakit up" by his Highness as he shall think expedient. – His Majesty, having accepted the said office of arbiter, and having appointed this day to both parties for giving in their claims, and hainv undertaken to pronounce his decret by 17th instant, both parties oblige themselves to fulfil the same without appeal."

(*Reg. Privy Council, Series* I. VI. 467)

The register ends abruptly at the end of this entry, and there are no records of any of the proceedings of Council up until the 8th of October, so the outcome of the arbitration is not known. However, Gorthie was later sold by George's son, George, to a Sir David Murray.

George Lundie of Gorthie died before 1610, when his son George was retoured as his heir (*Inq. Spec. Ret. Perth,* No. 212). On the 22nd of May 1610, sasine was registered from 'Hon.ble Magister Georgius Lundyne de Gorthie', Catherine Gorthie his wife, 'Georgius Lundye eorum senior filius et haeres appareus et Helena Lundyne ejus sponsa', to Mr William Rynd Junior, burgess of Perth, of an annual rent of £40 scots alienated to him, to be uplifted furth of all and whole the lands and Barony of Gorthie (*Sec. Reg. Sas. Perth,* v.1).

George had issue:

1   ***George Lundie younger of Gorthie***
2   ***Robert Lundie.*** In 1603, Robert, designed as the 'lawful son of George Lundye of Gorthie' acted as attorney, when John Lundie of that Ilk was given sasine of an annual rent of 500 merks by his brother german Sir James Lundie. Robert also received the infeftment on behalf of John Lundie of that Ilk. He died before 27th November

1619 (*Inq. Spec. Ret. Perth,* No. 275). He had issue:

    i George Lundie, was served as heir to his father in 1619, in an annual rent of 100 merks from the Barony of Gorthie (*Inq. Spec. Ret. Perth,* No. 275). It is thought by the author that George may well be George Lundie, clerk of Dysart, and further details can be read about him in section six, 'In Dysart.'

3   ***David Lundie***, He was heavily involved with a feud between the Lundies and the Murrays. He slaughtered a Johne Murray, and was later killed by Sir Andrew Murray of Balviard. The insuring feud was submitted twice before King James VI for arbitration (1600 and 1602) (*Scots Peerage*, VIII. 190; *Reg. Privy Council.* Series I. VI. 83, 467).

4   ***Walter Lundie,*** appears in the register of the Privy Seal a number of times after 1600, with regards complaints and actions made by him in respect to debts owed to him.

> "Holyrood House 11th October 1608
>
> Complaint by Waltir Lundy, son of Mr George Lundy of Gorthy, that Mr James Ross, minister at Forteviot, and George Moncreiff and George Cochran, indwellers in the Kirktoun of Maler, remain unrelaxed from a horning of 9th May 1607 for not paying him 1400 merks as principal and £100 of expenses – Compleaner appearing personally, decree as above against defenders."
>
> (*Reg. Privy Council, Series* I. VIII. 178)

> "Edinburgh 1st June 1609
>
> Action by Waltir Lundy, son of George Lundy of Gorthie, against Alexander Gairdner in Newtoun of Huntingtour, and Robert Grant, merchant burgess of Perth, for remaining unrelaxed from a horning of 16th February last for not paying complainer 200 merks as principal and 40 merks of expenses. Also action against Mr James Ross, minister of Forteviot, and Adam Hepburne of Polkmylne, for remaining unrelaxed after a horning of 24th April last for not paying complainer 600 merks as principal and £50 of expenses. Pursuer appearing by Archibald Douglas, defenders are apprehended for non-appearance."
>
> (*Reg. Privy Council, Series* I. VIII. 290)

Edinburgh, 14th Feb. 1611

Complaint by Waltier Lundy, son of Mr George Lundy of Gorthy, that Johnne Ros of Magdalinis, minister at the kirk of Blair, as principal, Mr James Ros, minister of Forteviot and Adam Hepburne of Polkmylne, remain unrelaxed from hornings of 24th April 1609 and 15th November last for not paying the complainer 600 merks and £15 of expenses – Pursuer appearing, decreet against the said Johne Ros (the only defender cited) as above.

(*Reg. Privy Council, Series* I. IX. 132)

"27th of March 1612

Complaint by Waltir Lundy, son of Mr George Lundy of Gorthy, that Sir Robert Creichtoun of Cluny remains unrelaxed from a horning of 26th May 1610 for not paying him 1000 merks. – Pursuer appearing by William Pitcairne, decree as above against the defender for not appearing."

(*Reg. Privy Council, Series* I. VIII. 253)

It is interesting to note that Sir James Lundie, brother of John Lundie of that Ilk, was also persuing Robert Crichton of Cluny, the previous year (*Reg. Privy Council, Series* I. IX. 132). Reference to Walter can also be found in the Particular Register of Sasines for Perth, and the Register of the Great Seal volume seven, p 564.

5   *John Lundie* (*Reg. Great Seal.* VII. 564)

6   *Marion Lundie*, spouse of Patrick Inglis of Byris (*PRS Perth*). Their marriage contract is dated the 13th and 15th of May, 1605. He was first married to Jane Drummond, the daughter of James Drummond of Cardney.

7   *Katherine Lundie*, married George Oliphant of Archailzie, with the contract dated the 21st of July 1609. Katherine was his second wife, with George being previously married to Margaret Clephane, the daughter of James Clephane of Hilcairnie. Katherine and George had issue.

As aforementioned, George also had a son, Humphrey Murray, to whom in 1599 he assigned a bond due from the Laird of Pitferran of 1000 merks.

GEORGE LUNDIE, YOUNGER OF GORTHIE

George, designed apparent of Gorthie, appears in several bonds of caution around the year 1590.

"Edinburgh 4th August 1590
Caution in 1000 merks by James Guthrie of Gagy, as principal, and George Lundy, apparent of Gorthy, and William Airth, portioner of Auchtermuchtie, as sureties for him, that he will not harm Johnne Traill, burgess of Dundee."
(*Reg. Privy Council, Series* I. IV. 518)

"Edinburgh 7th August 1590
Caution by George Lundy, apparent of Gorthy, Williame Grahame of Claveris (Clawerhous), as principals, and David Abircrumby of Pitelpie, as surety for the former, and Robert Maxwell, portioner of Lamylethame, as surety for the latter, in 1000 merks each, that Johnne Traill, burgess of Dunde, shall be harmless of the said principals."
(*Reg. Privy Council, Series* I. IV. 519)

"Edinburgh, 28th September 1590
Caution by Johnne Trail, burgess of Dundee, as principal, and Johnne Arbuthnott of Lentushe (Legisland), as surety for him, in £500, and by Williame Leslie of Dyis for him, and for Gilbert Ramsay of Leggisland in 300 merks, that George Lundy, apparent of Gorthie, shall be harmless of the said Traill and Ramsay. Caution in £500 by Williame Rollock, of Balegie, burgess of Dundee, for Robert Flesheour, burgess there, that he will not harm George Lundy, apparent of Gorthie."
(*Reg. Privy Council, Series* I. IV. 535)

"Edinburgh 22nd July 1591
Band of Caution by Mr George Lundy, apparent of Gorthie, for Thomas Fotheringhame, apparent of Powrie, in 2000 merks, and for Christopher Moncur, Robert Broun, Thomas Fotheringhame, servitors in Powrie, Johnne Ramsay

at the Mylne of Balmuir, Thomas Nicholl there, Robert Mitchelsoun in Myrtoun, William Keill, Thomas Oliver, Adam Smyth in Brychteis, Henry Auchinlek in Murrois, Thomas Auchinlek, his son, George Nicholl and Gilbert Mitchelsoun in Ballothroun, in 300 merks each, that David Maxwell of Teilling, Gilbert Ogilvy of that Ilk, Coline Campbell of Lundie, Johnne Smyth and Johnne Tailyeor, tenants of the said David Maxwell of Teilling, Andro Wilkie, Johnne and James Wilkies his sons, tenants to the said Gilbert Ogilvy of that Ilk, and Johnne Smyth, tenant to the said Coline Campbell of Lundy, shall be harmless of the persons forsaid. Subscribed at Densyde, 20th July, before Williame Grahame of Clawrous (Claverhous) , David Abircrumby of Gourdie, and James Lundie in Newbiggining."

(*Reg. Privy Council, Series* I. IV. 658)

"Edinburgh 24th May 1593

Andro Lundy of Condeland for George Lundy, apparent of Gorthie, 1000 merks not to harm patrik, Lord Drummond, James Commendator of Inchafray, George Drummond of Blair, ...(and many other Drummonds named). James Moneypenny of Pitmillie for Mr George Lundy of Gorthie, £2000, to the same effect, - the said principal, and George Lundy, his son and apparent heir, becoming sureties in relief. Mr George Lundy of Gorthie for David and Robert Lundyis his sons £1000 merks, to the same effect."

(*Reg. Privy Council, Series* I. V. 590-1)

"1594

Registration, by Mr Alexander Peblis, advocate, as procurator, of band by Mr George Lundy, apparent of Gorthie, for Thomas Fotheringhame, elder of Pouric, not to harm Andro Moncur of that Ilk, Wiliame Grahame of Baldovie, or William Grahme of Claverous, under pains in letters to that effect. Subsrcibed at Wester Denesyde, 20th September, before James Guthrie of Gagy, Rolland Gorthie and Henry Auchinlek."

(*Reg. Privy Council, Series* I. V. 638)

The feud with the Murray family detailed in the paragraphs describing his father's life, was not the only one involving the House of Gorthie. In 1606, George was summond by the Lords of the Privy Council, along with James Lundie of that Ilk, Sir James Lundie, Robert Lundie of Balgonie, David Lundie of Newhall, and Andrew Lundie of Conland, in order to quell a feud between the Lundies and the family of Learmonth (*Reg. Privy Council.* Series I. VII. 212). Full details can be read in section three: the history of the House of Lundie, under James Lundie of that Ilk who was laird at the time.

George appears twice in the register of the Privy Council in 1607. On the 1st of January he appeared charged by his father of keeping him a prisoner, possessing himself of his living, and il-treating his person.

> "Edinburgh, 1st January 1607
> George Lundy, apparent of Gorthie, appearing and giving in a copy of the letters raised by Mr George Lundy of Gorthy, his father, charging him to enter his said father before the council this day in order to his liberation, and also to answer for possessing himself of the whole of his father's living and for seizing his person and detaining him in strait firmance, protests in respect of the non-appearance of his father either personally or by procurator, that he shall not be held to answer farther until again warned. The Lords admit the protest."
> (*Reg. Privy Council.* Series I. VII. 292)

In May George, along with his brother John, and younger son George, was accused of attacking one Patrick Ross, when he came to Gorthie. The claim was not proved:

> "Edinburgh 21st May 1607
> Complaint by Patrik Ros, messenger, as follows:- Having been employed by Andro Andirsoun in Over Gortie, to execute a decreet obtained before the commissary of Dunkeld against David Dow in Gortie, he had passed upon the 10th April last to the mains of Gortie occupied by the said David, and, with the consent of George Lundy of Gortie, master of the said ground, had poinded a stack of oats in the said David's barnyard. He had entered the stack in Dow's barn in order to "thrasche the

samen," when George Lundy, apparent of Gortie, Johne Lundy, his brother, George Lundy, younger son of the said George, Johne Andirsoun, miller in Gortie, and Robert Alexander there, with others, all armed with swords, long staves and other weapons, set upon him, pursued him for his life, and would have slain him if ha had not "wan to his awne horse and fled his way." The defenders had not only so deforced him in the execution of his duty, but had intromitted with a black cloak of his worth £30, a hat worth £4, and a great mass of letters, besides the corn in the said barn. Complainer appearing personally, and the said George Lundy, apparent, appearing for himself and the other defenders, the Lords assoilize all the defenders because the pursuer has failed in his proof."

(*Reg. Privy Council.* Series I. VII. 368)

In 1608, on the 12th of May, George and his son George, were compained against by an Andrew Anderson in the Newtown of Gorthie, quite probably the Andrew Anderson in Over Gorthie refered to above. He claimed on oath that George and his son, with others, came to his house, broke the doors, struck him on the head, causing him to fall, removed him from his house, and seized his goods. This complaint was made to the Lords of the Privy Council. Both Andrew Anderson and George Lundie appeared before the Lords, whereupon they refered it to a new judge (*Reg. Privy Council.* Series I. VIII. 85).

George was married twice: First to Helen Lundie, who died before the 14th of August 1607 (*Edin. Comm. Court*): Second to Jenna Stirling, daughter of Henry Stirling 2nd of Ardoch (*Reg. Mag. Sig.* VII. 1101). The contract of the second marriage was dated the 3rd of February 1611 (*NAS*, GD24). On the 17th of May, 1611, he granted an annual rent from the mains of Gorthie, in favour of Sir David Murray, brother of Sir William Murray 9th of Abercairncy. This was in part payment of a 10,000 merk debt due by George to James Murray, Sir David's brother. George's brothers, Walter and John, were witness to the charter (*Reg. Mag. Sig.* VII. 564). On the 3rd of August 1614, George sold the lands of Gorthie to the said Sir David Murray, with the consent of his mother, eldest son George, and wife Jenna (*Reg. Mag. Sig.* VII. 1101).

George, now designed 'Sometime of Gorthie' appears in the register of the Privy Council of Scotland in 1618, due to his 'Riotus conduct in Perth:'

> "Edinburgh 21ˢᵗ 1618
>
> Petition by the Kings Advocate, the Provost and bailies of Perth, and Johnne Mathew of Balhoussie:- On 1ˢᵗ December last "being the publict fair and marcat keipit with the said burgh callit . . . Andersones Fair," an unseemly tumult was caused by George Lundy, sometime of Gorthie, . . . Guthrie, apparent of Kincardrum, Mr George Graham, son of the laird of Claverhouse, and others, to the number of nine. They, "having spent maist pairt of the day in the bestlie excessie of filthie drukkinnes," issued from a tavern about 12 o'clock at night, and with drawn swords "cuttit down the haill marcat standis being standing and sett up upon the streitis of the said burgh for the merchantis hanting to the said mercat during the tyme." It happened that the said Johnne Mathew, who had been at supper with Andro Gray, Dean of Guild, and was returning with his servant boy "to his awne chamber within the burgh," was overtaken by the said persons and cruelly used. He and the boy would have been slain, "wer not, be the providence of God, the commoun bell being rung, at the sound quhairof Andro Conquerour, ane of the bailies of the said burgh, come furth out of his bed and hous to haif tane ordour for keeping of his Majesties peace within the said burgh. . ."
>
> (*Reg. Privy Council* Series I, XI. 620).

He died before 1619 (*Inq. Spec. Ret. Perth,* No. 275). Some fifty or more years after his death (1671) one sixth of the lands of Monyfooth, described as formerly pertaining to George, then John Graham of Claverhouse, were resigned by James Marquess of Douglas in favour of John Lord Balmerino. George had issue:

1   ***Male Lundie,*** died before 1614. In 1607, George (following), is described as the younger son (*Reg. Privy Council.* Series I. VII. 368); but by 1614 he is described as the eldest and heir (*Reg. Mag. Sig*. VII. 1101).

2   ***George Lundie***, married Eupham Bruce, daughter of Alexander

Bruce, 6th of Cultmalundy, before March 1608 (*PRS Perth*).

3 ***Helen Lundie***, married William Thomeson in Cairnyie (*PRS Forfar*).

4 ***Jean Lundie*** (*PRS Forfar*)

5 ***Anna Lundie***, married Michael Ramsay of Forth (*PRS Forfar*). She was still alive by 1657 as on the 5th of May of that year she gave her consent to a charter of Michael Ramsay of Forth, the natural son of Michael Ramsey of Forth, whereby he granted a charter to Alexander Halybutoun, elder of Balgillo, merchant burgess of Dundee, of the lands of North Ferry with the teinds and fishings on the Tay at North Ferry, near Brughtie Craige, in the regality of Arbroath and sheriffdom of Forfar (*Hunter Charitable Trust Collection, Resteneth Lib. Forfar*).

Gorthie House

The Barony of Gorthy was within the Parish of Fowlis Wester in Perthshire, and many places in that area still bear the Gorthy name. Looking at a current OS map of the UK, travelling west along the A85 from Perth, after about six miles one comes across the Newinn of Gorthy, The Mains of Gorthy, Newton of Gorthy, the Nether Mains of Gorthy, and slighty to the north, Gorthy Wood. Gorthy House, the seat of the family, was located just to the East of Gorthy Mains, but no longer stands. Its location can be seen on the 1st edition of the OS six-inch map of Perthshire from 1867, seen by the forested area and the building called Newmill (as stated due east of Gorthy mains). The ruin is thought to have been inside the forestry enclosure. On today's map the forested area can still be seen, but is not labelled.

Although Gorthie House no longer stands today, details of it do appear in the 1791 and 1845 statistical accounts of Scotland. In the 1791 account the Rev. Mr. Stirling indicates that at this time the house was still standing. At this time the estate was held by Moncreiff of that Ilk, and the estate was the second most valuable, by means of rents raised, in the parish. By the time of the second statistical account, this time by the Rev. Alexander Maxtone, the house had been demolished.

> "At the distance of a mile east of the manse, once stood the castle of the Earl of Strathearn, on the east side of a den in which the burn of Dury runs. The site was peculiarly appropriate for this Celtic Chief, the great proprietor and chief magistrate of the district. The house of Gorthy was situated to the south east of this, on the side of another den of the same name with itself. It is now demolished, but the lawn is still marked by venerable trees with which it was ornamented."

Section Four

Other Landed Branches

The History of the Landed Cadet Branches of the Family of Lundie: That of the Houses of: Auchtermairnie, Baldastard, Breriehill, Bruntshiels, Clatto, Demperstoun, Glaswell, Formerly Kinnoull, Huttonspittle or Spittle, Inverlochtie alias Spittle, Langraw, Larg, Lungar, Podester, St. Monans, Strathairlie, Todrig and Little Todrig, Wester Denhead and The Wester Volts of Whitsome

The House of Auchtermairnie

ROBERT LUNDIE OF NEWHALL

Robert was the eldest son of William Lundie of that Ilk and his second spouse Elizabeth Lundie. He was the first of the family to hold the lands of Auchtermairnie. On the 6th of February, 1596-7, he married Isabel Leslie, daughter of James Leslie, master of Rothes by his spouse Margaret Lindsay, daughter of Patrick Lindsay 6th Lord of the Byres (*Scots Peerage*, VII. 296) . Robert and his father William bought the lands of Newhall, Lethame with the mill and mill lands, the lands of Segy, and lands of Segyhill for 40,000 merks in a contract dated 1595. The first 2688 merks were paid in 1597 whereupon a contract was made between Mr. Williame Lundy of that Ilk, Elizabeth Lundy, his spouse, and Robert Lundy, their son, with consent of his father as his administrator and tutor, of the first part, and David Wemeis (Wemyss), son of the late David Wemeis of that Ilk, on the second part.

This contract stated that in consideration of the payment of the 2688 merks Scots, the lands were to pass to William Lundy and his spouse, and the longer liver of them for all the days of their lives. Thereafter it would pass to Robert Lundy and the lawful heirs male of his body, whom failing, to David Lundy, his brother german, and the lawful heirs male of David's body. If these should fail, the lands could pass to Robert's nearest and lawful heirs and assignees (*NAS*, GD86/325). The original agreement over the purchase of these lands occurred in 1589. On the 24th of January 1589, Andrew Leslie, 5th Earl of Rothes, granted a charter to William Lundie of that Ilk, Elizabeth Lundie of that Ilk, and their 1st legitimate son, Robert. This charter, signed at Leslie, stated that the lands, failing heirs male of Robert, would pass to his brother german Andrew, failing legitimate heirs male of his body, to his brother german David. Failing legitimate heirs male of David Lundie, the lands would pass to any heirs of Robert. This original charter was confirmed under the Great Seal on the 8th of July 1594 (*Reg. Mag. Sig.* VI. 117). By the time of the later contract of 1595, Robert's brother Andrew was deceased.

In 1601 Robert was appointed, along with James Lowrey and Michael Balfour, Lord Balfour of Burleigh, by King James VI to proceed to France on a mission "in certain effairis concerning his majestie and then commone wele of his realme" (*Scots Peerage*, I. 539).

> "Holyrood House, 3rd April 1601
> The King, having directed Sir Michael Balfour of Burley, one of his masters of Household, with Robert Lundie of Newhall, and James Lowrie, burgess of Edinburgh, to proceed to France and other places beyond sea, "in certaine effairis concerning his Majestie and the commone wele of this realme, and als in sindrie his Majestseis particular effairis and serviceis," and being unwilling that they should be prejudiced in any way of their actions and causes during their absence, hereby supersedes, with advice of his council, all actions raised or to be raised against them before any judge, till their return within this realme and for 14 days afterwards, provided always that, if it be found that Lundie and Lowrie depart for their own affairs, and not in the service of Balfour, then this act shall have no force in their favour."
> (*Reg. Privy Council.* Series I. VI. 231)

On the same date as the extract above was written, Robert, whilst present at the Royal Court, along with Patrick Balfour of Pitcullot, acted as surety to the sum of 10,000 merks for David Betoun, fiar of Creich. This sum was to ensure that the said David would enter into ward within the city of St. Andrews by the 7th of April, "until he satisfy his Majesty anent the disobedience professed to his Highness, and the matters questionable between the said David and the Comptroller; also to observe the Kings peace and good rule in the country." (*Reg. Privy Council.* Series I. VI. 680)

Robert went abroad with Sir Michael, but may never have returned. He made his will in Bordeaux (23rd June 1602) and died in October of that year. His brother german David Lundie was served as his heir in 1603. Isabel Leslie Survived him, and married George Hamilton of Greenlaw (*Scots Peerage*, VII. 296; *PRS Fife and Kinross*). Robert left no issue.

DAVID LUNDIE OF NEWHALL AND AUCHTERMAIRNIE

On the 23rd of March 1603 David was served as heir male, of tallie and of provision to his brother German, Robert Lundie of Newhall in the lands of Newhall; the land of Lethame in the Parish of Crail; the land of Auchternairn (a.k.a. Auchtermairnie); the land of Kennoquhie; the land of Lelethan and Auldie in the Barony of Leslie; the land of Gilstoun in the Barony of Lundy; and part of the town and lands of Innergellie in the regality of St Andrews (*Inq. Spec. Ret. Fife*, No. 128).

In July 1603, his brother John Lundie of that Ilk, as principal; with Sir Duncan Campbell of Glenurquhy, Andrew Lundie of Conland, Andrew Ayton of Denmure,George Lundie of Gorthie, William Grahame of Claverhous, and David Sibbald of Lethame, as sureties in £20,000; was ordered to keep in company with David, and to produce him whenever required before either the Lords of Privy Council or the Justice general (*Reg. Privy Council.* Series I. VI. 794).

On the 11th of May the following year; following on a precept of Clare Constat by David, Earl of Crawford; David received an instrument of sasine as heir of the deceased Robert Lundy of Newhall, his brother, in the lands of Newhall in the sheriffdom of Fyiff (Fife), barony of Fynnhevin (Finnhaven) (*NAS*, GD1/640/11). On the 26th of August, 1610, a bond was issued by Alexander Coninghame of Wast Barnis to Robert, 9th Lord Lindsay, that a tack, dated 26 August 1610, by Robert to Alexander of the teinds of the barony of West Barnis in the parish of Crail should not prejudice a tack to

David Lundie of Newhall of the teinds of David Lundie's lands in the barony of West Barnis (*NAS*, GD20/1/372).

David was tutor to John, Earl of Rothes. In 1613, John, Earl of Rothes granted a charter, with the consent of Alexander, Earl of Dunfermline, Chancellor; his tutor, David Lundy of Newhall; Agnes and Elizabeth Lundy, David's sisters; Andrew Ayton of Dunmure, husband of Agnes; and Mr Andrew Ayton, advocate, husband of Elizabeth; to Thomas Inglis, burgess of Edinburgh, and Janet Geddes, his spouse, of two annualrents from the lands of Parkhill and Insches in the Regality of Lindores (Lindoris) in warrandice of lands of Hiltess, following on a contract among the said parties (*NAS*, GD172/1434). On the 30th of March, 1616, Mr. Patrick Lindsay, an indweller and Cupar, resigned into the hands of Lord Lindsay, the lands of Newhall, in favour of David Lundie of Newhall. In that same year there was a decreet of the court of session against him, discharging him from levying duties upon the fishings at the port of Randerston, which is close to Newhall (*East Neuk*, p 56).

An extra, and most probably false, generation is commonly placed in the account of this family. It has been suggested that David had two sons, Robert Lundie of Newhall, and David of Auchtermairnie. His son Robert is suggested to have died before 1629, with his son David being served his heir. This also implies that David Lundie himself died before 1629, as his son's were then the landowners, rather than being designed younger of Newhall and Auchtermairnie. However, in 1632, George Lundy, son of Robert Lundie in Dysart, is given a gift of the escheat of David Lundie "sumtyme of Newhall, now of Auchtermairnie." He was escheated on account of non payment of various debts in bonds and contracts, some made as early as 1619, where he is designed as 'of Newhall.' So David of Auchtermairnie after 1630, is the same man as David of Auchtermairnie pre 1630, rather than father and son (*Reg. of Signatures*, Liii, fo. 271). Extra evidence to rule out this generation is that there is no record of either a Robert Lundie or David Lundie being served heir to their father David in any of his lands; but, there is clear evidence of the succession from William Lundie of that Ilk, to his son Robert; to Robert's brother David (whom we are now discussing); and to his son John, who received sasine of Newhall and other lands in 1629 (*NAS*, B9/14/25). The reason for this misunderstanding is clearly as a result of David being served as heir to his late brother Robert Lundie of Newhall, in the lands of Maristoun (Mireston) in 1630; 27 years after he was served as his heir in Newhall etc. (*Inq. Spec. Ret. Fife*, No. 1570). Why there was this large time delay one cannot really say. Robert is believed to have obtained these lands from the Pitcairns. In 1631 David was given a charter of these lands of Mireston (*East Neuk*, p 56).

The debts referred to in the previous paragraph were quite large, and to a number of people. David owed 351 merks plus expenses to Walter Borthwick of Grangemure, from a bond dated 14th of March 1614; 1000 Merks, plus expenses, to Ninian McMorane, portioner of Kingsbarnis, from a bond granted by David on the 21st November 1627; 1000 merks, plus 300 merks expenses, to Heroit of Rasmagry and Landellis of Coull, contained in a contract between Patrick Heriot portioner of Lelethane as principal, with David Lundie and Heriot of Rasmagry as cautioners, and David Landellis of Coull and Henry and William Landellis his sons, in August 1919; and a further 1000 merks with 100 merks expenses to Ninian McMorane in an obligation of the 11th of March 1627 *(Register of Signatures, vol Liii fol.271)*. For these debts he was denounced as a rebel, and put to the horn; perhaps a good reason why he gave sasine of most of his lands to his son John when he did. The George Lundie referred to here, who received the goods of David, was later to be the town clerk of Dysart, and can be read about in section six.

David appears quite regularly in the Presbytery book of Kirkcaldy, as one of the heritors of that Parish, and most interestingly due to a disagreement between him and the Minister of the Parish, a Mr Frederick Carmichael.

> *"Dysert, October 10, 1633.*
> The whilk day Mr John Litiljohn exercised . . . The **laird of Newhall** in the Parochine of Kinnoquhie compeiring demanding some questions anent the chuseing of the elders and distributions of the poore folks money in Kennoquhie, the Presbytrie appoynsts Doctor Andro Lawmonth and Mr Robert Cranstown to goe to Kennoquhie and tryc thc mattcrs controverted upon betwixt the Laird and the minister, and to agree them, and report thair anser.

> *Kirkcaldie, May 1, 1634.*
> The whIlk day . . . John Williamson compeiring, lamented the pitiful and distressed estaite of John Balcanquhill and his

companie, the brethren promieses diligence. Mr Frederik Carmichel shewing that his congregation of Kennoquhie ane unable and some of the unwiling to contribute for the releif of the forsaid captives, demandit whether or not in such a caise any thing might be take out of the box with consent of the sessioun to that or the like occasioun. The brethren ansers : he may. The said Mr Frederik compleans that **David Lundie, Auchtermairnie**, does not behave himself naither in sessioun nor in uther ways as he sould, he haveing causs sowmoned him befoir the Presbytrie to anser fot the samyne : called, compeired not : to be sowmonit to the nixt day, pro 2. The said Mr Frederik demandit of the brethren whidder or not dureing the said Davids so caryage and misbehaviour in the sesioun and process aganest him, he may pass by his voit in sessioun The bretren ansers : he may.

Dysert, May 8, 1634
The whIlk day . . .Kathren Fyell was relaxit from excommunicatioun the last Sabbath in Kennoquhie, and resaved.
David Lundie of Auchtermairnie being sowmonit, called, compeired not ; ordained to be sowmonit the next day, pro 3. . . .

Kirkcaldie, May 15 1634
Compeired **David Lundie of Auchtermairnie** being sowmonit. The minister, Mr Frederik Carmichel compleanes upon him be claime layeing sundrie and divers misbehaviours to his charge. The said **David Lundie** desyres of the brethren that they wold visite the Kirk of Kennoquhie, that all things controverted betwixt him and the Minister may be Hard and judged be the brethren. The said Mr Frederik is content with this provision that if the brethren cannot agree, then that he may goe forward in his process aganest him, whereto thai agree and appoynts this day fyftein dayes for the visitatioun, and Mr Robert Douglas to preach thair, whik sal serve for his exerise. John Balcanquhill and his companie remembrit.

Kennoquhie, May 29, 1634.

The visitation of the kirk of Kennoquhie holden within the kirk thairof, upon the 29 day of May 1634 years, be Mr John Calmers thair chosen Moderator, the Parson of Dysert, Doctor Andro Lawmonth, Mrs Robert Cranstown, John Tullus, James Symeson, Robert Douglas, David Anderson, Harie WIlkie, Thomas Melvill, Thomas Powtie, and Frederik Carmichell, minister of the said kirk. The edict returned indorsat. All things belongeing to ane ordinar visitatioun being passed by, in respect this was appoyntit for the trying of controversie betwixt the Minister Mr Frederik Carmichell, and *David Lundie of Auchtermairnie*. The parties compeires viz., the said Mr Frederik giving his claime, compleaneing that the said *David Lundie* had wronged him, speaking verie disdainefullie and slanderouslie of him, quhIlk claime being read, conteined many contumelious and injurious slanderous speeches, bot in speciall thir :- That he could learn nothing of him bot pryd, malice, and averice, etc. The brethren demandit amongst themselfs what course wer best to be taken in tryeing of the things alledgit ; it was concludit that Master Frederik his claime should be read, and the said *David* posed upon everie particular therein contained, and he to answer thairto, whIlk being read, and the said *David* posed, as said is, confessed, that he said he saw nothing to learne in his minister bot pryd, avarice, and invye. The said Frederik also nominat witness for proveing of the same viz., Martin Balfour, aganest whom the said *David* objectit that he could not be witness aganest him in respect that he and he wer under law burrowes and so he was passed, further he nominates James Pitcairne, John Ramsay, James Archibald, James Roger, Henrie Landales, Robert Duire, Walter WIlkie who all being admitted and sworne, deopned as follows : - James Pitcairne deponed that he hard *David Lundie* say that he could learne nothing of his minister bot pryd, avarice, and envy. John Ramsay, James Archibald, James Roger, Walter WIlkie, Thomas Archibald all deponed affirmative ad idem. James Archibald also declared that none of the meane sort of the elders durst speak in sessioun for him, and that he boasted the gudman of Kilmuks, also Walter WIlkie declared that he boasted of him in the kirkyard. The Presbytrie finding Mr Frederiks claime both confessit and proven, they demaund of the said **David** if he will byde by the said speaches who anserit he would prove him proud and avaritious. The brethren persaveing his reasons to be weak and not able to prove his allegeances discharges him to come onie more to the sessioun, till he agree with the minister, and aither to prove his allegeances aganest the minister, or ells to secumbe in the matter and gives him ane moneths space to prove the samyne."

Sometime between 1633 and 1635, David was charged with molestation and malicious damage, after a complaint by Martin Balfour, portioner of Lathen. David, contrary to an act of Council, was said to prevent the said Martin Balfour from leading his corn, and did injury to the said Martin's property (*Register of the Privy Council of Scotland*, Series II. V., 471). The rather violent nature of David suggested by this conduct is not misplaced. On the 23rd of July 1635, David's wife, Maria Cockburn, was forced to put a case to the Lords of the Privy Council of Scotland due to his shameful and barbarous behaviour towards her. The extract from the register is given below.

> Edinburgh, 23rd July, 1635
> *Decreta April 1635 – February 1639, p44-45.*
> Complaint by Marie Cockburne, lawful daughter of the deceased Sir John Cockburne of Ormestoun, Justice Clerk, and spouse of David Lundie of Achtermearnie, as follows:- Some . . . years ago she was married to the said David Lundie and has borne him six children. She has behaved herself in all dutiful respect to him, "lookeing for ane ansuerable meiting on his part. Nevertheles it is of truthe that the said David agais the dewties of mariage and respect quhilk he owed to the gentlewoman's birth, hes this long tyme bygane verie shamefullie and barbarouslie abused her, with the particulars quherof she is loath to trouble his Majesties Council. But now, at last he hes withdrawin from her meat, drink and all others necessars, hes served inhibitions agains her, discharged his tenants to ansuer her anie thing for entertenanment of her and her children thair naturall lyves, and at last hes shot the gentlewoman and her children to the doores and putt them to beggarie so as they are lyke to sterve." Both

pursuer and defender compearing and having been heard, the Lords, "understanding and being trewlie resolved of the unnaturall and unkynd behaviour of said David Lundie towards his said spous, and that they cannot for the present cohabit togidder in that Christian harmonie quhilk becometh thame," modify to the pursuer for he entertainment four chalders of victual, half bear and half meal, with 200 merks of silver and five dozen fouls to be paid to her yearly during her separation from her husband, from the south-east side of the lands of Achtermearnie possessed by James Melvill as tenant thereof, her entry to be at this present crop of 1635; and this without prejudice of any provision formerly made by the defender to the rest of her children.*(Reg. Privy Council, series II, VI, 68)*

Far earlier than this, in 1618, David was also accused by William Myrton of Cambo of assaulting his herd boy. The Lords of Privy Council found the accusation to be true, and sentenced David to time in the Edinburgh Tolbooth:

"Holyrood House 30th July 1618

Complaint by Williame Myretoun of Cambo, as follows: - On 24th July instant, David Lundie of Newhall went up to George Clerk, pursuer's herd boy, when he was tending his master's cattle, "and demanding of him quhose man he wes, he then tirved the boy, and with a sword belt beltit and leischit him to the effusioun of his blood in greite quantitie, bidding him come and tell the said complenair and to ask of him how he liked of suche doings." Defender thereafter sent for Patrik Hereot, his servant who, "without salutation or uther respect," told pursuer that his master had sent him "to schow him that he had beltit and lisheit his man." The said David and his said servant "walkit ane houre or tua upoun the bra foiranant place and yairdis, making provocatioun unto the said complener to come furth." Pursuer and defenders appearing personally, the Lords find the charges proven upon the confession of defenders, and order them to be committed to the Tolbooth of Edinburgh, therein to remain during their Lordships' pleasure."

"Complaint by the forsaid Lundie of Newhall as follows: On the foresaid Williame Mertoun of Cambo went up to . . . servant and herd of pursuer, and of Alexander Gibb, his tenant at Lethame, while he was tending his masters cattle, threw him down, pulled a tether from him, and therewith with his feet and hands unmercifully struck him, The said William has divers from time to times since avowed "to gif the boy twyse alsmekle, in caise ony complaint wer evir maid thairupon." – Parties appearing, the Lords assoiliae defender, because he has denied the assault, though he admits that, "finding a boy in his fensit waird, with a horsse, he gave him a chope with his gloves allanerly."
(*Reg. Privy Council.* Series I. XI. 423-4)

David and Maria had issue:-

1   **John Lundie**, who succeeded

2   **Agnes Lundie**, (named as a probably daughter in Wood's *East Neuk of Fife*) married Lt. Col. David Wemyss in 1649.

3   **James Lundie at Easter Newton**. He had issue:

i   *William in Lundie Myln.* On the 6th of April 1650, William was named as curator of the minor John Lundie, son of the late John Lundie of Auchtermairnie (*Inq. Ret. de Tut.*, No. 770). William was twice married, his first spouse being Elspeth Aidie, daughter of John Aidie. During the period of their marriage, on the 28th of April, 1666, William bought off his father-in-law, John Aidie, a part of Bayrehills, near to St. Andrews. He received infeftment of this property the same day, and it was confirmed by Archbishop Sharpe. He later sold this property, in 1672, to Mr Patrick Lentron, brother of the then deceased Provost Lentron. Elspet Aidie died in July 1668 – "1668, Jul. 8 – Elspet Adie in Lundy Mill, spowse to William Lundin ther, depairted owt of this life att hir dwelling howse, and was interred the 9 of July att the Kirk of Largo in the day tyme. Mar. 1669, hir husband took a second fitt of distraction, and it continowed with him abowt 5 or 6 weeks" (*Lamont's Diary*, p 207). After her death, he remarried to Helen Lithel – "1669, Awg. 15, being the Sabath; - William Lundin in Lundin Miln in Fyffe, married for his second wife, Helen Lithel, Robert Lithel, merchant in Edb, his sister, then waiting on the Old Lady Lundin. That night they supped at Lundin, and dyned the nixt day, and went home privatly att night. (Remember, this marriage was first proponed be him to her on a Sabbath day at Largo Kirk, and afterwards accomplished ther on a Sabath after sermon privatly, be Mr John Awchinleck, m. ther.) Also notice, that the said Helen Lithell was spoken of att the tabell of Lundin one day after dinner, before the deceased Elspet Adie, his first wife, was interred, to be a fit woman for his second wife. (In this intervall of widowhead, he tooke a second fitt of distraction, the first being before he was first married.)" (*Lamont's Diary*, p 211). By Elspeth Aidie he had three sons, by Helen Lithel, he had a daughter:-

a   *John*, baptized on the 20th of December 1650.

b   *James*, baptized on the 9th of September, 1654. He was apprenticed in 1672 to John Waker, bookbinder and stationer in Edinburgh (*Index Reg. Deeds*, Mack, XXXI. 247; Scottish book trade index; *Reg. Appren. Edin.*).

c   *William*, baptized on the 28th of December, 1655

d   *Sophia*

It should be noted that Lundie-Mill has been associated with other family members other than William, but whose genealogical relationship is yet unknown. For example a Richard Lundie in Lundie-Milne had his testament proved on the 9th of February 1587 (*Edin. Tests.*); Christian, lawful daughter of Umphra Lundie at Lundie Mill had her testament proved on the 1st of December 1633; and Elizabeth Swyne, relict of Umphra Lundie at Lundie Mylne had her testament proved on the 18th of June 1607 (*Ed. Comm. Court*).

ii   *John of the Eallie*

4   **Anna Lundie**. She appears in the register of the Privy Council of Scotland, in August 1672, along with her nieces, making a complaint against a Mr John Alexander for attempting to defraud her of her life savings. An extract from the Register concerning this mater is given below.

> "*Decreta, August 1672 – January 1678, pages 62-64*
>
> Complaint by Anna Lundie, sister lawful of the deceased

John Lundy of Auchtermarnie, and Margaret and Helen, and Mary Lundie, her nieces, lawful daughters of the deceased John Lundy, her brother, and Mr William Annand, one of the ministers of Edinburgh, spouse to the said Helen, "and assigneyes afterspecifit, for their interes," as follows:- Whereas Sir Alexander Carnegie of Pittarro and his cautitioners are addebted to the complainer by bond in the sum of 4000 merks with interes, which is the whole fortune she has wherewith to maintain herself and pay her debts, yet in June 1670, she was induced by John Alexander, W.S., "to subscryve ane assignation to him and Anna Alexander, his sister, of the said bond and at the same tyme to subscryve a testament nominating them her executors and legatours bot with this expresse condition that the said compleaner should be master of these papers and be at friedome otherwayes to dispose upon the said soume at any tyme befor hir deceise, and accordingly she did ever sensyne keip the said bond, assignation and testament in her owne custody underlyvered until the month of Apryle instant that it having pleased God to visit her by siknes, and being in the house of the said John Alexander in Edinburgh, without fear of fraud or hazzard, yet it is of verity that the said John Alexander, at the leist some of his family, by his direction did in a most fraudulent maner search the compleaners pocketts (she being lyeing sick) for the saids wrytts and seized upon the same, and some tyme after, she having missed them and having questioned the said Alexander and the rest of his family for the same, they, to palliat the said fraud and cheat, made a pretendit search for the saids wryttes in the bed and rowme where the compleaner then lay, and in the mean tyme the said John Alexander, having caused dowble the saids papers, did cause putt the same at the compleaners back within her bed, expecting that she should have made no furder search in the said matter finding the number to be the same and the subscriptions at the end therof so lyke the principall; bot she, having some suspition of cheit and decoit therein, did cause take more particular notice and upon tryeall the compleaner did find that the said John Alexander had abstracted the principall papers and most deceitfully and basly had putt the saids dowbles in the place thereof and either hes or intends to abstract or destroy the saids principall papers or to compon with the debotor or to take some other indirect course to cheir the compleaner of her fortoun, to the ruine and undoeing of her and her creditors and the saids compleaners, her neices, to whom she made over her right by assignation for payment of her debts and alimenting her during her lyfetyme; and therfore in all equity and reason the said John Alexander ought and should not only be decernedimediatly to depositat the said principall bond, assignation and testament in the hands of the Clerks of his Majesties Privy Councill to be made furthcomand to all parties having interes, as accords of the law, bot for the said fraud and ryot examplary punished in his person and goods to the terour of uthers to committ and doe the lyke in tyme coming." Charge having been given to him, the said Anna Lundy having compeared by Mr Laurence Charters, advocate, her procurator, and the rest of the pursuers personally, and John Alexander having also compeared personally, when the Lords, having considered the complaint and the judicial declaration of the said defender, whereby he, in presence of Council, did acknowledge "that he tooke out the forsaid principall bond, assignation and nomination lybelled out of the pocket of the said Anna Lundy while she was lyeing sick in his owne house without her knowledge or consent, and that in place thereoff he putt the double of the saides wryttes into her pocket without her knowledge," which principal writs he produced, ordain the said writs to be delivered to the said Anna Lundy as her own proper writs to be used and disposed of by her at her pleasure, and recommend the Lord Register to see them delivered; and they supersede inflicting any censure or punishment on the defender till next Council day. The Lord Register saw the writs delivered accordingly."

(*Register of the Privy Council of Scotland*, Series III. Volume IV. pages 43-44)

5 *Jean Lundie*, spouse to Thomas Alexander, portioner of Drumeldrie (*P.R.S. Fife and Kinross*, XI, 305).
6. *Child* (*Reg. Privy Council*, series II, VI, 68)

JOHN LUNDIE 3RD OF AUCHTERMAIRNIE

John was married to Isobel Law of Brunton, the daughter of James Law of Brunton (*PRS Fife*). He was given sasine of the lands of Newhall, Lalathin and Kenoquhie on the 9th November, 1629 (*NAS*, B9/14/25), note this is well before his father's death. Around 1616, he and fourteen other "gentilmen and barones of the shirefdome of Fyif and magistattis of the buchtis thair" petitioned the Privy Council against the unfair sale of English Beer, and enforcement of a previous act "prohibiting the importers of English beers from selling it dearer that eighteenpence the pint" (*Reg. Privy Council*. Series I. XIV.) He died on the 13th of January 1650, at his father-in-law's house, in Brunton. From there he was carried to Auchtermairnie, and interred at Kennoway parish church. His wife later re-married, 12th February 1652, to William Bruce, commissar of St Andrews (*Narrative of the Shipwreck and surprising adventures of Richard Lundin*). John and Isobel had issue:-

1 *John Lundin, 4th of Auchtermairnie*, who succeeded his father, but at the time of his death was underage. In 1650, there is an act of parliament to give the power to sell part of his lands (*East Neuk*, p 57). He died unmarried on the 22nd of April 1661. "1661, Apr. 22 – The laird of Achtermairne, called John Lundy, depairted out of this life at the Easter Newton, in his uncles house, and was interred at Kennoway church, the 25 of April in the day time. He died a young man, neuer married so that his second brother James, did succeide to the estate" (*Lamont's Diary*, 135).

2 *James Lundin, 5th of Auchtermairnie*, baptised on the 14th of December 1641, in Kennoway. He succeeded his brother, and his details follow.

3 *Margaret Lundin*, baptized 11th May 1643, in Kennoway.

4 *George Lundin*, baptized on the 2nd of June, 1645, in Kennoway.

5 *Helen Lundin*, baptized on the 12th of May 1648 at Kennoway. She married the Rev. William Annand, minister of Edinburgh, on January 14th 1670 – "1670, Jan 14 – Mr Hannah, one of the ministers in Edb. married Helen Lundin, the old Lady Achtermairny in Fyffe, surnamed Law, hir second dawghter. They wer married privatly in Leith, without proclamation. That night they supped qwietly at

Jean Jafras in Edb. the Lady Achtermairnys qwarter for the tyme, and the nixt day went home to his own lodging. This mariage was acomplished after a short resolution; for the same day fowrtnight after he saw hir he was wedded to hir. He told he stood not upon hir portion for he said he was content to take hir although she had nothing" (*Lamont's Diary*, p 216). He was the son of Mr. William Annand, minister of Ayr. Helen was buried on February 20th 1687 (*FASTI*). She and William had issue:

  i *Barbara*, buried on the 28th of March 1687.

6   **Mary Lundin**

CAPTAIN JAMES LUNDIN 5TH OF AUCHTERMAIRNIE

    Baptized on the 14th of December 1641; he married Agnes (Anna) Law, daughter of George Law of Brunton, on the 8th of December 1666 – "1666, Dec 8. bein Saturns day, - John [James] Lundy of Achtermairny in Fyffe, married Agnes Law, the deceassd George Law of Brunton in Fyffe, his only daughter: They were married by Mr Andro Bruce, minister of Kilrinny, privatley without proclaimation at the kirk of Abetsan, by ane order from the Archbishope of St Androws to that effect. Jul. 1 1667, she was browght to bad of a son att Achtermairny in the 7 month, viz 2 monthes and some days before the ordinary tyme" (*Lamont's Diary*, p196). James was on a commission for adjusting the valuation of the shire of Fife (1681-1684) (*Register of the Privy Council of Scotland*, Series III. VII., 382; VIII., 331); and was a commissioner of supply for Fife in 1690 (*General Index to Acts of Parliaments of Scotland*). He was enrolled as a Burgess and Guildsman of the City of Edinburgh, 27th March 1698. On the 1st of September 1699, he granted a 19-year tack to John Archibald, portioner of Drummaird, along with John Thomson in Balbreikie, and Robert Philp, tenant in Easter Newtoun (SC20/33/7 Pp 123-24). On the 28th of December 1700, he granted a 7-year tack of the Cottar-shod of Auchtermairnie to Thomas Bisset (SC20/33/7 Pp 186-87).

    He died in 1726. His legitimate children were:-

1   **son**, died prematurely, 1st July 1667 (*Lamont's Diary*).

18. The Arms of Lundin of Auchtermairnie

2 *John Lundie*, lieutenant in Col. Fielding's, and Col. Grant's Regiments. He died unmarried in Edinburgh in 1721 (*East Neuk*, p 57).

3 *Mary Lundin*, married James Lamont of Newton, shipmaster at Elie, on 13th May 1697. He predeceased her. She afterwards re-married to John Lamont, surgeon in Largo. John Lamont had three daughters, but it is not known if Mary was the mother (SC20/33/12).

4 *David Lundin 6th of Auchtermairnie*, who succeeded, and whose details follow.

5 *Robert Lundin*, apprenticed to William Ross, merchant Burgess in Edinburgh on 16th June 1708 (*Reg. Appren. Edin.*). From a bond granted to him by his brother David, then of Auchtermairnie, we see that Robert, as his brother, was an advocate (SC20/33/12). He had issue:-

i Captain James Lundin, married his cousin, Ann Lundin, heiress of Auchtermairnie. They had issue, for which see Ann.

ii daughter

iii Ann Lundin, married Richard Smith. She became the heiress of Auchtermairnie on the death of her cousin Anne after 1781. She had issue:-

    a   *Christopher Smith*, later Lundin, of Auchtermairnie (of more later)

    b   *Margaret*, married Lachlan McLean of Torloish

    c   *Ann*, died unmarried

6 *Christopher Lundin*, shipmaster at Leven. Baptized 29th January 1692. The Sheriff Court of Fife records that he granted factorie to Christopher Seton, writer in Kennoway; on the 9th of February 1725 (SC20/33/10). He was married to Allison Kendall (B41/7/5; B41/7/4). He had issue.

i Margaret Lundin, died before January 1751.

ii Mary Lundin, married Thomas Adamson, customs officer in Leven. She was served as heir general to her sister Margaret on the 3rd January 1751.

iii Janet Lundin, married John Ross, shipmaster in Leven; contract dated the 8th of September 1777 (SC20/36/13).

7 *Margaret Lundin*, married Alexander Arthur, surgeon, on the

23rd of April 1717.

8 **William Lundin**, (*Index Reg. Deeds*, Dal. LXXVIII., 1250).

Illegitimate Children.

1 **Patrick Lundin**. Shortly after the date of his marriage to Agnes Law, James Lundie of Auchtermairnie and Agnes Wishart were named as the parents of Patrick "begotten in fornication" (*Lundins of Fife*).

DAVID LUNDIN 6TH OF AUCHTERMAIRNIE

David succeeded to Auchtermairnie in 1726 upon the death of his father. He was an advocate. It is most probable that he is the David Lundin, advocate, who appears on record as factor for the 'Earl' of Lundin around 1722 (SC20/33/10). David died before July 1751. He married Elizabeth Lindsay in 1728 (*East Neuk*, p 57). They had issue.

1 **James Lundin**, died without issue (*Browns of Fordell*)
2 **Elizabeth Lundin**, died without issue (*Browns of Fordell*)
3 **Ann Lundin 7TH of Auchtermairnie**, whose details follow.

ANN LUNDIN 7TH OF AUCHTERMAIRNIE

She succeeded her father David upon his death, being served as heir of provision general on the 10th of July 1751. . At the time of her succession, deeds on register by her curators and Tutors show that she was a minor (*Sheriff Court of Fife Deeds*, SC20/36/6; SC20/33/12). She married Captain James Lundin, her cousin, and also heir male to her father. They had one daughter, who died before her parents. The Estate passed to Ann's cousin, Captain James's sister, Ann Lundin (Smith).

1 **Elizabeth**, baptized 24th October 1764 (*Lundins of Fife*), died unmarried 1781.

CHRISTOPHER LUNDIN 9TH OF AUCHTERMAIRNIE

Son of Richard Smith and Ann Lundin 8th of Auchtermairnie, he became Laird upon the death of his mother in 1790, and thus changed his name from Smith to Lundin. He died in 1801, and was succeeded by his son Richard. His testament/probate will is held at the national archives at Kew. A deed registered with the Sheriff Court of Fife, on the 24th of April 1806, shows that sometime prior to his death Christopher gave a years tack of the South Mains of Auchtermairnie to Henry Leckie, son of Thomas Leckie, tenant in Collairnie (*Sheriff Court of Fife Deeds*, 20/33/16).

He was twice married; first to Elizabeth Cassells. They had issue:

1   *Mary Lundin*, baptized on the 26th of February, 1785. She must have died before her father, as in his will, Ann is named as his eldest daughter.

He married secondly Rachel Johnstone, youngest daughter of Andrew Johnston of Rennyhill and Euphemia Clephane, on the 14th of April 1789. They had issue:-

1   *Ann Lundin*, born December 24th 1789

2   *Richard Lundin 10th of Auchtermairnie*, of whom next.

3   *Andrew Lundin*, baptized on the 13th of January, 1793. He died young

4   *Anne Lundin*, born 30th December 1793, died unmarried

5   *Euphemia Lundin 11th of Auchtermairnie*, she succeeded to Auchtermairnie upon the death of her brother Richard. Her full details will follow on from his in the text.

6   *Christopher Lundin*, baptized on the 17th of August 1795. He died in 1818 at sea, unmarried.

7   *Margaret Marianne Lundin*, baptized on the 9th of March, 1797. She died unmarried.

8   *Elizabeth Lundin 12th of Auchtermairnie*, who inherited Auchtermairnie from her sister Euphemia, and whose details will be discussed in full after her sister Euphemia.

9   *Amelia-Rachel Lundin*, baptized on the 17th of August 1800. She died 24th September 1864.

CAPTAIN RICHARD LUNDIN, 10TH OF AUCHTERMAIRNIE

Born on the 18th of March 1791, he succeeded his father on his death in December 1801. At the time of his father's death, Richard was a minor.

His father's testament names several persons who may have been appointed as his children's curators and tutors in the event of him dying when they were young, which of course was the case: these included a Major General William Douglas MacLean Clephane of Carslogie; Lt. Col David Clephane of the twentieth Regiment of foot; Andrew Johnstone esquire of Rennyhill; Major George Johnstone of the fourty-forth regiment; Robert Johnstone esquire, merchant in Dundee; Henry Clephane, writer to the signet; and Andrew Clephane, youngest son of the deceased George Clephane of Carslogie. Richard was served as heir of provision special to his father, in Auchtermairnie, including Lalethan, Aldie and others, in the Barony of Leslie, on the 24th May 1803. In June 1803 Henry Clephane and Andrew Clephane were appointed his Guardians. He received the basis of his education at Kennoway Parish School, and before the age of 20 had entered the army. On the 30th of March 1814, having passed the age of 21, he was granted, in London, charge of his affairs. He was again served heir to his father, this time as heir male of provision general, on the 29th of November 1824. On that same date he was served as heir of male provision general to Ann Lundin of Auchtermairnie, his grandmother. On the 20th of December 1830, he was served as heir in general to his father.

Around 1810, when a Lieutenant in the 73rd Regiment, Grenadier Guards, he travelled with his regiment to Australia. After two years there he was given leave by the Governor of Australia, Major-General Macquarrie, to take a years leave of absence and return to Great Britain. He took passage on the merchant ship Isabella, sailing on the 4th day of December 1812. On route the ship hit rocks off the Falkland Islands, and the crew and passengers were shipwrecked and castaway upon a deserted small outlying island.

> "Between eleven and twelve o'clock, February 8, I was aroused by the noise and confusion I had heard upon deck, and hastening there, soon found sufficient cause for alarm. The land, which we had been running straight upon, appeared through the gloom (there being no moon), to be very high and only a short way off. The people were exerting themselves under the direction of Captain Brookes, who ever retained his presence of mind, in taking in sail and trimming the yards, to keep close to the wind. This being done, and seeing a prospect of weathering the land (to which we could not imagine how we had got so near), Brookes

retired to put on some additional clothing, when I heard the alarm from the head of the ship, "Breakers on the weather bow;" I hurried below to call Brookes, and had scarcely reached deck again, when the ship struck upon a sunk rock with dreadful force. Raised again by the swell, she struck with redoubled violence, so as to oblige every one to lay hold of something, to keep them from falling. She made at the same time considerable way, the rocks being too low to stop her, and the sea breaking with great violence over the rocks around us, whose hideous aspect was partly hid by the darkness, save when here and there the point of a rock reared his rugged head close to us. The sea, as far as could be seen, was one sheet of foam. Such of the crew as had presence of mind to attend orders, were sent aloft to take in all sail, so as to lighten her, as we were in great dread of being broken into pieces by the ship striking so repeatedly; we were however, in a short time so far relieved by her sticking fast. When nothing farther could be done, I had time to attend those around me. A man named Maddison, a gunner in the navy, returning home passenger, seemed most alarmed, and eager to get out a small boat for the preservation of some of the people, and to be in readiness in case of emergency. A few of us had now, with much exertion, got the boat into the water, and proceeded to make ourselves useful in some other part of the vessel. Our great fear was that her bottom had been beat out, and that when she got into deep water, she would sink. . . ."

It appears that although the ship ran aground in rather unpleasant conditions, the proximity of the calamity to land meant that all persons survived. However, Richard and his fellow travellers found themselves upon a tiny island "*Eagle Island*" (now called Speedwell Island) with no signs of human inhabitation, and only the small amount of food saved from the wreck of the ship on which to survive.

"We now had time to examine the country, and endeavour to find what part of the Islands we had been cast upon, which, after all our researches, we could not but conjecture. We found the island to be of an oblong shape, lying north and south, about

25 miles in circumference, surrounded in every direction by rocks and islands. Towards the north, it is separated by a passage about six miles in breadth, from what appeared a large extent of land; and on the west, where we landed, about four leagues off, the land extended as far as the eye could reach. About a mile and a half from our shore, in that direction, is the reef of rocks upon which we had struck, and which were now an object of dread, and mater of astonishment, how we could possibly have escaped, and drifted to the spot most convenient of any on that side of the island. They appeared even at high water, considerably above the surface; between which and the shore the water is covered by sea-weed, impenetrable except by ship; so that if we had struck on the other side of it we must all have perished. We at the same time decried, on the opposite coast (where the land is very high), a large opening, which we conjectured to be the southern entrance to the Falkland Straits, to which we were led by an old map of the Falkland Islands, belonging to a passenger; the ship charts being on too small a scale to be of service to us. We then began devising means of procuring relief, in our most melancholy situation; but rested our principal dependence on the known experience of Captain Brookes. We called to remembrance, that these islands were nearly the cause of rupture between Britain and Spain, respecting the right of possession, and that the English had had a settlement to the northward, called Port Egmont. We therefore supposed, that as England had given up her claim, that Spain might have taken possession. Our object now was to find out this settlement, make known our situation, and procure a vessel, either to convey away the people, or to proceed to Monte Video, and represent our case, where we would undoubtedly find relief. In the event of finding no settlement on the islands, to make the bold attempt of reaching the main-land in the boat; if we did not succeed, it was only exchanging one death for another; as so many people could not be supposed to exist for a very long period, the provisions every day decreasing."

On the 22nd of February 1813, in order to save the lives of the persons on the island, Richard Lundin, along with a Captain Brookes, a retired sea-captain; the mate of the wrecked ship; a marine named Wooley; an American named Ford; and a Portuguese national Jose Antonia; boarded a make shift vessel, that the carpenter of the wrecked ship had put together (no more that 18 ft in length), and attempted to sail to the main settlement of the Falkland Islands in order to find aid. After some degree of confusion about the exact location of the island they were wrecked upon, and battling with stormy seas, the six men reached the settlement they had been looking for. However, there luck was not in, and the town had been totally deserted by the Spanish. There was therefore no chance of finding any aid to their predicament on the Falkland Islands, and so they needed to take upon themselves the risky journey of sailing on the open ocean, from the Falklands, to the main land of South America, and the city of Monte Video. This journey, especially with the small craft they had, was incredibly perilous, and could have easily ended the six men's lives. Before hitting the open sea, Richard Lundin left the following note in the abandoned settlement:

"*Spaniards & Christians, should this ever meet your eye, know that 52 British subjects, have been shipwrecked upon one of these desert Islands, in latitude.....and longitude.....six of whom, in order to obtain relief, have endeavoured to reach the main-land in a boat. If they fail in this undertaking, their companions will, in all probability, be left to perish. If you find them, the boat has been lost; if not, we have brought them relief. March 8, 1813.*"

They made land on the 24th of March, but not before Richard had seriously burned his feet due to an accident with hot water in their cramped cooking conditions. Upon reaching the continent, they sailed up the River Plata towards Monte Video. The time of their arrival coincided with a civil war in what we would now think of as Argentina and Uruguay, and upon landing close to their target, Monte Video, the six members of the rescue party were accosted by soldiers of the revolutionary party of the army of one General Artigas.

"We had not waited long, though very impatiently, when our friends were seen returning, accompanied by two or three dozen ragged fierce-looking people, all on horse back, and some of them armed with fusils; Brookes, very dejectedly, told us to pull down the colours (to which the people also pointed), observing that after all our hardships and dangers, we would in all likelihood be sent to end our days in the mines, as, from what he could make out, the countries were at war.

With the little Spanish I was master of, I enquired if the English and Spaniards were no friends; to which, with readiness, they answered, NO! Four or Five now jumped into the boat, which was fast aground, while the others surrounded us, but used no violence – they said some soldiers had been sent for, whom they soon expected. Our new acquaintances now became very inquisitive and covetous. One of them took a fancy to Wooley's cap, which he did not dare refuse. My old trousers (which I was changing for another pair) met with a similar fate. I certainly parted with them without much reluctance, by way of securing the good offices of my ragged friend. Not satisfied with this, he made several applications for other parts of my wardrobe, to which, however, I turned a deaf ear, pretending not to understand him. Our appearance was indeed little calculated to command respect; we were as directly ragged and miserable looking creatures, as could be seen anywhere. I had now become quite tired of their importunities, and I determined to awe them into a little respect. I therefore put on my old regimental jacket (which I mentioned having brought). The sight of this produced an almost instantaneous effect; every one being more respectful than another to Signor Captain. Supposing we were hungry, by the manner they observed us eating some mouldy biscuit, one of them went away in a quest of fresh beef for us. We saw now about a dozen men galloping towards us. He who appeared commander stepped forward, and in very good English began a conversation. He was made fully acquainted with our adventures, and on his part informed us, that we were about ten miles from the Buenos Ayres army besieging Monte Video, which was held by the Royalists; and that it would be necessary for me, as an officer, to attend him to his colonel, who commanded a post at a short distance. This I was very willing to comply with on many accounts; one of which was, the hope of getting my feet dressed, which were excessively painful. We made a comfortable meal of some stewed beef that had been provided for us, and at four o'clock I set out with my new friend, who informed me he was a captain, although his present appearance rather belied his assertion – there being little difference between his dress and that of his soldiers. This he accounted for by stating the difficulties they lay under of procuring suitable clothing, from their distance from the capital, and no other town where they could be supplied. He entertained me with an account of his skirmishes with the Spaniards, plentifully interspersed with details of his own valour, and the feats he had performed during the war. He seemed to have a very contemptuous opinion of his own associates, though infinitely preferable to that of the Spaniards, regarding the English as in all respects superior to both. The alarm of our arrival having soon spread, we met several parties, all hastening to the place of our landing. After two hours' riding, we arrived at a cluster of huts, where the commandant parlied with us, and then desired us to proceed to the next post. From that we were turned over to another, and another, each officer forwarding us to the next in seniority, until at length we found that we would be obliged to proceed to the head quarters of General Artigas."

General Jose Artigas is regarded as the national hero of Uruguay. On the 18th of May 1811, two years prior to his meeting with Richard Lundin, Artigas defeated the Spanish forces that held Uruguay (then as part of the united provinces of the Rio de la Plata), and only left them in possession of Monte Video. This city was still under siege by Artigas when Richard Lundin arrived, and continued as such up until 1814, but due his victory over the Spanish in the rest of the country, the 18th of May is now a national holiday in Uruguay.

Richard dinned with Artigas at his house, and was subsequently taken to General Rondeau (Rondiou as Lundin writes), who was, at least on paper, Artigas's superior. Here he remained for a short while as the general's guest. This general, like Artigas is also looked upon now as a hero of the revolution in this area of South America. An Argentine soldier from Buenos Ayres, he was eventually elected the preliminary President of the free Uruguay on the 17th of September 1828, a position he resigned in 1829.

The fact that Monte Video was under siege created a few problems for the rescue plan of asking the city's governor for assistance, and for a ship to take back to the Falklands. Although General Rondiou was willing to send up a flag of truce to allow the party to enter the city and ask the governor for assistance in rescuing the other 46 persons left on the island (which included a lady and her child which had been born just before setting out from Australia), in all probability, as a result of the siege, the Governor would not have been able to provide the boat they required to take back to the Falklands and carry out the rescue. On this consideration, the six men decided to continue on to Buenos Ayres, which was a further 120-mile journey. After a rest of a few days, they boarded their small boat, and commenced this journey, arriving at Buenos Ayres on the 31st of March.

"Thus, after a passage of thirty-eight days from the time we sailed from the wreck, eighteen of which we had been out of sight of land, in seas proverbial for storms, did we, only through the mercy and assistance of the Almighty, reach our destined port is safety. I was next morning conducted to Captain Heywood, who I found as anxious and eager for the speedy relief of our people, as I could possibly desire, but was sadly puzzled for the means. He told me he wished most anxiously he could take his frigate down, but found it impossible, being placed there as much in a diplomatic character, as for the protection of the trade; at any rate, he could not undertake so hazardous a passage to endanger the specie he had on board. Nor were there any other ships of war on the station, except a brig, that had come in this morning dismasted, and otherwise so much damaged that she was to be condemned. He, however, sent orders to hold a board of survey upon her; and although the report was extremely unfavourable, seeing no alternative, he ordered all the carpenters that could be collected from other ships and ashore, to refit her with all despatch. In the mean time, the report of our arrival having spread among the English merchants, they came flocking from all quarters to see us. I was politely pressed to take up my residence at the house of Mr McNiel, one of the most considerable of them, and Brookes was invited to that of a resident English surgeon. The landlady of the inn where Captain Heywood lived, came to me, and asked if I was one of the people who came in the boat. Being answered in the affirmative, she begged I would accept a room in her house, free of all expense, and where I should have every comfort provided for me; and she actually extended that kindness to the mate, who lived with her a month or six weeks, and experienced the greatest kindness and hospitality; and when he left her, received both clothes and money. This person, whose name was Clarke, was originally a prisoner in the Jane Shore, which had been seized by the convicts on their passage to New South Wales, and carried to Buenos Ayres. She had established a very respectable character and fortune, and had married a man who commanded the few ships the Buenos Ayres government was master of. I now found myself very comfortably settled in a most hospitable house, – my host a very excellent gentlemanly man, where every attention I could possibly desire was paid to me; I was also greatly relieved by having my feet dressed, which I could not now put on the ground. Nor were they quite recovered for a month afterwards, being only able to hop about a little, during the two or three last days of my stay at Buenos Ayres. My companions in danger were also well disposed of, Wooley was taken aboard the frigate, where in three days his appearance changed wonderfully for the better, in consequence of the good treatment he experienced. Ford and Jose Antonio, had hired themselves to different employments, where they got high wages, and were well contented to remain. They each got twenty dollars from the sale of the boat, as a trifling recompense for the part they had all acted. Captain Brookes took his departure for England in a merchant-ship, four days after our arrival. I was sorry to part with him, considering the dangers we had shared together, and regarding him as, in a great measure, the means appointed by heaven for our preservation.

By the active exertions of Captain Heywood, the brig was so far repaired as to be ready for sea in a fortnight – and on the 16th April, I again found myself on the water, on board the Nancy, Lieutenant D'Arando. We anchored the first night close to the frigate, where our commander was ordered to send his useless hands, that there might be room enough in his brig for all our poor sufferers. I here saw Wooley, and asked if he was getting ready to return with me to the Islands. When he heard this he put on a very piteous face, and earnestly entreated that I would not insist upon him going; his present quarters he found so much more preferable. He soon became all smiles and good humour, when he found I was only jesting with him; there being certainly no necessity for punishing him."

Richard, being the only member of the six men who left on the rescue mission who returned to Eagle Island, arrived there to find the island still populated with the cast-aways of the shipwreck he had left behind, and so all the exertions upon the sea had been worth the pain. The Island population was subsequently rescued, and Richard finally managed to return to Great Britain, via Rio de Janeiro, landing at Falmouth on the 2nd of December of that year.

Further details of this story can be read in *"The Narrative of the shipwreck, & surprising adventures, in 1813, of Captain Richard Lundin, of Auchtermairney, parish of Kennoway, Fifeshire, as related by himself."* a copy of which can be found in the National Library of Scotland. It is from this book that the above extracts are taken. The plight of the persons left on the island can be read in "*The Wreck of the Isabella.*"

After turning 21, Richard took on the responsibilities of a land-owner. A posthumous introduction to his narrative states that "Richard, as a landed proprietor, magistrate, and country gentleman, was as highly respected as he had been in the army. He greatly improved his estate, was kind and generous, attentive to the poor, and anxious to do good to all. While thus actively employed, he was suddenly cut off by a fatal malady." Captain Richard died un-married on November 30th 1832. The testaments of Richard Lundin, Esq., heritable proprietor of the Lands of Auchtermairnie are registered with Cupar Sheriff Court, and are dated the 6th of April 1833. His sister Euphemia succeeded him.

EUPHEMIA LUNDIN 11TH OF AUCHTERMAIRNIE

Baptized on the 10th of January 1794, she inherited Auchtermairnie on the death of her brother Richard. She died, unmarried, on the 27th of February 1855. The estate passed to her sister Elizabeth. A large obituary of hers appeared about a month after her death in the Illustrated London News, in the section 'Obituaries of Eminent Persons.' The details of this are transcribed below:

Miss Lundin of Auchtermairnie

"This excellent lady died at her residence in Edinburgh at the age of fifty nine, last month. The family she was the representative of is one of the oldest, and was, at one time, one of the most influential in Scotland. Its possessions extended over the greater part of the counties of Forfar and Fife, where estates and villages are still called by the name of Lundie. The family can be traced up to the time of Malcolm Canmore, King of Scotland, the earliest period in Scottish family history that any documents are extant. The Lundins were, probably, as Chalmers believes one of those great Anglo-Norman families that settled in the neighbourhood of the Forth and Tay. In the reign of William the Lion, one of his sons married the heiress of Lundin and too the names with her estates. From this period the Lundins of Lundin enjoyed, in uninterrupted succession, their possession and influence for the long period of nearly five hundred years. Near the middle of the last century the estates were inherited by a female, who married the Earl of Perth, but the estate of Auchtermairnie still continued in the possession of a younger branch of the original stock, as we hope it long may. Miss Lundin succeeded, in 1832, her brother, Captain Lundin, who died unmarried. She is succeeded by her sister, who is married and has a large family. The arms of Lundin of Lundin were the Royal arms of Scotland, which they were permitted to wear, as being descended from Royalty. The arms of Auchtermairnie were those of the family before the connexion with the sovereign, and are still worn by the present generation. The motto "Tam Genus" shows that faith and power were their most cherished inheritance. The estate of Lundin in Fifeshire is at present owned by a large insurance company, Auchtermairnie remains in the family.

The article also included a picture of the arms of Auchtermairnie, the details of which are discussed towards the end of this chapter.

ELIZABETH LUNDIN BROWN 12TH AND LAST OF AUCHTERMAIRNIE

baptized on the 28th of November, 1798. She married the Rev. Robert Brown on the 15th of June 1827. She inherited the estate of Auchtermairnie on the 27th of February 1855, after the death of her sister, after which she, her husband, and family, adopted the name Lundin along with that of Brown. The Reverend Brown was born in May 1792, the second son of the Rev. James Brown; minister of Newburn in Fife, and later of Newbattle in Edinburgh; and Helen Adam. He was licensed by the Presbytery of Haddington on the 26th of March 1816; presented to the parish of Largo, county of Fife, by General Durham; and ordained on the 28th of June 1821. On the Session in 1843, Mr. Brown ceased to hold the living, and became Free Church minister of Largo; he was author of the parish in the New Statistical Account of Scotland; A ward in the East Neuk; and A Letter to the Moderate Brethren (*Browns of Fordell*, p75). Elizabeth died on the 12th of February 1868. After her death the Rev. Robert Lundin-Brown married, at Breslau, on the 28th of September 1870, Marie Wilhelmina Henriette Pauline, elder daughter and co-heir of Colonel Louis von Corvin-Wiersbitskij, Prussian Royal Artillery, and Pauline, his wife, nee Baroness Knobelsdorff. Her only sister married Eberhard von Leukanos, Lord of Schrine, in Silesia, and has issue. Mr. Lundin-Brown died at Largo 9th April 1877. After his death, the following notices in reference to him appeared in the public press, and is taken from the *Brown's of Fordell*.

DEATH OF REV. MR. BROWN, OF LARGO.

In the death of the Rev. Robert Lundin-Brown, the Free Church minister of the fishing village of Largo, Fifeshire, which took place on Monday, another of the rapidly diminishing band of pre-Disruption worthies has passed away. He was in his 85th year, and his labour in the ministry extended over a period of more that half-a-century. He was ordained in 1821, and was settled in Largo as a established Church minister, but left the Establishment at the Disruption, and to the people who adhered to him he continued to minister. In his long lifetime he was enabled to do many works of usefulness, and was a faithful pastor. One notable incident in his life must not be omitted in a notice of Mr. Brown. It was he who rescued Dr. Candlish from a watery grave in Largo Bay. Dr. Candlish was a passenger on board the steamer running from Leith along the East Coast. He was going to land at Largo, and in order to this it was necessary to come ashore in a small boat. The water in the bay was decidedly rough, and the boat was swamped at some distance from the beach. Candlish, among others, was precipitated into the sea, and the subject of this notice, who was waiting on the shore, dashed into the water, and at great risk to himself, laid hold of his friend, and delivered him from a position of imminent danger. Mr. Brown was twice married, and his second wife survives him.

Elizabeth Lundin, and the Rev. Robert Brown had issue:

1 *James Lundin Brown, M.D.*, born on the 4th of April 1828, he was christened on the 15th May 1828 in Largo. He married, on the 21st February, 1871, Sarah, daughter of T.O. Stevens of Obern Hill, Bristol. She died on the 22nd of December that year. Dr. Lundin-Brown died on the 2nd of May 1872, at Malvern.

2 *Richard Lundin Brown*, born on the 7th of November 1829, he was christened at Largo on the 20th of December 1829. He married on the 13th of April 1871, Margaret, daughter of Charles Maitland Christie of Durie, a Deputy-Lieutenant of the county of Fife, and Mary Butler, his wife, daughter of the Honourable Robert Lindsay of Balacarres. At the time of writing of '*The memorials of the Browns of Fordell . . .*' in 1887, he is described as the representative of the Lundin's of Auchtermairnie. He died on the 5th of December 1905, at 4 Middelshad, St. Andrews. His funeral was held on the 9th of December, leaving St. Andrews at 12.00 noon, and arriving at Kennoway at 2:30 pm. (*Scotsman*, 8th December 1905).

i Elizabeth Mary, born on the 16th of November 1872. She married, on the 31st of October 1900, at the Royal Hotel in Princes Street, Edinburgh, Mr Joseph H.H. Dase. The ceremony was performed by the Rev. J.R. Burt, minister of Largo. She is described in the wedding announcement as the 'only child of Mr and Mrs Lundin Brown, East Newport, Fife, and granddaughter of the late C.M. Christie of Durie, Fife.' (*Scotsman* 1st November 1900). She died in 1976 without issue.

3 *Helen Lundin Brown*, christened at Largo on the 1st of July 1832. She married on the 28th of February, the Rev. Thomas Stothert, Free Church minister at Lumphanan, in the county of Aberdeen. He was the younger son of the late William Stothert of Cargen and Blaiket, in the Stewartry of Kirkudbright, a Deputy-Lieutenant, and Captain in the Coldstream Guards. Helen died at Pau, on the 24th of December 1880. She had no issue. Mr. Stothert married, secondly, on the 14th of September 1882, Grace Catherine, daughter of Rear-Admiral Duncan Campbell of Barbreck, in the county of Argyll.

4 *Rev. Robert Christopher Lundin Brown*; born on the 17th of November 1833, he was christened at Largo on the 12th January 1834. He was vicar of Lineal-cum-Colemere, county Salop, and later vicar of Rhodes, county Lancaster, in 1874. He also spent some time in British Columbia as a missionary, and was the author of the following works:

1) "Klatsassan. and other reminiscences of missionary life in British Columbia":

2) "British Columbia. an essay":

3) "Christmas":

4) "The Dead in Christ: a word of consolation for mourners":

5) "The Life of Peace":

6) "Light from the Cross. Sermons on the Passion of our Lord. Translated from the German":

7) "The Sinlessness of Jesus an evidence for Christianity. ... Translated from the sixth German edition."

8) "The Epistle to the Philippians ... From notes supplied by Mr. R. Lundin Brown" by Rev. William Lincon:

9) "Commentary on the Sermon on the Mount. ... Translated from the fourth revised and enlarged edition, by R. L. Brown" by F. Tholuck.

The Rev. Robert Lundin-Brown died, unmarried, on the 16th of April, 1876, in Clapham, Surrey.

5 *Emma Elizabeth Lundin Brown*, christened at Largo on the 2nd of October 1836. She died at the hospital for Women, 30 Soho Square, Middlesex; on the 10th of April, 1878. She was a spinster.

6 *William Clephane Lundin Brown*, born on the 29th of August 1836, he was christened at Largo on the 29th of August 1838. He was a civil engineer by profession. He married on the 3rd of April 1878,

Eliza, daughter of Evans Prout, of Willow Grove, county Haldimand, Ontario. They had issue:

i   Emma Elizabeth Lundin Brown, born on the 10th of January 1879, in Hamilton, Wentworth, Ontario. She married Merton Leonard Raney, in Vancouver, Canada, on the 6th of August 1912. She died without issue.

ii   Helen May Lundin Brown , born on the 10th of January 1879, in Hamilton, Wentworth, Ontario. She married David Glover in Penticion, Canada, on the 20th of October 1923. She died without issue.

iii Agnes Wilhelmina Lundin Brown, born on the 13th of August 1881 in Oneida, Haldimand, Ontario. She died without issue

iv   Theodore Lundin Brown born on the 13th of August 1881 in Oneida, Haldimand, Ontario. She died without issue

v   Margaret Euphemia Lundin Brown, born on the 5th of June 1888 in Pelham Twp, Welland, Ontario. She married Roy Beverly Seely in Ashcroft, Canada on the 27th of May 1920. They had issue.

7   **Arthur Brown**, christened at Largo on the 1st of June 1840. He was in the Honourable East India Company's Naval service, and died un-married in India in 1868.

Sometime between 1855 and 1880, the estate of Auchtermairnie was sold off 'piecemeal to different parties, and the Mansion House, which was beautifully situated, commanding an extensive prospect, and surrounded by old ancestral trees' was demolished, 'and the trees uprooted' (*Narrative of the Shipwreck and surprising adventures of Richard Lundin*).

Heraldry

"Lundin of Auchtermemy, descended from the family of Lundin, caries the old coat of Lundin, viz. paly of six pieces, *argent* and *gules*, on a bend *azure*, three cushions *or*, all within a bordure indented of the third; crest, a hand, proper, holding a cushion argent: motto, *Tam genus quam virtus*. L.R.",
          from Nisbets *Heraldry*.

Although the family of Auchtermairnie bore the arms as just described, it would appear as if the lairds unofficially adopted the new arms of Lundin of that Ilk. The silver Ewer, shown above, was made by James Gordon, one of Aberdeen's leading Goldsmiths, around the year 1770. It is in the possession of Aberdeen City Council, who acquired it from a silver dealer in 1980 (*Aberdeen Archive No. ABDAG 1041*). It is engraved with a crest and motto. The crest depicts a right hand clutching a sword; the motto reads "DEI DONO SUM QVOD SUM". The motto is that of Lundin of that Ilk. This silver Ewer has been attributed to Christopher Lundin of Auchtermairnie. The reason for this provenance is due to the similarity between the crest on the ewer, and the markings on a punchbowl that came up for sale in 1923. The punchbowl, decorated with flower sprays, also featured an armorial: Or a lion rampant gules within a double tressure flory counter flory sable all within a bordure compony argent and azure; crest, out of an antique crown Or, a lion affronteé gules holding in the dexter paw a sword erect and in the sinister a thistle slipped all proper; supporters, two lions rampant guardant gules collared or, with the motto 'Dei Dono Sum Quod Sum.' This punchbowl came from a service made for Christopher Lundin of Auchtermairnie, (*Chinese Armorial Porcelain*, D. S. Howard, 843).

The use of the arms of Lundin of that Ilk by Auchtermairnie dates from much earlier than this. On the 16th of April, 1719, James Lundin of Auchtermairnie presented a silver communion cup to the Kirk Session of Kennoway. This communion cup, which now resides with the parish of Markinch, bore the arms of Lundin of that ilk.

Opposite: 19. Silver Ewer made for Christopher Lundin
By James Gordon

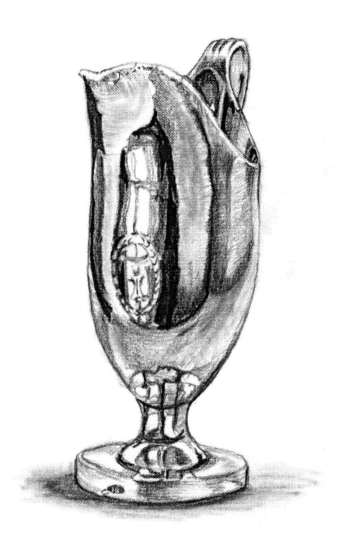

The House of Baldastard

The lands of Baldastard are located about three miles due north of Largo, in Fife. The family of Lundin of Baldastard (Baldastart, Baldaster or Baldastar) descend from the family of Lundie of that Ilk through a son of Walter Lundie of that Ilk, and Elizabeth Lindsay. The lands of Baldastard came into the family through the marriage of a great-grandson of Walter, through this line, to the heiress of the family of Ireland of Baldastard.

JAMES LUNDIE IN BALCORMO MYLN

The grandson of Walter Lundie of that Ilk, suggested through his son James, he was a tenant in Balcormo Mylne (*Lundins of Fife*). Balcormo was part of the Barony of Lundie, and many references to this land can be found in the section of this text discussing Lundie of that Ilk. James was named, with four others, all kinsmen of the Lundies, as curator of Thomas Johnston, grandson of William Lundie of that Ilk, through a judgement of the Lords of Council and Session, on 13th March 1616. He married Marion Greig who died in January 1617. Her testament is registered with St. Andrews Commissary Court on the 10th March 1617. They had issue (*Lundins of Fife*).

1   *James Lundie in Balcormo Myln*
2   *William Lundie*
3   *Robert Lundie*
4   *John Lundie*
5   *Agnes Lundie*, in 1656, designed as the sister of James Lundie in Balcormo Mylne, she is recorded as giving a discharge concerning the Barony of Lundie (*NAS*, GD160/283, No. 6)

JAMES LUNDIE IN BALCORMO MYLN

James was married to Margaret Trail, the sister of the Laird of Blebo-Hole. James died 25th August 1650, and was interred in Largo Church on the 28th of August (*Lamont's Diary*, p 22). Margaret Trail was provided with a life interest in Balcormo Mylne (*Lundins of Fife*) They had issue:-

1   *John Lundin, 1ˢᵗ of that name of Baldastard*, of whom next.
2   *James Lundin*
3   *Robert Lundin*, married Ann Moncreif, 14th February 1668, but died without issue – "1668, Feb. 14 – Robert Lundin in Balcormo Mill, in the parish of Largo, married An Moncriefe, Mowrney-pys dawghter; the marriage feast stood in hir fathers house nire Achtermowghty. Jul. 8, 1670, he depairted owt of this life att Bacormo mill, and was interred at Largo K. the 9 of Jul. in the afternoon: he died of consumtion" (Lamont's Diary, p 204).

JOHN LUNDIN, FIRST OF THAT NAME OF BALDASTARD

John was married to Barbara, the eldest daughter, and heiress of John Ireland of Baldastard and Bessie Scott, on the 2nd of March 1660:

> "1660, Mar. 2, being Fryday – Johne Lundy in Bacormo mille, the deceasd Ja. Lundy ther, his eldest son, married Barbara Ireland, the deceased John Ireland of Baldastart, his eldest daughter, (with ane eye to have the lands of Baldastart with hir); the marriage feast stood at Bacormo mille in his mothers house. . . Sept. 20, 1660, the said Barbara Ireland was brought to bed of a daughter called Sophia (about 10 of 11 weiks afor the ordinar time, in respect of the day of the marriage only.) Nov. 21, 1661, in the morning, the chelde died, and was interred on the said day at Largo church." (*Lamonts Diary*, p 120).

John Ireland had died on October the 11th, the previous year, so John Lundin became the laird of Baldastard upon this marriage. Although the name of the son of Walter Lundie of that Ilk, ancestor of John Lundin of Baldastard is not known, the descent of this cadet of the Lundie family is recorded in John's grant of arms. The following extract is taken from Nisbet's Heraldry.

> "John Lundin of Baldester, who's great grandfather was a lawful brother of the ancient family of Lundin, assumed the new coat of Lundie, and quartered it with the old arms of Lundie, thus recorded in the Lyon Register, quarterly, first and fourth the arms of Scotland within a bordure gorbonated, *argent* and *azure*, as being the arms granted by King Charles II. to the family of Lundin; and specially adapted to their descent form Robert of Lundin, natural son to William the Lion King of Scotland, and brother to King Alexander II. The second and third quarters are, paly of six, *argent* and *gules*, on a bend *azure*, three cushions of the first, as the coat formerly used and borne by those of the name, and all within a bordure *azure*; crest, a dexter hand open, and charged in the palm with an eye, all natural: motto, *Certior dum cerno*; so recorded in the Lyon register, 14th January 1698."

20. The Arms of Lundin of Baldastard

John was a strong supporter of the Covenanters, and in 1672 was prosecuted a number of times for attending conventicles. He was a commissioner of supply for Fife, appearing as such in acts of Parliament in 1690, 1695 and 1705 (*General index to the Acts of Parliament of Scotland*). In 1689, he complained to the King and Queen, as recorded by the Privy Council, about the behaviour of his minister. In 1690, he and his son John were appointed justices of peace for Fife (*Register of the Privy Council of Scotland*, Series III. XIV., 101-2; XV., 473.) On November 29th 1701 he was a member of the Largo Church Session that caused Alexander Selkirk (the prototype of Robinson Crusoe) to attend Church the following day to confess his sin for causing a family brawl and to be rebuked from the pulpit for his indiscretion (*Lundins of Fife*). In 1707 John Lundin, designed 'elder of Baldestar' is recorded as being paid by St. Leonard's College, University of St. Andrews, for lime (*Univ. St. And. Munim.*). John had issue:-

1   *Sophia Lundin*, born on the 20th of September 1660, and died on the 21st of November 1660 (*Lundins of Fife*).
2   *John Lundin 2nd of Baldastard*, of whom next.
3   *James Lundin in Balcormo Myln*. He married, first, Elizabeth, daughter of John Haldane of Myretoune, on the 26th of February, 1691/2. By her he had one son (*Lundins of Fife*):
   i   *John*, baptized 8th January 1693, who died in the West Indies without issue in 1715.
James secondly married Janet Gourlay, daughter of Thomas Gourlay tenant of Bandirren (*NAS* GD20/1/816), on the 26th of January, 1694, in Newburn. They had at least 15 children in the subsequent 22 years (*Lundins of Fife*):-
   i   *James*, baptized 29th November 1695. He married first Christian Rhymer in Falkland on 29th November 1717 and has issue:
      a Sophia, baptized 11th June 1721.
      b Margaret, baptized on the 5th of January 1724.
James secondly married Magdalene Condie, daughter of Robert Condie in Dalkeith by Margaret Laurie on 14th September 1727. Before 1758, James was a gardener for Lundin of that Ilk, after that date he was residing in Drummochie (*Sheriff Court of Fife Deeds. SC20/36/12*). James also had issue by Magdalene (*Lundins of Fife*):

a John, baptized on the 14th of July 1728. He died young.

b Henrietta, baptized on the 14th of September 1729.

c John, baptized on the 9th of January 1732, married Margaret Reid, with issue:-

    i   *Rachel*, baptized on the 6th of February 1756

d James Lundin in Drummochy, baptized on the 3rd of February 1734. He married Christian Henderson, July 16th 1758, with issue:

    i   *James Lundin in Drummochy*, baptized on the 18th of April 1762. He was served as heir general to his father 'James Lundin in Drummochy, on the 3rd of October 1831.

e Patrick, baptized on the 28th of March 1736

f Elizabeth, baptized on the 25th of September 1737. She married James Henderson, on the 1st of September 1753.

g Magdalene, baptized on the 4th of September 1740. She married Ebenezer Coutts, Bailie in Drumochie, on December 20th 1769. She was buried on the 28th of March 1810.

h Rachel, baptized on the 24th of September 1742

i Robert, baptized on the 17th of July 1744. He married Helen Briggs, daughter of William Briggs, baker in Elie, and Helen McIntosh. Robert was a Tailor in Drumochie. He had issue:-

    i   *Helen*, baptized 27th July 1774. She married Commander James Welsh R.N. in 1794 and died in 1802. They had issue and are the great-great-grandparents of G.T. Welsh, author of "Lundins of Fife"

    ii   *Robert*, baptized 11th August 1776, died in 1794.

    iii   *Magdalene,* born in 1778, married John Crevie in 1799 and Commander James Welsh, R.N., 10th July 1810.

    iv   *Rachel*, baptized 19th October 1782, died 1825

    v   *Henrietta*, baptized 19th October 1783, died 1791

    vi   *Elizabeth*, born in 1785

    vii   *Jane*, born 1789

k Anna, her birthdate is not known, but she is listed as a daughter of James in a disposition and assignation by him, dated the 23rd of September 1758, where he records the legacies he was to leave his wife and children. From this disposition it would appear as if only seven of his children were still alive by this date; James, described as eldest son; Robert; Henrietta; Marjory (perhaps either Margaret or Magdalene); Elizabeth; Anna and Sophia (*Sheriff Court of Fife Deeds.* SC20/36/12).

ii Robert, baptized on the 15ᵗʰ of January 1698, died young

iii William, baptized on the 14ᵗʰ of February 1699, died young

iv Elizabeth, baptized on the 9ᵗʰ of June 1700

v Barbara, baptized on the 25ᵗʰ of October 1701 She married John Sibbald on the 31ˢᵗ of April, 1727. John was dead by 1738 (SC20/36/7). They had issue:

  a   *John Sibbald*, wright in Kennoway.

  b   *James Sibbald*

  c   *Janet Sibbald*

  d   *Isobel Sibbald*

vi Thomas, baptized on the 24ᵗʰ of January 1703

vii Anne, baptized on the 14ᵗʰ of March 1704

viii Robert, baptized on the 26ᵗʰ of November 1706

ix Martha, baptized on the 1ˢᵗ of January 1708, and buried on the 13ᵗʰ of May 1773

x Margaret, baptized on the 2ⁿᵈ of January 1709, died young

xi Patrick, baptized on the 5ᵗʰ of March 1710. He is probably the Patrick Lundin featuring in the Dysart Deeds, as a tenant in Coats. This record shows a Patrick Lundin, tenant in Coats, granting a disposition, assignation and translation, in favour of his spouse Margaret Macke; his daughter, Janet Lundin; and his sister, Martha Lundin. This is dated the 24ᵗʰ of June 1755 (*NAS* SC20/36/9).

xii Christian, baptized on the 8ᵗʰ of July 1711

xiii Mary, baptized on the 9ᵗʰ of November 1712

xiv William, baptized on the 4ᵗʰ of April 1714

xv Margaret, baptized on the 1ˢᵗ of September 1717

xvi Anne, baptized on the 26ᵗʰ of October 1718

JOHN LUNDIN 2ᴺᴰ OF BALDASTARD

Around 1693, John was chamberlain of the forfeited estates of Cragie (*NAS*, E58/3). On the 21ˢᵗ of January 1701, Patrick Thomson of Deninoon granted him factory on the (*St Andrews Deeds* CC20/11/7). He was tacksman of the Earl of Roseberry's estate in Fife around 1707 (*Index Reg. Deeds*). He married Ann Livingston, the daughter of William Livingstone, merchant burgess of Edinburgh, on Thursday the 21st April 1692. Mr. James Kirkton, minister of North West Parish, Edinburgh, performed the ceremony. They had issue:

1   ***John Lundin heir to Baldastard***, baptized on the 29th of June 1696.
2   ***Anna Lundin***, baptized on the 4th of June 1697
3   ***James Lundin***, baptized on the 3rd of July 1698. He must have died young.

Anna must have died shortly after the birth of James, as John married Christian Durham, on the 25th of December 1700. Christian was the third daughter of Alexander Durham 3rd Baron of Largo; himself the second son of James of Pitkerow, by Margaret Rutherford, the daughter of Sir Thomas Rutherford of Hunthill. Around 1707 John was a factor for collecting the Royal rents in the Stewartry of Fife (*Univ. St. And. Arch.* Ms 36929 Box6/106; Box6/129; Box6/132; Box6/133. He also had issue by Christian Durham:

1   ***Robert Lundin***, baptized on the 23rd of January 1702 in Largo.
2   ***Margaret Lundin***, baptized on the 16th of March 1705 in Kennoway.
3   ***Captain Archibald Lundin***, baptized May 1709. He was married to a Mary Brown.
4   ***James Lundin***, baptized on the 8th of February 1711, at Anstruther Wester.
5   ***Alexander Lundin***, twin brother of James, baptized on the 8th of February 1711, at Anstruther Wester.

Whether John was succeeded by one of his sons is not yet known, but by 1782, Baldastard was held by George Steel. The lands of Balcormo were sold in 1755 as part of the Lundin estate. They passed to Duddingston of Stanford, and in 1765 were in sold by him to Alexander Shaw W.S., to be later acquired by Ker of Carskerdo (*East Neuk*).

The House of Breriehill

DAVID LUNDIE OF BRERIEHILL

David was a younger son of Sir Thomas Lundie of Pratis. David first married Elizabeth Lundie, daughter of Robert Lundie 1st of Balgonie, Lord High Treasurer of Scotland, and relict of Sir John Lindsay of Pitcruvie, Master of Lindsay, sometime after 1525. He secondly married Helen, daughter and heir apparent of Adam Stewart of Breriehill. In 1540, according to the annals of Dunfermline, the Abbot of Dunfermline granted a charter to David Lundie and his spouse Helen Stewart.

The following text is taken from the Annals of Dunfermline:

"George, archdecon of St. Andrews, and Commendator of Dunfermline, concedes to Helena Stewart, daughter and apparent heiress of Adam Stewart, of Brerhill, and David Lundy, sponso dictae Helena, the lands of Breryhill adjacent to the burgh of Dunfermline on the east part, and the lands of Mylhillis on the east part of the 'Newrow' croft, commonly called the 'Newraw-crofts;' the lands of Penelandes on the east part; the lands of Spittel on the south part; and those of Elliotshill on the west part. Also a small parcel of land, commonly called the 'Cluttis' croft, adjacent, within the regality of Dunfermline; and the narrow crofts in the burgh of Dunfirmline, on the west part of the lands of Halbank; and the north part of the lands of Brerehill, on the east and south parts; and the lands of Halbank adjacent, in the regality of Dunfermline."

David was one of a number of persons found guilty of involvement in the slaughter of James Borthwick, John Anderson and John Balzeat, during a disagreement between the laird of Ardross, and the Prior of Pittenweem. As a result, on the 11th of October 1531, a gift of the goods belonging to David, both movable and unmovable, was given to David's brother, Walter Lundy of that Ilk, by the King (*Reg. Sec. Sig.* II. 1029). David predeceased Helen, who re-married to James Herper in Drumtuhill in the Parish of Dunfermline. David died before 1592 as, on the 8th of March that year, an instrument of sasine was made in favour of Laurence Adesoun, baker, indweller in Leith, of the lands of Pennylandis in the parish and regality of Dunfermling, sheriffdom of Fiffe, under reservation of liferent to Helen Stewart, widow of David Lundy of Breryhill (*NAS*, B34/20/47-9). Helen died before February 1603.

David and Helen had issue:-

1   *Rev. George Lundie*, succeeded

REV. GEORGE LUNDIE OF BRERIEHILL

Sometime in 1565, he was given a Feu-Tack of the Abbey lands of Breryhill, Pennylands, Cloudscroft, Hallbank, and croft of New Raw (*Annals of Dunfermline*). He was a reader in the Regent's House in February 1568. He was admitted to the Parish of Newburn in 1570, at which point he is also described as minister of the Parish of Largo. He subsequently transferred to the parish of Dalmeny in 1574. At this time, until 1577, he also had under his charge the parishes of Aldcathie, Abercorn and Cramond. In the Assembly 1575, the Bishop of Dunkeld was complained upon for having written a letter to Rev. Lundie to serve equally four kirks, by course, on the Lords day upon pain of deprivation. In 1576, a Richard Brown was appointed as a reader to help the Rev. Lundie. On the 11th of April 1580, James VI presented Rev. Lundie to the vicarage of Dalmeny. In 1586, George is mentioned as principal on a bond of caution for 300 merks, put up be James Rig of Carbarrie, in order that George will not harm a Mathew Keir, servant to Harry Stewart of Cragyhall, his tenants or servants (*Reg. Privy Council*, Series I. IV. 132).

From details of "ministers troubled in the execution of their offiece and possession of their manses and glebis" it would appear the George had trouble with Harry Stewart of Craggyhall's brother James. In 1590 it was stated that "George Lundie wes cruellie persewit of his lyiff be James Stewart, brother to the Laird of Craigiehall, four yeiris syne, and yit insistis in his malice" (*Reg. Privy Council*. Series I. XIV. 374)

George transferred to minister the Parish of Pentland on the 21st of November 1587, but continued to reside at Dalmeny. On the 8th of July 1592 he was transferred and installed to the Parish of Pencuik Roslin. George died before the end of the year (*Edin. Tests.*). He was married to Katherine Loch, by whom he had issue:-

1   *George Lundie*, who succeeded
2   *James Lundie*, baptized 8th May 1577
3   *Susanna Lundie*, baptized 5th November 1578
4   *Margaret Lundie*, born 1st June 1580 in Dunfermline.

GEORGE LUNDIE OF BERRIEHILL

In 1592, he was served as heir to his father, George Lundie of Berriehill in, amongst other things, the land of Berriehill, the land of Pennyland, ¼ of the land of Ovirgrange Wester in the Parish of Kinghorn and the land of Halbank (*Inq. Spec. Ret. Fife*, No. 1512). On the 17th of March 1596, George and his spouse granted a charter in favour of Laurence Adisoun, baker and indweller in Leith, of an annualrent of £20 Scots furth of the 5 acres of land called Pennielandis lying near the burgh of Dunfermlyne in parish and regality thereof, in the sheriffdom of Fife. They gave sasine on the 13th of May that year. This charter was later confirmed by King James VI and Queen Anne, Lady of Dunfermline, in 1611. George later sold the lands to James Spens of Wormiston (*East Neuk of Fife*).

Lundie of Bruntshiels.

JAMES LUNDIE OF BRUNTSHIELS

James appears in the register of deeds in 1697. (RD. 4/81/321). This may well be another spelling of Bruntshcolls, which is an estate asociated with the Lundie family through the marriage of Anna Lundie, daughter of Captain James Lundie of Drumeldrie (himself the brother to John Lundie 8th of Strathairlie), to Nathaniel White of Bruntscholls in 1680.

Lundie of Clatto

The lands of Clatto are within the Parish of St. Andrews, Fife. They came into the possession of the Lundie family when they were purchased in 1667. At that time it is believed there was a castle at Clatto. Reference to this castle is first made in 1550, with a charter making reference to the 'fortalice of Clatto.' Whatever this building was, it no longer exists (*Fife, pictoral and historical*, I., 217).

GEORGE LUNDIE IN SALTGREIN

The fourth son of John Lundie of that Ilk, except for an agreement made between Robert Maitland, later Lundin, and George's brother John, and George himself, George should have become Laird upon the death of his brother John Lundie of that Ilk (*Lundins of Fife*). He married a Margaret Lundie, the daughter of Robert Lundie 8th of Balgonie (*PRS Fife and Kinross*, X. 41; *Lamont's Diary*, p 86). He died before 1655 (*East Neuk of Fife*, p 51). They had issue:-

1   *James Lundie of Clatto*.

2   *Margaret Lundie*, the eldest daughter, married Alexander Nairne, a St. Andrews man, and bailie of the Earl of Wemyss, on October 26th 1666, at Saltgrein. The marriage feast was at St. Andrews (*Lamont's Diary*, p 193). She died before 1670 (*East Neuk of Fife*, p 51).

3   *Eupham Lundie*, died on the 11th of August 1664, at Ardross, of "the Cruells in hir knee, which issue did run some yeirs before hir death." She was interred on the 12th of August in Crail (*Lamont's Diary*, p 171).

4   *Catherine Lundie*, died in 1662 (*East Neuk of Fife*, p 51)

5   *Magdalene Lundie*, the youngest daughter married Thomas Trail of Blebo-Hole, June 19th 1663. The marriage feast was held at Lundie, and her 'portion,' that he received upon marriage, was 500 merks, which was resting with Lady Lundie (*Lamont's Diary*, p 163). On the 4th of June 1663, John Traill of Bleboholl, granted a charter in favour of Thomas Traill, his eldest son, and Magdalen Lundie, daughter of deceased George Lundie, brother german of deceased John Lundie of that Ilk, his future spouse, of the lands of Bleboholl to be held de me of the said John Traill. This charter followed a contract of marriage of the same date between the said John Traill, Thomas Traill and Magdalen Lundie, with consent of Mr. James Lundie her brother german (*NAS*, GD7/2/121-2). A letter written by Magdalene to Lady Margaret Lundin still survives. It concerns two hundred and fifty merks Scots, which comprised a years interest of five thousand merks Scots, held by Lady Lundin, and belonging to Margaret and her brothers and sisters. This letter was witnessed by John Lundin Baylic in St Andrews, and Mr Allan Lawmonth (*NAS*, GD160/282, No. 13).

Margaret died before 1681 (*East Neuk of Fife*). She had issue;
    i   John Trail
    ii Thomas Trail
    iii James Trail
    iv Margaret Trail

JAMES LUNDIE OF CLATTO

At the time of his father's death he, and his sisters were all minors. Lamont's Diary records their choice of curators – "James Lundy, sone to the deceased George Lundy in Saltgreine, with his two eldest sisters, did nominate and choose 7 gentlemen for to be ther curators. This was done att Cuper, before Balfarge, shriffe of Fyfe, in the Tol-booth of Cuper, att the ordinary time of the sitting of the shyrra court. The persons chosen were these, viz. James Lundy of Straerlie; Mr George Weyms, Principall of St Leonards Colledge in St Androus; James Preston, sone to the Laird of Erdree; J . . . Lundy of Drums, and Andro Lundy, his brother; Dauid Lundy of Conland, and James Lundy in Saltgrein, his brother; (thir two last are uncles to the said cheldren.). Ther means is five and twentie thousand marks, in the hands of the Laird of Lundy, and elder brother to the said George Lundy. Jun. 5, 1665, the said James Lundy, two youngest sisters nominated the forsaid 7 gentlemen for ther curators also. (in the forsaid place at Cuper), with the Laird of Ayton, (bot he refused att that time to acept)" (*Lamont's Diary*, p 86). James married Margaret Bethune, daughter of Andrew Bethune of Blebo, in 1663 (*East Neuk of Fife*, p 51). In 1667 he purchased the estate of Clatto – "1667 – The yeir before, Mr James Lundin in Blebo, formerly mentioned, bowght the lands of Klatto, nire to itt, from Robert Hamilton, owner of itt, apparent aire of Kilbrackmont, it stood him abowt 10,800 merks Scots, and was estimat abowt 600 merks a yeire" (*Lamont's Diary*, p 199). Soon after James's purchase, there appears in the records a Thomas Lundie of Clatto. He appears as a grantee of a discharge on the 22nd of December, 1673 (*Index Reg. Deeds*, Dal. XXXVI., 439). His relationship to James is unknown. James died before 28th August 1691. He and Margaret had issue (*Lundins of Fife*):
1   ***Catherine Lundie***, baptised August 11th 1666.
2   ***James Lundie***, died before 1709.
3   ***Alisone Lundie***, alive 1708

4   *John Lundie*
5   *Mary Lundie*

In the description of the testament of James, eldest son of James Lundie of Clatto, he does not appear with the designation 'of Clatto'. It is not known what happened to this estate upon the death of James Lundie of Clatto.

Lundy of Demperstoun

ANDREW LUNDY OF DEMPERSTOUN

On the 17th of April, 1491, Robert Lundy of Balgonie granted a charter in favour of Thomas Schethum of that Ilk, of an annualrent of 13 merks out of lands of Schethum south of the River Leven. Amongst others, this charter was witnessed by an Andrew Lundy of Demperstoun (*NAS*, GD26/3/32). The lands of Demperston were shortly afterwards held by Scott of Balwearie. Sir William Scott of Balwearie, who was married to Janet Lundie, the daughter of Sir Thomas Lundie of Pratis, granted an annual rent of these lands to his nephew, John Lundie, the heir apparent of William Lundie of that Ilk, before 1532.

The House of Glasswell, formerly of Kinnoull.

MALE LUNDIE
1   *Robert Lundie*, merchant burgess of Dundee. On the 21st of May, 1629; at Cartoquhy, Auchmelchy; James, Lord Ogilvy, gave a bond to Robert Lundie, merchant burgess of Dundee, for 2000 merks Scots. This is the same date that James gave bond to Robert's brother Thomas. Robert gave discharge of this on the 12 of November 1634 (*NAS*, GD16/42/152). On the 19th of November, 1644, he was censured for running away from the City of Dundee, when the Marquis of Montrose and his army approached. He was outlawed for deserting the town, and had his assets seized in order to pay a 400 merk fine. On the 13th of January the following year, a fine of 300 merks was taken from him. He died before September 18th 1661, his

nephew, Thomas Lundie, minister of Rattray was served as his heir (*Gen. Retour*, No. 4499).

2   ***Thomas Lundie***, minister of Alyth, of whom next.

THOMAS LUNDIE, MINISTER OF ALYTH

Thomas was born in 1579; he received an M.A. from St. Andrews University in 1598. Most probably he is the Thomas Lundie who appears author of the book "Vtrum Romanus sit Antichristus necne?" published through St. Andrews University by R. Waldegrave, Edinburgh, in 1602; held by the National Library of Scotland. He was admitted as minister to the parish of Alyth in 1602. He married Jean Blair, daughter of Patrick Blair of Ardblair by Elizabeth Ramsay, herself the daughter of George Ramsay of Banff by Elizabeth his wife, daughter of Laurence Mercer of Aldie (*Scots Baronage; Blairs of Balthaylock and their Cadets*). Johanna died of fever on the 22nd of May, 1636, aged 43. Thomas died "as though of a fever brought on by grief" on the 8th of June 1636. He was "revered for his piety and renowned for his blameless character." A monument was erected to them both in Alyth Church, by the Rev. J. Robertson, in 1748, who was minister of Alyth at the time (*Stat. Acc. Scot.* 1845). The account described it as a plain stone monument, located near to the pulpit. The church this monument was in was pulled down soon after that particular account was written, and today (2005) very little now remains. Luckily attached to one of the remaining walls of the ruin is the remains of the plaque in question. As the church is now open to the elements, this has taken its toll on the monument, and the inscription (in Latin) is hard to make out. What is very important to note is that above the plaque are carved the ancient arms of Lundie (three pallets surmounted of a bend charged with three tasselled cushions): halved with those of Blair (for Thomas's wife Jean). This carving is still in a fine state of repair.

On the 20th of June, 1622, at Cloway, a contract of wadset was made between Sir David Ogilvy of Cloway, kt., with the consent of Euphame Young, his spouse, on the one part, and Mr. Thomas Lundie, minister at Alicht and Jean Blair, his spouse, on the other part.

Sir David wadset to Thomas and Jean, in conjunct fee, the lands of Morentie and, in special warrandice thereof, an annualrent of 300 merks Scots furth of the lands of Cloway and Cortoquhy, under reversion for 2500 merks Scots. A Charter de me followed thereon. This was dated the same.

Thomas and Jean were given sasine of the lands of Morentie, on the 3rd of January, 1623. This was registered in the P.R.S Perth on the19th of February, 1623. They were given sasine of the said annualrent on the 8th of November 1624. Which was registered P.R.S. Forfar, on the 11th of November 1624. An instrument of requisition by Thomas Lundie to Sir David and James, Lord Ogilvy, to redeem these lands, was given on the 31st of January 1625.

On the 20th of January, 1626, at Morentie, Nether Kirk of Airlie, a contract of wadset was made between James, Lord Ogilvy, with the consent of Isobel Hamiltoun, his spouse, on the one part and Mr. Thomas Lundie, minister at Alyth and Jean Blair, his spouse, on the other part whereby Lord Ogilvy wadset to Thomas and Jean, in conjunct fee, the lands of Morentie and, in special warrandice thereof, annualrent of 300 merks Scots furth of the lands of Cortoquhy, under reversion for 2500 merks Scots. Thomas and Jean gave discharge and renunciation of the foresaid lands and annualrent to James, Lord Ogilvy, in name of Sir David on the 20th of January 1627. This was registered in the General Register of Sasines on the 1st of February 1627 (*NAS*, GD16/12/188-189). On the 21st of May, 1629, dated at Cortoquhy, James, Lord Ogilvy, with John Ogilvy of Galay and Alexander Lyndesay at the mill of Ratwall as cautioners, gave bond to Mr. Thomas Lundie, minister at Alycht and Grisel and Magdalen Lundies, his daughters, for £1000 Scots (*NAS*, GD16/42/153). On the 9th of July that year, dated at the Kirk of Kingoldrum, James, Lord Ogilvy gave a second bond to Thomas Lundie, for £81 6s. 8d. Scots in payment of all buildings erected by him on the lands and mains of Morentie (*NAS*, GD16/42/156).

Sometime between 1627 and 1628, Thomas was put at the horn, for not paying his taxes (*Register of the Privy Council of Scotland*, Series II, II., 522). Sometime between the 15th and 27th of August, 1632, at Alyth, James, Lord Ogilvy, with Alexander Ramsay of the mill of Innerqueich, Alexander Ramsay in Alyth, John Rattray in Balquhome and Archibald Campbell in Balloch as cautioners; gave a heritable bond to Mr. Thomas Lundie, minister at Alyth and Jean Blair, his spouse, in conjunct fee, of annualrent of 250 merks Scots furth of lands unspecified on principal sum of 2500 merks Scots (*NAS*, GD16/1/44). Between the 18th and 27th of December, 1633, James, Lord Ogilvy, with Sir John Ogilvy of Innerquharritie and Sir Patrick Ogilvy of Inschmerteine as cautioners, gave a heritable bond to Mr. Thomas Lundie, minister at Alyth, of annualrent of 300 merks Scots furth of lands unspecified on principal sum of 3000 merks Scots (*NAS*, GD16/1/45).

He had issue:

1 **Thomas Lundie**, minister of Rattray, whose details follow.

2 **Grizel Lundie**, baptized on the 9th of January, 1625

3 **Isobel Lundie**, baptized on the 9th of January, 1625

4 **Magdalen Lundie**, baptized on the 14th of March 1627

5 **Jean Lundie**, married George Chalmers, portitioner of Banchory

6 **James Lundie**, baptized on the 6th of April 1630, apprentice to John Fish, merchant in Edinburgh, 10th of February, 1647 (*Reg. Appren. Edin.*).

7 **Robert Lundie**, baptized on the 6th of April, 1630, died young

8 **Robert Lundie**, baptized June, 1634.

It should be noted that around this same time, a James Lundie married Janet Niven on the 11th of June, 1626, in the Parish of Alyth, Perth, Scotland. It is very probable that James was related to Thomas.

THOMAS LUNDIE OF KINNOULL, MINISTER OF RATTRAY

Educated at the University of St. Andrew's, M.A. July 1635. He was presented to the sub-chantry of Dunkeld in 1636, and admitted prior to the 9th of May 1637. He was succentor of Dunkeld Cathedral in 1637. By 1648, he was minister of Rattray, being presented to the kirk, parsonage and vicarage of Rattray, by Charles I (*NAS*, GD385/Bundle 229) . He is designed as such when giving discharge to James, Earl of Airlie, of a bond (dated 22nd and 26th July 1636), on the 5th of June, 1648 (*NAS*, GD16/42/243).

On the 11th of May 1649, Thomas was a Chaplain to the army: On the 9th of August the same year, he received a charter of confirmation under the Great Seal, of a charter granting to him the lands of Parkheid in the Parish of Blair, Perthshire; lands previously belonging to Ireland of Parkheid (*Reg. Mag. Sig*. IX. 2116): On the 30th of November 1649, he had gift of the Treasury of Dunkeld from King Charles I: He joined the Protesters in 1651, becoming a member of their Presbytery: He was served as heir to his father on the 12th of January, 1653 (*Gen. Retours*, No. 3732).

On the 22nd of November 1659 he subscribed to "The testimony to the truth of Jesus Christ; or, to the doctrine, worship, discipline, and government of the Kirk of Scotland; and to the National Covenants, against the prevailing errors, heresies, blasphemies, &c. &c. By the ministers of Perth and Fife."

REVEREND and dear brethren, being informed that you are upon thoughts of causing print the Testimony, given by you in behalf of the doctrine, worship, discipline, and government of the kirk of Scotland, and of the national covenant, and solemn league and covenant, and the work of uniformity in religion, and against the errors, heresies, and blasphemies of the times, and the toleration thereof, &c. And taking to our serious consideration the manifold dangers that do threaten religion, and the work of God in these nations, especially in this church, with the continuance and increase thereof day by day: We could not but encourage you therein; and for the exoneration of our own souls, join with you as joint witnesses in those matters. We could have wished, and we know, so also could ye, that there had been a new draught fitted in every thing, to the present state and condition of the time, and to the workings of the spirit of delusion therein: and in a special way taking notice of that unhappy petition lately subscribed and promoted by some few of our countrymen, in behalf of that vast toleration that is now on foot in these nations; a petition that we are the more bound to witness against, because it is commonly reported, and we believe, not without ground, to be subscribed by Mr. Thomas Ireland, who did once profess himself to be of our number, whose miscarriage in that particular, as we desire to be humbled before God for it, so we judge it our duty, and we know also, so do ye, to bear witness against it before the world; but knowing that it would take a long time before a new draught of a testimony could be condescended upon, by these that live at such a distance, especially in the winter season; we thought it better to encourage you to publish this, and to take hold of the present opportunity of signifying our consent thereunto, than to delay, being altogether uncertain what the present confusions might bring forth. That we did not at the first subscribing join therein, was not upon any dissatisfaction upon the matter which it contains, we being abundantly clear in that from the beginning, but some of us were cut off from the occasion, by physical impediments, and others knowing that there was at that time some endeavours and expectation of and address to be made by several synods, to the civil powers, for remedying of the evils which you then thought fit to witness against, in such way, they judged it more expedient for the time, to delay the giving of any such testimony, until these addresses should prove ineffectual: and there being now no access thereunto, we are very free to homologate your Testimony, and do hereby declare our consent and adherence to the same, desiring that it may be construed of the world, and accepted of God, not only as yours, but as ours and yours jointly: So commending you to the grace of God, we continue

Your very affectionate brethren in our Lord Jesus Christ,

Mr. Thomas Lundie, minister at Ratray.
— James Symson, minister at Airth.
— George Murray, minister at Fouls.
— Robert Rule, minister at Stirling.
— Thomas Hogg, minister at Lerber.
— Thomas Glass, minister at Dunkell.
— James Strachan, minister at Dunkell.
— Gilbert Menzies, minister at Fortengel.
— Patrick Campbell, minister at Killin.

The original testimony that is referred to here, by ministers in Fife, is around 20 pages long, so for brevity is not included.

He was summoned before the Privy Council on the 24th of March 1663 for not obeying its Act of the 1st of October 1662 and "still labouring to keep the hearts of the people from the present government of Church and State." The full extract from the register of the Privy Council is given below.

Acta July 1661 – November 1667, pages 243-244

The Lords his majesties privy Council, being informed that there are severall ministers within the dioces of Dunkeld who not only, contrar to the order of Councill dated at Glasgow the first October last, doe continow at their former residences and churches, bot in manifest contempt thereof and contrar to the indulgence granted to them be the late act, dated 23 December last, doe persist in their wicked practices, still labouring to keip the hearts of the people from the present government of Church and State by their pernicious doctorin; and more particularly that Messrs Patrick Campbell, minister at Kilinne, Jon Andersone at Ochtergaven, Francis Person at Kirkmichael, David Graham at Forgundeny, Georg Halliburtoun at Duplin, Richard Forrett at Ava, John Miniman at Abernytt, Jon Cambell at Teling, David Campbell at Menmwir, Thomas Lundy at Ratry, Robert Cambell at Mullen, John Cruikshank at Regortoun, Thomas Glasse at Litle Dunkell, Andro Donaldson at Dalgety and Thomas Blak at Lesly are cheiff instruments in carying on that wicked course, therefor the saidis Lords of Councill ordains letters to be direct to charge the fornamit persons and everyone of them to remove themselves, thair wyves, bairnes, families, servants, goods and geir furth and frae their respective duelling places and manses and outwith the bounds of the presbyteries where they now live, and that they doe not take upon them to exercise any part of the ministeriall function either privetly or publictly; and alse command and charge them and every one of them to compear before the saidis Lords the . . . . . day of . . . . . to ansuer for their former disobedience, with certification.

Series III, Volume I. pages 650-651: (1663)

He was deposed by the bishop in October 1664. He was seized in the lands of Powburn Scotstoun and Kirktoun in 1666. Thomas died before 14th July 1670. He features in an interesting book entitled "Some predictions or prophesies, of severals of the Reverend and worthy servants of the Lord, viz. Mr. Thomas Lundie, Mr. Samuel Rutherford, Mr. John Welsh, Mr. Richard Cameron, Mr. Alexander Peden ... : To which is added, a letter written by Mr. John MacClelland ... Likewise, an account of an apparition in the Castle of Edinburgh, in the year 1651 or 1652.," which was published in 1739, and is held by both the British Library and National Library of

Scotland (as is the testimony which is quoted above). His 'prophesy' reads as follows:

> "Mr *Thomas Lundy*, a godly Minister at *Rattery* in the North, and his Sister, a Lady in that Country, who died *anno* 1693, gave the following account to a godly Gentleman.
>
> This that followeth is written word for word, without either adding or pareing, out of a book, entituled, *A brief refutation of the errors of toleration, erastinism, independancy, and separation*, delivered in some sermons from I *John* iv. preached in the year 1652, by the revered Mr. *James Fergusson* late minister of the gospel at *Kilwining*.
>
> In his second use, of his refuting toleration, he saith, Hence see what an account those magistrates have to make, who make no use of their power this way for God, if they get their own houses built, cares not for his: If rebellion against themselves be curbed, cares not for the curbing of rebellion against God.
>
> This was the sin of the parliament of *England* though they entered into a Covenant with the Most High God, that they would suppress error and heresy, they never employed their power that way; and that because they durst not for angering of their army, and therefore God hath suffered their army to overturn them, and set themselves, and whom they please, in their place: And now they, by their practice, give toleration to all, and this is the way to strengthen them. I say, in the name of the Lord, if they repent not, it shall be the way to ruin them, a people swearing in their low condition to root out heresy &c. and God blessing them from that day; and within a few years carrying themselves as if they had sworn to do the contrary, to suffer all, encourage all, in spite of all the devils in hell, to vent what blasphemies they please, and for their encouragement, to give them surety, that no power in *Britain* shall hinder them. Was there ever such affront done to God? Think ye, that he will sit with it? No, if he should make the one half avengers of a broken covenant, against the other, he will not. It is noted of *Asa*, 2 *Chron.* xiv. 5. God's way, to keep magistrates sure, and their kingdom quiet, is to be zealous against false worship: No, but (say they) the way is not to anger heretics,

they are the surest pillars of our common-weath, but wo to, and will be to that common-wealth that is builded on such pillars. And if *Scotland*, or any party in it join with them on these terms, our wo is but coming. He is jealous God chiefly in the mater of his service, as is clear from the second command.

The said Mr. *Thomas Lundie*, after some sickness, and seeming to recover again, which comforted; but one morning staying longer in his chamber than ordinary, his sister, the foresaid lady, knocking at his chamber door, who opening it, she found him more than ordinary weighted, she ask'd him the reason, seeing he was now better; whereupon, smilling he said, sister, within a few hours I will be taken from you. But alas! for the days I have seen upon Scotland, the Lord has let mess see the French going with their armies through the breadth and length of the land, marching to their bridles reins in the blood of all ranks, and all that for a broken covenant, but neither you nor I will see it."

Thomas married Anna Somerville who died July 1682. Her testament is recorded in the Commissary court of St. Andrew's on the 6th October. They had issue:-

1   ***Thomas Lundie of Glasswell***

2   ***Anna Lundie***, married George Kerr of Labothie, merchant of Dundee (*PRS Forfar*).

3   ***Margaret Lundie,*** married Alexander Leslie (Lessly) of Glasswell (*Index Reg. Deeds*, Dal. LXX., 295, 344). They were married on the 25th of March, 1675, in Edinburgh.

THOMAS LUNDIE, 1ST OF GLASSWELL, FORMERLY 2ND OF KINNOULL

Christened on the 28th of September 1660, at Rattray, Perth; he was served heir to his father, Thomas Lundie of Kinnoull, January 7th 1686 (*Gen. Retours*, No. 6695). In 1690 he appears in an act of parliament, named as a commissioner of supply for Forfar (*General index to the acts of parliament of Scotland*). He was also a factor for the managers and commissioners on the estate of James Marquis of Douglas (*Index Reg. Deeds*, RD. 4/90/528).

He married Margaret Colvill on 10th August 1686. Margaret was the only daughter and heiress of David Colvill (brother to Robert 2nd Lord Colvill of Ochiltree; the 1st Lord Colvill of Ochiltree being his uncle), and Margaret Berkley, (daughter of Michael Berkley). They had issue:

1 *Robert Lundie*, born on the 16th of November 1690, Edinburgh Parish, Midlothian. He predeceased his father.

2 *Margaret Lundie*. In the testament of her father, she is described as the only surviving daughter of himself and Margaret Colvill. The testament makes reference to a bond of one thousand pounds, granted to Margaret Barclay, her grandmother, by David Beatoun of Balfour, younger, which was assigned to Margaret Lundie, on the 17th of April 1692.

3 *Thomas Lundie*, christened on the 12th of May, 1693, Edinburgh Parish, Midlothian. He predeceased his father.

4 *David Lundie*, christened on the 16th of August, 1694, Edinburgh Parish, Midlothian. He predeceased his father.

5 *George Lundie, 2nd of Glasswell*, he succeeded his father to Glasswell, and his details follow.

Thomas later married Janet Bruce on the 9th of June 1701. On the 20th February 1708 Thomas, designed, 'Thomas Lundy of Glasswell, bailie of the regality of Kirriemuir,' gave a discharge to Alexander Wedderburne of that Ilk, for all fines due to the court of Kirriemuir, for his absence of the head courts (*NAS*, GD137/3152). Thomas died in August 1716. His tetament was proved on the 16th October 1717, (*Brechin Comm. Court*). He also had issue by Janet:-

1 *John Lundie*, christened 15th January 1702, Dundee, Angus. He was a merchant in Dundee, He died, unmarried before 27th March 1730.

2 *Janet Lundie*, christened on the 2nd November 1703 in Dundee.

3 *Katherine Lundie*, christened on the 20th December 1704 in Dundee.

4 *male Lundie* christened on the 26th May 1707 in Dundee.

5 *William Lundie*, christened on the 26th May 1711 in Dundee.

GEORGE LUNDIE, 2ND OF GLASSWELL

Born on the 16th of June 1696, in Edinburgh Parish, Midlothian; he succeeded his father, being served heir general, on the 2nd of October 1718. On the 7th of March 1721, he was served as heir general to his grandfather, David Colvill, Nephew of Robert Lord Colvill of Ochiltree. On the 10th of September 1728, he was served heir of provision general, to Robert Watson, son of John Watson, merchant in Perth. In the same year he disponed the lands of Glasswell and Tairbirns to John Brown, a merchant in Dundee (*Petition for Robert Fletcher of Balinsho*).

George was still alive in 1766. Crail Deeds record him, in a settlement, living in St. Andrews; and designed 'late of Glasswell,' (*Crail Deeds*, B65/5/5 Pp 182-87; B65/22/37).

- - - - - - - -

Remembering that Glasswell was withing the Parish of Kirriemuir, in connection to this family we should take note of a *JOHN LUNDIE*, who was a farmer in that Parish, and so may well have been a descendant of the Glasswell line. He had one son, David Lundie, who married an Elizabeth Lawson daughter of the late John Lawson, farmer in the parish of Humbie, on the 7th of January 1739, in South Kirk Parish, Edinburgh (*Ed. Reg. Mar.*).

And also another *JOHN LUNDIE*, who had three children christened in that parish in the early 18th century:
1   *John Lundie*, christened on the 29th of June 1737.
2   *David Lundie*, christened on the 1st of January 1739.
3   *Charles Lundie*, christened on the 30th of October 1753.

I will also make mention of *JOHN LUNDIE*, a weaver on the Loanhead of Lour, Parish of Forfar, adjacent to Kirriemuir, who is listed in the muster roll the Forfarshire or Lord Ogilvy's regiment, in the rebellion of 1745.

The House of Huttonspittle and of Spittle

The name Spittle generally originates from lands belonging to a hospital, 'spital lands'. Spittle lands have already been mentioned in the discussion of Lundie of that Ilk, Lundie of Breriehill and Lundie of Balgonie. It is not an uncommon name for lands. There are two Lundie families designated as 'of Spittle'. The first is Lundie of Spittle, or Hutton Spittle, in the Parish of Hutton, Berwickshire. The second is Lundie of Spittal, in Fife. In the later case, the lands are also known as Innerlochtie, and the family as Lundie of Innerlochtie; this will be discussed under the title Innerlochtie; here we shall concern ourselves with the former family from Berwick.

ALLAN LUNDIE OF HUTTONSPITTLE

Minister of the Parish of Lessudden, also known as St. Boswells. He studied at St Salvator's College, and had his degree from the University of St Andrews on the 10th of December 1586. During his time at St. Andrews, 1595, he was clerk to the Presbytery there (*Univ. St. And. Munim.* SS110G10.25). James VI presented him to the Vicarage of St. Boswells on the 7th of April 1596. He was charged by the Presbytery on the 20th of September 1608 "with negligence in his calling, and not ministering the communion, overstrait in exacting the vicarage, ane player at cardis, blamit with beiring companie, and impatient of reproof and admonition" – "the brether admonish him gentlie". Being also admonished on the 3rd of April 1610, "to attend his ministrie, and increase in diligence, to be earnest for repairing his kirk, to teach in the afternoon, and to abstain from carding, all which admonitions he took verie weel", he was transferred to Hassendean in 1610, which was changed for Channelkirk in 1611, and Hutton and Fishwick in 1614. He was no longer minister there in 1636, as by this time his son was minister there (*FASTI*). On the 17th June, 1634, James Home of Cowdenknows, disponed to Mr Alan Lundie, minister at Huttoun, and James Trotter, merchant, burgess of Edinburgh, room and lands in the east end of town of Fogo, extending to 3 husbandlands and 7 acres, in town and territory of Fogo, sheriffdom of Berwick (*NAS*, GD158/163). Allan died on the 24th August 1648 (*Index Retours 1700-1851*). His ancestry is yet unknown. He was married to Agnes Trottar (*PRS Berwick*). They had issue:

1   *James Lundie*, of whom next
2   *William Lundie*, most probably William Lundie of the Wester

Vaults of Whitsome (see that family), (*PRS Berwick, FASTI*)
3   John Lundie of Todrig and Little Todrig (see that family).
4   Andrew Lundie
5   Elizabeth Lundie, married John Dicksone of Newbiging (*PRS. Berwick*)

JAMES LUNDIE, 2ND OF HUTTON AND SPITTAL

James was presented to the combined parish of Fishwick and Hutton, by the crown, in 1636. He was deposed, with the approval of the assembly, in 1649 (*Dec. Court Sess. Till 1764*; III. 213-5) . He married Katherine Home of Abbey St. Bathans. They had at least two children. On the 7th of December 1675, a bond was registered which he had granted to his brother William, and Agnes Lundie, spouse to Mr Patrick Smith, minister of Tweedmouth (also minister of Chirnside) (*Dur*. XXXX. 80.). Although the relationship between James and Agnes is not known, one asumes it to be prety close (sister/niece/daughter).

1   James Lundie, 3rd of Huttonspittle, whose details follow.
2   Alexander Lundie. (*Index Reg. Deeds*, Dur. LXVI. 34).

JAMES LUNDIE, 3RD OF HUTTONSPITTLE

On the 17th of August 1683, James Lundie of Huttonspittle was served as heir to his grandfather, Allan Lundie, minister of Hutton, in the lands of Spitle in the Sheriffdom of Berwick (*Inq. Spec. Ret. Berwick,* No. 413). On the 22nd of December, 1668 there is a disposition by Alexander Trotter of Eistend of Fogo to Mr. James Lundie of Hutton Spittell, and Alexander Lundie, his youngest son by his first wife (*NAS*, GD158/163). One of is wives was Janet Home (*PRS Berwick*).
1   James Lundie, 4th of Huttonspittle, succeeded his father (*PRS Berwick*)
2   Alexander Lundie, youngest son by first wife, alive in 1668 (*NAS*, GD158/163).
3   Katherine Lundie, married James Lundie, son of John Lundie of Todrig (PRS Berwick).

JAMES LUNDIE, 4ᵀᴴ OF HUTTONSPITTLE

On the 5ᵗʰ of October 1695, James Lundie of Huttonspittel was served heir to his father, 'Magistri' James Lundie of Huttonspittle (*Gen. Retour*, No. 7619). He appears again in the Retours Service of heirs, on the 20ᵗʰ December 1701, when again being served as heir to his father; and also on the 4ᵗʰ of November 1703, being served as heir special to his great grandfather, in the lands of Hutton Spittle. James Lundie of Hutton Spittle died before 31ˢᵗ July 1711, (*Lauder Commissary Court*). He was married to Margaret Christieson, they had issue:

1   *James Lundie, 5ᵗʰ of Spittle*, whose details follow.

2   *Jean (or Jane) Lundie*, married to Alexander Christison portitioner of Hutton (*PRS Berwick*)

3   *Katherine Lundie*, married David Denholm of Cranshaws (*Scot. Hist. Rev.* I. 461). Katherine died in 1748, her spouse in 1717. Katherine's testament is registered with Lauder Commissary Court on the 14ᵗʰ of June, and 9ᵗʰ of August, 1748. They had issue:-

i   *James Denholm of Cranshaws.* He succeeded his father, and upon the death of his uncle, James Lundie of Spittle, he laid claim to his estate as nearest heir.

ii   David Denholm

iii   Walter Denholm

iv   Margaret Denholm

v   Jean Denholm

JAMES LUNDIE, 5ᵀᴴ OF SPITTLE

James was married to Mary Mow, daughter of John Mow of East Mains. James died before the 15ᵗʰ of May 1739 (*Lauder Commissary Court*). Mary remarried to William Stow upon which he took the name of Lundie. It seems strange for the family holding the estate following James's death to take upon the additional name of Lundie, without any blood ties to the family, however, none have yet been found.

Stow-Lundie of Spittal

DAVID STOW

On the 29th of September 1680, David married Anne Selby. David's father was also a David Stow. Anne is believed the daughter of Oliver Selby. David died in 1733, and was buried on the 16th of January of that year in Holy Cross Church, Berwick. They had issue:-

1   *William Stow (Lundie)*, of whom later

2   *Richard Stow*, christened on the 14th July 1682, Holy Cross, Berwick. He married Mrs. Margaret Coulson on the 26th August 1708, in Stannington, Northumberland. He died in 1744.

3   *George Stow*, christened on the 6th April 1684. He married Sarah Watson on the 26th June 1715 in Tynemouth, Northumberland. He died in 1687, being buried at Holy Cross Church Berwick on the 26th of January that year.

4   *David Stow*, christened in November 1690 at Holy Cross Church, Berwick.

5   *Anne Stow*, christened on the 30th June 1695, at Holy Cross Church, Berwick.

6   *John Stow*, christened on the 6th October 1698, at Holy Cross Church, Berwick.

WILLIAM STOW (LUNDIE) OF SPITTAL

As Mayor of Berwick in 1745, he appears designed as William Stow Lundie, rather than simply William Stow, taking the name of his mothers first husband, for reasons (as discussed above) as have yet to be established (*NAS*, GD158/2574). He was twice married: firstly to Anna Blake; they married on the 14th of February 1727 at Norham in Northumberland: Secondly to Mary Mow sometime between 1732 and 1736. He had issue by both wives:

By Anne Blake:

1   *Ann Stow*, christened on the 14th of October 1729, at Holy Cross church. Berwick. She died two years later and was buried on the 30th of July 1731 at Holy Cross.

2   *David Stow*, christened on the 9th of March 1732 at Holy Cross Church, Berwick. He died two months later and was buried on the

20th of May of that year, at Holy Cross.

By Mary Mow

1   ***Blake Stow (Lundie)***, of whom later

2   ***Sarah***, christened on the 16th of January 1736 at Holy Cross church, Berwick. She married the Rev. John Foster, and died in 1824.

3   ***Isabel***, christened on the 30th of August 1737, at Holy Cross church, Berwick.

4   ***Ann***, christened on the 9th of July 1741, at Holy Cross church, Berwick. She married the Rev. William Johnston Temple on the 6th of August 1767 at Holy Cross church, Berwick. She died on the 14th of March 1793, in Cornwall

5   ***William***, born on the 11th of February 1740, he was christened on the 14th of March that year at Holy Cross church in Berwick. He died in 1740, being buried at Holy Cross on the 5th of October 1740.

BLAKE STOW LUNDIE ESQ. OF SPITTAL

Born on the 21st of September 1739 in Twizedale, Northumberland; he was christened on the 24th of October that year in Holy Cross Church, Berwick. He was twice married: firstly to Mary Foster, on the 10th Of October 1772: Secondly to Sarah Plank, on the 6th of March 1779, at St. Martin in the Fields. He died on the 19th of August 1808, being buried at Holy Cross Church, Berwick. His testament at Lauder Commissary Court is dated the 26th of November 1809. His probate will, held at Kew, is dated the 9th of January 1809. He has issue by his first wife:

1   ***Rev. William Stow Lundie of Spittal***, who succeeded his father in Spittal, and whose details follow.

2   ***James Stow Lundie***, christened on the 24th of November 1774, at Berwick. He must have died without issue, as his sister Mary was closest heir to his elder brother William.

3   ***Mary Stow Lundie***, christened on the 18th of October 1775, at Berwick. She must have died very young.

4   ***Mary Stow Lundie***, christened on the 22nd of November 1777, at Berwick. She married the Rev. William Compton. She succeeded

her brother William to Spittal.

5   *Elenora Stow Lundie*, Christened on the 25th of July 1778 at Edinburgh Blotter, Edinburgh, Midlothian.

6   *Martha Stow Lundie*, implied as a daughter of Blake Stow, died in 1851, in East Grinstead, Sussex (*Eng. Wales Civ. Reg. Ind.*, 1a, 354).

7   *John Stow Lundie*. By 1804 he was serving with the British Army in the 41st Regiment of Foot. He appears as Mess President of the 41st on the 2nd of November 1804. At this time the Regiment was based in Canada, and the Mess in Quebec. In 1805 Ensign John Stow Lundie, was part of a party of several British Officers attempting to capture two deserters within the U.S.A. The other officers involved were a Captain Adam Muir, Lieutenant Henry Brevoort, and Lieutenant Porter Hanks; with one of the deserters named Morrison. On the 14th of December 1805, the British party came across Morrison somewhere out in Michigan. Morrison evaded their capture through the help of one Thomas Nowlan, and escaped to Detroit. He was followed to Detroit by the party of officers, who subsequently tried a second attepmt at capture. It is said that they "rushed violently into thee house of Conrad Sick, a citizen of the United States, armed with swords and pistols, which they presented to the family, and laid hold of the aforesaid Morrison the British deserter, and dragged him forcibly out of the house," (*Trans. Supr. Court. Mich.* II. 89). It is said that Captain Muir attempted to shoot Morrison, but ended up shooting himself; Lundie faught with Conrad Sick; Brevort hurled abuse at the gathering citizens; and Lieutenant Hanks protected the former three from the aforementioned gathering citizens. Morrison however escaped, and the four British Officers were arrested by the local Marshal. They were charged with assult and battery; and on the 18th of September 1805, a 12 man jury was ordered for their trial. Lieutenant Hanks pleaded guilty as charged, but Ensign John Stow Lundie, Captian Muir and Lieutenant Brevort refuted the charges. Following trial, they were all found guilty (*Trans. Supr. Court. Mich.* I. 358-9).

In 1827, John appears in *The Times* as a bankrupt. At the time he was living in Copthorne, Sussex. He was then a builder. He must have died without issue, as his sister Mary was closest heir to his elder brother William.

REV. WILLIAM STOW LUNDIE OF SPITTAL

Christened on the 21st of December 1773, at Berwick, he was ordained a minister on the 19th of September 1802 (*Durham Univ. Arch*: DDR/EA/CLO/3/1802/5). On the 20th of April 1809, he was served as heir of line and provision special, to his father, in Hutton-Spittal, Claribad, and others. He died before 1837, and was succeeded by his sister Mary.

MARY STOW LUNDIE OF SPITTAL

She succeeded her brother William to Spittal upon his death, being served as his heir of talzie and provision general on the 29th of November 1838. She married the Rev. William Compton, M.A. on the 9th of November 1801, at Carham in Northumberland. He was minister of Carham. He adopted the name of Lundie, and died in 1843. They had issue:

1   *Rev. William Compton Lundie of Spittal*, who succeeded to Spittal, and whose details follow.

2   *Ellen Compton Lundie*, born on the 9th of April, 1804, christened on the 12th of April that year.

Compton-Lundie of Spittal

REV. WILLIAM COMPTON LUNDIE OF SPITTAL

Graduating from University with a Master of Arts Degree, he was, like his father, minister of Carham in Northumberland. He was born on the 5th of February 1803, in Carham, and christened there on the 13th of the month. He was served as heir talzie special, to his mother in "Spittal called Hutton Spittal and the lands of Clanbad," on the 29th of November 1838. He died on the 11th of February 1871, at Spittal House. On 14th April 1871, the testament of the Rev. William Compton Lundie of Spittal, in the County of Berwick, Master of Arts, who died at Spittal House, is proved and registered with Duns Sheriff Court. He married Margaret Mary Ord, (daughter of the Rev. Craven Ord), in 1848, in Kings Norton, Staffordshire (*Eng. Wales Civ. Reg. Ind.,* 18, 291). She predeceased him. Their children erected a large monument to their memory in Hutton Churchyard.

1   ***William Compton Lundie of Spittal***, who succeeded his father, and whose details follow.

2   ***Stow Compton Lundie***, born 1854. He married Maria Hull on the 7th of June 1875, in Rothsay, Bute. She died in 1900, in St Thomas, Devon (*Eng. Wales Civ. Reg. Ind.*, 5b, 30). By 1891, Stow and his family were living in Tavistock, Devon. He was still living there in 1914, as shown by his son Kenneth's military papers. Stow and Maria had issue:

i Stow Harold Compton Lundie, born 1877, in Herefordshire, England.

ii Cuthbert Ord Compton Lundie, born 1879, in Fiddington, Bridgewater, Somerset, England. . He emigrated to Canada in 1912, and died aged 77 on the 7th of December 1956. He had issue:

a Stow Compton Lundie, born around 1913, he died in Vancouver on the 18th of June 1977, aged 64.

b Major Anthony Compton-Lundie, born around 1915, he died aged 30, in the Second World War, on the 21st of April, 1945. He was a member of the Canadian Scottish Regiment, and died when commanding D-company of his Regiment during the assault and liberation of Wagenborgen in Holland. His grave (number III. G. 14) is in the Holten Canandian War Cemetary.

c Erica Compton Lundie

d Gladys May Compton Lundie

iii Eric William Compton Lundie, was born on the 17th of September, at Keenthorne House, in Fiddington, Bridgewater, Somerset, England. He became a South African citizen. He fought in the First World War as a private in the 2nd Regiment of the South African Infantry; service number 17769. He died at war, on the 31st of October, 1918, and is buried in Mont Huon Military Cemetary, Le Treport, grave No. VII. L. 4A. He is also listed on the War Memorial in Whitchurch church yard.

iv Glady Compton Lundie, born in 1885, in Fiddington, Bridgewater, Somerset, England.

v Arthur Compton Lundie, born in on the 17th of May 1886, at Keenthorne House, in Fiddington, Bridgewater, Somerset,

England.

vi Kenneth Compton Lundie, born on the 14th of December 1888, in Bristol, England. He emigrated to Canada, and signed up for the Canadian Overseas Expeditiary Force at the start of the First World War. His papers list his occupation as a farmer in the Calgary area of Alberta.

3 Annie Compton Lundie, implied, was married in Barnstable, Devon in 1883 (*Eng. Wales Civ. Reg. Ind.*, 5b, 861)

WILLIAM COMPTON LUNDIE OF SPITTAL, BERWICK; AND COONOR, EXMOUTH

He was born 1851, and married Emily Hall, (the daughter of William Hartroop Hall, of Marpool Hall, Devonshire), on the 5th of August, 1873, in Christ's Church, Ealing, London. In the 1881 and 1891 Census he appears as a Magistrate. In the 1891 Census, living in Coonor Lodge, Devon, his household consists of himself, his wife, his two daughters, five servants, one governess, his mother-in-law, and nephew Kenneth Lloyd. He appears in The Times of the 26th of October 1881, on a subscription list for the Berwickshire Coast Disasters Fund. He died on the 18th of March, 1923, at Exmouth (*The Times,* 19th March, 1923). He had issue:

1 William Craven Compton Lundie, born 1877, Dawlish, Devon. In the 1891 census he was listed as being a boarder at Renton School in Derbyshire.

2 Eva Emily Compton Lundie, born 1878, Scotland. She died unmarried before the 20th of October 1960. On that date, details of her will were published in *The Times* (page 7). They show her estate was valued at £15 018. She left her share in her residence, Windsor House, and share in its sale, to the Christian Alliance for Women and Girls.

3 Margaret Clare Compton Lundie, Born 1880, Exeter. She married Cecil John Snowdon, the third son of Canon Snowdon of 15 Mount-Avenue, Ealing. The wedding ceremony took place on the 5th of January, 1936, at Holy Trinity Church, Exmouth. It was performed by the Rev. Basil Pattern, a cousin of Margaret, assisted by the Rev. S. H. Copleston and Rev. S. Freeman (*The Times*, 6th January 1905)

The House of Inverlochtie, alias Spittal

The lands of Inverlochtie (Innerlochtie), alias Spittal (Spittell), are in the parish of Markinch, Fife. In 1510, these lands were held by Allan Couttis of the Spittale. On 6th March of this year, these lands passed to Sir Andrew Lundie of Balgonie, for £160 Scots, and an annual rent of 12 merks from the lands of Schetheme, for a chaplainry and chaplain in the Parish kirk of Markinch for the soul of the late Andrew Wemyss (*NAS*, GD26/3/56). The next year they were incorporated under a Royal charter into the Barony of Balgonie. These lands were held by subsequent Lairds of Balgonie, until around 1616, when they were occupied by Richard Lundie, brother to Robert Lundie 7th of Balgonie, son of David Lundie 6th of Balgonie.

RICHARD LUNDIE, 1ST OF INVERLOCHTIE

Son of David Lundie 6th of Balgonie and Lillias Oliphant, he was married to Sara Wemyss. On the 12th of June 1610, Richard Lundie and his spouse, Sara Wemyss; as brother of the deceased Robert Lundie of Balgonie; were granted a charter of the lands of Spittell, in the barony of Balgonie, by Robert Lundie of Balgonie (*NAS*, GD26/3/106). This initial contract cost Richard 6000 merks, and included a cause whereby Robert Lundie of Balgonie might redeem the lands. Six years later, in a contract dated 15th June, 1616; Richard Lundie, brother of the late Robert Lundie of Balgonie, and his spouse Sara Wemyss; who were already in possession of the lands of Inverlochtie, alias Spittell, by payment of the fore mentioned 6000 merks; paid an additional 4000 merks to Robert Lundie of Balgonie whereby Robert ratified the previous alienation of the lands of Inverlochtie to Richard and Sara, renounced the clause of reversion, and bound himself to infeft Richard and Sara anew (*NAS*, GD26/3/121). This was contract was confirmed by a Charter to Richard and Sara, from Robert Lundie of Balgonie, of the same date (*NAS*, GD26/3/122). Richard died before 10th March 1619. He had issue:-

1   *Robert Lundie, 2nd of Inverlochtie*, succeeded his father.
2   *Richard Lundie, 3rd of Inverlochtie*, succeeded his brother.
3   *Margaret Lundie*, married John Hamilton, merchant Burgess of Edinburgh
4   *Helen Lundie.*

ROBERT LUNDIE, 2ND OF INVERLOCHTIE

Robert succeeded his father, being served as heir general on the 29th of June 1625 (*Gen. Retours*, No. 1202). He married Janet Lundie, the daughter of John Lundie 6th of Stratherlie. Their marriage contract is dated the 3rd of June, 1635; at which date John Lundie of Stratherlie was dead (*NAS*, GD26/3/217). On the 30th July of that year, Sir Alexander Leslie of Balgonie, kt.; major-general in Lower Saxony; issued a precept of Clare Constat, in favour of Robert Lundie; as son and heir of deceased Richard Lundie of Inverlochtie, alias Spittell; of the lands of Innerlochtie (*NAS*, GD26/3/215). Shortly afterwards, in accordance with their marriage contract, Robert granted to his spouse, the lands of Inverlochtie, in life rent; 12th December, 1635. A Charter by Alexander, Earl of Leven, confirmed this (*NAS*, GD26/3/217). Robert Lundie of Spitall, is listed as one of the heritors of the Paris of Markinch, in 1636. Some time between 1637 and 1642, Wadset was given by Sir William Murray of Blebow and Euphemia Ogilvy, his spouse, to James Sibbald in Bonsyd and Margaret Key, his spouse, of the Mylnetoune of Blebow. A tack thereof was given to Sir William, and assignation of their rights (Margaret Key and William Sibbald, her son), was given to Robert Lundie of Spittell (*NAS*, GD7/1/41). Robert died before the 16th of May, 1644. He left no issue, and was succeeded by his brother Richard. Janet Lundie later married a Major Richard Lundie.

RICHARD LUNDIE, 3RD OF INVERLOCHTIE

On 16th May 1644, a precept of Clare Constat was granted by Alexander, Earl of Leven, General of Scottish army in England, in favour of Richard Lundie as brother and heir of the deceased Robert Lundie of Inverlochtie alias Spittall, of the lands of Innerlochtie (*NAS*, GD26/3/222). In 1646, 29th November, there are letters of Horning against Janet Lundie, wife of the late Robert Lundie of Spittell, by Richard, for payment of 160 merks yearly, by Janet to Richard, for his yearly maintenance; and also for his right to teinds of the lands of Spittell (*NAS*, GD26/4/808). Two years later Richard married Christian Blair, daughter of Margaret Bonar; the contract dated 3rd August, 1648 (*NAS*, GD26/4/813). As part of this contract Richard was paid 1000 merks.

After the Earl of Leven granted the precept of Clare Constat in favour of Richard Lundie, Richard seems to have come to an arrangement with Duncan Wemyss in Boreland, over the ownership of this land. On 15th August, 1644, Richard disponed to the said Duncan Wemyss, the lands of Inverlochtie; this was confirmed by a charter of the same date. Again on this date, there is a Bond of reversion, by Duncan Wemyss, to Richard, of the lands of Inverlochtie, following payment of 500 merks (*NAS*, 26/3/224-6). Richard died before 1650, and was succeeded by his sisters Helen and Margaret as portitioners.

MARGARET AND HELEN LUNDIE, PORTIONERS OF INVERLOCHTIE

On the 10th of December, 1650, Margaret Lundie, the spouse of James Hamilton, a merchant burgess of Edinburgh, was granted a precept of Clare Constat by Alexander, Earl of Leven, as sister and heir portioner of the deceased Richard Lundie, of half of the lands of Inverlochty (*NAS*, GD26/3/229). In 1651, Margaret disponed her half of the lands to David Wemyss of Balfarg. In these contracts and bonds, she also promised that if Margaret's sister Helen died, and Margaret was heir, that she would dispone this second half to David Wemyss as well. This was judicially ratified in 1654 (*NAS*, 26/3/231-233, 235). These lands thus ultimately passed to David Wemyss in 1658.

Lundie of Langraw

JOHN LUNDIE OF LANGRAW

By the early 1600's, the lands of Langraw were held by the family of Ramsay of Langraw. In 1629, there is record of George Ramsay younger of Langraw, and his son and apparent heir William. Eugenie Ramsay, most likely a daughter of Ramsay of Langraw, had by 1637, married one John Lundie. On the 20th of June that year, John, designed as 'in Langraw' was charged and convicted, by the Lords of the Privy Council of Scotland, with the assault of a George Henderson. The details of the case, taken from the register of the Privy Council of Scotland (Second Series, VI., 461-2), are shown below.

Edinburgh 20th June, 1637
Decreta April 1635 – February 1639, p345.

Complaint by George Hendersone, servitor to Sir James Lundie, and the said Sir James for his interest, as follows:- On 27th March last, as the said George was returning from the plough about 7 o'clock at night, he met John Lundin, in Langraw, ... Ramsay, his spouse, and Katherine Hind, their servant, who, without any offence done by him to them, "feircelie sett upon him, tooke his pleuche gad frome him, gave him manie bauch and blae straiks thairwith in diverse parts of his bodie; and the said John Lundin himselfe brake a great tree in peaces upon the compleaner and woundit him on the face to the great effusion of his blood at mouth and nose." Further, on 1st April, thereafter the said . . . . . Ramsay and Katherine Hind, and Harie Scot, tenant of the said John Lundin, at the instigation of the said John Lundin, came to the said George Hendersone while he was at his plough for the purpose of taking his life. "And the more easilie to effectuat thair intention the said Harie come in a freindlie shew to the compleaner and talked with him saying he sould be his warrand and nothing sould ail him; and with that er ever wes awar drew frome the pleuche and frome all his wapons and then callet for the said Kathernie, who had tue great graip shafts carying under her plaid, and tooke one of thame frome her, and the said . . . . . Ramsay tooke one of the pleuche gads lying on the ground quhairwith she gave the compleaner a number of cruell straiks on the backe, he being haldin at this tyme the said Harie Scott, who also, when she wes tyred, gave the complainer a number of straiks thairwith, and so birsed and bruised his haill bodie as he hes ever lyne bedfast sensyne in great paine and dollor, to the hazard of his lyff." Charge having been given to these persons complained upon, and the pursuers compearing but not the defenders, the Lords, after hearing the deposition of witnesses, find that John Lundin "tooke and gad frome the said George Hendersone and strake him thairwith on the heid, and thairafter brake a stalff on his face to the effusion of his blood"; and that . . . . . "Ramsay,

Katherine Hird and Harie Scot strake, hurt and woundit the compleaner in manner abonewritten and bruised him as he hes ever lyne bedfast sensyne under the cure of chiurgians," for which insolence they fine the said John Lundin 100 merks; . . . . . Ramsay his wife, £40; Katherine Hird, 40 merks; and Harie Scot, £40, to be paid by them to the said George Hendersone; and they also ordain the sad John Lundin to pay the chirgeons charged with the curing of the said George. They further ordain that the whole defenders to be charge to enter into ward within the tolboth of Edinburgh until they pay these fines, and are liberated by their Lordships, Hird and Scot on a charge of six days, and John Lundin and his wife, in respect of their present sickness, on a charge of fourteen days, and that upon pain of horning.

In 1643, a Mr Thomas Christie, with the consent of William Ramsay, son and heir of George Ramsay younger of Langraw, resigned the lands of Langraw in favour of John Lundie (*Reg. Mag. Sig.* IX., 1514).

Lundie of Larg

ANDREW LUNDIE OF LARG

He appears in the Register of deeds in 1668.

Lundy of Lochside

JOHN LUNDY OF LOCHSIDE

On the 12th of July 1600, John Lundy of Lochsyde acted as surety in 500 merks each, for Henry Mathew, Andrew Crawford and John Ramsay, all in Muredrum of Ardestie, not to harm Henry Ramsay of Arduny and John Ramsay in the Lawis (*Register of the Privy Council of Scotland*, Series I, VI., 657). Note that 'Lochtyside' appears as a part of the Barony of Balgonie around 1622 (*NAS*, GD26/3/131); but also that Ardestie, Ardownie and Laws are located close to Denside, an area associated with George Lundie, younger of Gorthie.

The House of Lungar

Lungar (Lumgair) is located in the Parish of Dunnotar, in the Mearns. The family of Lundie of Lungar descended from a youger son of the Baronial House of Benholm. The family's first association with these lands dates from 1551, when on the 18th of November that year, William Lundie, 3rd of Benholm was given a gift of the ward and nonentry of the lands of Lungar, following the death of Sir John Erskine of Brechin (*Reg. Sec. Sig*. IV. 1419)

JOHN LUNDIE IN LUMGAIR

John was a younger son of Andrew Lundie 2nd of Benholm (see that family). His elder brother, William Lundie 3rd of Benholm, succeeded their father Andrew, but his line ended in a daughter. Upon the death of William Lundie 3rd of Benholm's daughter, Elizabeth, it seems as if John was the rightful heir at least in part, to the estate of Benholm. However, for some reason, he resigned both his, and his son Robert's right and title to the estate of Benholm in favour of the right honourable Robert Keith of Benholm, 'their master'. The resignation is dated 20th April, 1602 (*NAS*, GD4/94). Two years earlier, 6th May, 1600, John, then in the Nether Knox of Benholm; in a contract with the fore mentioned Robert Keith of Benholm; acting as assignee for his six brothers and two sisters; renounced all right to goods and gear, and specially to a sum of 2000 merks bequeathed him by Dame Elizabeth Lundye, lady of Benholme; for which Robert was to pay him 300 merks (*NAS*, GD4/93). John was married to Cristain Strathauchin. She died before 17th June 1591, as her testament is recorded in the Edinburgh Commissary Court on this date. John had issue:-

1   *Robert Lundie of Lungar*

2   *William Lundie*, brother-german to Robert. He seems to have had a desire to regain the inheritance lost in the agreements his father made with Robert Keith, as on 19th January 1630, a William Lundie is registered as heir male to his uncle Robert (alias William) Lundie of Benholm (*Gen. Retours*, No. 1710). This would also imply that his elder brother's line was extinct.

ROBERT LUNDIE OF LUNGAR

Robert was married to Catherine Mortimer. He died before the 6th of October 1612, as on this date William Lundie, brother-german to Robert Lundie of Lungar was served as guardian to the estates of the minors, John, Joanna and Issobelle Lundie, children of the late Robert Lundie of Lungar (*Inq. Ret. de Tut.*, No. 1290). Catherine died before December 3rd 1614. Robert had issue:-

1   *John Lundie of Lungar*
2   *Joanna Lundie*
3   *Issobelle Lundie*

JOHN LUNDIE OF LUNGAR

John was served as heir to his father, Robert Lundie of Lungar January 15th 1613 (*Gen. Retours*, No. 8497).

Lundin of Podester

JOHN LUNDIN OF PODESTER

John appears in the Register of Deeds in 1706 (RD. 2/92/847).

Lundie of St. Monans

SIR ANDREW LUNDIE OF ST. MONANS

On the 28th of January 1618, James Philip, factor to Lord Lindores, petitioned the Privy Council, craving letters to be ordained in order to relieve the tax burden of Lord Lindors by making several defaulters pay their share. One of these persons was Sir Andrew. His share was six chalders for the tiends of Woddilbie and half lands of Scheillis (*Reg. Privy Council*, XI. 623).

The House of Stratherlie.

ANDREW LUNDY, 1ST OF STRATHERLIE

Andrew was a younger son of Sir John Lundy of that Ilk. He married, prior to 1507, Janet Melvill, the daughter and heiress of William Melvill of Carnbee. Although the lands of Stratherlie were within the barony of Lundy, they were held in feu-ferm by William Melvill, with Lundy of that Ilk as superior. It was through this marriage that Andrew Lundie obtained the lands. On the 10th of May 1497, a notarial instrument of precept of sasine was directed towards Andrew and David Anstruther, and William Strang, by Alexander Spens of Pittencrief, the principal bailie of William, Lord of St. John, 'commandour' of Torphichen. The bailies were charged with infefting 'Jonet Melvill, daughter and heiress of the late William Melvill of Carnbee', as his nearest and lawful heir, in the temple lands of Carnbee, in that barony, and the temple lands of Stratharlie, called Sandy Hillock, in the barony of Lundy and sheriffdom of Fife. Sasine of these lands was given on the 13th May 1497 to John Oliphant of Kelly as procurator for Janet Melvill (*Laing Charters*, No. 231).

On the 17th of June 1507, Andrew's brother, William Lundy of that Ilk directed a precept of sasine to Thomas Strang, Thomas Couston and William Anderson, as bailies, for infefting his brother 'Andro Lundy and Jonet Mailvyn, his spouse', in conjunct fee of the sixth part of the lands of Stratharly with pertinents, lying in the barony of Lundy, (*Laing Charters*, No. 265). On the same date, William directed to the same bailies a precept infefting his brother and his wife in the lands of Tuetis [Teuchats] in the barony of Lundy in warrandice of a sixth part of the lands of Strathairly. Both writs were signed at St. Andrews (*Laing Charters*, No. 266). Seven years later, on the 7th of April 1514, Andrew's brother, William Lundy of that Ilk, as superior of the lands of Stratharlie, gave sasine, with his own hands, to Lawrence Grey and his spouse Margaret Gourlay, the nearest heirs of a one-twelfth part of the lands of Stratharlie with pertinents. They thereupon resigned the same for new infeftment in favour of Andrew Lundy of Stratharlie and Jonet Mailvill, his wife. The notarial instrument narrating this information was witnessed by among others a Mr William Lundy (*Laing Charters*, No. 299). On the 6th of May 1522 Andrew was appointed as Sheriff depute of Fife (*Sheriff Court Book of Fife*). He had issue:

1   *John Lundy, 2ⁿᵈ of Stratherlie*, whose details follow.

2   *James Lundy*. He appears twice in records with his brother. The first is concerning his part in the slaughter of James Borthwick, John Anderson and John Balzeat, for which he and his brother were escheated in 1531, but pardoned in 1538 (*East Neuk*). The second is when he and his brother appear in the local records of Dysart on the 24th September 1542.

JOHN LUNDY, 2ND OF STRATHERLIE

He appears as Laird in 1531 when he, and his brother James, were denounced as rebels, put to the horn, and had their goods escheated, for their part in the slaughter of James Borthwick, John Anderson and John Balzeat. On the 15th of October that year, a gift of their goods, movable and unmovable, was given by the King to Walter Lundy of that Ilk (*Reg. Sec. Sig.* II. 1029). On the 23rd of July 1538, they both obtained remission for this crime (*Reg. Sec. Sig.* II. 2114; *East Neuk of Fife*, 281-3).

In 1540, John Lundy of Stratharlie witnesses a premonition of redemption by Robert Douglas of Lochleven of the lands of Thorntoun of Fossoway (*NAS*, GD150/1057). On May the 6th of that year, at Lathalland, John Lundy (spelt Lwyndy) delivered to Alexander Spens of Lathalland 200 merks (in specified coins) for redemption of an eighth part of lands of Lathalland from Simon Waid, an indweller of Anstruther, and another eighth part from David Hwntar of Newtoun. In return Alexander promised to infeft John Lundy in an eighth part of his lands of Lathalland in warrandice of 18 bolls of victual to be paid annually to John Lundy, together with 7 merks. This requirement was duly acted in the books of the official principal of St Andrews. Following this, on the 13th of May, on ground of lands of Lathalland, in the presence of Henry Jhonsoun, Stephen Criste, Alexander Peirsoun and Simon Iirland; Alexander Spens of Lathalland gave sasine propriis manibus to John Lundye of Stratherlie of an eighth part of lands of Lathalland, in the sheriffdom of Fife, in warrandice of payment of the victual contained in the aforementioned act in the books of the official principal of St Andrews. On the 9th of November Alexander Spens of Lathalland gave sasine a propriis manibus to John Lundy of Stratherlie of a sixteenth part of lands of Lathalland in warrandice of payment of 50 merks according to an act made in books of the official principal of St Andrews (*NAS*, GD1/

1042/7).

John's Kinsman, Walter Lundy of that Ilk, son of John's cousin Thomas Lundin of Pratis, gave sasine to John, with his own hands, of the lands of Strathairlie, in the barony of Lundin and shire of Fife, on the 2nd of March 1542-3. This was witnessed by among others a Richard Lundyn (*Laing Charters,* No. 471). A few months later, on the 30th of July, Walter granted a charter in favour of John, his heirs and assignees, of the lands of Stratharlie, in the barony of Lundin and shire of Fife, which had been resigned by John for new infeftment. Under the charter John was to hold these lands from Walter for services used and wont. The charter was dated and signed at Lundie in Fife, on the 30th of July 1543. It was witnessed by, among others, John Lundyn, son and heir of Walter Lundy of that Ilk (*Laing Charters*, No. 482).

John died sometime before 1544 as the testament of John Lundie of Strathairlie was proved around 1544. He had issue, and was succeeded by his eldest son Andrew (*NAS*, GD1/1042/7):

1   *Andrew Lundy, 3rd of Stratherlie*, whose details follow.
2   *John Lundy 4th of Stratherlie*, who succeeded his brother Andrew, of whom details follow his brothers.

ANDREW LUNDY, 3RD OF STRATHERLIE

After succeeding his father he caused William Cranstoun, professor of sacred literature, provost of the collegiate church of St. Salvator within the city of St Andrews, and principal official of that see, to transume from the protocol book of John Chalmers, notary public, a sasine, dated 9th May 1537. This sasine was in favour of his father, John Lundy of Stratharlie. The said sasine followed on a precept by Walter, Lord of St. John, which was given by David Balfour of Evenstoun, templar bailie, and was of the templar-lands of Carnbee in the barony of Lundy, and also the templar-lands of Stratharlie, called Sandy Hillock, in the barony of Lundy and sheriffdom of Fife. The said William Cranstoun then confirmed the sasine on the 4th of May 1545 (*Laing Charters,* No. 496). On the 15th May 1551, Walter Lundy of that Ilk, as superior of the lands of Stratharlie, gave sasine of the lands of Stratharlie in the barony of Lundy, with his own hands, to 'Andrew Lundy, first born son and heir of the late John Lundy of Stratharlie.' This was witnessed by among others a George Lundy (*Laing Charters,* No. 579).

He died without issue before the 26th February 1564 (*Laing Charters*, No. 768). He was succeeded by his brother John. His testament was proved on 4th July 1573 (*Edin. Tests.*).

JOHN LUNDY, 4TH OF STRATHAIRLIE

He had succeeded his brother Andrew to Stratharlie by the 26th of February 1564. On that date a precept of Clare Constat by James [Sandilands] Lord of St. John, was directed to George Balfour of Evinstoun, as bailie, for infefting John Lundy, 'now of Stratharlie', as the lawful and nearest heir of his father, the late John Lundy of Stratharlie, in the templar-lands of Carnbee, and in the templar lands of Sandehillok, in the shire of Fife. John was given sasine following this, on the 15th of March 1564 (*Laing Charters,* No. 768, 769).

In 1572, 10th June, he established his right as the lawful heir of his grandmother, Janet Melvill. A Retour of Inquest was taken in the city of St. Andrews before, Patrick Lermonth of Daisy, Knight, provost; James Lermonth, president; and Mr Alexander Sibbald, a bailie of St. Andrews. In the inquest, Andrew Rouch in Newburn; Martin Dischington in Newburn; William Dischington; George Lundy in Fawfield; John Dudingston, younger, in Mill of Murecamhouse; Walter Hereot in Lalethame, Alexander Smyth, William Giffart; Andrew Lundy; David Scott; Robert Murray; Andrew Crastaris; Andrew Mortoun; William Geddy; and Thomas Balfour; citizens of St. Andrews, declared on oath that John (John Lundy of Strathharlie) was the lawful and nearest heir of his grandmother, the late Jonet Melvill, daughter and heir of the late William Melvill of Carnbee (*Laing Charters,* No. 871).

On the 2nd of June 1574 John was paid 450 merks by James Spens of Lathallan for redeeming an annuity payable out of the lands of Easter Lathallan (*Scots Baronage*).

At this time the lands of Strathairlie appear to have been in three parts. One third held by John Lundy of Strathairlie, one third held by Sibbald of Rankelour, and the final third held by Lindsay of the Mount. All were within the barony of Lundy, and all were held of Lundy of that Ilk as superior. Sibbald of Rankelour had been in possession of one third of Strathairlie since at least 1544, where a James Sibbald of Rankelour, described as the Frank tenementar of Walter Lundy of that Ilk, is recorded as having paid his composition for the tenandry for a third part of Strathairly (*Laing Charters*, No. 454). Lindsay of the Byres held one third of Strathairlie since at least 1498. As has been discussed in the details of Lundy/Lundie/Lundin of that Ilk, in October, 1498 John, 3rd Lord Lindesay (Lindsay) of the Byres; resigned into the hands of William Lundy, baron of the barony thereof, in favour of Patrick Lindesay of Byris, his brother (and later 4th Lord of the Byres), a third of the lands of Strathairlie. The next year, on the 8th of May, William gave sasine of these lands in favour of Patrick, 4th Lord Lindesay of Byres, (*NAS*, GD20/1/323-324). These lands were held by Lindsay of the Byres from the laird of Lundy for ward and relief (*Laing Charters*, No. 1261).

John lundie, 5th of Strathairlie, purchased a further one third of the lands of Strathairlie, from Alexander Sibbald of Over Rankelour. In a contract dated the 27th of June 1586, signed at Over Rankelour, Alexander Sibbald of Over Rankelour, with the consent of his son and heir apparent, Andrew Sibbald, agreed to sell his one-third of the lands of Stratharlie, excepting ten acres lying to the east of Largo Kirk, to John Lundy of Strathairlie for 2000 merks, and to infeft John in these lands, which were to be held of Mr William Lundy of that Ilk, superior of the same (*Laing Charters*, No. 1128). According to this contract, on the 4th of November 1586, Alexander Sibbald resigned these lands into the hands of his superior, Mr William Lundy of that Ilk; who subsequently gave sasine to John Lundy of Strathairlie. The resignation was performed at 'the hall of Lundy,' and sasine was given to Strathairlie 'at the principal messuage of Stratharlie' (*Laing Charters*, 1133, 1135). John received a charter, granting and confirming this one-third part of Stratherlie (minus the ten acres near the Kirk of Largo) to him and his heirs by 'Mr William Lundie of that Ilk, superior,' which was dated and signed at Lundy, on the 1st of June 1593. It was witnessed by, Magnus Ayton; Robert Schedo; and James Gourlay; who were all servants of William Lundie of that Ilk (*Laing Charters*, No. 1260).

In 1593, all of the lands of Strathairlie were united under the control of this family. On the 10th of June that year, James Lord Lindsay of the Byres gave a discharge narrating that he had set in feu-farm to Andrew Lundy in Stratharlie (eldest son and heir of John Lundy of Strathairlie – to be discussed shortly) his third part of the lands of Stratharlie, in the barony of Lundy and the shire of Fife. These lands were to be held in feu-farm for ten merks scots, and 6s. 8d. of augmentation yearly. The discharge states that the lands were being held by the granter from the laird of Lundy for ward and relief; but now, for certain reasons, the granter discharged the grantee of all feu-farm and other duties of the lands. This was dated at Edinburgh on the 10th of June 1593, and signed by Lord Lindsay; Sir David Lindsay of the Mount, knight, Lyon King of Arms; and Andrew Lindsay, his brother, as witnesses (*Laing Charters,* No. 1261).

On the 7th of February 1597, John Lundy of Stratharlie and John Johnsoun, miller of the mill of 'Johnesonis myln,' appeared before the notary public (Mr Thomas Wod, of St Andrews diocese) and several witnesses (Robert Lundy, Nicholas Bell and Thomas Archibald, all in Stratharlie, Thomas Johnesoun in Johnesoun's mill, and Andrew Bonsie there). In front of this gathering, John demanded from John Johnsoun the 'watter maill' and duties, etc., which he believed were owing to him for the water dams of Johnson's mill in years past. Johnsoun replied that he had paid the yearly duties to Andrew Lundy, tacksman of Stratharlie (most probably John Lundy's son and heir); but nevertheless offered to agree with John Lundy, and to pay him in future the usual dues for the 'licence and tollerance of the said water dammes.' This offer John Lundy wholly rejected without present payment of all bygone dues, and new conditions for the licence. John Lundy then directed the notary to read and intimate to the miller the letter of the licence etc., which had been previously granted to Cristain Lundy, tenant of Johnson's mill, and John Auchmouthie, her spouse, given for her life-time only (dated at Stratharlie, 2nd April 1562). After this was read, John Lundy discharged Johnsoun of the licence of the uppermost dam, 'callit the 'mid dam,' in all time coming, and immediately thereafter'. John Lundy, according to the custom passed to the ground of the dam, 'dammit in and standing upon the said John Lundy's proportie of Stratharlie, to the great hurt and skayth of his heritage, as he affirmit, and did cast down the saymn, and that without any manner of stop or stay of the ganging of the said mylne.' (*Laing Charters,* No. 1324).

John was at least twice married. His first wife was Helen Dudingston. A Notarial instrument of Sasine dating from the 13th of June 1577, narrates that John Johnston of Johnston-mill passed to the tenement of the mill, in the shire of Fife, and regality of Dunfermline, and will his own hands gave sasine of the mill, mill lands etc., to John Lundy of Strathairlie and Elen Dudingston, his spouse, in terms of a feu-charter to them (*Laing Charters,* No. 948). Helen died before the 13th of May 1579, on which date her testament is proved (*Ed. Comm. Court*).

His second wife was Agnes Morton or Myrton, to whom he was married by 1587. A Notarial instrument dated the 5th of January 1587, narrates that John Lundy of Stratharlie and Agnes 'Myuirtoun', his spouse, in terms of a contract between them, with John Johnston in Morsturphie as their cautioner, and John Dudingston in Murcammows, gave sasine to John Dudingston of an annual rent of £20 scots from the third part of Stratharlie which had been resigned by Alexander Sibbald of over Rankelour. This was witnessed by David and Archibald Simsones, burgesses of Dysart; William Johnston; John Hagy in Tempil of Stratharly, and John Munnian in Stratharly (*Laing Charters*, No. 1137).

John had issue and was succeeded by his son Andrew:

1   *Andrew Lundie, 5th of Strathairlie*, whose details follow.
2   *James Lundie*, On the 12th August 1589, James, son of John Lundie of Stratherlie registered as apprentice to a Robert Middleton, a Taylor in the city of Edinburgh (*Reg. Appren. Edin.*).
3   *Christian Lundie*, named as a probable daughter by Rev. Wood in his *East Neuk of Fife*.

ANDREW LUNDIE, 5TH OF STRATHAIRLIE

On the 23rd of June 1593, Andrew, and his spouse Mariota Ballinghall were given sasine of a third part of the lands of Stratharlie, by William Lundy of that Ilk. This part of the Strathairlie lands had been resigned by Andrew's father John, in favour of Andrew, but reserving John's liferent (*Laing Charters*, No. 1263). Mariota died before the 6th of June 1597, as that is the date her testament was proved (*Edin. Tests*). It is thought that he had two further wives. The first was Helen Wood, who died before 1608, as in this year the Edinburgh Commissary Court records the testament of Helen Wood, spouse to Andro Lundy of Stratharlie. His third wife was Jean Borthwick. In 1618 they were infeft in a tenement in Pittenweem (*East Neuk of Fife*, p 95). He had issue:-

1   *John Lundie, 6th of Strathairlie*, who succeeded, and whose details follow.

JOHN LUNDIE, 6TH OF STRATHAIRLIE

He is the only known child of Andrew Lundie 5th of Strathairlie, his mother most probably being Mariota Ballinghall. He married Agnes Kay, the daughter of James Kay of Pinkerton, minister of Dumbarton. In fulfilment of their marriage contract, dated the 26th of October 1601, his father, Andrew Lundie 5th of Strathairlie, resigned into the hands of John Lundy of that Ilk, as superior, an annualrent of six chalders of victual, upliftable from the lands of Stratharlie, for new infeftment in favour of Agnes Kay. John Lundie of that Ilk subsequently gave Sasine of this victual, which was leviable from the lands of 'John Lundy, senior of Strathairlie,' John 6th of Strathairlie's grandfather. These actions were done in the garden of Stratherlie, on the date of the contract (*Laing Charters,* No.1374). It was also in fulfilment of this contract that John and his spouse became infeft in the lands of Strathairlie. On the 13th of October 1604, John's father produced a procuratory directed towards James Kay, a writer, for resigning the third part of his lands of Stratharlie into the hands of John, Lord Lindsay of the Byres, as Lord superior of the said third part. This was in order for new infeftment in favour of John, reserving his father's liferent. The writ was signed by John's father at Anstruther as 'fiar of Strathairlie (*Laing Charters,* No. 1470). At the end of the month, John was given sasine of the other two thirds of Strathairlie. On the 30th October 1604, John's father resigned into the hands of his superior, John Lundy of that Ilk, these two parts of the lands of Strathairlie in favour of John Lundy, designed 'younger, of Stratharlie.' This resignation was made reserving Andrew Lundy's liferent, and the liferent of six chalders that sasine of had been given to Agnes Kay in 1601. Sasine was given to John on the same date. The lands included the house of Nether Strathairlie, which the writ states was given to be occupied by 'John Lundy, senior of Stratharlie' (John Lundie, 4th of Strathairlie) until his death. Sasine was recorded in the secretary's register for Fife on the next day (*Laing Charters,* No. 1472). Two charters were then given to John following the resignations by his father. On the 1st of November 1604, John Lundy of that Ilk, as superior, granted a charter 'in favour of John Lundy, son and apparent heir of Andrew Lundy, fiar of Stratherlie, and to the heirs begot between him and his wife, Agnes Kay, the two parts of the lands of Strathairlie, templar-lands etc., reserving liferents.' This was done at Lundy, and was witnessed by among others, David Lundy in Largo; and William Lundy in Fawfield (*Laing Charters,* No. 1473). A charter of the final third part of Strathairlie was given by John, Lord Lindsay on the 20th of February 1605. Lord Lindsay granted 'in feu-farm to John Lundy, son and heir apparent of Andrew Lundy of Stratherlie, a third part of the lands of Stratherlie, barony of Lundy and shire of Fife for ten merks of former feu-dute and 6s. 8d. for augmentation' (*Laing Charters*. No. 1478). Sasine following on this charter was given on the 8th of May 1605 (*Laing Charters*, No. 1483). John was given sasine of the templar-lands of Strathairlie, reserving the liferent of his grandfather, John Lundy 4th of Strathairlie, by Robert Williamson of Muriston, heritable proprietor and lord superior of all the templar-lands in Scotland, on the 9th of April 1610 (*Laing Charters*, No. 1572).

John died before 1622, as on the 27th June 1622 King James the sixth gave the gift of the marriage of his eldest son and heir to James Kay (probably Agnes Kay's father) (*Laing Charters*, No. 1908). He left issue and was succeeded by the aforementioned son.

1   *James Lundie, 7th of Strathairlie*, whose details follow

2   *Janet Lundie*, married Robert Lundie of Inverlochtie (alias Spittal), with the contract dated 3rd of June 1635 (*NAS*, GD26/3/217). After the death of Robert, she married Major Richard Lundie. It is not impossible that this was Robert's brother, and heir in Inverlochtie. In 1649, Major Richard was given the chage of fencibles in Stirling and Clackmannan (*General Index to the Acts of Parilaments of Scotland*).

3   *Katherine Lundie*, married first Robert French, town clerk of Kirkcaldy; secondly William McGill, Dr of Physic at Kirkcaldy (*PRS Fife and Kinross*, XIII, 210; XIV. 140, 489; XVIII. 309; XIX. 83); and third, on the 28th February 1662, Alexander Hamilton, a lister in the linktoun of Abbotshall (*Index Reg. Deeds, Mack*. IV., 787).

JAMES LUNDIE 7TH OF STRATHAIRLIE

A minor at the time of his father's death in 1622, he appears in the general retours establishing himself as heir to his father 'John Lundie, Feoditarius de Stratheilie,' on the 25th of November 1629 (*Gen. Retours*, No. 1545).

James became contracted to marry Margaret Orrock, the eldest daughter of Alexander Orrock of that Ilk on the 3rd of November 1630. The contract was between James Lundy, apparent of Stratharlie, with the consent of his mother, Agnes Kay, who was now spouse to Robert Douglas of Drumgarland, and the aforementioned Robert Douglas of Drumgarland his interest, on one part, and Alexander Orrock, fiar of that Ilk, for himself, and for Margaret Orrock, his eldest daughter, and for her own interest, on the other part. The contract stated that James and Margaret would bind themselves to marry each other before the 22nd of November that year, with James pledging himself to obtain infeftment in the lands of Stratharlie, as heir to the late John Lundy, his father, and to secure his intended spouse in her liferent and other provisions (*Laing Charters*, No. 2070).

It would appear however that John's superiors in at least two thirds of his lands of Strathairlie, namely Lundie of that Ilk, were more than reluctant to give him the infeftment he was duly entitled to as his father's heir. On the 15th of October 1632, a Precept was produced by King Charles the First, 'requiring Sir James Lundie, knight, franktenementar of that Ilk, and John Lundie, fiar of that Ilk, the superiors of the lands, to obey former mandates, and without further delay to give sasine to James Lundie, son and heir of the late John Lundie of Stratharlie, in the lands of Stratharlie' (*Laing Charters*, No. 216). Following this, the heads of the House of Lundie were not willing to provide John the infeftment. On the 16th of November 1632, James appeared before Sir James Lundie of that Ilk and John Lundie 'fiar of that Ilk,' at ' the manor place of Lundy,' with the Royal Precept. Upon presentation it is recorded that John Lundie fiar of that Ilk refused to obey the Precept (*Laing Charters*, No. 2118). It would be six months later (4th and 6th of March 1633) that 'Sir James Lundie, knight, and John Lundie of that Ilk', issued a Precept of Clare Constat for infefting 'James Lundie of Stratharlie, as heir of his father, the late John Lundy, in the lands of Stratherlie.' This was dated at both St. Andrews and Lundy, and signed 'S. James Lundine, J. Lundin of yt Ilk' (*Laing Charters*, No. 2125). Sasine was given on the 30th of March that year (*Laing Charters*, No. 2127).

It is not known whether James had the same difficulties with obtaining infeftment from the Lindsays for the third of the lands of Strathairlie they were superiors of, but certainly he had to wait for it to happen. It was not until the 1st of January 1635 that a Precept of Clare Constat by was given by John Lord Lindsay of Auchter Struther (or of the Byres) , for infefting James Lundie of Stratherlie, as heir of his father, in Lord Lindsay's third of the lands of Stratharlie (*Laing Charters*, No. 2160).

Although James was now infeft in his father's lands, it was not until the 18th of July 1638, that he appears as officially served as heir to his father, John Lundie of Stratherlie, in the lands of Stratherlie (*Inq. Spec. Ret. Fife*, No. 477).

In 1649, James was on a committee of war for Fife (*General index to the acts of parliament of Scotland*). He was captured by Cromwell's troops on the 11th of May 1654, but was soon released (*Lundins of Fife*). On the 20th of September 1656, James Lundy of Stratherly with consent of Margaret Orrok, his spouse, granted a charter to John Lundy, of Stratherly, his eldest son, and heirs of John Lundy by Mary Ramsay, his future spouse, of a third of the lands of Stratherly (*NAS*, GD20/1/332). He died in 1661 – "1661, Oct. 3 - Old Straerly, called James Lundy, depairted out of this life at Bamungo, who was liuing ther for the tyme, who died of a flux. His corps were brought to Straerly upon the Sabath, in the afternoon, and sett without doores ther all night, till Moneday, att ane of the clock, being 7 of Oct. at which tyme they were lifted and carried to Largo church, where they were interred within Lundy isle" (*Lamont's Diary*, p140).

He had issue:-

1 *John Lundie 8th of Strathairlie*, succeeded his father after his death in 1661.

2 *Captain James Lundie of Drumeldrie*, designed as the second lawful son of James Lundie, elder, in a charter to him granted by his brother John in 1660 (*NAS*, GD103/2/173). He was twice married: His first wife was Elspeth Henderson in Hatton, whom he married on the 6th of August 1658. She was the daughter of the deceased 'Good-Man of Hatton.' The marriage feast was held at her mother's house in Nether Pratis (*Lamont's Diary*, p 107). By Elspeth he had issue. After the death of Elspeth he married Margaret Edie. It is believed he had no issue by his second wife. There were at least two occasions during his brother's life, that James bought from his brother various parts of the Strathairlie estate. Rev. Wood in his *East Neuk of Fife* indicates this was a means to advance his brother money in order to pay of his brother's large debts. In 1660 he paid 8000 merks for the land of Keirs and Damside, and in 1668 he paid 10,000 merks for the land called the Mains of Strathairlie. Further details of these transactions can be read under his brother's life.

James was at one time (1668-78 for certain), Chamberlain to the powerful Lord Lovat. On the 8th May, 1668, Hew, Lord Fraser of Lovat, gave tack to James Lundie, his chamberlain, of his whole lands and baronies of Abertarffe, Stratherrick, Beauly, Strathglass, lordship of Lovat, and fishings of River Beauly, for the ingathering of the rents thereof. From this tack exemption was made of the Mains of Lovat, which were in the possession of Master Symon Fraser. For his pains James Lundie received 300 merks yearly in addition to his expenses. The tack was dated at Fortrose (*NAS*, GD176/520). On the 11th May, 1677, Kenneth Earl of Seaforth, Sir George McKenzie of Tarbat and Hugh Fraser of Belladrum, who had at that time acquired titles to the late Lord Lovats Estate, obliged themselves to dispone to James Lundy, brother to Stratherly the said Lord Lovats Estate for payment to him of £1800 Scots (*NAS*, GD305/1/148/205). By 1691, James was working as a factor in Innergellie (*NAS*, RH15/56/32).

In 1678, the Register of the Privy Council of Scotland records him as being robbed of a horse and other effects. The extract from the register is given below. It gives one of the reasons for him being chosen as the victim of this robbery as his support for the government of the time, that of King Charles II. It is interesting that his two brothers, the Rev. Robert Lundie minister of Leuchars, and Rev. Alexander Lundie, minister of Cupar, are penalised for their loyalty to the Stewarts, after the revolution of 1688.

Decreta February 1678 – September 1681, page 414

Complaint by James Lundy, brother to Stratharlie, and Daniel Achmoutie of Drumeldire, as follows:- James Smythe, grieve in Lundy, Alexander and James Balfoure, tenants in Gilstoun of Lundy, Thomas Nesse, tenant in Nether Praters of Lundy, Alexander Madieson, servant to the Laird of Feinzies, John Scott, now tenatn in Fau[ll]field, Mr Arthur Couppar in Abercrombie, William Robertson, weaver in Kinneucher, and John Mount in Branckstoun, having, upon the first rising of the rebels in the West in June, 1679, not only traitorously abandoned their loyalty to his Majesty by joining with them, but added thereto robbery and violence, and they, on June, 1679, a Sabbath day, came by night to the complainers' houses and threatened to burn the same if they got not access, and by their violence having procured entrance, they stole the goods underwritten, viz. from the said James Lundy a horse worth 300 merks, a pair of fine pistols worth 10*l* sterling, a 'massie' silver hilted sword with a buff belt having great silver buckles thereon, worth 10*l* sterling, a French fowlingpiece worth 5*l* sterling; and from the said Daniel Auchmoutie two horses worth 400 merks. These things they did merely because the complainers were loyal and well-affected to the present government. Charge having been given to the said Thomas Nesse (and the others whose names follow his, but not mentioning those proceeding him), and none of them compearing, the Lords ordain them to be put to the horn and escheat.

    (*Register of the Privy Council of Scotland*, Series III. VI., 521-522)

James appears in the Register of the Privy Council of Scotland in December 1685, when he was appointed to command the Fifeshire militia. He appears also in 1689 and 1690, as holding the position of bailie of Kirkcaldy (*Register of the Privy Council of Scotland*, Series III. XI., 60; XIV., 147-149; XV.). The acts of the Scottish Parliament show him as a commissioner of supply in 1690, and a subtacksman of the annexed excise of Fife and Kinross in 1695 (*General index to the acts of parliament of Scotland*); a job he seems to have had since at least 1688 (*Index Reg. Deeds*, Dal. LXIX., 1257). In 1697, James was a factor appointed for collecting rents and duties on the lands, which belonged to George Lord Melville. On the 23rd November that year he gave tack to William Orrock, son of David Orrock, tenant in Tilliebridles, of room and lands of Cormie Hill in the Parish of Abbotshall (*NAS*, GD26/5/57). He was also this year, (23rd of November), given a bond by David, Earl of Leven, for 19,000 merks (*NAS*, GD26/4/266). In 1702, he contributed funds to the repair of St. Leonard's College, of the University of St. Andrews (*Univ. St. And. Monim.*).

James Lundie died in 1705, when still a factor in Innergellie. He has issue, only daughters; who, subsequent to James's death, received an annual rent of 400 merks Scots from the lands and barony of Royston as a result of a bond by their father to George, Viscount Tarbat (later Earl of Cromartie). The bond dated from the 1st of August 1687

(*NAS*, GD305/1/117/442). 5000 merks Scots from this bond had been assigned, by James, in 1701, to Robert Lundin of that Ilk. In 1607, the total sum assigned to Robert Lundin of that Ilk, due to interest, had risen to 8095 merks Scots. This he renounced and consented that the amounts should instead be paid by the Earl of Cromartie to James Lundin's children. (*NAS*, GD305/1/147/114).

i Mary, baptized on the 9th of February 1679. She married her cousin Andrew Lundin, 2nd February 1700, in Largo, Fife.

ii Anna, married Nathaniel White of Bruntscholls, bailie of Elie, in 1680. Details of their marriage contract are preserved in the Laing Charters:-

"Contract matrimonial between Nathaniel Whyt of Bruntscholls, with consent of his mother Margaret Small, relict of the late John Whyt of Bruntsholls, on one part, and Anna Lundy, second daughter to James Lundy, brother-german of John Lundy of Stratharlie, with consent of her father, on the other part. The said Nathaniel and Anna bind themselves to marry each other while Nathaniel obliges himself to infeft his future spouse in liferent in the half of the lands of Bruntscholls, with half of the mill, also in and annual rent of 180 merks from that part of the lands of Ardross, with houses, etc., 'buildit upon the sacher (or saucher) thairof,' possessed by John Warrander, tenant, and from those acres occupied by Henry Bennet, indweller in Ealie, also from those acres occupied by Alexander Bennet, tenant in Balcleavie – all lying in the barony of Ardross, parish of Elie, and shire of Fife – in which Nathaniel was infeft on 13th May 1676, by a precept of Clare Constat by William Scott, elder of Ardross, and William Scott, fiar, superiors of the lands; also to infeft in liferent in a high tenement or house, with yard, etc., extending to four roods of land, lying within the said burgh of Ealie, 'boundit betwixt the commone rennel leiding from the port of Ealie to the mercat croce therof upon the eist, the sea fluid [and] comone way betweine upon the south, and land of Mr John Carmichell, now of William Scott of Ardross, upone the west, and the comone way upon the north pairts,' in the burgh of Ealie, barony, etc., as above. With other provisions. Dated and signed at Ealie and

Lundie-Milne, 24th and 25th March 1680. Witnesses, Alexander Gilespie, skipper in *Ealie*; Mr Henry Henderson, lawful son of John Henderson in Kilbracmount; John and Allan Lamont in Lundy-Mill; and James Cornfitt [or Coufrett], cooper in *Over Largo*.

    [*Laing Charters*, No. 2790]

    She was served as heir portioner special, to her father on the 5th June 1705, in parts of Strathairlie.

iii Margaret Lundin. She was served as heir portioner special, to her father on the 5th of June 1705, in parts of Strathairlie.

iv Isabel Lundin, married her cousin Humphrey Lundin, on the 14th of April 1705. She was served as heir portioner general to her father on 5th August 1705. She died before the 9th of August 1719, on that date her testament was proved at Edinburgh Commissary Court. Humphrey predeceased her. They had issue:

a   *Isobel Lundie,* born on the 26th of June 1707, in Edinburgh Parish, Edinburgh, Midlothian.

b   *James Lundie*, born 28th November, 1708. It is assumed that he and his sister died young as his aunt Sophia Lundin, was served as heir general to her brother, (his father) in 1731.

v Sophia Lundin, married Michael Lundin of Drumes. She was served as heir portioner general to her father on the 5th of August 1705.

3   **Margaret Lundie**, born around 1638, she married the Laird of Briggs in 1661 (*East Neuk*): "1661, Jul 1, being Saterday . . . Hamiltone of Briggs, a Lowthian gentelman, besyde the Quens-Ferry, married Margaret Lundy, old Stratherlys eldest dawghter; the marriage feast stood at Bamungo, in hir fathers house. In Dec. 1662, he depairted out of this life in Lowthian, about the same tyme that his wife was brought to bed of a son" (*Lamont's Diary*, p 137). She may well be the child of James Lundie of Stratherlie who was baptised on the 22nd of December 1638 at Largo. This baptism being witnessed by among others a James Lundie in Bonsie. Another 'child' of James was baptized at Largo on the 12th of September 1640, this was again witnessed by James Lundie in Bonsie. For this second child, James Lundie of Stratherlie was not present at the baptism, as he was 'being at the south,' so George Lundie in Saltgrein held up the child for baptism (*Largo Register, NAS*, GD50/185/57).

4   *Rev. Robert Lundie*, born around 1644, he was educated at the University of St Andrews, receiving his M.A. on the 18th of July 1664. He was ordained by James Sharp, Archbishop of St. Andrews in September 1669, at the Ferry near Dundee (*Lamont's Diary*, p 213). He was shortly afterwards, that same month, admitted by the Presbytery of Kirkcaldy to second charge in the Parish of Dysart, the first minister being a Mr John Anderson. He transferred, and was admitted (privately) to the parish of Leuchars in September 1684. As with his brothers, he was a Staunch Jacobite, and continued to publicly pray for King James VII, after the ascension of King William III and Queen Mary II., to the throne. For such reasons he was deprived in 1689.

"Anent a petitione given in to the Lords of his Majesties Privy Councill be the parishioners of Leuchars in Fyfe, viz., James Stivensone of Cowbackie, Robert Meldrum in Balmullo and John Hendersone in Leuchars, for themselves and in name of the saids parishioners, and Sir John Dalrymple, younger of Stair, his Majesties Advocat, for his Highnes interest, shewing that in obedience to the saids Lords proclaimatione anent ministers they have caused call M[r] Robert Lundie, minister at Leuchars, to compeir and answear before saids Lords upon the twentieth instant for his not reading and obeying the proclaimatione emitted by the Estates of this kingdome upon the threitinth of Apryle last for praying for their Majesties King William and Queen Mary, and seing that the said M[r] Robert Lundie hade not only contempteously disobeyed to read the said proclaimatione and to pray for their Majesties, but alsoe continues to pray for the late King James and therby endevours to alienat the hearts and hearers from their obedience to their present Majesties, and that they hade also cited witnesses to the said day for proveing of the premisses, as the executiones therwith produced would testifie, and therefore humbly craving the saids Lords to cause call the said Mr Robert Lundie and the witnesses to the effect they might be examined upon the poynts above mentioned, as the said petition bears: . . . . .

(*Register of the Privy Council of Scotland*, Series III, XIV., pages 71-72)

The Rev. Robert married Mary Symson; daughter of George Symson, Bailie in Dysart, and granddaughter of Archbishop Spottiswood; in August 1672. Rev. Robert died before 1705 (*Reg. Appren. Edin.*). They had issue:

i   David Lundie, baptized on the 1ˢᵗ of January 1676 in Dysart.

ii   Rachel Lundie, baptized on the 20ᵗʰ of July 1684 in Dysart.

iii   Robert Lundie, bapised on the 12ᵗʰ of July 1686 in Leuchars. On the 10ᵗʰ of February 1715, he was appointed as tutor to Andrew, James and Robina Lundie, children of Andrew Lundie of Strathairlie (*Index of Tutories and Curatories Lawful*). By occupation, he was a joiner in Edinburgh

iv   Charles Lundie, christened on the 28ᵗʰ of August 1688, in Leuchars; he was registered as an apprentice to James Peakoke, barber and perriwigmaker, on the 24ᵗʰ of October 1705 (*Reg. Appren. Edin.*).

5   *Rev. Alexander Lundie*, minister of Cupar, baptized 21ˢᵗ December 1649. He was educated at the University of St. Andrews, receiving his M.A. on the 24ᵗʰ of July 1669. He passed trials before the Presbytery of Glasgow and had a testimonial for licence on the 5ᵗʰ of June 1672. He was ordained to the Parish of Orwell before the 3ʳᵈ of October 1677, and was subsequently transferred to the Parish of Carnbee. He was presented to this parish by Sir Robert Dalyell, tutor to Alexander, Earl of Kellie, with the consent of Mary the Dowager Countess of Kellie, in March 1881, and admitted on the 27ᵗʰ of April that same year. On the 4ᵗʰ of May 1683 he was transferred from Carnbee to the parish of Wemyss, being elected to this post by the town council of Edinburgh on the 16ᵗʰ of March 1683. He transferred to the parish of Cupar in 1686, being presented by Arthur, Archbishop of St. Andrews in that July (*FASTI*). Alexander was a Jacobite. On the 29ᵗʰ of August 1689 he was deprived by the Privy Council for not reading the Proclamation of the Estates. An extract from the register of the Privy Council of Scotland detailing this mater is given below.

Acta, May 1689 – November 1689, page 260-261.

"Anent to the petitione given in and presented to the Lords of his Majesties Privy Councill be Thomas Lockhart, Joseph Knox and James Clidsdale, present baillies of Couper, and William Peag, deacon of the conveener of the Trades for the said burgh, for themselves and in name of the remanent parishioners of the paroch of Couper and Sir John Dalrymple, younger of Stair, his Majesties Advocat, for his Highnes interest, against M[r] Alexander Lundie and M[r] William Wilsone, ministers at Couper, shewing that wher by the law of God and by the principells and constitutiones of every weell governed natione all persones are bound to give due obedience unto and wish weell and pray for such whom they owe just obedience and true alledgance as their soveraingne, especially to such who have been the glorious instrument of our delyverie from popery and the pernicious inconvenincies that accompanie and arbitary power, and that by the municiple constitutiones of this realme all the subjects therof are obleidged to pray for their lawfull soveraigne; and particularlie by an act of the Meeting of the Estates of the date the thretein day of Apryle j[m]vi[c] eightie nine years all ministers who are in ane eminent maner obledged to discharge that dutie are therby expressly commanded to read a proclamatione of that date and publictly to pray for King William and Queen Mary as king and queen of this realme upon the dayes particularlie therinmentionit under the paine of being deprived and lossing of their benefices, and that they by that same proclaimatione all the leidges certified that they presume not to own or acknowledge the late King James the Seventh for their king nor presume upon their highest perill by word, wryting in sermones or in any other manner of way to impunge or dissowen the royal authoritie of William and Mary, King and Queen of Scotland; and by ane act of the saids Estates of the date the twentie third of Apryle last all ministers are obleidged to read a proclaimatione of that date whereby the Estates did grant warrand for a voluntar contrabutione to be collected throw the wholl kingdome both in paroch churches and meeting houses for the releiff of many distressed Protestants that ware fledd out of the kingdoms of France and Ireland for shelter and relieff, under the certificatione therin mentionit; and lastly by ane proclaimatione dated the twentie sixt day of Apryle last by past all ministers be south the river of Tay are ordained to keep the sixt day of May then nixt to come as ane day of solems and publict thanksgiveing to Allmightie God for delyverie from popery and arbitrary power, and are particularlie appoynted to read and intimat the samen from their pulpits as the acts and proclaimationes fully expresses: And true it is that the said Mr Alexander Lundie and Mr William Wilsone, ministers at Couper, was so farr from evidencing the just sense they ought to have read to his Majesties preservatione of our religione and of our releiff from those grivious circumstances the nation groaned under, which ware brought about by the seasonable and expensive charge of so dangerous ane interprize, that when the said proclaimatione of the Estates was sent to him, at least came to his hands or at least of which he had knowledg off, he was so farr from testifieing his gratitude and giveing due obedience therunto that nether the day appoynted by the said proclaimatione nor at anytime since hes he read the samen or Prayes for their Majesties King William and Queen Mary, and in high and manifest contempt of the last proclamatione anent the publict thanksgiveing the very hour appoynted for the exerciss of that divyne service did he command and suffer his servants to labour, diverting them or any others from gineingobedience therunto; and instead of reading the said proclaimatione for a contributione for the French and Irish Protestants he most barbarouslie, unchristianly and uncharitablie did stopt hinder and impedd the reading and proclaimeing of the same and did not make or permitt to be made any contributione aither at the church doors or by the elders throw the paroch; and in sight of the certificatione contained in that proclaimatione and act he actually prayed and daylie prayes for King James and for his hapie restoratione to his thron and for the confussione of his enemies; and seeing that the continuatione of such a persone in the ministeriall functione might prove very pernicious and extreamly disadvantageous to the interest of the present government; and anent the charge given to the said Mr Alexander and Mr William Wilsone, defenders, to have compeired before the saids Lords to have heard and seen decreit and sentance given and pronunced against them in manner to the effect underwrittin, as the warrand for the citatione granted by the saids Lords and executione of the charge given therupon more fully bears: The said Thomas Lockhart, ane of the saids persewars, for himself and in the name of the parishioners of the said parochin of Couper compeirand personally with . . . . ., their procurator, with concourse of his Majesties Advocat, and the saids Mr Alexander Lundie and Mr William Wilsone, defenders, compeirand alsoe personally, the which lybell and executions therof with the acknowledgement aftermentionit of the saids Mr Alexander Lundie and Mr William Wilsone that they had not read the proclaimatione nor prayed for King William and Queen Mary being read, heard and considered be the saids Lords and they therwith well and ryplie advised, the Lords of his Majesties Privy Councill have found and declaired and heirby finds and declairs that the said Mr Alexander Lundie and Mr William Wilsone hes lost and amitted their right to the benifice at the said kirk of Couper, and therfore the saids Lords have deprived and heirby deprives him therof and declared his church vaccant, and have discharged and heirby discharges the said Mr Alexander Lundie and Mr William Wilsone from preaching or exercissing any other part of the ministerial functione within the said parochin of Couper allenarly, and ordaines them to remove from their manses and gleibs at Mertinmiss nixt; and that becaus upon reading of the said lybell the persewar haveing offored to prove by the defenders their own acknowledgment that they hade not read the proclaimatione of the Estates nor prayed for King William nor Queen Mary in the terms therof, the said Mr Alexander Lundie and Mr William Wilsone did acknowledge the samen, and therfore the saids Lords gave and pronounced their decreit and sentance in the said matter in finding, declaring, depriveing, discharging, decerning and ordaining in manner abovewrittin, and ordains letters of horning on fyftein days and other executorials, etc."

(*Register of the Privy Council of Scotland*, Series III. XIV., pages 129-131)

In 1692 he was imprisoned in the Tollbooth for not Praying for

William and Mary, and also actively praying for the deposed King James VII. He was released after four days as he was "far from the means of subsistence, and his wife lying dangerously ill at home with a family of small children." Having begged the council's pardon, he was prohibited from exercising the ministry until he qualified himself by Act of Parliament. This incident appears in Chalmers Domestic Annals of Scotland.

> "Soon after, the Council judged, in the case of Mr Alexander Lundie, late minister of Cupar, who stated that, 'having a mixed auditory, he prayed so as might please both parties,' This style of praying, or else the manner of alluding to it, did not please the Privy Council, and Mr Lundie was ordered 'to be carried from the bar, by the macers, to the Tolbooth, there to remain during the Council's pleasure.' Having lain there four days, far from all means of subsistence, while his wife was ill of a dangerous disease at home, and his family of small children required his care, Mr Lundie was fain to beg the Council's pardon for what he said, and so obtained his liberation also, but only with a discharge from all clerical functions till he should properly qualify himself according to act of parliament."

The Rev. Alexander married a Miss Crawford. They had issue as indicated below. Alexander died on the 23rd June 1696. His elder brother, James Lundie of Stratherlie, was served as guardian of the estates of the minors, Anne and Maria Lundie, daughters of Alexander Lundie, minister at Couper on 29th September 1696, (*Inq. Ret. de Tut.*, No. 1157).

   i   Anna Lundin, died before October 1725.

   ii   Mary Lundin, was served heir to her sister Mary on the 21st of October 1725. She married John Orrock, the second son of Alexander Orrock of that Ilk, the contract being dated the 2nd of October 1728 (RH11/27/37 Pp 25-29; RH11/27/38 fol 213-18).

   iii   James, baptized July 3rd 1687 (*Lundins of Fife*)

6   **Anna Lundie** (*East Neuk*).

7   **Eupham Lundie**, baptized on the 26th of September 1653 (*East Neuk*).

8   **Agnes Lundie**, married Edward Jolly, son of David Jolly, cordier London, servitor to the King, on the 30th March 1672, (*Index Reg. Deeds*, Dal, XXXII., 364).

JOHN LUNDIE 8TH OF STRATHAIRLIE

He married Maria, daughter of the Rev. Robert Ramsay on 25th September 1656, at Abbotshall, Fife; and succeeded his father after his death in 1661.

It would appear that John held an estate that was very much encumbered with debt. Rev. Wood in his East Neuk suggests that a couple of payments made to John, by his brother James, for various parts of the Strathairlie lands, were to help pay off these debts. The first of these transactions took place in 1660, where his younger brother James paid 8000 merks for the lands of Keirs and Damside. This is recorded in great detail in a disposition from the time.

1st and 2nd of June 1660.

Disposition by John Lundie, fiar of Stratherlie, with consent of Mary Ramsay, his spouse, and also with consent of his father and mother, James Lundie of Stratherlie, and Margaret Orrock, his wife, in consideration of 8000 merks Scots paid by James Lundie, brother-german of the granter, and Elspeth Henriesone, his spouse, selling and alienating to the younger James and Elspeth, their heirs, etc., those portions of the lands of Stratherlie call the Keiris [possessed by David Tod] and the Damside [possessed by Patrick Boyd], being the east part of the lands of Stratherlie, lying in the parish of Largo and sheriffdom of Fife, with privilege of transporting ' wair from the wair sea' to the lands, 'with divits in the braes under the linkis' for building and repairing houses, and pasturage for two horses and two cows and their followers, ' be south and be eist and under the braes of the linkis,' the said lands of Keirs and Damsyde being bounded thus: - 'Haveing the landis of Monturpie on the eist, north and eist, and Drumeldrie milne burne, also on the eist and south eist, and the linkis of Stratherlie on the south, and ane fur coming down from Monturpie throw the Mucklat to the meidow be the eist place of Stratherlie, and going eist the meidow-heid to ane know callit the Hippielaw, and down be the eist the Hippielaw be ane erin lyned fur to the aker callit the Smithis aker, and goeing from thence west the north side of the Smithis aiker to the end of the Hawklaw, goeing down be ane ern fur by the west side of the Hawklaw to the head of the Weitlandis, and from thence west to the end of the Strangishaugh, and from thence southward as far as the Longlandis of the Strangishaugh, and from thence westward to the Shortlandis of the Strangishaugh, and from thence southward be the eist fur of the heading of the Shortlandis of the Strangishaugh to the aiker callit Crysties aiker, and from thence westward be a fur betwin Crysties aiker, and from thence southwards to the linkis on the west pairtis.' And the granter binds himself to infeft the grantees in the said lands, th be held from him of his superiors, to writ – 'the two pairt theirof' to be held of the Right Honourable Margaret Lundie, now Lady Lundie, for services due and want, and for ward, relief, and marriage; and the other third part to be held of John, Earl of Crawfurd and Lyndsay, in feu-farm for 29s. 4d. Scots yearly, as the proportional part of ten merks 6s. 8d. payable for the third part of the whole lands of Stratherlie. Disposition dated at Innerleven and Anstruther Easter on 1st and 2nd June 1660. Witnesses John Orrock in Balweirie mill; Robert Henrieson in Pitcorthie; Andrew Martine, bailie of Anstruther Easter; Andrew Symsone, clerk thereof; and Magnus Aytoun, clerk of Burntisland.

(*Laing Charters*, No. 2544)

John then granted a charter of these lands to his brother on the same day. One assumes that the lands of Keirs and Damsyde were in the third of Strathairlie with the Lindsays as superior, as the charter was confirmed on the 6th of June 1665 by John, 17th Earl of Craufurd, 1st Earl of Lindsay (*NAS*, GD103/2/173). Following the disposition and charter, on the 2nd of June 1660 'James Lundie, son lawful to the deceased George Lundie, who was brother german to the late John Lundie of that Ilk', gave sasine of the lands as mentioned in the disposition above. This was recorded at Cupar on the 6th of June 1660, and witnessed by 'David Tod, tenant in Keiris; Alexander Gatkarar in Burntisland; James Anderson, servitor to William Tod, tenant in Stratherlie (*Laing Charters*, No. 2545).

The second transaction occurred in 1668. On this occasion, James Lundie paid his brother John 10,000 merks for the lands called the Mains of Strathairlie. This was under reversion of the same amount (*Laing Charters*, No. 2628). Again this is well described by a disposition of the time.

Disposition by John Lundie of Stratherlie, heritable proprietor of the lands, with consent of Marie Ramsay, his wife, and of Margaret Orrock, his mother, relict of his father, the late James Lundie of Stratherlie, in consideration of 10,000 merks, alienating to James Lundie, his brother-german, his heirs and assignees, that portion of the granters lands and mains of Stratherlie possessed by Thomas Mackie and David Adamson, bounded as follows:- 'Beginning at the west end of that piece of land called Christies aker, and north nook or corner of it, and from that, westward and north-west the north side of the middle of the stauk coming to the midle of the burn of Stratherlie, and from thence up the middle of the burne northward and eistward under the yairds and planting of Stratherlie to the burne brae as far as the planting goes, and from the eist corner of the planting northward be the dyke biggit for keiping the young planting, and thence westward be the same dyke to the west corner of it, and from thence west be the south side of the heading untill the march of the landis of Largo, and from thence northward to the landis of Morturpie' with the same privilages of transporting sea 'wair' and others (as mentioned in the last disposition). The granter binds himself to infeft the grantee by charter to hold of his superiors, as in next writ. He also binds himself to transfer a tack or lease qccquired by his father, of the parsonage and vicarage teinds of the parish of Largo, of date 29th October 1602, leased by the late Mr. John Auchinleck, minister of Largo, with consent of the late Andrew Wood, elder of Largo; to the now deceased Andrew Wood, younger of Largo, for the space of two liferents and three nineteen years. Letters of disposition written by Magnus Aytoun in Burntisland, and dated at Stratherlie, 21st January1668. Witnesses, Mr John Auchlinleck, minister at Largo; John Halkstoun, burgess of Burntisland; and said Magnus Aytoun.
(*Laing Charters*, No. 2626)

Charter by the said John Lundie of Stratherlie, in terms of the above disposition, to James Lundie, his brother-german, of a portion, duly bounded and described, of the lands called the

Mains of Stratharlie [see lasst writ]: To be held of the granters superiors. Reddeudo, to the granter, 2d Scots yearly, if asked only, as feu-farm; to Margaret Lundie, lady of Lundie, for two parts of said lands, ward and relief, etc., and to the Earl of Crawford, for the other third of the lands, 35s yearly as feu-farm. dated at Stratharlie, 21st January 1668. Witnesses as in preceeding writ. [Indorsed is a confirmation by Dame Margaret Lundie of that Ilk, superior of part of the lands, of her portion of the lands. Dated at Lundie, 16th July 1677, of which charter Mr. Alexander Orrock of Cassindonat is writer, while William Lundie, son lawful to the late William Lundie of Lundie-Mill, is among the witnesses].
(*Laing Charters*, No. 2627)

Following the charter by John to his brother, sasine was given the following day by John Halkstoun, mealdealer, burgess of Bruntisland, as bailie, and recorded at Cupar on the 12th of February, 1668. (*Laing Charters*, No. 2629). Both of these transactions are also described in Lamont's Diary.

"1660, June 1 – James Lundy, who married Elspet Henderson in Haton, brought from his brother, young Straerly, in the parish of Largo, four chalder of victuall of the lands of Straerly, called Keirs and Dame-syde, laying on the esat side of Straerly; it stood betwuixt eight and nyne thousand makrs Scots. Jun. 2, the young Lady Straerly, surnamed Ramsay, went to Enster, and renunced, judicially, hir interest of the saids lands in favours of hir brother in law. The wryter of the sureties was Manse Ayton, clerke in Bruntelland; the place where the said sureties were subscriued was in Salt-greine, in James Lundys house, (son to the deceased Laird of Balgonie)" (*Lamont's Diary*, p 123).

"1668 – About the end of Jan. James Lundin, Straerlys brother in Fyffe, gave in to his brother Str., in money and by bond, ten thousand merkes Scots, for to pay his debt; for which he had a wadsett of 5 chalder victwall more in Straerly, only redeimable by Straerly himself, or his aires. (This with the former 4 ch. that he had before, makes 9 ch. in all.)" (*Lamont's Diary*, p 204)

John died in 1690 (*East Neuk,* p95). Note however that this same reference claims John left no issue. A charter granted to Andrew Lundin 10th of Strathairlie, by Robert Lundie of that Ilk, in 1737, wherein Andrew is designed eldest grandson and heir of John Lundie [7th] of Stratherlie, shows this cannot be the case. John and Margaret had issue.

1 *Andrew Lundin 9th of Strathairlie*, of whom later
2 *Humphrey Lundin W.S.*, described as the brother of Andrew in Rev. Wood's *East Neuk*. He married his cousin Isabel, daughter of James Lundie of Drumeldrie, on the 14th of April 1705, and died before 1720. They had issue (*see Isabel*).
3 *Sophia Lundin*, was married to John Watson, minister of Whittinghame (*RD.* 2/104/545). She was served as heir general to her brother Humphrey on the 26th January 1732.

ANDREW LUNDIE 9TH OF STRATHAIRLIE

He succeeded to Strathairlie upon his father's death, and married his cousin Mary Lundie, daughter of James Lundie of Drumeldrie, on the 2nd of February 1700.

On the 8th of October 1703, he granted a charter to 'Margaret Geddie, relict of Robert Dalrymple, tenant in the Temple of Stratherlie, and Mary Dalrymple, her daughter, in fee, of a house and yard, lying within the Temple of Strathairly, with David Thomson's yard and march stones therein on east, the road to the hill called Templehill on south, the yard of William Black, weaver, on west, and the highway through the town of the Temple of Strathairlie on north – all temple-lands and in the parish of Largo: To be held for an annual feu-duty of £1, 12s. Scots.' This was done at the Seatown of Largo, and witnessed by John Dalrymple, son of Robert; Walter Brabner in Largo, and Andrew Brabner (writer of Deed), servitor to Mr Samuel Gray, writer in Edinburgh (*Laing Charters*, No. 3009).

Much of the estate that Andrew inherited was in debt, and a large part was held by his uncle, (and father-in-law) James Lundie of Drumeldrie. Upon James Lundie of Drumeldrie's death, his five daughters inherited his lands, which included the lands of Keirs, Damside and Mains of Strathairlie, all of which were part of what was the Strathairlie estate. For unknown reasons, the daughters and heirs of James Lundie of Drumeldrie, transferred their rights to these lands to Andrew. On the 13th of March 1705, Anna Lundin, one of the five heirs-portioners of James Lundin, conveyed to Andrew her fifth part of her father's lands of Keirs and Damsyde, also her fifth part of 300 merks annualrent of 5000 merks in a bond by the late Kenneth, Earl of Seaforth (*Laing Charters*, No. 3018). She then transferred her rights of one fifth of the Mains of Strathairlie to Andrew on the 21st of May 1705 (*Laing Charters*, No. 3022). Four days later, her sister Mary, Andrew's spouse, with his consent conveyed to Walter Brabner, writer in Largo, her fifth part if her father's lands. That same day Walter then translated the same back to Andrew (*Laing Charters*, No. 3020, 3021). The claim of the other sisters was transferred the following year. On the 22nd August 1706, 'Isobella, Sophia, and Margaret Lundin, three of the heirs-portioners of the late James Lundin, with consent of Humphrey Lundin, writer in Edinburgh, husband of Isobel,' conveyed to Andrew all their rights to their three fifth parts of the Mains of Strathairly and the other lands their father bought of his brother. These lands had been granted to the five sisters reserving the liferent of Margaret Edie, the relict of their father. In the transfer of rights to their father's lands, the three sisters bound themselves to free Andrew of a proportion of the liferent of the said Margaret Edie. Isobel is recorded as giving her oath of consent, before Patrick Hume of Balsibrig, commissary depute of Lauder on the 23rd of August that year (*Laing Charters*, No. 3028).

Just as Andrew's grandfather had come across difficulties in gaining infeftment in his lands from Lundie of that Ilk, so did the heir portioners of Andrew's late uncle, and thus Andrew himself in the lands. A Precept from the chancery of Queen Anne, written on the 20th of July 1705, was directed to Robert Lundie of that Ilk, superior of the lands, for infefting Anna, Margaret and Mary Lundie, in two third parts of the Mains of Strathairlie and in two third parts of Keirs and Damside as heirs of their father, the late James Lundie of Drumeldrie, 'who died last vest in the lands' (*Laing Charters*, No. 3024). Andrew appeared before Robert Lundie of that Ilk, in 'the hall of Lundy' on the 29th of September 1705. As procurator for Anna, Margaret and Mary Lundie, he demanded infeftment on their behalf in two third parts of the Mains of Strathairlie and other lands according to the precept from Queen Anne. Robert refused to sign the writ, nor would he sign a precept presented for his signature. Andrew is then said to have protested 'for coast, skeath and damage,' and that his offer may stop the nonentry and process of declaration at Lundie's instance (*Laing Charters*, No. 3026). In 1706, (25th October) Robert Lundie of that Ilk was bound by obligation to 'receive Andrew Lundin of Strathairlie as his vassal in that part of the lands of Strathairly which belonged to the late James Lundin, to which Andrew had right by disposition be the heirs-portioners.' This Obligation was done at Drumochy and witnessed by among others, Humphrey Lundin, writer in Edinburgh, Andrew's brother (*Laing Charters*, No. 3030). The Precept of Clare Constat was finally given by Robert Lundie of that Ilk, to all five of James Lundie of Drumeldrie's daughters, in all of his aforementioned lands, on the 5th of October 1708; Again Andrew's brother was a witness. Sasine was given on the 20th of December the same year (*Laing Charters*, No. 3046, 3047).

The lands of Strathairlie were finally united again, in the possession of Andrew in 1713. On the 15th of October, 1713, Mr. David Lundin, advocate, (David Lundin of Auchtermairnie) acting as procurator for Andrew Lundin of Strathairly, resigned into the hands of Robert Lundin of that Ilk, his superior, Andrew's lands of Strathairly (except Keirs and Damside and the Mains of Strathairly). David, also acting as procurator for Ann, Isobel, Sophia, Margaret and Mary Lundie, the heirs-portioners of the late James Lundie of Drumeldrie, with consent of Humphrey Lundin, writer, husband of Isobel, and the Andrew, husband of Mary, resigned their lands of the Keirs, Damside, and Mains of Strathairly, into Robert Lundin of that Ilk's hands, all for due infeftment to be given to Andrew. The new infeftment was then given by Robert Lundin of that Ilk. All this was done in the dwelling house of Alexander Chisholm, writer in Drummachil (*Laing Charters*, Nos. 3069, 3070)

Andrew died around 1714, leaving nine children, who were all minors at the time. Andrew was succeeded by his son Andrew, but it is interesting to note that failing his own issue, the estate of Strathairlie was set to pass to a Mr Andrew Anderson of Balhame. On the 13th of September 1705, Andrew had granted a disposition to Andrew Anderson stating that for the love and favour which Andrew had and bore towards Mr Andrew Anderson of Balhame, and 'certain other weightie causes' moving him, he disponed to him (failing the heirs of his own body) all lands heritages moveable good &c. belonging to him at the time of his death, under the burden of paying debts, and also under the burden of the liferent provision granted by Andrew Lundie to Mary Lundin his spouse. This was done reserving power of revocation of the disposition. It was recorded with the Commissariat of St. Andrews on the 24th of January 1715 (*Commissariat of St. Andrews Deeds*, vol vii; *Laing Charters*, No. 3025; *NAS*, CC20/11/7).

His nine children were:-

1   **Andrew Lundin, 10th of Strathairlie**, whose details follow.
2   **Robina Lundin**, baptized on the 26th of January 1701
3   **John Lundin**, baptized on the 20th of October 1702 in Largo. It is suggested he died young.
4   **Marron Lundin**, baptized on the 9th of December 1703 in Largo.
5   **James Lundin**, baptized on the 20th of July 1708 in Largo. Still alive in 1744 (*Lundins of Fife*).
6   **Kenneth Lundin**, baptized on the 31st of July 1709, it is suggested he died young (*Lundins of Fife*).
7   **Humphrey Lundin**, baptized on the 15th of January 1711 (*Lundins of Fife*).
8   **Kenneth Lundin**, baptized on the 20th of January 1712 (*Lundins of Fife*).
9   **Michael Lundin**, baptized on the 2nd of December 1713 (*Lundins of Fife*).

ANDREW LUNDIN, 10TH OF STRATHAIRLIE

At the time of his father's death, and so his succession to Strathairlie, he was a minor. Amongst his curators were Michael Lundin of Drums, and Robert Lundie, son of the Rev. Robert Lundie (Andrew's great uncle) (*NAS*, B41/7/3). Robert Lundie was also tutor to Andrew's siblings, James and Robina. As no other siblings are mentioned, it may well suggest that the others died young. On the 26th of July 1715, James, Robina, and their tutor, 'Robert Lundie, joiner in Edinburgh,' issued a summons against Andrew, designed 'now of Strathairlie.' James, Robina and Robert, the pursuers in the case, plead to the Lords of Session that their father had died intestate but that their brother Andrew had served himself as heir to the whole estate. They stated that they had often desired of Andrew, as their elder brother, to make provision for them, but he refused. Andrew, as defender, is said to have answered this charge by stating that although the estate was worth £1395 Scots of yearly rent, it was burdened with debts and with interests to two liferenters (Lady Smiddiegreen and Mrs. Whyte). The Lords of Session gave decree for modified aliment to the pursuers of 100 merks yearly to each, to be increased at the deaths of the liferenters (*Laing Charters*, No. 3078).

On the 11th of October 1737, James Lundin of that Ilk granted a Precept of Clare Constat in favour of 'Andrew Lundin, now of Strathairlie,' infefting him as the eldest grandson and nearest lawful heir of his grandfather, the late John Lundin of Strathairlie, in the two part lands of Strathairlie, and others. This was done at Lundin, and witnessed by Patrick Lundin, the granter's brother-german. Sasine was given on the same day (*Laing Charters*, No. 3136). On the 11th of September 1744 Andrew resigned these lands back into the hands of James Lundin of that Ilk, for re-infeftment in favour of himself and his heirs (*Laing Charters*, No. 3164). Andrew granted a bond, registered the 23rd of October 1740, to the Kirk session of Markinch (*NAS*, SC20/36/7). On the 4th of August 1760, he granted a charter to the Trustees or Patrons of the Hospital of Largo, of a portion of the lands of Strathairlie, bounded by the lands of Monturpy, belonging to the Hospital on north and east, the Laird of Largo's lands on the west, and the King's highway leading eastwards from the Kirk town of Largo on the east. This charter was granted in exchange for 500 merks, and was witnessed by Andrew's son Robert (*Laing Charters*, No. 3209). On the 11th of September 1760, he granted three 19 year tacks of Strathairlie to a Mr. George Ayton (*NAS*, SC20/36/10). He died around 11th December 1776. His testament, registered with St. Andrew Commissary Court, is proved the 21st November 1786.

He married, on the 2nd of July 1734, Anne Oliphant, the second youngest daughter of George Oliphant of Prinlaws (*NAS*, SC20/36/6); they had issue:-

1   *Mary Lundin*, born on the 17th of May 1735, and baptized on the 22nd of May that year in Largo. She most probably died before her father, as a bond by her father, registered just after his death (14th of December 1776) is for the provision of his *two* daughters, Margaret and Anne Lundin (*NAS* SC20/36/13).

2   *Margaret Lundin*, baptized on the 1st of February 1737. She died unmarried before the 27th of May 1814. Her testament appears, as Miss Margaret Lundin, daughter of the late Andrew Lundin, Esq. of Strathairly, in the register of Testaments of Edinburgh Commissary Court, on that date.

3   *Anne Lundin*, born on the 28th of February, 1739, in Largo,

Fife. She died before the 30th of September, 1819. Two testaments, dated the 20th of September 1819, and the 21st of November 1820, are registered with Edinburgh Sheriff Court Inventories, under the name Ann and Anne Lundie, respectively, daughter of Andrew Lundin Esq. of Strathairly.

4 *Major James Lundin, 11th of Strathairlie*, whose details follow.

5 *Andrew Lundin*, born on the 17th March 1742 in Largo.

6 *George Lundin*, born on the 25th of June 1744 in Largo.

7 *Robert Lundin*, baptized on the 6th of August 1745. It is believed he married and had a son who was buried in 1769 (*Lundins of Fife*).

8 *John Lundin*, born on the 23rd of September 1747 in Largo.

9 *Phillip Alexander Lundin*, born in on the 5th of December 1751. He had issue (*Lundins of Fife*):

i   *Phillip Lundin*

ii *David Lundin*

MAJOR JAMES LUNDIN, 11TH OF STRATHAIRLIE

He was baptized on the 17th of August 1740 in Largo. He sold the estates of Strathairlie shortly before 1789; by this year a Mr David Briggs appears proprietor. Major James died in 1813 (*Eask Neuk of Fife*).

The estate of Strathairlie lies just east of Largo. The house, illustrated on the next page, still stands, but is now a corporate headquarters.

House of Todrig and Little Todrig

JOHN LUNDIE, 1ST OF THAT NAME OF TODRIG AND LITTLE TODRIG

John was the son of Allan Lundie of Huttonspittle, minister of Hutton. On the 24th of August, 1681, John Lundie was enrolled as a Burgess and Guildsman of the City of Edinburgh, by an act of Council. He married Jean/Jane Home. He had issue:

1 *Agnes Lundie*, married Thomas Rougheid of Whitsumhill (*PRS*

21. Strathairlie House

Berwick). Thomas's mother was a Jean Lundie (Dur. LXXXVI. 24). Agnes and Thomas had issue:

   i Thomas Rougheid of Whitsumhill

2 ***Christian Lundie***, married Thomas Kerr, Portioner of Hutton (*PRS Berwick*)

3 ***James Lundie of Little Todrig***, whose details follow.

4 ***Jean Lundie***, married John Majorbanks of Dedriggs. They had issue:

   i John Majorbanks of Dedriggs

JAMES LUNDIE, 2ND OF LITTLE TODRIG

He married Katherine Lundie, daughter of James Lundie of Huttonspittal. He died sometime before 1687. On this date King James VI of Scotland, as *ultimus haeres* of James Lundie of Little Todrig, made a grant of Little Todrig to David Crawford (*Abstracts of Records of the Secretary's office*, 1687-88; *NAS*, GD50/185/57)

One should note that in 1684-5, a Jean Lundie in Little Todrig took the oath of abjuration (*Reg. Privy. Council*, Series III., X., 481).

Lundie of Wester-Denhead

GEORGE LUNDIE OF WESTER DENHEAD

On the 22nd of November 1616, George Lundie of Wester Denhead was contracted to be married to, Helen Graham the daughter of Agnes Lundie and William Graham of Claverhouse (*Scot's Peerage*, III. 322). Little, if nothing, is known of George's ancestry and children, other than speculative guesses.

Helen Graham's mother, Agnes Lundie, was the daughter of Robert Lundie of Balgonie and Conland, so one might well surmise a link between George and the Balgonie Lundies. There was also a close relationship between the Graham's of Claverhouse and the Lundies of Gorthie, from location of estates and personal interaction. George Lundie, younger of Gorthie, son of George Lundie of Gorthie and Katherine Gorthie of that Ilk, appears connected with Wester Denside, located one mile east of Monikie in Forfar, and a few miles away from Myrton of Claverhouse. William Graham of Claverhouse, George Lundie of Gorthie, and his son George Lundie younger of Gorthie, appear in record on a number of bonds together (see House of Gorthie for further details). When George younger of Gorthie was complained about for drunken and riotous behaviour in Perth, one of his companions was George Graham, the second son of William Graham of Claverhouse and Agnes Lundie; and later to be the Laird himself.

There are various places of the name Wester Denhead, but the most probable location for George's estate is Denhead located between the aforementioned Monikie and Denside. As well as the association with Lundie of Gorthie, this area has a number of Lundies living in the vicinity. A James Lundie with his spouse Isobel Balbirney were living in Denside prior to 1577 (*Ed. Comm. Court; Ind. Cal Deeds XXII. 281*). Located a mile due south of Denhead is Newbigging, another area associated with the Lundies of Gorthie, as James Lundie in Newbigging (also with the Laird of Claverhouse) was witness to a bond of caution by George Lundie, younger of Gothie (*Reg. Privy Council, Series* I. IV. 658). John Lundie of Lochside had associations with Ardownie and Ardestie, located less than a mile south of Newbeggining, 2 miles south of Denhead.

With all of this information one might well surmise that George Lundie of Wester Denhead was a desendant of the House of Gorthie, with a high probability of him being the son of George Lundie younger of Gorthie; and Helen Graham being his second wife.

Lundie of the Wester Vaults of Whitsome

WILLIAM LUNDIE OF THE WESTER VAULTS OF WHITSOME

He was married to Margaret Home. It is quite probable this is William Lundie who was prior to 1680 designed as a portitioner of Simprine. This William was also married to a Margaret Home. She was the daughter of David Home of Crocerig. His father was probably Allan Lundie of Huttonspittle. He had issue:

1   *Allan Lundie*. He predeceased his father, and died before January 1711.

2   ***Jean Lundie*** (*Index Reg. Deeds*, Dur. LXVII., 376).

3   ***Agnes Lundie***. She was married to Thomas Hastie, a writer in Dunse. She was served as heir portioner general, along with her sister, to he brother, Allan Lundie on the 18th January 1711. On the 15th October 1730, she was served as heir portioner, along with her sister Agnes, to her father.

4   ***Margaret Lundie***. She was married to Abraham Lamb, late of Horse Guards Blue, - - master in the Duke of Bolton's regiment of Horse. She was served as heir portioner general, along with her sister, to her brother, Allan Lundie on the 18th January 1711. On the 15th October 1730, she was served as heir portioner, along with her sister Agnes, to her father.

Section Five

Other Well Documented Branches

As well as the Lundie branches holding landed estates in Scotland, there are also a number of other branches, not associated with a particular estate, or even region of Scotland, whose member's lives have been recorded and documented in a fair degree of detail. Many of these families have strong Military, Ecclesiastic, Scholastic and or Medical Connections. In most cases it is not specifically known how these branches descend from the Barons of Lundie, but they all have a long association with Scotland.

John Lundie, Professor of Humanities at Aberdeen University, and his descendants.

PROF. JOHN LUNDIE, M.A.

He was elected a regent of King's College in Aberdeen in 1626, and was a humanist there in 1629 (*Fasti Aberd.* lxxxiv). He was created Professor of Humanity in 1631. On the 16th March 1634, he was appointed by Patrick, Bishop of Aberdeen, chancellor of the University, to the office grammarian at Aberdeen University. He was appointed to teach Grammar, Poetry, Rhetoric, instruct the students in learning morals, and chastise delinquents (*NAS*, GD86/537). In November 1638 he represented his university at the general assembly at Glasgow (BAILIE *Correspondence*, Bannatyne Club, I. 135, 169). Having already subscribed to the covenant, he refused the King's covenant of October 1638. When attending the general assembly, John appears to have received small powers from the university, but getting wind that he was a covenanter, the assembly gave him those powers which the university of Aberdeen withheld, with the result that he exceeded his powers, and got into trouble on his return with the Aberdeen authorities, to whom he subsequently 'pleaded guiltie and confessed his error' (SPALDING, *Hist.*). According to Charters (*Cat. of Scottish Writers*) Lundie wrote 'very many poems and the comedie of the 12 patricians in the Latin tongue.' Besides the Oratio Eucharistica et ecomiastica in benevolos

Vniversitatis Aberdonenses benefactores fautores et patrones . . . havita xxvii. Jul. 1631,' Aberdeen 4to (Marischall College Library), he wrote the 'Carmen dedicatorium in commendationem totius libri,' prefixed to Bishop Patrick Forbes's 'Funeralls,' in which are other verses from his pen both in English and Latin (pp. 370, 414) (*Dictionary of National Biography*).

A short extract of some of his poetry is transcribed below. It was published alongside that of his brother-in-law, Alexander Gardyne, by the Abbotsford Club in 1845.

An. 1635. 1 Januar.
Goodmorrowe for my New Yeirs Gift.
To Mr. Da. Leich.

The first goodmorrowe (as ve vse to say)
Procurs the first propine on neue yeirs day.
Billie, goodmorroue, by mu soul! goodmorroue.
This bygon yeir which first began thy foroue
In tyms being buried, Janus heir
Coms and proclames a fair neu joyfull yeir.
Hence, therefor, al thy melancholike passions ;
Hence, hence, thy deipest , fadest cogitations.
Reserve thy self for better things, and burrie
In deip oblivion vrath's consuming furie.
My Janus heir requests the never remember
The fade disasters of foul December.
As for that other passion, thy supreme,
Which in lou's books hes enternis'd thy name,
Quench not ; but fitt it for some braver project,
And for some firmer and fairer object
Salute our primare ; for my blushing muse
To take such task upon hir doth refuse.
Shoe knous his will, his knoulege, iugment fage,
Outstrip his tym – anticipat his age.
Thairfor sho's forc'd for to imploy some other :
And quho;s so merit as you, his frind, hir brother.
The first goodmorroue, as ve vse to say,
Procurs the first propine on neue yeirs day.

The Princiapl re-salits with his Propine.

In lieu of guerdon, loue a gratefull mind,
And by this token poor pure loue esteime.
Lou's prospect makes a myte a montane seim.
Look throch it, and O quhat a store you'l find.
If madest malice hade not clipt my vings
I'd long ere noue due and gryter things.

The Author returns the Principale thanks.

Lo! heir my Muse befor your altar stands
Presenting thanks unto your sacred hands.
Your countenance, Sir, or yoor gracious smill
Could recompenced had hir rustike styll,
That it vold pleis youe vith your learned lines
T' impart the pleges of true lou's propins;
Yovr loue, yovr lou's effects I never wanted,
But vith yovr lin's my muse vas not aquanted.
Oft tyms youe haue in gryt magnificens
Enrich'd hir vith yovr pourful eloquence ;
Oft tyms in Stagirit's fair meads yove fedd hir ;
Oft tyms throch Ramus' Cyclads haue youe ledd hir ;
Oft tyms vith Atlas youe haue made hir beir
Th' vnveering vaight of the first moving sphear :
And vith Endymion his Latinian bray's,
To passe the nicht in chest Diana's play's ;
Yea, by yovr pour oft tyms I sein hir make
The rouling rounds of heavens vast globe to shake ;
And by your cuning in hit practise nimble,
Shoe can make all this louer round to trimble.
Thes shoe could doe befor, but noue yovr measurs
Acquaint hir with the sveit Vrania's pleasurs.
Roks seim to haue ears, and floods their furie stoping,
Stand fix'd as voods quhil voods and meads go hoping ;
Yea, noue the heavens rapt vith thy sveitest tonge,
Listning league of their Pythagorean song,

Sooner shall boistrous Boreas shake his ving
From Niger's lake and moistie Auster spring,
From Scotland's frostie Hebrid's then thy fame
Shall parish, or oblivion rase thy name.
In spyt of malice (which thy fame vold bound)
Thy temples still vith laurels shall be crowned.

A reply to Mr. Da. Leich S. his lyns.

QUHENCE sloue thy streams ? I'm fure from Phous fontane,
And from the tou tops of the Aonian montane.
Thy happy vain in lou's sveit subject yeilds,
Such floods overfloving the Boeotian feilds,
That fenns and plains overspred vith rivers be,
Yea Parnasse seims a valey vnto me.
No marvell. Scarce yet borne, thy cradle prest
Sveit Philomels to couch their tender nest.
Vithin thy mouth the bees to build did striue,
And arch the chambers of their hony-hyue ;
And sveit Vrania in hir arms infolding
Thy tender bodie, smylingly beholding
Hir father's darling with a vorld of kisses,
Into thy soul shoe brath'd a thusand blisses.
Then roking the but sostlie quhil shoe brings
Hir babe asleip this sveit baloue sings :
MIlk be thy drink, and hony be thy food,
And al things that can be doe men's bodie good ;
In als gryt plentie thy soul possesse them,
In als gryt plentie as Apollo hes them.
That quhen thou grous at last and soars and springs,
Not with Icarian but Dedalian vings,
Al that in lou's sveit subject loue to sing,
May to thyn altar henceforth ofrings bring.
No merval then, if thus thy heavenly measurs,
Rapt human souls vith mor than human pleasurs,
Much lyk Meander or much lyk our Po.
Heir straich they runne, and their they turning go,

Glade to go on, more glaid to turne and wynd them,
Glaid of neue sichts, more glade of thos behind them :
As if they vere affected with desyr,
And brunt with Beutie's much beuiching fyre.
Peneus, I grant, and old Apidanus,
Eas, Enipeus, and svift Inachus,
Having their souls rapt throch their crystal ey's,
Did sundrie tyms their Naiads idolize.
But heir's no object which may moue thy streams,
To stay or veip or strain forth sorouing theams.
Therefor go an and look no more behind the,
Or tell me quhy thoue lous to turne and wynd the.
If thoue be seik my muse shall come and eas the ;
I thoue be quhole vith lyns shoe vous to pleis the :
And if if chanch hir self in such casse be,
Shoe sveirs to seik non other Leich but the.

On Neu Yeirs Day I gave ane Dictionar of 400 Languages to M. Al. Gardyn, vith this Inscription.

Vnto the father of the Muses songs,
I give this treasure of four hundredth tongs,
A rare propyne, farr rairer he thtat gaue it,
But thryse more rair is he quho nou must haue it.

M. Al. Gardyne replys.

Amphyon-lyk that pinns Apollo's harp,
And theron fynlie friddins flatt sharpe,
And thoue ane other Delius in our dayes,
Rich in conceptions rair receave this prais,
That vith thy Polyglot to me thoue gaue,
It vas thyn oven, and thoue thyn oven shall haue.

Another to M. D. L. S.

The glyding currant of th' affections go,
Much lyk Meander turning to and fro,
Quhen in his pryd throch Lidian feilds he flees,
To pay tribut to his fathers seas;
The loftie flood proud of his pourfull train,
He turns his courser from the main again,
And stands overcharged with a vorld of joy,
To veiue the grandour of his grand convoy.
　　　　Much lyk our Po, quhose course runs
　　　　　　straicht and plain
From Pallas' mount t' Apollo's bouns again,
Seing no object all along the vay,
Of vorth to mak his Princelie troups to stay,
Holds straicht his course, and scorns to look behind him,
Or to our contrey suains to turne and vynd him,
But quhen Appollo's police he espy's,
He turns his cotch, and al his troups he stays.
Sometymes he stands, sometymes his merch advances,
From bank to bank he capers, cuts, and dances,
And scarse beleving such things their to be,
Which both he heirs, and vith his eys doth see,
He stands amazed, vandring to and fro,
Stagring throch joy a much inebriat Po;
And if that nature forc'd him not remoue,
Doubtless his streams should dry at lenthe throch loue,
For quhen in end he mounts his coatch of bleue,
He crys tenn thusand-thusand tyms adeue.
Look on my floods, Deir Leich, and thou shall see
The liulie portrait of Leich constancie;
They in their turning haue a braver proiect,
Leich loue is mor, tho not so rair his obiect;
They scorne to turne them to a sylvan Dryade,
Leich in lou's church doth idolize a Naiad:
Naiad, Oread, or quhat euer shee be,
Leich in his loue respecteth non but shee.

They loue no quher th'ar lou'd. A svain
Leich loues, and yet Leich is not lou'd again.
This constancie, Deir Leich, I can not loue it,
Yea, all the Muses iointlie disaprove it,
And vith the al to re-advance thy fame,
No more to loue, or loue some rairer dame.
The send the an heir then the Phenix rarer,
Vyfer then Pallas, then the ivorie fairer,
Cleirer then cristall, quhiter then the snoue,
Constant in loue more then the turtle doue;
Shoe is not Helene or Hermione,
Cressid, Creusa, nor Penelope,
She is not Leda, not Laodomia,
She is the Muses fairest Vdemia.

John Lundie was twice married. His first wife was Helen Gardyne (*Reg. Sasine. Aberdeen*), sister of Alexander Gardyne the Poet, and Elizabeth Gardyne, sometime wife of Alexander Morisone of Bognor. The date of this marriage is not certain, but certainly prior to 1636, when in his poems as seen before, Alexander Gardyne is described as his brother-in-law. By her he had issue:

1   *Rev. James Lundie,* minister at North Leith, born around 1640. Details of his life and descendants follow later.
2   *Alexander Lundie*, lister (dyer) burgess in Aberdeen. He married Elspeth Gordone, and had issue:
  i James Lundie, christened on the 17th of June 1669, in the parish of Saint Nicholas, Aberdeen.
  ii Marjorie (Mary) Lundie, christened on the 10th of February 1671, in the parish of Saint Nicholas, Aberdeen. She died before the 15th of July 1736. Her cousin The Rev. Archibald Lundie, minister of Saltoun was served as heir to her and her father, which suggests that her siblings died before this without issue.
  iii Elizabeth Lundie, christened on the 15th of October 1674, in the parish of Saint Nicholas, Aberdeen.
  iv George Lundie, christened on the 30th of October 1676, in the parish of Saint Nicholas, Aberdeen.

v   Helen Lundie, christened on the 9th of February 1680, in the parish of Saint Nicholas, Aberdeen.

John married secondly, on the 12th of July 1647, at Gordon's Mill, Margaret Gordon, by whom he had issue *(Dict. Nat. Biog.)*.

3   *John Lundie*. From Prof. John's poems, it would appear as if his son John predeceased him.

REV. JAMES LUNDIE, MINISTER OF NORTH LEITH

He was born around the year 1640. Graduated master of Arts from King's College Aberdeen in 1657; he was ordained to the Parish of Tron, as second charge, in 1663; he was transferred to St Giles Parish, Edinburgh in 1688; transferred to the Tollbooth Parish, Edinburgh, in 1672; transferred to the Parish of Tron in Edinburgh, this time as first minister, in 1675; he transferred to the parish of Dalkeith in 1680, but was deprived on account of the Test. On the 5th of September 1687, he was presented to the Parish of North Leith, Edinburgh, by the inhabitants, and admitted soon after *(FASTI)*.

He appears in the records for the Parish of South Leith on the 22nd of November 1692. "This day Mr. Jo. Law one of ye minrs. of Edr. came to ye session and required Patrick Glass, Nottar, whom he brought along wt him to read a paper which he said was a commission from the pbty of Edr. impowering him and Mr. Ja. Lundie minr. of North Leith (who came not alongst with him) to discharge our session to proceed to a new election and yt ye pbty declared our session to be no session nor could chuse none but yt that was ye only session qrof Mr Wishart was Moderator…" James Lundie came himself to this session in South Leith on the 22nd of December that year.

Rev. James died on the 31st of March, 1696, aged 56, and was buried in North Leith Churchyard, Coburg Street, Edinburgh. According to Robertson in his *South Leith Records*, a 'magnificent tombstone' marked James's grave, which was restored around 1911. Sadly a thorough search of this churchyard (2003) revealed that if this tombstone is still standing it could no longer be read, and thus discerned from other ancient stones. There are several in that churchyard where the faces are illegible. However, it is some small degree of consolation that the details of the inscription on this monument were preserved in the text: *"An Theater of Mortality: Or, the*

Illustrious Inscriptions extant upon the several monuments, erected over the dead bodies, (of the sometime honourable persons) buried within the Gray friars church yard; and other churches and burial places within the City of Edinburgh and suburbs: collected and Englished by R. Monteith, M.A." The original Latin inscription and translation, transcribed from this text are given below:

> "North Leith Churchyard
> The Reverend Mr. James Lundie's Monument.
> John Chap. 5. verses 28.29. at length.

Siste gradsum Viator. Hic jacet Dominus Jacobus Lundinus, Theologus admodum Reverendus, & verbi divini Minister eximius; Præ.clarum exemplar spectatæ morum probitatis, veræ Pietatis, Christianæ Humilitatis, Modestæ Gravitatis, cerræ Amicitiæ, & humanæ Urbanitatis; Perpetuæ Fidei, Curæ & vigilantiæ, in munere Pastorali; Quo, cum annos octodecens, in Ecclesia Edinburgena, anum in Dalkethensi, summa cum laude & bonorum favore functus affet, Conscientiæ suæ side commotus ab anno MDCLXXXI ad annum MDCLXXVII a publico ejusdem exercitio cessavit. Postea vero, mutato retumstaeu, unanimi Ecclesiæ Lethensis Septentrionalis suffagio, ad Animarum curam ibidem admotus eam tenuit annos VIII. menses V. Obijt Prid Cal. April. Anno Dom. MDCXCVI. ætatis 56.

Charissimo patri Posuit filius natu maximus Dominus Archibaldus Lundinis, verbi divini Minister, apud Saltoun. Volat irrevocabile tempus.

On the back, within a large round Wreath, is written
Revel. 14. 14 at length.
M.
I. L.
Stay passenger. Here lyeth Mr. James Lundie, a very Reverend Divine; and a notable Preacher (or minister) of Gods Word; A most famous Patterno of a good life, true piety, christian Humility, modest Gravity, from Friendship, and courteous Civility; of a constant Faithfulness, Care and vigilancie, in his ministerial Function, which when he had discharged for the space

of 18 years in the Church at Edinburgh, one year at Dalkeith, with great Commendation, and the favour of all good people, He moved by a principle of Conscience, ceased from the public exercise of his Ministry from the year 1681, to the year 1687. But afterwards the state of affairs being altered, by the Unanimous Call of the Church at North-Leith, he was advanced to the Cure there, which he officiat in the space of 8 years and 5 Moneths. he dyed on the last day of March, in the year of our LORD, 1696. His age 56.

His eldest son Mr. Archibald Lundie, minister of God's word, at Saltoun, errected the Monument to his dearest Father's Memory. Irrecoverable Time flies away."

Details of James's monument also feature in Nisbet's *Essay on Additional Figures and Marks of Cadency, &c.* Ecclesiastics in Scotland were entitled to carry the plain coat of arms of their chief families, so as minister in Scotland, James was entitled to carry the plain coat of arms of the Lundie family. Nisbet describes his Tomb as showing the ancient arms of Lundie (Paly of six *argent* and *gules*, over all, on a bend *azure* three cushions *Or*).

The Rev. James married Catherine Chrystie, daughter of James Chrystie of Whytehouse, on the 2nd March 1671. They had issue:-

1   *James Lundie*, baptized on the 4th of June 1672, probably buried 5th February 1674.
2   *Rev. Archibald Lundie*, whose details follow.
3   *Margaret Lundie*, born on the 24th of April 1675.
4   *Jean Lundie*, baptized on the 25th of June 1676.
5   *John Lundie*, baptized on the 22nd of December 1677.
6   *Andrew Lundie*
7   *Janet Lundie*, baptized on the 8th of March 1679.

The Rev. James married secondly, Agnes, daughter of James Wilkie of Cammo, and widow of Henry Morison W.S. James died on the 31st of March 1696. Agnes Wilkie died in January 1692. They had issue:-

1   *James Lundie M.D.*, baptized on the 7th of May 1686, and died in 1777. He is probably the 'late Dr. James Lundie, physician in Haddington,' whose daughter Margaret Lundie features in the Scots magazine of August 1806 (*NAS*, GD50/185/57).

REV. ARCHIBALD LUNDIE, MINISTER OF SALTOUN

The second son of the Rev. James Lundie, he was baptized on the 20th of January 1674. He was educated at the University of Edinburgh, graduating M.A. on the 13th of July 1691. He was ordained on the 24th of September 1696. He married Jean Menzies of Cramond, on the 2nd of February, 1699, at Saltoun, East Lothian. He was minister of Saltoun, in East Lothian, for 64 years, until his death on the 4th of November, 1759. Dr Alexander Carlyle, minister of Inveresk, visited Archibald, and briefly refers to this visit in his autobiography:

> "The next I went to was old Lundie of Saltoun, a pious and primitive old man, very respectful in his manners, and very kind. He had been bred an old Scotch Episcopalian, and was averse to the Confession of Faith: the presbytery showed lenity towards him, so he did not sign it to his dying day, for which reason he never could be a member of Assembly"

> *(Autobiography of the Rev. Dr. Alexander Carlyle)*

Archibald was served as heir general to his father on the 20th December 1700 (*Gen. Retours*, No. 8199). On the 21st July 1736, he was served as heir special to his uncle Alexander Lundie (styled dyer in Old Aberdeen), in four crofts of land, lying within the city of Old Aberdeen; and heir general to his cousin, May Lundie, daughter of the said Alexander. He and Jean Menzies had issue:-

1   *Rachel Lundie*, christened on the 9th of January, 1720, at Saltoun, East Lothian, Scotland.

2   *Rev. John Lundie*, minister of Oldhamstocks in Haddingtonshire. He was born on the 3rd of September 1704. He was educated at Edinburgh University and licensed by the Presbytery of Haddington on the 18th of April, 1732. He was presented to the Parish of Oldhamstocks by Lord Alexander Hay of Lawfield, and ordained on the 19th of July, 1733 (*FASTI*). He was twice married: First to Helen Lundie. By her he had issue:

   i   *Archibald Lundie*, born on the 5th of November 1741, died 26th

September 1747

ii Isabel Lundie, born on the 5th of March 1743 and christened on the 16th of March that year, at Oldhamstocks. She married the Rev. Henry Cant, minister of the dissenting congregation at Spittal, Durham, on the 25th of June 1787, in Edinburgh. She died before the 7th of October, 1791.

Helen Lundie died on the 17th of December 1744. The Rev. John remarried to Helen Hepburn, daughter of John Hepburn of Humbie. She died on the 15th January 1777. He died before the 13th of July, 1787.

3   *Isabel Lundie*, baptized on the 15th of August 1706, at Saltoun, East Lothian. She married William Bannatyne, minister of Yarrow (*FASTI*).

4   *Rev. Henry Lundie*, minister of Trinity Parish Edinburgh. He was educated at Edinburgh University; Licensed by the Presbytery of Haddington on the 24th of June, 1740; ordained to the Parish of Monzie on the 10th of May 1743; transferred to the parish of Abercorn on the 24th of September 1747; called to the parish of Saltoun on the 13th of August 1756, transferred and admitted to the parish of Trinity in the City of Edinburgh on the 15th of June 1758 (*FASTI*). He married, on the 19th of November 1749, Christian Menzies, daughter of Dr. John Menzies, a physician in Dumfries (*Ed. Mar. Reg.*). The Rev. Henry Lundie died on the 1st of January 1800, his wife Christian died on the 10th of November, 1810. They had issue:-

i Archibald Lundie W.S., was born on December the 22nd 1751 and was christened on the 29th of that month, in Abercorn, West Lothian. He married his cousin, Jane Lundie on the 30th of November, 1782, at St. Cuthberts, Edinburgh. He was served as heir general to his father on the 1st May 1800. He died on the 4th of May 1841. She died sometime before the 9th of July 1841, as on that date her testament ins proved (*Ed. Sheriff Court*). Archibald and Jane Lundie had issue:

a Henry Lundie, born on the 16th of November, 1783, in Edinburgh.

b Christian Lundie, born on the 15th of January, 1786, in Edinburgh.

c Janet Isabella Lundie, born on the 28th of May, 1787, in

Edinburgh. Assumed she died young as another child born 10 years later has the same name.

d Jean Lundie, born on the 20th of January, 1789, in Edinburgh.

e Katherine Campbell Lundie, born on the 18th of January, 1791, in Edinburgh.

f James Lundie, baptized on the 18th of March 1793, in Edinburgh.

g Archibald Lundie, baptized 13th October 1795, at Edinburgh. He died, a midshipman, January 18th 1815

h Janet Isabella Lundie, born June 4th 1797, Edinburgh.

i Agnes Lundie, born February 10 1799, Edinburgh.

One of Archibald Lundie's daughters is thought to have married, on the 26th of November 1804, at Madeira, Andrew Wardrope, a merchant. They also had a daughter on the 28th of February 1806 (*Scots Magazine*, 1804; April 1806)

ii Catherine Lundie, Christened on the 3rd of June, 1753, at Abercorn, West Lothian.

iii Jean Lundie, christened on the 10th of November, 1754, at Abercorn, West Lothian

iv John Lundie, born on the 1st of December 1755, and christened on the 11th of January 1756, at Abercorn, West Lothian, Scotland.

v Margaret Lundie, born on the 4th of May 1757, and christened on the 8th of May that year, at Abercorn, West Lothian. She died on the 20th of December 1759.

vi Robert Lundie, born on the 13th of June 1760, in Edinburgh Parish, Edinburgh. He died on the 1st of June 1767.

5   ***Andrew Lundie***, born on the 14th of December 1708; he was buried on the 27th of March 1716.

6   ***Archibald Lundie***, born on the 3rd of December 1710.

7   ***Rev. Cornelius Lundie***, minister of Kelso. He was born on the 11th of August 1716. He was ordained, and married, on the 27th August 1762, Mary Ronald, the daughter of William Ronald of Williamscraig. She died 1st May 1801. They had issue:-

i   Mary Lundie, born on the 13th of January 1764; christened at Kelso on the 5th of February that year. She married the Rev. John Wood of Crookham in July 1784.

ii Archibald Lundie, born on the 15th of July 1765; christened on the 28th of July, 1765, at Kelso; he died in Nice on January the 23rd 1789.

iii Jean Lundie, born 18th May 1767; christened on the 7th of June that year at Kelso.

iv Margaret Lundie, born on the 25th of January 1769; christened on the 5th of February that year; she died 12th June 1787.

v Rachel Lundie, born on the 27th of November 1770; christened on the 2nd of December that year, at Kelso; she died 14th November 1771.

vi William Lundie, born on the 19th of July 1772; christened on the 2nd of August that year; he died 8th January 1774.

vi Rev. Robert Lundie of Kelso. Born on the 4th of July 1774 and christened on the 17th of the month, at Kelso. Further details of his life will be discussed in full shortly.

vii Elizabeth Lundie, born on the 26th of April 1776; christened on the 19th of May, 1777 at Kelso; she died on the 22nd of February 1795.

viii Marion Lundie, born on the 11th of August 1777; christened on the 24th of August, 1777, at Kelso; she died on the 4th of February 1786.

ix Catherine Lundie, born on the 16th of May 1779; christened on the 30th of May, 1779, at Kelso; she died on the 1st of October 1841.

8 *James Lundie*, minister of Erskine. He was born 1716-17, and appointed to Erskine in 1742, succeeding the Rev. Walter Menzies who had died the previous year. He married Christian Ballantyne of Kellie, daughter of Archibald Ballantyne of Kellie, on the 26th of August 1745. He died on the 2nd of January 1769, whist still in his post. His testament is registered with Glasgow Commissary Court (7th August 1769). Shortly after the death of Rev. James Lundie, his widow's brother, James Ballantyne of Kellie, died (November 6th 1679). Christian was his heir, and succeeded her brother to Kelly (*History of Renfrew*). James and Christian had issue:-

i James Lundie, born on the 20th of September 1746, and died when abroad.

ii Archibald Lundie, born on the 14th of July 1748. On the 14th of March, and 17th April, 1794, whilst a merchant in Jamaica, he was served as heir of provision special, to his grandfather, Archibald Ballatyne of Kellie, who died in 1712, in Dykes, Milrig, St Phillanswell &c. and the Temple lands of Skelmorlie, in Ayrshire.

iii Walter Lundie, born on the 28th of March 1750; christened on the 30th of March that year, at Erskine, Renfrew. An M.D in Jamaica

iv Janet Isabella Lundie, christened on the 5th of July 1753; she married Andrew Wardthorpe, a surgeon, on the 30th of November 1778 (*Reg. Mar. Ed.*).

v Jane or Jean, born on the 24th of December 1755; christened on the 27th of December, 1755, at Erskine, Renfrew; she married her cousin Archibald Lundie, with issue. She died 23rd April 1826.

9 *Katharine Lundie*, christened on the 9th of January, 1720, at Saltoun, East Lothian, Scotland.

REV. ROBERT LUNDIE, MINISTER OF KELSO

Second son of Rev. Cornelius Lundie and Mary Ronald, he was born on the 4th of July 1774, and christened on the 17th of the month, at Kelso. He appears as quite a famous Scottish minister; as a result of his own works; those of his wife and children; and the company and society he was moved in. He corresponded with much of the 'academic intellect of Edinburgh' of his day, stemming from his time spent at the University there. Much of this correspondence has been preserved and is now held by the National Library of Scotland, donated by his granddaughter. Further details of these papers can be read towards the end of this section under the title of 'Lundie Papers.' The Rev. Matthias Bruen of New York, upon visiting Rev Lundie and his family in 1817 wrote "I have acquired at Kelso, at least one of the kindest friends, which, so long as sin is in this world, we can hope God will give us to comfort us in our state of Pilgrimage" (*Poets of the Church*). He was later to be the subject of a biography written by Rev. Lundie's wife Mary. The National Gallery of Scotland holds a portrait of the Rev. Robert, drawn by Turner.

Robert was ordained on the 26th of March 1801 to the Parish of Gordon. In 1807, he transferred to Kelso. On the 27th of April, 1813 he married Mary Grey, daughter of George Grey of Sandyhouse. One of the Rev. Roberts sermons is documented in:

"Gleanings of R. Lundie's "Pastoral Address" to his beloved flock ... With a sermon [on Genesis v. 24] preached at Kelso after his death, by ... J. Baird, etc." This can be found in the British Library.

He was served as heir general to his father on the 15th March 1809; and heir general to his mother, on the 7th of May 1819. The Rev. Robert died before 1832. After this Mary re-married to Dr. Rev. Duncan of Ruthwell (the founder of savings banks). Robert and Mary had issue:-

1 *Mary Lundie*, born on the 26th of April 1814. She married the Rev. W.W. Duncan, and died on the 5th of January 1840. She is the subject of the book, "Mary Lundie Duncan". Further details of her life will be discussed later.

2 *Cornelius Lundie*, born on the 25th of May 1815, and died on the 12th of February 1908. Further details of his life will be discussed later.

3 *Susanna Isabella Lundie*, born on the 6th of May 1817; christened on the 8th of June 1817, at Kelso; and died on the 14th of August 1826

4 *Rev. George Archibald Lundie*, born on the 31st of December 1819. He was a missionary in Samoa, where he died in September 1841, and is author of a book related to his work there: "missionary life in Samoa".

5 *Jane Catherine Lundie*, born on the 1st of December 1821, she married the Rev. Horatius Bonnar and died on the 3rd of December 1884. Further details of her life will be discussed later.

6 *Rev. Robert Henry Lundie M.A., D.D.* Christened on the 5th of December 1824. He was the Minister of St. Andrew's Church, Fairfield, Liverpool. Further details of his life will be discussed later.

MARY LUNDIE (DUNCAN)

The eldest daughter of the Rev. Robert Lundie of Kelso and Mary Grey, she was born on the 26th of April 1814 in Kelso. She married the Rev. W.W. Duncan minister of Cleish (son of Rev. Henry Duncan who is often described as father of the savings bank) in 1836, having two children together.

She produced a number of poems, pieces of music and short writings, almost all with a religious tone. Her Hymns include, "Jesus, Tender Shepherd, Hear Me," "Lo! Round the Throne a Glorious Band," and "My Savoir, Be Thou Near Me." She was the author of "Rhymes for my Children." She died on the 5th of January 1840 and is buried in Cleish, Kinross, Scotland. A marble plaque in Cleish Parish chuch is placed in her memory:

To the memory of
MARY
DAUGHTER OF THE LATE
REV. ROBERT LUNDIE OF KELSO
AND WIFE OF
THE REV. W. WALLACE DUNCAN
OF CLEISH

....
IN THE MORNING OF LIFE
THE SWEET AFFECTIONS OF HER HEART
AND EVERY ENERGY
A POWERFUL AND
HIGHLY REFINED INTELLECT
WERE CONSECRATED, BY THE HOLY SPIRIT
TO THE SERVICE OF
JESUS CHRIST

....
LOVED ALIKE IN PERSON AND CHARATER,
SHE DISCHARGEDWITH FIDELITY THE DUTIES
OF A WIFE AND OF A MOTHER,
AND PRAYERFULLY SOUGHT TO IMPROVE
EVERYOPERTUNITY OF USEFULNESS
AMOUNG THE PEOPLE OF THE PARISH;
TILL,
UNEXPECTEDLY, BUT NOT UNPREPARED,
SHE FELL ASLEEP IN JESUS
ON THE 5TH DAY OF JAN.
A.D. 1840
AGED 25

She is the subject of the book, *"Memoir of Mary Lundie Duncan; being Recollections of a Daughter: by her Mother."* It is this posthumous memoir that made the 'pious' life of Mary so famous. Her mother wrote several other books including "Memoirs of the Life and Character of the Rev. Matthias Bruen," "History of Revivals of Religion in the British Isles, especially in Scotland," and "America as I found it".

From the 5th edition of Mary's biography, an Appendix was included which, amongst the poems and hymns written by Mary, included a "Sketch of her character by her correspondent in London."

"My opinion is merely the echo of that expressed by a circle of intimate friends, who, whenever her name was mentioned, universally agreed in their estimate. All speak with love and admiration of the rare combination of excellencies she exhibited. Her piety, natural dispositions, intellectual attainments, accomplishments, and personal attractions, would, if held separately, have distinguished their possessors in society, but when united in one individual, like the colours in the heavenly bow, each beauty added to the rest.

"To begin with the evanescent qualities, I am glad a portrait was not attempted. It would have been too much to hope for a likeness. It is not a matter of surprise that it should be difficult to transfer to canvas those features, chiselled in the highest style of Grecian beauty, and lighted up as they usually were, with an expression almost seraphic – and is better than nothing unjustly purporting to be a representation should appear. I well remember, when at school, a weight having accidentally fallen on dear Mary's head, she was obliged to recline on a sofa; the fright had sent away the colour from her cheeks, and she lay with eyes closed. We were all seated around the table with our drawing. My own pencil relaxed for a few minutes to gaze on that alabaster face, as I thought I had never seen anything so beautiful. On glancing round, each eye was found attracted to the same spot, and an involuntary murmur of admiration escaped every lip. This little incident has often been referred to by those who were present, and I confess it among my most vivid recollections. Perhaps to many it may appear unworthy of being mentioned, as beauty is such a secondary thing in reality. Still to deny its great influence betrays little knowledge of human nature; and as it often forms a strong temptations to its possessor, a deliverance from the snare is an additional proof of the power of divine grace, and is such a worthy record. We have the authority of one of our most celebrated clergymen, for the declaration, that 'since beauty is the gift of God, and a good gift, the beautiful woman is accountable to Him for the use she makes of her beauty, as the man of intellect is for the talents bestowed on him.'

"The term holy, which can seldom be used in reference to individuals dwelling in this world of sin, always seemed singularly applicable to dear Mary. She was one of the few in whom, for days together, you might endeavour to trace her actions to their source, and find they originated in right motives, - any one who has tried such an experiment will know that the result is not common. The godlike disposition to promote the happiness of every sentient being, was displayed in acts of kindness to every person and living thing within her reach. Large indeed were the sympathies of that unselfish heart.

"Refinement of mind and taste was perhaps her most striking characteristic. The one purely natural, as it must ever be, the other partly owing to her early and intimate acquaintance with the best classic authors in her own language. The companionable qualities were appreciated even by those who had ho opportunity of judging of the deeper parts of her character. She had a most happy mode of imparting information – that suggestive manner, which seems to give superiority to the hearer. Her store of general knowledge was very large, and she was at great pains for it's constant increase. Not a visit was paid, a book read, or the prospect of a lovely landscape enjoyed, without an after investigation as to the amount of new ideas and images received. Her enthusiastic enjoyment of the beauties of nature and poetry, might have tempted one to suppose that an atmosphere of poetical excitement was that which she constantly breathed. But a more minute acquaintance with her character produced the conviction that she had a just appreciation of more solid pursuits united to very active habits, founded on a principle of duty.

"Her industry was indefatigable. During my visit to her after her marriage, when her delicate health seemed to call upon her to take rest, from six in the morning until midnight she was unceasingly occupied. And when we remember that her natural was not of that bustling, energetic kind which delights in action, but decidedly of a meditative cast, surely we must acknowledge and admire the strength of principle which obtained so complete a mastery over constitutional tendencies. Many who are conscious of possessing far greater bodily stamina, would shrink from much which she encountered in her visits to distant cottages in stormy weather – or in preparations for classed when her aching head much needed repose. But with her, at all times, mind nobly conquered matter."

As previously mentioned Mary wrote a number of poems, of which several are included in the appendix of later editions of "Memoir of Mary Lundie Duncan." Three examples of her poems are now given. The first was written when at school in London. After hearing various derogatory comments about the country of her birth she wrote this 'Address to Scotland' in response.

Address to Scotland

Thou art the country of my birth,
And wheresoe'er I rove,
Thou art the spot of all the earth
I'll never cease to love.

Thou art the land where first my eyes
Were open to the day;
Where first I heard the lullabies
That soothe my pains away.

And first among the glassy dales
My infant footsteps strayed,
And first in thy beloved vales
My happy childhood played.

And first beneath thine azure sky
I learned thy sacred name
Which breathes of immortality,
And feeds love's holy flame.

The morning and the evening breeze
That o'er thy valleys stray,
Played round me when I bent my knees

And raised my heart to pray.

Oh! there's a charm in those sweet scenes,
Which now are past away,
That o'er me steals like early dreams
Of life's first opening day.

And every spot of that sweet land,
Where childhood's years were passed,
Is bound my love's most tender band,
That with my life must last.

Scotland! though many a mile may lie
Between thy shores and me,
Ne'er can that sweet affection die
That knits my heart to thee.

Little brother (Poem)

Little brother, darling boy,
You are very dear to me!
I am happy - full of joy,
When your smiling face I see.

How I wish that you could speak,
and could know the words I say!
Pretty stories I would seek,
To amuse you every day -
All about the honey bees,
Flying past us in the sun;
Birds that sing among the trees,
Lambs that in the meadows run.

Shake your rattle - here it is -
Listen to its merry noise;
And when you are tired of this,
I will bring you other toys.

Lo! round the throne, a glorious band (Hymn)

Lo! round the throne, a glorious band,
The saints in countless myriads stand;
Of every tongue redeemed to God,
Arrayed in garments washed in blood,
Arrayed in garments washed in blood.

Through tribulation great they came;
They bore the cross, despised the shame;
But now from all their labours rest,
In God's eternal glory blest,
In God's eternal glory blest.

They see the Saviour face to face;
They sing the triumph of His grace;
And day and night, with ceaseless praise,
To Him their loud hosannas raise,
To Him their loud hosannas raise.

"Worthy the Lamb, for sinners slain,
Through endless years to live and reign;
Thou hast redeemed us by Thy blood,
And made us kings and priests to God."

O may we tread the sacred road
That holy saints and martyrs trod;
Wage to the end the glorious strife,
And win, like them, a crown of life,
And win, like them, a crown of life!

Mary Lundie and William Duncan had two children:
1   *Mary Lundie Duncan,* born on the 28th of May 1837, in Cleish.
2   *Henry Robert Duncan*, born on the 18th of February 1839, in Cleish.

CORNELIUS LUNDIE

The eldest son of the Rev. Robert Lundie minister of Kelso. He was born on the 25th of May 1815 in Kelso. Cornelius was long connected with the railways of the united Kingdom. He worked for the Blyth and Tyne Railway Company up until 1860, whereupon he joined the board of the Rhymney Railway. He worked here up until the age of 93, when he died. Here he worked as the "General Manager, Engineer, and Locomotive Superintendent," but in 1905 (at the age of 90) he retired from this position of effectively running the railway, to solely take a position on the board, where he held the title of Consulting Director. It is said however that even though he had now retired, he still continued to run the railway as before. In his capacity as a member of the board of the Rhymney Railway, he is featured in the Times upon several occasions (22nd March 1886, page 11; 20th February 1888, page 6; 27th of July 1888, page 3; 28th of July 1890, page 12). A short biography of Cornelius is given in the book "British Railway History: An Outline from the Accession of William IV to the Nationalization of Railways," by Hamilton Ellis, 1959. Here he is described as "a Scotsman of extremely managing type; his word was law and his autarchy was not to be questioned."

Cornelius died on the 12th of February 1908, the oldest railway director in the world. Although 'retired,' he had last been to his office only two days prior to this. It is said he was the last living man to have been acquainted with Sir Walter Scott. His obituary from 'The Scotsman,' dated the 13th of February1908, reads as follows:

DEATH OF A VETERAN RAILWAY DIRECTOR

PERSONAL ACQUAINTANCE WITH
WALTER SCOTT

Mr Cornelius Lundie, the oldest railway director in the world, and believed to be the last surviving person who had personal acquaintance with Sir Walter Scott, with whom he had lunched at Abbotsford, died yesterday at Cardiff, aged 93. He was born at Kelso, and after managing railways in Scotland and England, went to South Wales about fourty years ago. At the time of his death he was managing director of the Rhymney Railway Company.

An obituary also appeared in the Times on the 22nd of February 1908:

> Mr Cornelius Lundie, for 43 years manager of the Rhymney Railway, died at Cardif last week, at the age of 93. he often recalled visits paid to his father's manse at Kelso by Sir Walter Scott, and he is believed to have been the last link with the novelist. In company with his father and James Ballantyne, the printer, Mr Lundie once drove from Kelso to Abbotsford on a visit to Sir Walter Scott and had the honour of lunching with the great novelist and poet – at that time the "Great Unknown" as the secret was not out. Mr Lundie's father had long been in on the secret. Mr Lundie spoke of Sir Walter as having been the most genial of hosts, and well remembered the kindly manner of the great man – then a boy of about 14 years.

Cornelius is thought to have been twice married, and had at least one child:

1 *George Archibald Lundie*, born in 1843 in Australia, he married Mary Ann Brandon, on the 10th of June 1873, in Kingston, Jamaica. George was an engineer, and also involved with the railways like his father. In 1884 he was one of two engineers who drew plans for a railway from the Rhymney Railway East of Caerphilly to the LNWR Sirhowy Branch at Ynysdu (*Cardiff and Monmouthshire Valleys Railway: Parliamentary plans & sections, Session 1884*). George and Mary had six children together:
  i *Cornelius Ronald Lundie*
  ii *George Archibald Lundie*
  iii *Lionel Brandon Lundie*
  iv *Kenneth Grey Lundie*
  v *Robert Nicholas Lundie*
  vi *Ethel Lundie*

REV. DR. ROBERT HENRY LUNDIE M.A., D.D.

Christened 5th of December 1824, Kelso, he was another child of Robert Lundie minister of Kelso. The following details of his life come from "*Liverpool's Legion of Honour.*"

"Lundie (Rev. Robert Henry), M.A., D.D., has been respected during many years in Birkenhead and Liverpool as a Presbyterian minister of high character, considerable ability, and intense earnest; but recent changes in public opinion and in the action of the Watch Committee and the magistrates make him peculiarly notable as the apostle of a reformation which few years ago seemed hopeless. Without slighting the valuable co-operation of other ministers of religion, it must be recorded that he, beyond any other, has been both the hardest worker and the conscience, the lofty teacher speaking in the name of all that is most impressive, of those who were engaged in attempting to increase social purity and to lessen the mischeifs caused by intoxicants. Not satisfied with preaching duty and urging others to do theirs, he had also come forward as a citizen and ratepayer, and by every legitimate method open to a citizen and ratepayer has done more than his full share in the long-continued struggle against vested interest, political entanglements, and general inertia. No Christian minister in the city is more consistent, more influential, or more useful. Dr. Lundie's ancestry was likely to produce such a man. He comes from one of those Scotch families which may be classed as Levitical, being either the fifth or sixth in a direct line of Presbyterian preachers of righteousness. His grandfather was minister of the Parish of Kelso, and his father succeeded him, the ministry of the two extending over three quarters of a century. The later died when Robert Henry was a child; but subsequently the widow married the Rev. Dr. Duncan, of Ruthwell, the founder of savings banks, so that the lad again became an inmate of parsonage. His mother was also worthy of special honour, being the authoress of several works. Her son was educated at Edinburgh Hill School and University. He took his M.A. degree in 1848, and adopting with something more than the hereditary profession, in 1850 became minister of St. Andrew's Presbyterian Church, Conway-street, Birkenhead. Here he laboured acceptably, one result being the establishment at Rock Ferry of the cause now so important under Mr. Henderson; until after sixteen years he crossed the Mersey to become first minister of a newly-formed congregation at Fairfield, where he has remained until now. In both his charges Dr. Lundie has shown himself solid, competent, and effective. At Conway-street galleries had to be added; the Fairfield church has been twice enlarged. He is now surrounded by a network of useful congregational agencies, on each of which his individuality is impressed. He is not only a student and preacher, wise in private visitation, but a systematic and judicious administrator who gets through a vast amount of work with a clear head and without fuss. He is D.D. of Edinburgh University, and twice has been Moderator of the English Presbyterian Church. To him fell the honour of writing the life of Alexander Balfour. *The Presbyterian,* alluding to him in Jan, 1892, said, "Hardly any other man could be named who has laboured so Sedulously for the success of every Church enterprise. In church building and intercourse with other Churches he had been especially useful. In the Synod he has spoken in almost every important debate, and is always listened to with deference and respect." In Liverpool he is, outside Presbyterianism, president of the Vigilance Committee (which brought about the improvements already mentioned), and hon. secretary for the British and Foreign Bible Society and the Young Woman's Christian Association. Dr. Lundie's sister became the wife of the late Rev. Horatius Bonar, the Scotch hymn writer; his elder brother, Cornelius Lundie, is a C.E. in Glasgow. He himself married, in 1854, Elizabeth, daughter of Mr. Charles Cowan, then M.P. for Edinburgh; and now, while their children are men and women, an elder son is a successful physician in Edinburgh, and a younger son, Mr. Charles Cowan Lundie, is on the way to carry into one more generation the convictions, habits, and ministerial thoroughness which have made his father one of the most honoured moral and religious forces in Liverpool."

The Rev. Robert Lundie was married on the 4th of April, 1854, in Penicuik, Midlothian. He died in 1895. Apart from the Memoir of Alexander Balfour, mentioned in the previous extract, Robert Henry was the author of a number of other works, all of which listed can be found in either the British Library, the National Library of Scotland, or both:

1) "The late Mr. Bryce Allan. In memoriam"
2) " Seed-Corn in Belgium. Being a visit to the Belgian Churches"
3) "Take heed how ye hear"; or, good preaching not the only want of the age"
4) "Crown without the conflict; or, Musings on the death of children"
5) "I remember; I meditate; I muse. Sermon preached in Fairfield Presbyterian Church, in 1891."

He is also the subject of a memorial text "In memoriam, Robert Henry Lundie". This memorial text includes two articles from the *Liverpool Daily Post* published the day after his death; the first being his obituary; the second a further expansion on his influence on the life of the City of Liverpool. Both articles now follow.

"Never did any man impress himself more distinctly or usefully on the serious life of a great city than did the late Dr. Lundie – whose death we sorrowfully announce today – on that of Liverpool. And though he did it mainly by uncompromising warfare against the excrescences of a certain amenable trade – and though the most reputable members of such a body are prone to make common cause with the less reputable – we may say with confidence that in doing the great good which he accomplished Dr. Lundie made no enemies. The truth is that there is something more winning in quiet, calm, dispassionate resolution, based upon grave conviction, than in mere blandishments of manner. This doughty apostle of temperance and of public decorum never showed temper, or even vehemence. He was determined, but he was moderate. He conceded nothing, but so far as feeling went he conciliated all. In another part of to-day's paper we have stated emphatically, but without the least exaggeration, the results of Dr. Lundie's long, long campaign, and the methods by which he succeeded. For he did succeed. The fashion of Liverpool public bodies – and others – when they do not stolidly resist the demands of public opinion – is to turn round after they have mended their ways upon those who have compelled the reformation, and to attempt to carry the thing off by pretending that, as they are now behaving well, there never was any reason to find fault with them. In plain fact, the Liverpool Bench was for many years an opprobrium, both in the manner of licensing and in the manner of the enforcement of the law against offending licence-holders. It has now greatly improved. The improvement was compelled by Dr. Lundie and those who he led and largely inspired. No words can too honouringly or encomiastically express the indebtedness of the Liverpool community to this good and devoted Presbyterian minister, who feared not the face of man, high or low, rich or poor, and who has demonstrated that it is possible as it is beneficial for the law to be administered by the magistrates as to minimise every kind of social evil. Testimony is abundant and various that these manifestations of Dr. Lundie's fine qualities in public life expressed also by an analogy the essence and tone of his ministry in more spiritual things. He was beloved and revered by the whole Church to which he belonged, and his devout and earnest spirit made the congregation which he served an example to all. Dr. Lundie's "Life of Mr. Alexander Balfour" was one of the literary expressions of his noble and sympathetic Christianity, and all who, under any circumstances, knew him were won by his kindliness and brightness with which the manly and saintly traits of his character were illustrated in his daily conversation. Never was warrior more valiant or serene. he passes from our midst admired, lamented – a precious possession of his friends' remembrance, and acknowledged example of public and private duty, nobly and fruitfully done.

....

The Rev. Robert Henry Lundie, M.A., D.D., was born at Kelso, Scotland, in 1824. His father was the minister of Kelso, an office in which he succeeded his father – the grandfather of the subject of the present memoir. The ministry of these two worthy men extended over three-quarters of a century. At the age of seven Dr. Lundie was left fatherless. His widowed mother removed to Edinburgh. Afterwards she married the Rev. Dr. Duncan, of Ruthwell, known as the originator of savings banks. She was an able, not to say gifted woman, and a not unsuccessful authoress, and lived to the advanced age of eighty-seven. Meanwhile, growing up amid the same clerical influences, Dr. Lundie, after a course at the Edinburgh High School, entered the university of that city, and in 1848 took his M.A. degree. He decided upon entering the ministry, and in 1850, therefore, was ordained minister of St. Andrew's Presbyterian Church, Conway Street, Birkenhead. In that charge he spent sixteen years. His pastorate was marked by energy and success, and he took a chief part in founding the Presbyterian Church at Rock Ferry. In 1854 he married the daughter of Mr. Charles Cowan, then M.P. for Edinburgh. Ten years subsequently, being always interested an active in the founding of new charges, he took part in promoting the establishments of the congregation at Fairfield.

Fairfield Presbyterian Church was built in 1864. It cost £3,200, towards which Mr. John Graham, Mr. Bryce Allan, Mr. John Reid, and Mr. Alexander Balfour were liberal subscribers. The edifice was opened on the last Sunday in September, 1864, and was crowded morning and evening. Up to February, 1866, until which time the congregation was without a pastor, Dr. Lundie acted as Moderator of Session. In 1866, he undertook the pastorate, which he filled up to the time of his decease. His ministry was attended by success. In 1868 there was added to the Church a lecture hall, which cost £1,000, of which £600 was generously given by the late Mr. Bryce Allan. In June, 1871, a mission building was erected in Balm Street, Kensington, costing £2,000, the whole of which was defrayed again by Mr. Bryce Allan. In 1876 the Church itself was enlarged, transepts being added, at a cost of £2,000. The charge was defrayed by the congregation. The organ, opened by Mr. W. T. Best in October, 1884, was added at an outlay of £700, and more recently, in 1887, new entrance gates and a gallery were built, the sum expended being £600. Again, in 1890, the enlargement of the Kensington Hall was undertaken, and successfully carried out. The building was, at the same time, named after Mr. Bryce Allan, its donor.

These, however, are but the outward results of the pastorate of a painstaking student, a man of wide and liberal culture, a judicious and clear-sighted administrator, and a pastor whom these qualities combined mad wise in counsel and visitation. It was inevitable, therefore, that he should become influential outside the limits of his own individual work. In 1865 he was Moderator of the Synod of what was then called "the Presbyterian Church in England," but is now, and has been since the union with the United Presbyterians in 1876, the Presbyterian Church of England. Speaking of his work for the Presbyterian Church generally, the Presbyterian, in a brief notice published some two years ago, remarked:- "Dr. Lundie's fidelity and devotion to the interests of our Church have constituted a very marked feature of his character. He has taken an active and influential part throughout his whole career in the work of his Presbytery and Synod. Hardly any other man could be named who has laboured so sedulously for the success of every enterprise to which the Church has put her hand. In the departments of church building and intercourse with other churches he has been especially useful. In connection with the latter of these, Dr. Lundie possesses more than ordinary qualifications for success, as he is well acquainted with the continent, has been a great traveller, and has always taken a very warm interest in the welfare of foreign churches. In the Synodical Committees Dr. Lundie is looked up to as a wise and prudent counsellor, and in the Synod he has spoken in almost every important debate, and is always listened to with deference and respect."

Those who knew Dr. Lundie knew also how much his experience and recollections were enriched by his keen taste for foreign travel. For this he embraced every opportunity, and he knew Europe from the North Cape to Sicily; from Moscow to Madrid. One of his most popular lectures was a pleasant description of "A Run Through Russia." Another, entitles "Felix Neff," sketched his Alpine experiences. In the Alpine valleys he was known in many a Protestant pastor's family and congregation. Twice he crossed the Atlantic on visits to Canada and the United States. A journey through Palestine was undertaken in company with Dr. Norman McLeod. Such enlarged experiences made him a delightful social companion, who had keen powers of observation and much mundane shrewdness under his clerical exterior. He was specially familiar with the Waldensian Churches in Italy, and the Free Evangelical Churches in Belgium – a knowledge highly valued by the Synod.

In 1884, when the Synod met in Liverpool, he was again elected Moderator. he was a prominent member of the Synod committees on ministerial support, home missions, and intercourse with other churches, the Judicial Committee, and the Business Committee; and on all did a great amount of useful work, though in no sense an innovator. In point of years and length of ministry he was veritably the father of the Presbytery of Liverpool. He was reputed an authority on the laws and rules of the Presbyterian Church. With these and other multifarious duties pressing upon him, Dr. Lundie attempted little in authorship, but his selection as the biographer of the late Mr. Alexander Balfour, a work justly valued by those who can judge it, showed that he possessed undoubted literary powers. His pamphlets dealing with the "Responsibility of the Church in relation to great cities" and "Licensing Reform in Liverpool: Its vitiating elements," were important contributions to the pressing questions of the day. Among his fugitive pieces was a beautiful little poem on the death of his infant daughter. We quote two verses:-

Where'er I go L see a dimpled hand
That ceaseless beckons, beckons from above,
A silver voice, amid the blood-bought band
I hear, that woos me to the land I love.

A magnet now to draw my heart on high
Is she who sweetly here my cares beguiled:
In heavenly treasure, oh! how rich am I,
One home contains my saviour and my child.

Dr. Lundie received his degree of Doctor of Divinity from the University of Edinburgh in 1890.

Far more, however, than his position in the Presbyterian Church was Dr. Lundie prominent before the public association with which it has been customary to style "The Purity Crusade." Of this, more especially in its relation to licensing reform, he was more than any other individually the focus. He was chairman of that undoubtedly powerful body the Vigilance Committee. Now that the movement has been attended by success, it is more interesting briefly to recall the unpromising beginnings from which it sprang. With its initiation Dr. Lundie was above all identified. He was its active pioneer. His name was, however, first prominently before the public as leader of the determined, though eventually ineffectual opposition, offered to the licensing of a large public-house built by a firm of brewers at the further corner of a great tract of clay pits and waste land in the eastern outskirts of the city. The opposition was in effect aimed at the system of erecting suburban public-houses on what it was thought would proves eligible corner lots, in speculative anticipation of the streets of cottages which would speedily cover the surrounding waste. It failed, but what wonder? The now admitted abuses of licensing in Liverpool had, in point of fact, grown beyond the grasp of the police. The laissez-faire attitude of the bench, and the still more indifferent attitude of the Watch Committee, gave little zest to the police to undertake prosecutions in which, even in what would now be thought the strongest cases, they were on one pretext or another worsted. Indeed, it became almost an unwritten tradition in the Second Court at Dale Street never to fine a licensee if there was a means of avoiding it; whilst the power of transfer was sometimes grossly abused. The consequences need only be stated. The system did the licensed victuallers, as a body, no good. On the contrary, those of them worth of respect suffered from the presence of and odium of a hundred and one places of unenviable notoriety which thrived upon an illegitimate trade. Add to this fact that certain quarters of the city presented a very Gehenna of vice, and others a very Tophet of squalid intemperance, there can be no surprise that so earnest a man as Dr. Lundie was, felt himself, as he was on the very threshold of this state of things, stirred to do his upmost to secure reform. It was discouraging work. Time after time he attended at the Police Court on licensing days, squeezed up in the well of the court by hostile lawyers; hustled by public-house agents' clerks; protesting as a citizen amid the jeers or ironical applause of the body of barmen who filled the back of the court; facing the half-pitying smiles of an unfavourable bench. Truly his seemed a voice crying in the wilderness. And where appeared the means to break down an abuse which everybody – public authorities even – accepted as a matter of course, because of its very hugeness? In this solitary cleric, who dared to descend into the pit of the lions, because he dared not flinch. Even those who wrote him down a fanatic, admired his courage. But he was no fanatic. He never took, steadily refused to take, a pledge as a teetotaler; set his face as a flint against placing the temperate consumption of wines and beer in the orthodox catalogue of sins; would have nothing in common with the social espionage which thinks a great cause is advanced by petty means. His belief in moral force, which was supreme, lifted him above all this. it is true that, for the sake of example and consistency, he had become for many years practically a total abstainer, but he never abandoned his position that he sought not to substitute the consumption of tea and coffee for alcoholic beverages, but to promote temperance, to advance self-control, and to abolish abuses which debauched the people in place of properly meeting their needs.

Such a man, therefore, was exactly he whose example and courage would spread; and finally opinion found its expression in that influential deputation which, on the 26th June, 1889, headed by Dr. Lundie, expressed to the magistrates the public indignation that in a state of things which made necessary the arrest of over 15,000 persons annually for drunkenness, only one publican should have been convicted for permitting it. The Vigilance Committee, it is not generally known, originated in a suggestion of the late Sir James Picton, who at that meeting was chairman of the magistrates; and who suggested that the memorialists should form such a committee to obtain and lay before the bench such information as would assist them in their objects, since the bench had merely to adjudicate on such matters, and not to prosecute. The suggestion was at once acted upon, and with the results with which the public are familiar. The committee set to work, and secured, tabulated, and arranged its information; and through the services of an able solicitor, vigorously attacked at every licensing session the badly-conducted licensed houses. The collateral reform of the Watch Committee and the firm attitude of the bench complete the movement, which arrested the attention of the whole country. It is only necessary to add that the last four licensing sessions in Liverpool have resulted in the extinction of ninety-five licenses, and that of the thirty-two extinguished at the sessions of 1892 the Vigilance Committee were in thirteen cases the only objectors. Such is a too brief resume of twenty-three years of active, most active, effort in behalf of temperance reform. Dr. Lundie was the leading spirit in a band of reformers who revolutionised licensing administration in this city, but who have now to mourn in his death an irreparable loss.

His obituary also featured in the Scotsman on the 21st of January 1895:

Our Liverpool correspondent, telegraphing last night, says:-

The death took place to-day at Liverpool of the Rev. R.H. Lundie D.D., one of the best known ministers in the Presbytery Church of England, after an illness extending over several months. Dr. Lundie was a son of the manse, both his father and grandfather having been ministers of the parish of Kelso, where he was born in 1824. After graduating Edinburgh University in 1850, he was ordained minister of St Andrews Presbytery Church, Birkenhead. Here he laboured for sixteen years. He was transferred to the new charge at Fairfield Liverpool, where he has since remained. He was twice moderator of the Presbytery Synod, and was recognised as a valued councillor in connection with all Synodical committees. Having travelled considerably in the US, Canada, Palestine and European countries, he was a man of wide knowledge and culture. In 1890, he received the degree of Doctor of Divinity from Edinburgh University. He was a strong advocate of temperance principals, and was the leader of what is known in Liverpool as the "Purity Crusade," . . ."

22. Robert Henry Lundie, M.A., D.D.

Two weeks later, on the 9th of February, the same newspaper featured information regards a meeting in Liverpool to set up a memorial to Dr. Lundie:

> An influential meeting was held yesterday in Liverpool Town hall, under the presidency of the Lord Mayor, and with the Bishop of the diocese present, with a view to a memorial of the late Dr. Lundie, of Fairfield Presbytery Church, who was twice moderator of the Synod of the Presbytery Church of England. It was decided to found a scholarship and give other rewards to interest young people in day and evening schools in the duties and responsibilities of citizenship and in the subject of temperance. A sum of £500 is to be raised, and several handsome subscriptions were announced.

The scholarship mentioned in this text went on to be associated with Liverpool University, but has recently ceased to be used. As well as these social memorials, a large hall in Fairfield, Liverpool, was posthumously named after him, Lundie Memorial Hall, which included a building for Sunday Schools. A picture of this hall, drawn shortly after Dr. Lundie's death can be seen following this section of text, along with a picture of Dr Lundie and his wife. This building with obvious ecclesiastical links at its conception, is now used as a gymnasium. The author of this text sometime ago found at auction a marble plaque to the memory of Dr. Lundie, and wonders whether it did not originally come from the memorial hall.

As the obituaries and quoted texts state, Robert Henry married Elizabeth Hall Cowan on the 4th of April 1854, at Penicuik, Midlothian. They had at least four children.

1   *Dr. Robert Alexander Lundie*, M.A., B.Sc., M.B. C.M., FRCS (Ed.), born in 1855. He went to School at Liverpool College, and then went on to the University of Edinburgh, where he obtained his M.A. in 1875; B.Sc., in 1877; and M.B. C.B. in 1880. A medical doctor, his first appointment was as resident physician at the Edinburgh Royal Infirmary, from 1880-1. In 1881, he became resident surgeon at the same hospital. 1882, he worked as a surgeon on the Castle Line ship S.S. "Warwick Castle;" and was medical officer at the Cowgate dispensary in Edinburgh. From 1883 to 1902 he worked as a private assistant to Dr. Argyll Robertson; and from 1895 to at least 1914, he held the position of assistant medical officer at Longmore Hospital, in Edinburgh. He was also chairman of the Edinburgh and Leith division of the British Medical Association, an examiner in physiology, and a dental examiner B.C.S.

Robert was the author of a number of medical articles and texts, which include.

1) "A case of spontaneous pneumo-thorax and pneumo-pericardium" Read before the Medico-Chirurgical Society of Edinburgh, 3rd June 1891" Reprinted from the Edinburgh Medical Journal for September 1891:

2) "The treatment of myxoedema" Read before the Edinburgh Medico-Chirurgical Society at the discussion on myxoedema, 15th February 1893; Reprinted from the Edinburgh Medical Journal for May, 1893:

3) "A case of successful laparotomy for perforation of gastric ulcer Reprinted from Volume fourth of the Edinburgh Hospital Reports, Edinburgh, Young J. Pentland, 1896.

4) "Perforated Gastric Ulcer," *Edin. Hops. Reports*, 1896.

5) "Loss of Speech in a child," *Edin. Hops. Reports*, 1896.

6) "Gaseous Distension of Colon," *The Lancet*, 1897

7) "Dew Bows," (with Dr. C.G. Knott), *Proc. Roy. Soc. Ed.*, 1889-9

8) "Treatment of Intussusception," *Edin. Med. and Surg. J.,* 1906

9) "Spasm of Retinal Artery," *Ophthal Rev.*, 1906

10) "The correct anatomical form of bicycle pedals," British Med. J., 1905

The 1914 *Medical Who's Who*, lists his interests as fishing, cycling, walking, golf and chess. It shows his address as 55a, Grange Road, Edinburgh, and also indicates his professional interests were field botany, geology, as well as Ophthalmology. Aberdeen library holds letters of his dated 24th and 29th of March 1913 addressed to the Principal of that University, Sir George Adam Smith. He was married to Annie Sarah Moore, the daughter of Charles H. Moore, sometime MP for Edinburgh. She lived until the age of 93, passing away at their home, 24 Ormdale Terrace, Edinburgh, on the 22nd of December 1946 (*The Times*, 27th December, 1946). Robert died in 1918, in the St. Giles District of Edinburgh. They had at least two children:-

i *Major Robert Charles Lundie*, DSO, born in 1885. Fought with the 93rd Field Corps of the Royal Engineers in the 1st World War,

23 *Lundie Memorial Hall and Sabbeth School, Fairfield, Liverpool*

when he died (14th October 1918).

ii Kate Winifred Lundie, married Squadron Leader Robert Boog Watson R.A.F.M.S. on the 1st of July 1919. They were married by the Very Rev. Canon Lawrie, at the church of the Good Shepherd, in Edinburgh. Robert was the elder son of Chas. B. Boog Watson, of Napier Road, Edinburgh (*The Times,* 2nd July 1919). Robert predeceased Kate, passing away on the 2nd of May 1935, when in London. His funeral was held at Golders-Green, two days after his death (*The Times,* 3rd May, 1935).

2 *Catherine Cowan Lundie*, born in 1862; still alive 1881.

3 *Rev. Charles Cowan Lundie*, born in 1868. He followed his father into the church. He was author of the book "The Story of the Presbyterian Church of England at Parkgate and Neston, 1858-1933". He married, on the 15th of December 1909, Frances Eleanor Edmonson, elder daughter of Alfred Edmonson, Esq., of Walloway, Watermillock, Penrith. The ceremony was performed by the Rev. J. N. Eastwood B.A. of Penrith, assisted by the Rev. Oswald N. Ewing M.A., of Forrest Hull, and the Rev. John Hasdic B.D., of Tenruddock. At that time Rev. Charles was living at 18 Silverbeach Road, Seacombe. (*Scotsman,* 17th December 1909). He and his wife had issue:

i daughter, born on the 18th of December 1910, at Silverbeach Road, Seacombe (*Scotsman,* 21st December 1910).

4 *daughter*, died in infancy

JANE CATHERINE LUNDIE

The youngest child of the Rev. Robert Lundie minister of Kelso, she was born on the 1st of December 1821 at Kelso Manse. Like her sister Mary, she spent some time at school in London, being sent there in 1835. She married the Rev. Horatius Bonnar, a famed Scottish Hymn writer, who was pastor of the North Parish of Kelso, on the 16th of August 1843, in Kelso. As with her elder sister Mary, Jane Catherine also wrote Hymns. Below is an example that was first published in "Songs of the Wilderness," in 1843 (*An Anthology of Scottish Women Poets*). It also appeared later in "The Bible Hymn Book," which had been compiled by her husband.

Pass Away Earthly Joy.

Pass away earthly joy,
Jesus is mine;
Break every mortal tie,
Jesus is mine;
Dark is the wilderness;
Distant the resting-place;
Jesus alone can bless: --
Jesus is mine.

Tempt not my soul away, --
Jesus is mine;
Here would I ever stay,
Jesus is mine;
Perishing things of clay,
Born but for one brief day,
Pass from my heart away,
Jesus is mine.

Fare ye well, dreams of night,
Jesus is mine;
Mine is a dawning bright,
Jesus is mine;
All that my soul has tried
Left but a dismal void,
Jesus has satisfied,
Jesus is mine.

Farewell mortality,
Jesus is mine;
Welcome eternity,
Jesus is mine;
Welcome ye scenes of rest,
Welcome ye mansions blest,
Welcome a Saviour's breast,
Jesus is mine.

Indecently, the music for this Hymn was written by Theadore E. Perkins, and is entitled simply "Lundie". Jane Catherine Lundie Bonar died on the 3rd of December 1884, at 10 Palmerston Road, Edinburgh, and is buried in Cannongate Churchyard in Edinburgh. Jane Catherine Lundie and Horatius Bonar had issue. Of their children, five are believed to have died young. This may include some children not found in the records as they died so young as to have not been christened.

1   *Mary Lundie Bonar*, born on the 29th of July 1844, at Kelso, Scotland.

2   *Marjory Emily Jane Bonar*, born on the 30th of September 1849, at Kelso, Scotland.

3   *Elizabeth Maitland Bonar*, born on the 10th of September 1857, at Kelso, Scotland. She died in 1941, Newington, Midlothian

4   *Christina Cornelia Bonar*, born on the 28th of November 1852, at Kelso, Scotland.

5   *Horatius Niman Bonar*, born on the 2nd of April 1860, at Kelso, Scotland.

6   *Emily Florence Bonar*, born on the 26th of December 1861, at Kelso, Scotland. She married, on the 2nd of August 1894, at 10 Palmerston Road Edinburgh, the Rev. Duncan Clark Macnicol. The ceremony was performed by her uncle (Rev. Dr. R.H. Lundie) and the bridegroom's father (Rev. D. Macnicol) (Scotsman 3rd August 1894).

7   *Henry Robert Bonar*, born on the 17th of December 1865, at Kelso, Scotland.

The 'Lundie Papers'

The National Library of Scotland holds in its manuscripts collection a series of papers that relate to the descendants of Prof. John Lundie, through to his great-great-grandson Robert Lundie minister of Kelso. These papers were donated to the library by three parties. The first was a Mrs K.W. Boog Watson, a great-granddaughter of Robert Lundie minister of Kelso. In 1937, she presented papers and correspondence relating to Robert Lundie minister of Kelso, and his father Cornelius. These are listed under MS 1816 to 1818 'Lundie papers.' It includes letters between Cornelius Lundie and his sons Robert and Archibald; a book of Robert Lundie, minister of Kelso, containing copies of his correspondence; and a funeral book detailing deaths of many family members and copies of letters. This later book contains entries from as far back as 1696. The second benefactor is described simply as 'the Bonar family of Edinburgh,' and must descend from the marriage of Jane Catherine Lundie, daughter of Robert Lundie of Kelso, and Horatius Bonar. In 1953, they presented papers relating to the correspondence of this family between 1708 and 1840. These letters are held under the listing MS 9847-9. Typescript copies of many of the letters in MS 9847 and 9848 were previously donated to the library by Miss Elizabeth Maitland Bonar, daughter of Jane Catherine Lundie and Horatius Bonar; grand-daughter of Robert Lundie minister of Kelso. These are held under MS 1722 'Lundie Letters' and MS 1675, also 'Lundie Letters.' Miss E. M. Bonar published several articles in the Scotsman (13th April 1914; 21st December 1921; 15th July 1922) and one in the Kelso Chronicle (3rd August 1928) upon the contents of these letters.

Prior to the gift of these papers to the library, they survived the ravages of time stored in "an old leather-covered box, clamped with iron, and studded with brass nails." Although the description at the National Library gives the earliest date as 1696, Miss E.M. Bonar in her 1914 article states that this 'chest' held "letters, sermons, and professional orations," dating back to 1631, the time of Prof. John Lundie.

Although there are some early papers, most in the collection seem to date from the time of Robert Lundie, (son of Cornelius Lundie) minister of Kelso. In the earlier details of his and his son Cornelius's lives, it was briefly stated that Robert was well acquainted with Walter Scott, and that he "corresponded with much of the 'academic intellect of Edinburgh' of his day."

The collection of letters received by Robert certainly reflects this, with letters from persons such as the fore mentioned Sir Walter Scott, William Erskine (*a Judge in Bombay*), Henry Brougham (afterwards Lord Brougham – *Lord Chancellor*), Sir David Brewster (*scientist and writer*), John Leyden (*oriental scholar*), Robert Southey (*one of the lake poets*), Montgomery, the Duke of Roxburghe, James Falconar, James Graham (*poet*), Dr Thomas Brown (*Professor of Moral Philosophy*), Lord Jeffery Wilberforce, Dr Henry Duncan (*founder of savings banks*), Edward Irvine, Lord Buchan, Lord Mansfield, Dr Carson (*of Edinburgh High School*), Dr Andrew Thomson, Sir Henry Moncrieff, and Lord Lauderdale.

Robert Lundie's association with Sir Walter Scott probably dates from Scott's school days in Kelso, where he stayed with his aunt Janet, not more that 200 yards from Kelso Manse; but much of these other correspondents relate to Robert's time at the University of Edinburgh. One letter written by John Leyden gives and interesting insight to the world they lived in:

"How grave and philosophical an aspect you have in your letter. I can scarcely help figuring you to myself, in an arm-chair, with the most majestic of tye-wig, and a variety of other incongruous appurtenances. I have shortly got rid of my Latin discourse, and cannot bear the appearance of seriousness. It passed for and able discourse, because no one understood it, partly from designed and undesigned obscurity of diction, and partly from rapidity of lection. The Hebrew Society has sunk down in pace to the mighty dead, on account of the absence of the greatest part of its members. Mr Gillespie is to appear in the 'Edinburgh Magazine' in his lyrical character – an 'Ode to Winter' and an 'Ode to Loch Ken,' and an elegy on the death of a learned lady. Perhaps they may be accompanied by and ode of mine. Please present my congratulations to Mrs Bell if you see her. Had I received my invitation in due time, I should have approven myself volunteer laureate on the occasion. It is true that to me, who never fall in love, one name is as good as another, but I can perceive that there is a tremendous difference between Viola and Mrs Bell for a lyric ode; there is nothing to rhyme with it except the d- and hell. What are my companions doing? Erskine is interrupted in an 'Essay on the Evidences of Christianity,' by the ardent study of mathematics and natural philosophy; Reddie is writing his law thesis on 'Gifts.' Brown, having confuted Darwin's 'Zoonomia,' proceeds to prove the complete passivity of mind, and disprove latent heat. Brougham has nearly completed a paper on 'Optics' and an 'Utopia of Atheism.' Plato excluded poets from his 'Utopia,' but Brougham is content with excluding God Almighty."

Another letter by Robert Southey, one of the lake poets, reflects upon his work, and the ongoing war:

"The missionary chapters of the 'Quarterly' are mine, but there is difficulty of acquiring information. The articles in the 'Quarterly' are miserably bad, and the theological papers are generously deficient in the Christian virtue of charity. My own papers wherever they relate to sectarian history appear to me, when I see them in the review, as if they had been expurgated by a High Church board of censure. I look with much pleasure for Walter Scott's poem, and hope he will be as good a prophet as poet. For I know he will prophecy of good things. He, like myself, has had faith in the worst times. The recovery of Figuerias is the most important event that has happened since the surrender of Dupont; except the deliverance of Barcelona, it is the most important success that the Spaniards could have obtained."

Many of the literary correspondents also visited the Lundies in Kelso. E. M. Bonar describes how "Dr Chalmers, Southey, Sir David Brewster, Dr Andrew Thomson, Dr Henry Duncan, Sir Walter Scott, and James Ballantyne, his publisher, were some of the worthy visitors at the manse." There is the suggestion that Wordsworth was also visitor, and J.M.W. Turner is know to have been to visit Robert Lundie, as he painted his portrait. One of the visitors, William Erskine of Amandell, in a letter, describes how "Kelso is unfavourable to study; the country is too delightful, the society too agreeable."

These papers make up a remarkable record. It is a shame that other branches of the Lundie family do not have their history so well preserved.

Alexander Lundie in Fossoway, and his Descendants

ALEXANDER LUNDIE

Alexander was born around 1770 in a region of Perthshire that by 1841 had become part of Forfar (possibly Cupar Angus). He was the son of John Lundie, a schoolmaster, and Catherine McKenzie. From a strong recollection of a connection with the Lindsay family with Alexander's descendants it is thought that his father, John Lundie the schoolmaster, may well be a thus far un documented son of James Lundin of Drums and Katherine Lindsay of Kirkforthar. On the 23rd of July 1797, whilst living in the Parish of Muckhart, Alexander married Helen Crawford from the Parish of Fossoway. They had issue:

1   *John Lundie*, whose details follow.
2   *Margaret Lundie*, christened on the 19th of October 1800. She married Thomas Skindling, a coachman, on the 7th of February, 1830, at Alva, Stirling. She died on the 27th of October 1880, at Knock Cottage, Ferntower, Crieff, Perth. He died on the 13th of May, 1859. They are both buried in Alva, Stirling. They had issue:
  i   Mary Skindling, born in 1839, she died on the 17th of July, 1869. She had one son by Thomas Hogg. It is not known if they were married.
    a   Thomas Skandline Hogg, born on the 15th of July, 1854, christened on the 1st of December, 1854, at Alva, Stirling. He died on the 17th of December, 1873. He is buried in Alva.
  ii Thomas Skindling, died at the age of six, and is buried in Alva, Stirling.
3   *James Lundie*, christened on the 12th of January 1803. James was a farm labourer. He died on the 3rd of December, 1881, at Stirling district Asylum. His death certificate suggests that he had been ill some years. A slight discrepancy in the records gives James's age at his death as 68. He married Margaret Fyfe, the daughter of James Fyfe, a coalminer, and Margaret Hynd. She was still living in Dollar at the

time of her husband's death. She died on the 2nd of January, 1909 at Blairingone, Fossoway, aged 74. They had issue:

i Alexander Lundie, born around 1853, he married Margaret McCulloch, at the Parish Church of Culross, Perth, on the 31st of December 1874. At the time of his marriage his age was given as 22, and his profession as an agricultural labourer. He was living at Bicranside, in the Parish of Saline, Fife. His wife was the daughter of William McCulloch, a labourer, and Ann McCullock, whose maiden name was Dickie. She was 21 at the time of their marriage, living in the parish of Culross, and working as a Domestic Servant. The 1881 census gives Alexander's birth place as Dollar, Clackmannan, but no record seems to survive. At the time of the aforementioned census, he and his wife were living alone in Shiresmill, Culross.

ii John Lundie, born on the 14th of August, 1855, at Fossoway and Tulliebole, Kinross, Scotland. He died aged 22, in 1877, at Dollar.

iii Lundie (male), died aged nine hours on the 29th of March, 1857, at Dollarbeg, in the Parish of Dollar.

iv Lundie (male), born on the 29th of June, 1858, at Dollar, Clackmannan, Scotland.

v David Lundie, born on the 13th of May, 1864, at Dollar, Clackmannan, Scotland. He died aged 9 months on the 3rd of March 1865, at Dollarbeg, Dollar, after suffering from bronchitis for three weeks.

It is believed that Helen Crawford died, and that Alexander re-married on the 17th of May 1807, in the Parish of Fossoway and Tulibole, to Mary Scotland. The data in the old Parish records show that an Alexander Lundie married on this date, but show no details of his wife. Alexander Lundie and Mary Scotland had issue:

1   David Lundie, christened on the 20th of March 1808, in Fossoway and Tulibole. In the Christening record his father Alexander Lundie, is stated as living in the Waulkmiln of Tulibole. David was a labourer and eventually farm manager. By 1838, he was living in Tulliallan, Perthshire; 1841 he was living in Alva in Stirlingshire; he lived there at least until 1845. By the time of the 1851 census, he and his family were living in the parish of Dollar. He married Marjory (May/Mary) Reid, daughter of David Reid and May Sinclair. On

the 10th of January 1830, David and Mary were found guilty by the
Fossoway Kirk session, of antinuptual sex. They were both absolved
on the 24th of January (Fossoway Kirk Session *NAS*). David died
at 6.00 am on the 2nd of May, 1874, at the upper mains of Dollar.
The record gives his age at this time as 64 (two years out from his
birth date). Marjory died on the 22nd of August 1885, in Alloa,
Clackmannan, aged 74. They had issue:

i   *Mary*, born in 1830, in Perthshire. She had one illegitimate son
who died young:

a *Robert Lundie*, an illegitimate son, born in Dollar in 1852,
he died age 3 on the 24th of January 1855. No fathers name is
given on the death entry. At the time of his death, his mother's
profession is listed as a domestic servant. The informant was his
grandfather, David Lundie.

After Robert's death, she later married James Cook, in 1857, in
Dollar. She died at the age of 41, on the 14th of June 1872, at
Coalsnaughton, Tillicoulty, Clackmannan.

ii   *Helen Lundie*, born around 1831. She died unmarried on the
second of December 1911, at 16 Castle Street Edinburgh. This
was the same residence her sister Marjory was living at, and she
appears as informant. The death registration gives her profession
as a sometime caretaker, and age as 80. Notice of her death was
published in the Scotsman on the 4th of December. She had one
child, out of marriage, with an Alexander Sinclair:

a *Marjory Lundie,* born on the 12th of August 1857, at the
upper mains of Dollar. David Lundie the grandfather was the
informant.

iii *Alexander Lundie*. Born in 1834, in Powmill, Perthshire. He was
a ploughman, general labourer, and later gasworks labourer. He
married Margaret Simpson on the 17th of July, 1861, in Stirling. She
was the daughter of George Simpson and Isabella Ferguson. She
died on the 23rd of January, 1885, whilst living in the high street of
Alloa, Clackmannan. In 1874 Alexander was the informant of his
father's death; in 1885 the informant of his mother's. He died on
the 6th of November, 1912, at 118, Castleloan, Bo'ness, Lothian.
He had issue:

a   *David Lundie*, born on the 3rd of May, 1862 in Alloa,

Clackmannan, Scotland.

b Isabella Lundie, born on the 8th of February 1865, in Alloa, Clackmannan, Scotland. She is the only child of David and Margaret not listed as living with them in the 1881 census.

c George Lundie, born on the 10th of March 1867 in Alloa, Clackmannan, Scotland. He died aged 18, in 1885, Alloa, Clackmannan.

d Marjory Lundie, born on the 24th of February 1869 in Alloa, Clackmannan, Scotland. She married a William John Johnston in 1910, in Alloa, Clackmannan; he was a coalminer. Marjory died aged 73, on the 29th of September 1942, at Sandie Alloa. Her husband was the informant.

e Alexander Lundie, born on the 25th of May 1871, in Alloa, Clackmannan, Scotland. He died aged 13, in 1884, in Alloa, Clackmannan.

f Margaret Lundie, born on the 13th of December 1873 in Alloa, Clackmannan, Scotland. She died aged 11 in 1885.

g Andrew Lundie, born 1876-7. He married Robina Stien, in Clackmannan, Clackmannan, 1909. Andrew died at the age of 60 of prostate cancer, at County Accident Hospital, Alloa, on the 27th of June 1937. His usual residence was given as 25 – Crescent, Alloa. It is not known it he had issue.

h Janet Lundie, born 1878-9

iv Margaret Lundie, born on the 14th of October, 1838, at Tulliallan, Perth, Scotland.

v David Lundie, born on the 21st of January, 1841, christened on the 7th of February that year in Alva, Stirling. He married Agnes Richardson, on the 4th of April 1862; she was originally from Bannockburn. The 1881 census shows David, his wife Agnes, and son David, living in Curate Wynd, Kinross, Kinross shire.

a Agnes Lundie, born in May 1862, in New -, Alloa. In 1881 she appears in the census working as a servant at No. 1 Hart Street, Edinburgh St. Mary's, Edinburgh. She was unmarried at the time.

b Marjory Mason Lundie, born on the 21st of March 1865, in Alloa. She died aged 3, in Alloa, in 1868.

c David Lundie, born around 1868, in Alloa, Clackmannan.

vi James Lundie, born on the 28th of November, 1843; christened on the 17th of December, 1843, at Alva, Stirling.

vii Marjory (May) Lundie, born on the 25th of September, 1845; christened on the 30th of November, 1845, at Alva Stirling. On the 10th of November 1876 she married Charles Hamilton, at two South Grey Street Edinburgh. Charles was a butler, and son of Charles Hamilton, a carpenter, and his spouse Elizabeth Lee. She was still alive in 1911, where she appears as the informant on her sister Helen's death registration.

2   Thomas Lundie, christened on the 21st of January, 1810, in the Parish of Fossoway and Tulibole. He was an agricultural Labourer. He married Grace McAnsh, daughter of Alexander McAnsh, a labourer, and his wife Margaret Morgan. The 1841 census shows Thomas and Grace living at that time in Brigland in the Parish of Fossoway and Tulibole. He moved to Alva, Stirling in 1846. Thomas died at the age of 44, on March the 31st, 1855, in Alva, Stirling. He was buried in the Churchyard of Fossoway. Grace died on the 19th of October 1884, whilst living at 44 Johnstone Street, Alva, Stirling. The informant on her death was her nephew, Alexander Luke. They had issue:

i   Alexander Lundie, born on the 13th of September 1837, in the Parish of Fossoway and Tulibole. He died on the 26th of February, 1856, at Alva Stirling. He is probably buried at Fossoway Churchyard, the details on his death certificate are hard to make out.

3   Alexander Lundie, christened on the 9th of May, 1813, in the Parish of Fossoway and Tulibole.

4   Isabella Lundie, christened on the 9th of November, 1817, in the parish of Fossoway and Tulibole.

It is believed that Alexander married for a third time; the 1851 census shows an Alexander Lundie aged 78, living in Fossoway and Tulibole, with his wife Katherine, aged 76, and his son James, aged 48. Both James and Katherine were born in the Parish of Fossoway and Tulibole, Alexander is recorded as being born in Forfar, Perthshire. James is the correct age to be the son of Alexander, listed as child three of Alexander and Helen Crawford. James's occupation is given as a labourer; Alexander is listed as a pauper. This means that at that time he was receiving a small income from the Parish for sustenance.

Alexander died on the 6th of April, 1857, at the upper mains of Dollar. His son David informed the death. He is buried in Fossoway Churchyard.

JOHN LUNDIE

An agricultural labourer and weaver, he was born on the 12th of May, 1798, he was Christened on the 20th of that month, in Crook of Devon in the Parish of Fossoway and Tulibole. At this time his parents were living in the Walkmiln of Tulibole. He married, on the 27th of May, 1829, Agnes Brownlee, in Cumbernauld, Dumbartonshire. Agnes was the daughter of John Brownlee, a master blacksmith, and Agnes Brownlee, who were married on the 9th of December 1788, in Cumbernauld, Dumbartonshire. John Lundie died in 1863, at Chryston, Cadder, Lanark; Agnes died on the 6th of June, 1882, aged 75, at Woodside Cottage, Cadder Lanark. They had issue:

1 *Helen Lundie*, christened on the 20th of June, 1830, in Cumbernauld, Dumbartonshire. She died in 1863, in Cadder Eastern, Lanark.

2 *Rev. Alexander Lundie*, of whom next.

3 *Agnes Lundie*, born on the 1st of August 1835; christened on the 13th of September that same year in Cumbernauld, Dumbartonshire. She married John Cross on the 22nd of January, 1864, at Cadder, Lanark. John was an engineer. Agnes died on the 20th of November, 1917, at Lime Cottages, Muirhead, in the eastern district of Cadder, Lanark. Her husband predeceased her. They had issue:

   i *Agnes Cross*, born on the 4th of January, 1865

   ii *Ann Cross*, born on the 18th of August, 1866

   iii *Margaret Cross*, born on the 17th of July, 1870

   iv *Helen Cross*, born on the 19th of September, 1874

4 *John Brownlee Lundie*, born on the 1st of September 1838, in Chryston, Cadder, Lanarkshire. He married, on the 31st of December, 1867, in Falkirk, Janet Shaw. John was an Engineer. He died in 1919, in Dunfermline, Fife. He and Janet had issue:

   i *Jane Yeats Lundie,* born around 1869, she died, at the age of five, on the 8th of January 1874.

   ii *Helen Lundie*, born on the 26th of February, 1871. In the 1891 census, where she is listed as living with her parents, her occupation is described as a 'biscuit packer'. She married James McKenzie

Mitchell in 1895, in Falkirk, Stirling; he was an ironmonger. She died on the 30th of August 1916, in Falkirk. Her husband was the informant. They had at least on son:

a *James Mitchell.* Present at the death of his aunt, Agnes Shaw Lundie

iii Agnes Brownlee Lundie, born in 1873, she died on the 28th of January, 1874, aged five months, in Falkirk, Stirling.

iv Jane Yeats Lundie, born on the 15th of December, 1875, in Larbert, Stirling. In the 1901 census of Scotland, she appears as a visitor at the house of her younger sister Jessie (129 Barat St. Blackfriars, Stirling). In both that census and the one ten years prior, her occupation is given as dressmaker. She was still alive and unmarried in 1945.

v Agnes Shaw Lundie. Born in 1878, in Larbert, Stirling, she is described in the 1891 census as a message girl. She died, unmarried, on the 22nd of August 1939, at 7 West High Street Crieff, of natural causes, where her occupation is given as housekeeper. The death registration describes her usual residence as 28 Gourlay Street Kirkcaldy.

vi Jessie Lundie, born on the 21st of February, 1880 at 8:30 am, in the Landward District of Falkirk. At the time of the 1891 census she is listed as a scholar. She married Alexander M'Kendrick in 1900, in Blackfriars, Lanark. At the time of the Marriage, Alexander was a Police Constable; later Alexander was an inspector of Glasgow School authority. They had issue:

a *Dr. John Brownlee Lundie M'Kendrick.* He was born 1904 in Dennistoun, Glasgow. He started at Glasgow University in 1923 studying Medicine. At that time his address was Rotten Row, Glasgow. He died aged 32 in 1936, at Govan, Lanark.

b *Dr. Fowler M'Kendrick.*

c *Jessie M'Kendrick - (Mrs Ralston).*

d *Ellen Mckendrick - (Mrs Keith)*

5 *James Lundie,* born on the 13th of January 1842, at Chryston, Cadder, Lanarkshire. He died in 1866, in the parish of Cadder, Lanarkshire.

24. Rev. Alexander Lundie, minister of Torryburn

REV. ALEXANDER LUNDIE, MINISTER OF THE UNITED FREE CHURCH AT TORRYBURN

He was christened on the 30th of September 1832, in Cumbernauld, Dumbartonshire. He studied at the University and Free Church College in Glasgow. He was ordained at Torryburn in Fife in 1867. Some of his ministry was also spent in the Orkney Islands, where as a symbol of the congregations appreciation of his work, they gifted him a beautiful set of chairs made from Orkney Driftwood. His congregation in Torryburn, also to show their appreciation for the work of Alexander, gifted him a large slate clock, inscribed To Rev. Alexander Lundie, "presented as a grateful token of esteem by his attached congregation, Torryburn, 9th January, 1884."

The Rev. Alexander married, on the 26th of April, 1868, at the High Church in Glasgow, Lanark, Jessie Dunn Paterson. Jessie was born on the 12th of January, 1843, in Barony, Lanark, the eldest child of John Paterson, a grain merchant in Glasgow, and his wife Isabella Baird. Jessie died on the 30th of October, 1915, at Clarkston Road, Muirend, Cathcart, Lanark. Rev. Lundie predeceased her, passing away on the 23rd of May, 1906, at the United Free Church Manse, Torryburn. He died of Pneumonia. He is buried, along with his wife and children William, James, Daisy and Isabella (the younger), in Crombie Point Old Church Yard, where his parishioners erected a monument to his memory. His obituary, featuring in the 'Scotsman,' reads as follows (*NAS*, GD50/185/57).

"Died at U.F. Manse, Torryburn, Fife, on 23rd inst. Rev. Alex Lundie. Funeral on Thursday, 26th inst at 2 o'clock."

"The late Rev. Alexander Lundie, Torryburn.
The death was announced yesterday of the Rev. Alexander Lundie, who was ordained to the ministry of the Free Church, at Torryburn, 37 years ago. In the early days of his ministry Mr Lundie distinguished himself by his outspokenness on the temperance question. Previous to his Fife conducted – work at Portobello."

Alexander and Jessie had issue:
1   *Isabella Paterson Lundie*, born at 2.00 pm on the 29th of April,

Jessie Dunn Paterson:
Mrs Lundie

Rev. John Lundie

Agnes Bryce Paterson Lundie

Ella Lundie

Jessie Lundie

Andrew Paterson Lundie
and Alexander Lundie

Crawford Lundie

Isabel Dobson Taylor:
Mrs Lundie

John Taylor Lundie

25. Extended family of Rev. Alexander Lundie

1869, at the Free Church Manse, Torryburn. She only lived for three minutes.

2   Isabel Baird Paterson Lundie, born on the 30th of September, 1870, at Torryburn. She died at the age of 81, on the 16th of June, 1952, in Edinburgh, of old age. She never married. It would appear from family papers that she was an accomplished artist.

3   Rev. John Lundie M.A., born on the 1st of May 1872 at Torryburn. At the age of 18 (1890), he commenced his studies at the United College in the University of St. Andrews, which he attended for three years. In 1890-91 he studied 2nd Greek, 2nd Humanity and Latin, and first maths; 1891-2, he studied Logic, English Literature and 2nd Maths; and 1892-3 he studied natural philosophy and moral philosophy. He graduated M.A. from the Department of Mental Philosophy, in April 1893. He studied to become a minister of the United Free Church of Scotland, it is presumed at the U. F. College, Glasgow. This was the college his father attended. He appears in the 1901 census for Scotland, with his profession described as a Probationer in the U. F. Church. The census shows that he was staying with the Rev. James Ferguson and family, at the United Free Church Manse at Cupar, Fife. John migrated to Australia sometime before 1911, whereupon he became minister of St. Andrew's Presbyterian Church, in Esk in Queensland, up until 1916. He is said to have bicycled around his parish over 700 miles per year, in order to attend services (*Esk Presbyterian Church Centenary*). The Queensland Times of the 5th of April 1914, features details of the church AGM for that year, where Rev. John Lundie was presiding. "Minister since November last travelled over 700 miles by bicycle to attend services when thermometer never below 90." He ministered there until 1916, when the Rev. Mervyn Henderson succeeded him. By 1951 he was living in the Eastwood district of New South Wales (*letter to his nephew*). He was married, but had no children.

4   Agnes Bryce Paterson Lundie, born on the 10th of February, 1874, at Torryburn. She attended Dunfermline High School, but it is not certain where she attended University. She worked as a nurse in the First World War, after which she migrated to Australia. For a while she worked a bush nurse in the Cann River area of Victoria. She returned to Scotland, and died unmarried on the 8th of March

1952, at 62 King Street Stenhousemuir. She is buried in Dunfermline cemetery with her sister Ella and brother Alex.

5   *Ella Lundie M.A.*, born on the 30th of November 1875 at 10.00 a.m. at the Free Church Manse, Lower Torry, Torryburn. She studied; commencing in 1895; at United College, in the University of St. Andrews. In 1895-6 she was enrolled in Latin, Junior Maths and French; 1896-7, Logic and Maths; 1897-8, Natural Philosophy, Moral Philosophy, Chemistry and Practical Chemistry; 1898-9, Natural History and Practical Natural History, Junior and Practical Anatomy; 1899-1900, studying with a Taylor Thomson bursary, at the Medical Faculty, she was enrolled in Ordinary Physiology, Demonstrated Anatomy and Practical Anatomy. She graduated M.A. in the year 1889-9. Ella is recorded as having achieved Class honours in the winter session 1898-9 in Junior Systematic Natural History, and First Rank in Anatomy (Practical and Lectures). From the 1st of January 1914 until the 31st of December 1920, she served as a sister in Queen Alexandra's Imperial Military Nursing Service (*PRO*, WO 399/5037). She left Scotland for Australia sometime afterwards, moving to the New South Wales District, where her brothers John and Andrew were living. In 1925, she married Alexander MacVean, who was a sheep farmer. He died the following year. Ella returned to Scotland, where she died on the 5th of February, 1934, in Dundee. She is buried in Dunfermline cemetery with her brother Alex and sister Agnes.

6   *Jessie Dunn Paterson Lundie*, born on the 11th of May 1877 at the Free Church manse, Low Torry, Torryburn. She died of meningitis on the 29th of March 1897. She appears to have been known as Daisy. Notice of her death was published in 'The Scotsman:' "Died at F.C. Manse, Torryburn, suddenly on the 29th March, Daisy, youngest daughter of the Rev. Alex Lundie. Funeral today (Wednesday) 31st at 2 P.M." (*NAS*, GD50/185/57).

7   *William Paterson Lundie*, born on the 8th of August, 1878 at 12:05 pm, in Torryburn. He died at Torryburn, oat 3 o'clock in the afternoon, on the 21st of May 1879, after suffering for seven days with pneumonia.

8   *Dr. Alexander Lundie, Bsc., M.B., Ch.B., D.P.H., Late Captain R.A.M.C.* younger twin of William, of whom next.

9   *James Lundie*, born in Torryburn on the 28th of May, 1880, at 6.00 pm; he died at the manse, Lower Torry, at 10 o'clock in the morning of the 17th of April 1881, after suffering from a bowel illness for one month.

10 *Andrew Paterson Lundie, M.A.* He was born on the 22nd of May 1881, at 11:30 p.m. at the Free Church Manse, Lower Torry, Torryburn. He studied at St. Andrews from 1898 to 1901. In 1898-99, he was enrolled in Latin, Maths and French; 1899-1900, studying with a Taylour-Thomson bursary at the Faculty of Arts, he was enrolled in Logic and Natural Philosophy; 1900-1901 he was enrolled in English, Old English, Moral Philosophy and Political Economy. He passed the final examinations for Mathematics in March 1899; Latin in October 1899; Natural Philosophy in March 1900; Logic in October 1900; and Political Economy in March 1901. He graduated M.A., becoming a Classics Master. He emigrated to Australia in 1911, and married Mary P. Muir, in 1916, in Marrickville, New South Wales. Mary was the eldest of seven children of David Muir, a farmer near Esk. He was also the session clerk of St. Andrew's Presbyterian Church at Esk, where Andrew Paterson Lundie's eldest brother John was minister; and it is through this connection that Andrew and Mary met. Andrew died in 1945, Mary in 1976. They had issue:

i Alexander Paterson Lundie, born in 1918, in Ipswich, Queensland. He married Florence Mabel Johnson in 1939, in Burwood, New South Wales. They divorced in 1954, and he remarried, in 1972, to Charlotte Bruce, a widow with three children.

ii Daisy Lundie, died in 1920, in Wollongong, New South Wales.

iii Andrew Stanley Paterson Lundie, born 12th August 1920, in Fairy Meadow, New South Wales. He enlisted on the 22nd of January, 1940, for the second world War in Richmond, New South Wales. At the time he was living in Eastwood, NSW. He was a sergeant in the Royal Australian Air Force; service number 12084. He escaped Malaya before the Japanese took over, and was discharged on the 7th of January, 1946. At discharge he was posted to the 1st reserve personnel pool. He married Margaret, and had issue:

a Robert Lundie, a headmaster. Married Kathleen, and had three children, Rachel, Nicole and Jarrod.

b Pamela Lundie

iv David Crawford Paterson Lundie, born on the 25th of September 1922, in Wollongong, New South Wales. He enlisted for the Second World War on the 15th of August 1941, in Sydney Australia. He was a Flight Sergeant navigator in Lancaster Bomber Command (412986) RAAF. He died on a mission on the 13th of June 1943. At that time he was posted to 460 Squadron. For a while he was reported as 'missing' appearing as such in *The Times* of the 28th August 1943 (page 8). He is buried in IJsselmuiden (Grafthors) General Cemetery, in the Netherlands. Mention of David is made briefly in the text "Going with God," a Biography of the Rev. Alexander Casby, who was minister in Torryburn sometime after Rev. Alexander Lundie. Two weeks before his death, David visited Torryburn Manse, and a short account of this visit is given in the aforementioned biography .

"One afternoon a young New Zealand [Australian] Airman called at the Manse. He told us his grandfather was once minister of Newmills. 'You must be Lundie,' I said. His father had told him about Newmills Manse and an enormous stone built underground tank under a bedroom window near the back door. The airman explained his father and two uncles (most probably Alexander and Crawford) had been put to bed at eight p.m. and the bedroom window was locked. When all was quiet the boys tied a rope on the huge four-poster bed, opened the window and slid down to the ground. The boys would romp round with pals until nearly ten o'clock then shin back up the rope to bed. One night the boys were nearly caught. They hid in the tank, up to their knees in water. Young pilot officer Lundie was familiar with every corner of the manse. He loved going over every room, and relating stories his father had told him. He had lunch with us, then wrote a letter in my study to his parents in New Zealand [Australia] about his visit. The lad's uncle, Dr. Lundie of Cupar, called us a fortnight later to say his nephew had lost his life on an air mission over Germany. I wrote to his parents in New Zealand [Australia]. Some weeks later we had a reply saying the last letter they had received from their son was a precious one – that written in my study." *Note that the comments in brackets were added by the author of this text.*

v John Paterson Lundie, born on the 30th of January, 1925, in

Hurtsville, New South Wales. He enlisted for the Second World War, in Sydney Australia, on the 30th of January 1943. He was a flying officer in the Royal Australian Air Force; service number 432831. Pilot in a Kittyhawk fighter aircraft, he served in New Guinea and the Pacific, with the 76 Squadron Kittyhawks. He was discharged on the 8th of October 1945, his posting at that time being '2 operational training unit'. Afterwards he was a County Clerk. He married Ellen McPhie, at Wollongong in 1949, and had issue. He died of a heart attack in 1997.

 a Lynne Lundie, she died when around thirteen years old.

 b Jennifer Lundie

 c Christine Lundie

vi James Paterson Lundie, born on the 5th of July 1927, in Hurtsville, Sydney. A High School Headmaster. He married Margaret McCleary from Coleraine, Ireland. They have no issue:

vii Jean Harding Paterson Lundie. Elder twin of brother Douglas Paterson Lundie. She was born on the 20th of July 1929, Eastwood Sydney, New South Wales. A teacher, she married Noel Redman. The had no issue.

viii Douglas Paterson Lundie. Younger twin of Jean, born on the 20th of July 1929, Eastwood Sydney, New South Wales. He drowned in 1957.

11 *Dr. Crawford Lundie BSc. M.D. Late Captain R.A.M.C.* Born at 8.00 p.m. on the 3rd of March 1884, at the Free Church Manse, Lower Torry, Torryburn. He commenced his university education at United College in the University of St. Andrews, like so many of his siblings. In 1901-2, under a Patrick Kidd Bursary, at the Faculty of Arts, he was enrolled in Latin, Greek and Mathematics; 1902-3, studying with a Spence and portion of Cheape bursary, at the Faculty of Arts and Science, he was enrolled in Natural Philosophy and Practical Natural Philosophy, Chemistry and Practical Chemistry; 1903-4, with the same bursary, and at the same faculties, he was enrolled in Logic, Junior Honours Maths, Honours Chemistry, Honours Practical Chemistry; 1904-5 with Spence and Cheape bursaries, at the Faculties of Arts, Science and Medicine, he was enrolled in Senior Honours Maths, Applied Maths, Honours Natural Philosophy, Honours Practical Natural Philosophy, and Practical Anatomy. He graduated

26a. Marie Lundie, Mrs Jane Lundie, and Dr Crawford Lundie

26b. Andrew Paterson Lundie

BSc in October 1904, having passed examinations in Mathematics in March 1902; Natural Philosophy in March 1903; and Chemistry in March 1903; which would appear to qualify for an M.A., but continuing on, and additionally after passing Chemistry (higher standard) in October 1904, he graduated instead with the Bsc. He continued in education, and studied medicine at Glasgow University from 1908 to 1912, receiving his MB in 1912. The University records list him at the time living at 33 Linn Terrace, Muirend, Cathcart. He married in 1915, in Cathcart, Jane Wood. He received his M.D. from Glasgow University in 1919. Like his brother Alexander, he served in the Army, in the Royal Army Medical Corps. On the 15th of October 1919, he relinquished his rank as temporary Captain, to be confirmed as a full Captain (*The Times*, 15th November, 1919). A summary of some of his medical papers is included below.

1) "Observations on the sporulation of the syphilis organism as seen on the dark ground," C. Lundie M.D. Glasg., Late Captain, R.A.M.C. (T.C.); and F. H. Goss M.C., M.B., CH.B. Leeds, Captain, R.A.M.C. (S.R.); *The Lancet*, 194, 1025, (1919)

2) "Complement-fixation experiments in influenza," H. J. B. Fry M.D. Oxon., Captain, R.A.M.C. (T.). and C. Lundie M.D. Glasg., Captain, R.A.M.C. (T.C.); *The Lancet*, **195**, 368 (1920).

3) "Antileucocytolysins," C. Lundie; *The Lancet*, **203**, 922, (1924)

Crawford and his wife at some time emigrated to South Africa. They had one child.

i Dr. Marie Lundie, who died in South Africa after a long career in medicine, without issue.

Dr. ALEXANDER LUNDIE. BSc., M.B., Ch.B., D.P.H., Late Captain R.A.M.C.

He was born on the 8th of August 1878, at 12:30 pm, the younger twin of William Paterson Lundie, who died young. He studied at Dunfermline High School, and afterwards at United College, St. Andrews University. He commenced his university studies in 1895, the same date his sister Ella started her studies there. He was enrolled, 1895-6 in Junior Greek and Junior Maths; 1896-7 in Natural Philosophy, Chemistry and Practical Chemistry; 1897-8 in Advanced Chemistry, Natural History and Practical

Mrs. Isabel Lundie, Dr. Alexander Lundie
Their children Robert, Alexander and John

27. Family of Dr. Alexander Lundie

Natural History, Botany and Practical Botany; 1898-9 in Advanced Practical Chemistry, Advanced and Practical Natural History, Advanced Practical Botany; 1899-1900, with a Berry Medical Scholarship, in the Faculty of Medicine, Physiology, Anatomy and Practical Anatomy. In the 1898-99 session Alexander received Class Honours in Senior Systematic Practical and Natural History; was one of two students in First Rank in Practical Chemistry; and was second Rank in Advanced Botany. He is recorded as passing his final Zoology and Botany examination in October 1899, and subsequently graduating BSc. After finishing his studies at St. Andrew's he moved on to Edinburgh, where he studied from his bachelor of medicine and surgery degrees (M.B. Ch.B.). Later on in life he would also receive a doctorate in public health (D.P.H.) from the University of London.

In 1910 Alexander was appointed medical officer with the West African Medical Staff in the Gold Coast (what in now Ghana). Some time was spent travelling in the Ashanti region of the country, which is documented in stories written for his children. From his strong affections for this country, Dr Lundie later named his home in Cupar Fife after one of it's cities, Ahunda. From 1914 to 1921 he served with the Royal Army Medical Corps, as a Bacteriologist at the Aldershot Command; and the officer in charge of the School of Army Sanitation, again in Aldershot. He was twice mentioned in dispatches. On the 12th of March 1915, when on a temporary commission as Lieutenant attached to the Aldershot command, he appeared briefly in *The Times* as a result of his work on Meningitis.

"SERIOUSNESS OF "SPOTTED" FEVER

In answer to Mr. Bowerman, Mr. Tennat says there have been there have been no cases of cerebro-spinal meningitis at Tidworth since March 9.

The Lancet says that the Army Medical Department has been giving very serious consideration to the outbreak of this disease. The Journal describes the strict system of isolation and other precautions adopted in the various camps.

The opinions on the subject of Dr. A Lundie, Dr. D. J. Thomas, and Dr. S. Fleming, who are all attached to the Aldershot command, are given in the *British Medical Journal*. They state that the disease is more widespread that in usually recognised. It

28. Dr. Alexander Lundie

probably gives fair warning of its onset by catarrhal symptoms, and often goes no farther. In its second stage in may run a non-malignant course, giving plenty of time to arouse suspicion, and, if correctly diagnosed, would probably be cured by suitable treatment. During an epidemic routine examination of all sore throats would probably be of more value in stopping the disease than the examination of a vast number of alleged contacts."

Shortly after this article was published, on the 31st of August 1915, Alexander was raised from the rank of Lieutenant to Captain (*The Times*, 21st September 1915, p4). In 1921, after leaving the R.A.M.C., he worked at the ministry of pensions as the deputy commissioner of medical services (Pathology). In 1925 he was assistant medical officer for the Carnegie Trust; 1927, area medical officer for Fife Education Authority; 1931 executive Tuberculosis Officer for Fife County Council; and by the end of 1938, was the chief medical officer for Fife. From the same source as the information regarding his nephew David's visit to Torryburn, Ronald Caseby (although not in the biography), comes the following extract:

"In the autumn of 1938, Ronnie (son of the Rev. Alexander Caseby, the minister of Newmills and Torryburn) was nearing two years old. Dr. Lundie, Chief Medical Officer for Fife, called at the Manse. Many years earlier his father was the minister of my church. He loved seeing through our lovely home. However, his visit was something special. Torryburn, Newmills, High and Low Valleyfield – parents would not take their children to Torryburn Hall for immunisation against certain diseases. I said, "Leave it to me, I will initiate, we will take our six children to Torryburn hall at 11 am the following Saturday to be immunised and request that all other parents do the same." Dr. Lundie said that he would have a full staff ready.

As we promised we took our six children. Many parents also arrived. Our children came out of the hall; not in tears, but smiling. For six and a half hours the medical team toiled and at the end of the appointed session, I was told that 95% of the children in the area were immunised. "A record indeed," said Dr. Lundie, "and I am most grateful". No child out of the 95%

immunised suffered any discomfort and hundreds of Mums and Dads thanked me for my example in sending, or rather taking, our children first to the Torryburn Hall."

Alexander was the author of papers on Trypanosomiasis, Yellow Fever, Cerebro-spinal Fever and Tuberculin, and a list of some of his medical papers follows:

1) "The free use of amyl nitrite in pulmonary haemorrhage," Alexander Lundie M.B., CH.B. Edin.; *The Lancet*, **171** 427, (1908)
2) "The Pleomorphism of the meningococcus," Alex. Lundie M.B., CH.B. Edin, Lt., R.A.M.C., D. J. Thomas M.R.C.S., L.R.C.P. Lond., D.P.H. Oxon, Lt., R.A.M.C., and S. Fleming M.B., C.M. Edin., D.P.H. Camb., Lt., R.A.M.C.; *The Lancet*, **186**, 693-694, (1915).
3) "Account of Two New Tubercular Antigens," Alexander Lundie, Birmingham, 1924

On the 14th of October 1915, in the Union United Free Church of Clydebank, Alexander married Isabel Dobson Taylor. The ceremony was performed by the Rev. Colin M. Nicol, of the U.F. Church of Clydebank, and the Rev. Andrew M. Kelly of Fairfield U.F. Church in Govan. Isabel was born on the 20th of September 1892, at Old Kilpatrick. She was the eldest child (of four, also: Jessie McNab Taylor, Robert William Taylor and John Gregor Taylor) of John Taylor O.B.E., J.P., (who was Provost of Clydebank for 15 years, and M.P. for Dumbarton burghs from 1918 to 1922) and Agnes Gordon Wood. Isabel was an artist, and studied at Glasgow School of Art. An example of her work long stood in the Union Church, Clydebank; where a stained glass window she designed, donated to the church by her parents in memory of her eldest brother Robert William Taylor, who lost his life in WW1, was erected in October 1916. Sadly this church was destroyed by fire a few years ago, and has since been demolished. Isabel died at 2.45 pm, on the 13th of March 1927, aged 34, at 134 Park Road Rosyth, Dunfermline, of Acute Lymphatic Leukaemia.

Dr. Alexander Lundie appears in the book "Scottish Biographies 1938"; which as well as including a details of his medical career, as had been described above, states his other interests as fishing, travelling and motoring. Dr. Lundie died on the 20th of March 1951, at Dundee (*The Times*, 28th March, 1951). Both he and his wife, along with his sisters Ella and Agnes, are buried in Dunfermline Cemetery (plots 4326/4327 Eastern Div.) where a monument is erected in their memory.

Alexander and Isabel had issue:

1   *Col. Alexander Robert Taylor Lundie*, of whom next

2   *John Taylor Lundie*, born in 1920. He studied medicine from 1937 to 1939 at the University of St. Andrews, when he broke his studies to sign up to fight in the second world war. He died whilst on active service in Iraq, a lieutenant in the 3rd Battalion of the 8th Punjab Regiment. He is buried in Baghdad war cemetery, Iraq. John is also named on the war Memorial in Cupar, Fife.

3   *Dr. Robert Andrew Crawford Lundie, MB. ChB., D.P.M.*, was born on the 12th of October 1923, at 16 Kensington Road, Selly Park, Birmingham. In 1937 he was awarded a Foundation Scholarship by Fettes College, Edinburgh (*The Scotsman*, 7th July 1937, page 14), and so spent his senior school years there. By the time he had finished his school education, war had broken out, and so he went straight into the Royal Air Force, holding the rank of sergeant. Between May and June 1942 he was on pilot training. From July to December of 1942 he took the ab initio air bomber-training course at Wigton. January and March of 1943 he took the Air bomber instructors course at 1 A.A.S. Manby, and subsequently qualified (11th February 1943) as an air bomber instructor. After this training Robert was attached to 416 squadron at R.A.F Bottlesford. Here, from June to July 1943 he took part in several bombing raids over Germany, where he was the bomb aimer in a Lancaster Bomber. He returned to Wigton in August 1943 for further training, and in January 1945, moved on to the officers training unit at Stanton Hardcourt. By this time he held the rank of Warrant Officer. After a short course in R.A.F. Sandtoft in April 1945, Robert joined 116 Squadron in R.A.F. Kirmington. By June of that year he had been promoted to Pilot Officer, and was soon after promoted to Flight Officer. At Kirmington Robert's job was as Air Bomber, aiming the bombs in Lancaster bombers, in raids mainly over railway marshalling yards in Germany. Robert came out of the R.A.F. in 1946, and started the medical studies at the university of St. Andrews, which he had postponed due to WWII. He graduated MB. ChB. and then spent his houseman year in Dundee. From then up until 1958 he worked as a general practitioner, first in Doncaster, and later in Bradford. In 1958 he started work as a psychiatrist at

Bootham Park Hospital in York, taking a Diploma in Physiological Medicine sometime after. Robert worked at Bootham Park up until his death on the 13th of November 1975.

During his time at R.A.F. Kirmington, Robert met his wife Hazel Robinson, daughter of Charles and Nellie Robinson. At the time when they met Hazel was working as an inspector of the Lancaster Bombers at the A.V. Roe factory. They were married on the 20th of July 1946, in Cupar, Fife. Robert and Hazel had two children, John and Jane.

Col. ALEXANDER ROBERT TAYLOR LUNDIE. O.B.E., M.C., M.D., Bsc. M.B., ChB., DTM&H., FRC Path.

Born on the 7th of November 1916 at the Old Court House, Hale, Farnham Surrey, the eldest son of Dr. Alexander Lundie and his wife Isabel. He attended Dunfermline High School and Bell Baxter High School (in Cupar Fife), and went on to study at University College Dundee and United College, University of St. Andrews. Studying medicine, he received his MB ChB on the 30th of June 1939.

On the 7th of July this year he was given a short service commission as Lieutenant (on probation) in the Royal Army Medical Corps (*The Times*, 26th July 1939, p19), and was confirmed in this rank on the 14th of October (*The Times*, of same date, p4). Initially serving at the Royal Army Medical College and the Royal Herbert Hospital, he was posted as the Regimental Medical Officer to the 1st Battalion, Royal Welch Fusiliers at the out break of WWII, and served with the British Expeditiary Forces in France and Belgium until they were overrun by S.S. Panzer Troops on the 27th of May 1940. Alexander was taken prisoner of War, and remained 'awaiting re-patriation' until May 1944. Although now a POW Alexander was officially promoted to the rank of Captain on the 7th of July 1940. He was initially employed on medical duties at Oflag VII H, in Bavaria, where he set up a dysentery hospital, and was eventually to become a patient there himself. In November 1940 he was transferred to Marienburg in Prussia where he carried out general duties in the camp, but later found himself transferred to the main hospital where he was able to start some lab work. In May 1943 he was transferred to a POW camp in Danzig. Here he found himself able to organise some clinical pathology. On the 5th of May 1944, following the recommendation of a mixed medical commission, Alexander was repatriated upon medical grounds. After a short spell in a sanatorium at Elsterhorst in Bavaria, he returned to the United Kingdom via Sweden. Here he took charge of lying patients on the hospital train to Gothenburg, and their supervision onboard M.V. Gripaholm.

In November 1944, Alexander was posted to the Scottish Command Laboratory, and continued his training under Major-General Sachs and Brigadier Sir John Boyd. In September 1945, his medical category was raised, and he was posted as a graded specialist in pathology to Porton, where he served under Sir Paul Fildes and Doctor Henderson.

On the 29th of November 1945, Alexander was awarded the Military Cross (*London Gazette*, of same date). A short note featured in the Fife Herald and Journal of the 5th of December.

> "Capt. A.R.T. Lundie, R.A.M.C., eldest son of Dr. A. Lundie, Ahunda, Milbank Cupar, has been awarded the Military Cross for gallant and distinguished services in the field. A former pupil of Bell Baxter School, Capt. Lundie took his M.B. Ch.B. at St. Andrews University in June 1939 and joined the regular army the following month. He went to France with one of the first contingents of the B.E.F., and was taken prisoner when France collapsed. He was for some time in a P.O.W. camp in Poland. In September last year, he was repatriated, the first Cupar prisoner of war to be so released from captivity. A younger brother, J. T. Lundie, Punjab Regiment, died on service in India in 1942, and his youngest brother, Robert A. C. Lundie, has a commission in the R.A.F."

Alexander was promoted to Major on the 7th July 1947, and after a month at the Army Vaccine Laboratory (David Bruce Laboratories) he became a demonstrator of Pathology at the Royal Army Medical College. In September 1948, he was posted to the United States of America. From May 1949 to September 1951, he worked with the Medical Research Council Radiobacterial Research Unit, at Harwell. He also lectured regularly at the Royal Army Medical College. Between September 1951 and March 1952 Alexander attended the 51st Senior Officer's course at the Royal Army Medical

College, and then completed the senior specialist course in pathology, passing the examination in August 1952. Subsequently, on the 1st of September 1952, he left the United Kingdom for service with the Royal Navy Special Squadron in Australian Waters, and returned in November.

On the 11th of January 1953, Alexander was appointed as Assistant Director of Pathology, Eastern Command, and given the rank of Lieutenant Colonel. He was also officer in charge of the Eastern Command and London District laboratories. In September 1953 he was posted to the War office as Assistant Director General of Army Medical Services, where he served with Major-General Sachs and Major-General Archer, in A.M.D.8. During his spell at the War office he was also secretary of the Army Pathology Advisory Committee, concerned with the production of papers concerning Pathology; examining officers at the Royal Army Medical College; and lecturing and taking part in experiments also at the Royal Army Medical College.

Before 1956, Alexander was appointed to the chair in Pathology at Khartoum, but was unable to take up this post due to serious losses in the Army Pathology services. On the 21st of February 1956 Alexander was confirmed in the rank of Lieutenant Colonel (*The Times*, 27th February 1956, p12); and was awarded the O.B.E. on the 13th of June the following year. That September he was posted as the Assistant Director of Pathology to Southern Command, and the Officer in Charge of the Leishman Laboratories.

From September 1959 until September 1962 Alexander was the Assistant Director of Pathology for the Middle East and Near East Land Forces, with laboratories based in Dhekelia, Cyprus (command Lab.); Tripoli; Benghazi; and Malta. On the of 7th July 1962, Alexander was promoted to Colonel (*The Times*, 16th July, 1962, p7), and after attending the Wantage course on the medical use of isotopes, he assumed command of the army blood depot at Aldershot. His spell there was not long, as in November 1962, he returned to Southern Command for a second spell as Assistant Director of Pathology, and took command of the Leishman Laboratory. In November 1963 he submitted his thesis "Bacillary Dysentery The Military Disease" to the University of St. Andrews, for consideration for the degree of Doctor of Medicine: This was awarded the following June. Alexander had sometime previous submitted a thesis to the University of St. Andrews for BSc. entitled "The Medical Problem in Atomic Warfare". The date of submission is not known, but the thesis was accepted. A founder member of the College of

Pathologists (Now Royal College of Pathologists); after the award of his M.D. he was advanced to Fellow. Alexander was also a fellow of the Royal Society of Medicine; a fellow of the Royal Society of Tropical Medicine and Hygiene; a member of the association of clinical pathologists; a member of the British Medical Association; a member of the British Academy for Forensic Sciences; a member of the Pathological Society of Great Britain and Ireland; a member of the Society for General Microbiology; and an honorary member of the Association of Military Surgeons of the United States.

In September 1966 Alexander was posted to the Far East Land Forces as the Deputy Director of Pathology, and the officer in charge of the central pathology laboratory in Singapore. Dependant laboratories in his area were situated in Hong Kong, Malaysia and Nepal.

Col Lundie retired from the Army on the 7th of November 1969, remaining a reserve until the 7th of November 1974. He went on to work as Director of Immunology for the Evans Medical Company, based in Liverpool, and later as a Consultant Pathologist in the National Heath Service.

During his time in the Royal Army Medical Corps he produced a number of papers on tropical medicine, malaria and the medical effects of atomic and chemical warfare. These titles include:

1) "Discussion of Penicillin in Rhinology;" Hall I.S., Williams R.H.H., Mitchel J.F.O. *et al.*; *Proc. Roy. Soc. Med.* 39, 279, (1946).

2) "Some medical aspects of atomic warfare;" Lundie, A.R.T.; *Roy. Army. Med. Corps*; XIV, 5, 246-248 (1950).

3) "The present status of Hemorragic aspects of radiation injury;" Lundie A.R.T. (with E.P.Cronkite, D.P. Jackson and G.V. Lerey); *Proc. Internat. Soc. Hematol*, 549-551 (1950)

4) "Instrument requirements in Atomic warfare;" Lundie A.R.T. (with P.H. Halliday) *J. Roy. Army. Med. Corps*; XCV, 161-168, (1951).

5) "The treatment of radiation injuries;" Lundie A.R.T.; *Interim supplement to British Encyclopedia of Medical Practice*, 162 (1956).

6) "British Army Pathology Before and After Leishman;" Lundie A.R.T.; *J. Clin. Path.* 19, 408, (1966).

7) "Chloroquinie resistant Malaria in West Malaysia;" Lundie A.R.T. (with H.B.H McKelvey, D.H.H. Williams, H.S. Moore, and D.E. Warsley); *Brit. Med .J.*, 5632, 703-4 (1968)

8) "Malabsorption and Skin;" McKelvey T.P., Lundie A.R.T., Williams E.D. *et al*; *Brit. Med. J.*, 4 (5632), 702 (1968)

9) "Chloroquine-resistant P falciparium infections;" Lundie A.R.T.; *J. Clin. Path.* **22**, 509 (1969)

10) "Chloroquine-Resistant Falciparum Malaria among British Service Personel in west Malaysia and Singapore;" McKelvey T.P., Lundie A.R.T., Vanreenan R.M. et al; *T. Roy. Soc. Trop. Med. H.*, **65**, 286 (1971).

He married, on the 21ˢᵗ of August 1945, at the College Chapel, St. Andrews, Helen Elizabeth Wilson, only child of William Wilson M.B.E., and Margaret Georgina Brown (descendant of the Brown's of Currie – see '*The Family Craven*' by Rev. J. B. Craven). Helen had also studied at Bell Baxter School and St. Andrew's university. They were married by the Rev. John McPhail M.A. (*The Times*, 25ᵗʰ August 1945). They had three children together: Elizabeth Margaret, Isobel Mary, and Alexander Stewart. Isobel is the artist of various figures in this book, and her eldest son is the author. Colonel Lundie died in Ayr, on the 4ᵗʰ of October 1988; his wife, Helen Elizabeth (Betty), died on the 21ˢᵗ of April 2005 in Dalbeattie

Family of David Lundie, minister of Tongue.

JOHN LUNDIE

He married Elspeth Lamond, and had issue:
1   *James Lundie*, christened on the 12ᵗʰ of April 1840, in Kirkmichael, Perth.
2   *Eupham Lundie*, christened on the 27ᵗʰ of February 1842, in Kirkmichael, Perth.
3   *Mary Lundie*, christened on the 7ᵗʰ of July 1844, in Kirkmichael, Perth.
4   *David Lundie*, christened on the 23ʳᵈ of November 1846, in Kirkmichael, Perth. His details follow.
5   *Robert Lundie*, christened on the 28ᵗʰ of January 1849, in Kirkmichael, Perth.
6   *Margaret Lundie*, christened on the 1ˢᵗ of February 1852, in Kirkmichael, Perth.

REV. DAVID LUNDIE, MINISTER OF TONGUE,

David was born in Rhidorach, Glenshee, on the 23ʳᵈ of November

1846. He was educated at Perth Academy and the University of St. Andrews, receiving his M.A. on the 10th of April 1869. He was licensed by the Presbytery of St Andrews on the 8th of May 1872. His first appointment was as assistant at the Parish of Boarhills. In November 1872, he was ordained to the parish of Kinlochbervie. On the 31st March 1880 he was transferred, and admitted on the 27th March 1881, to the parish of Tongue. He married, on the 22nd of June 1881, Elspeth Fleming, the 2nd daughter of William Aitken Butter, farmer, from upper Kenly, St Andrews (*FASTI*). They had issue:

1   *William John Lundie*, minister of Eddrachillis, whose details follow.

2   *Lamont Duncan Lundie*, born 6th February 1883. She married, on the 14th of October 1903, at 37 Merchiston Crescent Edinburgh, Mr Sinclair Coghill, of the Sutherland Estate Office. The marriage ceremony was performed by the Rev. Thomas burns FRSE of Lady Glenachy's church (*Scotsman*, 16th October 1903).

3   *James David Lundie*, born 11th August 1892, he was a 2nd Lieutenant in the 5th Seaforth Highlanders.

REV. WILLIAM JOHN LUNDIE, MINISTER OF EDDRACHILLS

He was born on the 11th March 1882. He was educated at the Miller Institution, Thurso, and the University of St Andrews. He was licenced by the Presbytery of Tongue in April 1913, appointed assistant at Golspie; and ordained on the 6th of May that year (*FASTI*).

Family of John Lundie, schoolmaster Auchterarder

JOHN LUNDIE

The owner of a public school in Arbroath, he married Janet (Jess) Milln on the 29th of November 1811. He died on the 22nd of July 1850 in St. Vigeans. He and Janet had issue:

1   *Helen Lundie*, christened on the 24th of December 1812, in St. Vigeans, Angus, Scotland. In the 1841 census she appears living with

her parents in Inverbrothock, Arbroath, working as a dressmaker.

2   *James Lundie*, christened on the 29th of June 1814, in St. Vigeans, Angus, Scotland. In the 1841 census he appears living with his parents in Inverbrothock, Arbroath, working as a stationer. Between 1846 and 1852, his shop was located at 99, High Street, Arbroath. The premises later moved to 27, Reform Street, Dundee. He married Ann Wannan Honeyman on the 6th of December 1853, with proclamations in both the parishes of Saint Vigeans and Barry. She died on the 18th of April 1901; James predeceased her (*Dundee Probate*). After his death his wife ran the shop, and she was succeeded in the business by their son Robert. They had issue:

  i   Jessie Wannan Lundie, born on the 24th of December 1854, in Arbroath, Angus.

  ii   Anne Honeyman Lundie, born on the 29th of March 1856, in Arbroath, Angus.

  iii   Dr. John Lundie Bsc. Dsc, He appears in the "*Dictionay of American Biography*," described as an Engineer and Inventor. Born on the 14th of December, 1857, in Arbroath, the son of James Lundie and Anne Honeyman. He went to school at Dundee high school, graduating in 1873; spent four years on the office of the harbour engineer of the port of Dundee; went on to study at Edinburgh University, graduating Bsc in 1880, with a first prize in mathematical physics. He moved to the United States of America soon after, and was heavily involved in the building of railways. He worked upon many projects including the building of table rock tunnel; laying out the first low-level drainage system for Chicago; power handling of freight on the central Georgia Railway; the London Metropolitan Railway; using electric power on the Isthmus of Panama (in conjunction with the General Electric Company) and directing the affairs of the Panama-American Corporation. He developed a theory of "rapid acceleration" concerning the movement of trains, for which he presented a thesis at the University of Edinburgh in 1902, entitled "The Economics of Train Movement," and being awarded a Doctorate of Science. From this thesis comes the 'Lundie formula,' which is concerned with train resistance. In the course of this work he obtained several patents including; the Lundie Ventilated Rheostat (Patent No. 687,

569, Nov. 26 1901) and the Lundie Tie Plate (Patent No. 1065696, June 24, 1913). Subsequent to these inventions, John founded the Lundie Engineering Corporation, of which he was president. In 1921 he was appointed as technical advisor to the Central American Corporation. John was twice married. His first wife, Iona Oakley Gorham, whom he had married in 1906, died in 1925. In 1929 he married Mrs Alice Eddy Snowden, the widow of Dr. Albert A Snowden. John died on the 9th of February 1931, in New York.

iv James Lundie, born on the 15th of October 1861, in Arbroath, Angus

v George Watson Lundie, born on the 29th of December 1863, in Dundee, Angus

vi William Lundie, born on the 14th of February 1865, in Dundee, Angus

vii Georgina Wannan Lundie, born on the 8th of August 1867, in Dundee, Angus.

viii Robert Lundie, his birth date is not known, but the Lamb Collection, donated by A.C. Lamb to the Dundee Public Libraries, includes a small pocket calendar produced by Mrs. J. Lundie, bookseller and stationer in Dundee. The shop, started by her husband, is said to have been taken over by their son Robert, after his mother's death. He is most probably Robert H Lundie, whom one can see as a publisher of books and postcards in Dundee in the early 20th Century.

3   *Margaret Lundie*, christened on the 30th of May 1818, in St. Vigeans, Angus, Scotland. In the 1841 census she appears living with her parents in Inverbrothock, Arbroath, working as a dressmaker.

4   *Jessie Lundie*, christened on the 13th of March 1820, in Arbroath, Angus, Scotland.

5   *William Hannah Lundie*, christened on the 23rd of February 1822, in St. Vigeans, Angus, Scotland; of whom next.

6   *Ann Lundie*, christened on the 8th of February 1824, in St. Vigeans, Angus, Scotland. In the 1841 census she appears living with her parents in Inverbrothock, Arbroath.

7   *Alexander Lundie*, born around 1828; in the 1841 census he appears living with his parents in Inverbrothock, Arbroath, working as a stationer's apprentice

8   *George Watson Lundie*, christened on the 22nd of march 1831, in St Vigeans, Angus, Scotland. In the 1841 census he appears living with his parents in Inverbrothock, Arbroath.

WILLIAM HANNAH LUNDIE

He was christened on the 23rd of February 1822, in St. Vigeans, Angus. He was a schoolmaster at the Sheridan Trust School, Auchterarder. He married Mary Tasker. She died on the 21st November 1910, at 5 Buckingham Terrace, Ayr, at the age of 86. William Pre-deceased her, passing away on the 21st of January 1900, at Lochwinoch, Renfrewshire. His testate will was registered on the 30th of May 1900, at Paisley. They had issue.

1   *Rev. John Lundie*, Born on the 10th of December 1849, at Coupar Angus. He was educated at Auchterarder Sheridan's School; the University of Edinburgh, where he obtained his M.A.; and the United Presbyterian College. He was appointed as a missionary to Kattraria, South Africa on the 26th December 1876, and ordained for Foreign Missionary service by the United Presbyterian Presbytery of Edinburgh on the 4th of September 1877. This same year, on the 16th of August 1877, he married Rebecca Peachy Best. He retired from service on the 1st of January 1929, and died, at Nqqeleni, Umtata, South Africa, on the 14th of June 1935 (*FAST U.F. Church*).

   i   Elizabeth Lundie
   ii   Frank Lundie
   iii   Mary Tasker Lundie
   iv   Flora Lundie
   v   Marshall Lundie
   vi   Dr. Arnold E Lundie. He was married and had one son:
       a   *Dr. John Kayden Lundie.* He married, on the 15th of July, 1953, at St. James's Church, Gerads Cross, Mary, the elder daughter of Mr. and Mrs. R. Haynes of Gerrads Cross, Buckinghamshire (*The Times*, 31st March 1953; 18th July 1953). They had at least one son, who was born on the 31st of December, 1954, at Moedersbond Hospital, Pretoria.

2   *Helen Lundie*, born on the 14th of June 1851, at Coupar Angus.

3   *Rev. James Lundie*, **M.A.** born on the 10th of March, 1853,

at Coupar Angus. He died on the 21st of March 1890, at Calle Mendeznunez 30, Huelva in Spain (*Scotsman*, 22nd March 1890). He was at one time living at Sheddan Cottage, Auchterarder. His testament is registered at Perth, on the 31st of December 1890.

4 ***Dr. William Tasker Lundie M.A. Bsc. M.D.*** He was born in Auchterarder in 1855. He initially trained as a teacher, and later as a physician. He married, at the Willows, Relugas Road, Edinburgh, on the 14th of August, 1895, Elizabeth Lawson Auld, daughter of Mr Wallace Auld. The ceremony was performed by the Rev. T.S. Dickson, of Argyll Place U.P Church, assisted by the Rev. R.D. Mitchel of the E.U. Church Dalkeith (*Scotsman*, 15th August 1895). He died at the same address, on the 28th of June 1899. And had his funeral at one o'clock on Tuesday the 31st of June (*Scotsman*, 31st June 1899). His obituary, from the 1st of July edition of 'The Scotsman' includes a well-detailed obituary of this man, and so it is included for reference below.

"Scotsman, 1st of July 1899

By the death of Dr. William Tasker Lundie, Glengyle Terrace, the career of one of the most promising of Edinburgh's younger physicians has been prematurely closed. He was born in 1855 at Auchterarder, where his father was head of the Sheridan Trust School. Trained for the teaching profession, he also took the university courses in Arts and Science, graduating M.A. in 1883, and B.Sc. in 1886. For some time he was on the teaching staff of George Watson's Ladies College. Having long had a leaning towards the profession of medicine, he abandoned teaching, and at the close of his medical course graduated M.B.C.M in 1888. For two years he acted as House Surgeon in Craiglockhart Poorhouse, and began private practice in 1890. Being already well known to a large circle of friends, he soon established a large connection and his winsome personality and professional abilities made him a universal favourite among all classes with whom he was brought into contact. Dr. Lundie graduated as M.D. in 1893, and among other appointments, held the post of Chloroformist to the Edinburgh Dental Hospital. Dr. Lundie was married in 1895, and is survived by his widow and three children. His remains were interred in Grange Cemetery yesterday, in the presence of a very large gathering of mourners."

William and his wife had issue.

i Dorothy Jane Lundie, born on the 6th of May 1896, at 3 Glengyle terrace Edinburgh (*Scotsman*, 7th May 1896).

ii Evelyn Mary Tasker Lundie , born on the 3rd of June 1897, at 3 Glengyle terrace Edinburgh (*Scotsman*, 4th June 1897).

iii Edith Catherine Lundie, born in 1898.

5 **Marshall Lundie**, born on the 25th of March 1857, at Auchterarder.

6 **Catherine Pringle Lundie**, born on the 1st of June 1859, at Auchterarder.

7 **Andrew Tasker Lundie**, born on the 17th of August 1861, at Auchterarder.

8 **Jessie Lundie**, born on the 26th of August 1863, at Auchterarder. She married, at three Glengyle terrace Edinburgh, on the 10th of June 1891, the Rev. Henry B. Gray, of Lochwinnoch. The ceremony was performed by the Rev. T.S. Dickson, M.A. of Argyll Place U.P. Church, assisted by the Rev. J.B. Smith of Greenock (Scotsman, 11th June 1891).

9 **Alexander Brock Lundie**, born on the 16th of August 1866, at Auchterarder

Section Six

Families Associated By Region

There are far more descendants of the Lundie family bearing that name and its variants, than can now be linked to the different Houses and Branches described in the text so far. Many records of the Scottish Lundies, Lundins and Lundys are of course preserved in the Old Parish records of Scotland, now held by the General Record Office of Scotland. These however ignore those persons for whom no record of birth, marriage or death still survives, and for those who left Scotland and whose descendants now live elsewhere in the world. To simply list all the birth marriage and death notices for persons of the Lundie/Lundy/Lundin surname, would be an entire volume on itself, even if one just considered performing this task for Scotland. However, to do so would also be almost pointless to the reader, as such information is readily available on the Internet at websites such as www.familysearch.org, and www. scottishpeople.gov.uk. However, to supplement the information that the reader can access elsewhere, the following section includes information on people and small family groups, who feature in records other than just BMD, and can be associated together due to their locality. The dates of many of the people featured in this section date prior to the first surviving entries in the Old Parish Records for these areas. This is not an exhaustive list, but more an account of the extra information I have found whilst researching the previous sections, that I have not been able to link to the various other branches. **Section Seven** has a similar basis, but is based upon individuals who have no visible connection with other Lundie families, by area or other means.

In Benholm

Although upon the death of Elizabeth Lundie the barony and castle of Benholm passed into the hands of the Keith family, there remained in the area a number of descendants of this family. One of these families is that of Lundie of Lungar; this family, as discussed in the section three, descending from the brother of the last male Lundie Laird, William Lundie of Benholm. William Lundie of Benholm and John Lundie of Lungar had six other brothers and two sisters. Although an exact family relationship cannot be given between the following individuals and the family of Benholm at this moment, it is hoped that further information might, in the future, help to connect them together.

WILLIAM LUNDIE AT THE MYLNE OF BENHOLM, had his testament registered with the Edinburgh Commissary Court On the 14th of June 1565, (*Edin. Tests.*). Note that Benholm Mill is open to the public as a visitor attraction.

- - - - - - - - - -

ANDREW LUNDY IN THE NETHERKNOKIS OF BENHOLM had his testament registered with the Edinburgh Commissary Court On the 28th of August 1590 (*Edin. Tests.*).

- - - - - - - - - -

ANDREW LUNDIE IN OVER KNOX OF BENHOLM, appears in the Register of the Privy Council between 1604 and 1607, along with, the late *Andrew of Knocky*, *John in Knocky and William in the Nether Knox* (Reg. Privy Council, VII., 562, 591, 593, 594).

- - - - - - - - - -

MARGARET LUNDIE sometime spouse to Alexander Eldar in Stane of Benholm had her testament registered with the Edinburgh Commissary Court On the 9th of July 1597 (*Edin. Tests.*).

- - - - - - - - - -

ANDREW LUNDIE IN THE KNOX OF BENHOLM. On The 15th of September 1617, Sir Alexander Strattoun of that ilk issued letters of commission to an unknown person, granting that person the power to uplift from 'Andrew Lundie in Knoxe - assize boll and anchorage of port and haven of Gordoune' (*NAS*, RH15/37/57). Andrew has his testament registered with the Edinburgh Commissary Court On the 8th of July 1635.

- - - - - - - - - -

ANDREW AND WILLIAM LUNDIE IN THE STANE OF BENHOLM. On the 19th of April 1659, an instrument of sasine was given in favour of Robert Scott, son of deceased James Scott of Logy, of the lands of Stane of Benholm. This land consisted of 150 acres or round a bout, and at that time was possessed by Andrew and William Lundie. The sasine followed on a disposition, dated the 14 of March 1659, by the Commissioners to the estate of William, Earl Marischal, and others excepted from the act of pardons and grace to the people of Scotland. It was recorded in the G.R.S. 19 April 1659 (*NAS*, GD70/112). In 1672, two bonds are registered that were granted by Andrew Lundie elder and younger, in the stein of Benholm (*Mack.* XXX 255; XXVIII. 738). On the 27th of June 1676, Andrew Lundie in the Stein of Benholm was granted an indenture of apprenticeship (*Mack*, XXXIX. 376).

- - - - - - - - - -

On the 30th of September 1657, the testament of Catherine Barclay, spouse to Andrew Lundie in Knox of Benholm, is registered with Brechin Commissary Court.

- - - - - - - - - -

In Burntisland

THOMAS LUNDIE. A wright in Burntisland, he married Janet Collier on the 27th of December 1725, in Burntisland. Her father, Walter Colliar, was a freeman, and as a result of the marriage Thomas was admitted as a freeman of the wrights on the 23rd of July 1726. Janet's brother James Colliar, the eldest son of Walter, was also a wright in Burntisland, and was admitted freeman in 1712; her sister Agnes married John Paterson a freeman of the Bunrtisland Hammermen.

Thomas served as Deacon in 1731 and 1735. He had six apprentices, David Stocks in 1735; James Mores in 1741; John Watt, also in 1741; John Arnot in 1749; Walter Scot in 1765; and Mouray Walter in 1765. In 1729, his servant is listed as one Mitchell Waterston, and in 1731 a David Wishart was working for his as a journeyman. Mitchell Waterston was also the servant of Thomas's brother-in-law James.

Thomas and Janet had two children:

1   *Walter Lundie*, of whom next
2   *Margaret Lundie*, christened on the 24th of June 1729; she married David Dalrymple on the 9th of May 1763. Both her christening and marriage were in Burntisland. They had issue:
  i   *Janet Dalrymple*, christened on the 21st of October 1766

WALTER LUNDIE, son of Thomas and Janet, was christened on the 30th of July 1727, in Burntisland. Like his father, he was also one of the Burntisland Wrights. He was admitted as a Burgess on the 19th of December 1754. He had one known apprentice, James Hogan, who entered his apprenticeship in September 1769. Walter married Elizabeth Crawford on the 22nd of December 1754, in Burntisland. They had issue:

1 *Walter Lundie*, married Agnes Kennel on the 25th of March 1786, in Burntisland. Either Walter or his father appears in The Times on the 10th of February 1789, listed as one of the heritors and burgesses of Burntisland, in an address to the Prince of Wales, concering the illness of the King, and appointment of the Prince of Wales as Regent.

2 *John Lundie*, christened on the 7th of June 1763, in Burntisland Fife; by 1787 he had moved to the Parish of Greyfriars in Edinburgh, and was working as a mariner. He married Agnes Shoolbroad, the daughter of William Shoolbroad, a farmer at Kinross, on the 19th of June 1787. The marriage is listed in both Edinburgh and Burntisland. After the marrige, John returned to Burntisland, where his children were born:

i John Lundie, christened on the 16th of September 1787, in Burntisland. He is probably the same John Lundie who was apprenticed to Alexander Lyall in September 1803, and was afterwards admitted freeman of Burntisland. He was a cabinetmaker, and was listed in the Pigot Index in 1825 and 1837. he died on the 1st of May 1851.

ii Elizabeth Lundie, christened on the 30th of July 1788, in Burntisland.

3 *William Lundie*, christened on the 16th of December 1765, in Burntisland.

Sometime between 1850 and 1859, an Ann Stalker was served as heir to her Grandfather, Walter Lundie in Burntisland. It is not yet clear if this was Walter son of Walter, or Walter son of Thomas (*Index Retours*).

In Dundee

JOHN LUNDIE. He died sometime before 1548, as his daughter

Katherine, designed as the daughter of the late John Lundie in Dundee, appears in the Register of the Privy Seal as having died without an heir (*Reg. Sec. Sig.* III. 1729).

- - - - - - - - - -

THOMAS LUNDIE, treasurer of the Burgh of Dundee. He appears with this designation on a burgess ticket granted to William Rait, a physician in Dundee on the 9th of March 1744 (*NAS*, GD68/1/311)

- - - - - - - - - -

JAMES LUNDIE, a bookseller in Dundee, died before the 16th of February, 1769 (*Brechin Comm. Court*).

- - - - - - - - - -

JAMES LUNDIE, shipmaster in Dundee, married Janet Myles on the 12th of August 1782, in Dundee. They had issue.

1   *James Lundie*, was born on the 17th of April 1783, and christened on the 22nd of April 1783, in Dundee. He was a private in the 92nd Regiment of Foot, and died in the year 1809, in Spain. His testament was proved on the 14th of May 1817, and is registered with Edinburgh Commissary Court.

2   *David Lundie*, was born on the 18th of February 1874, and christened on the 24th of February 1874, in Dundee.

3   *John Lundie*, was born on the 28th of August 1786, and christened on the 2nd of September 1786. He was a Watchmaker in Dundee, with a business at the High Street of Dundee between 1809 and 1837 (*Old Scottish Clockmakers*). He married Margaret Mills, on the 24th of June 1807. Margaret was served as co-heir of provision general to her brother William Mills, a sailor in Dundee – on the 18th of July 1832. James died on the 29th of December 1865, when he had been residing at No. 4 Sibbald Place, Edinburgh. He had issue:

i Catherine Lundie, born on the 27th of February 1808, and christened on the 9th of March same year, in Dundee

ii Crichton Lundie, born on the 1st of March 1817, and christened on the 8th of March 1817, in Dundee. She married James Forsyth, Shipmaster in Dundee, on the 13th of March 1842, in Dundee. She died before the 3rd of February 1875, as on that date her testament is proved at Dundee Sheriff Court. Her husband pre-deceased her.

iii James Keiller Lundie, born on the 28th of September 1818, and christened on the 8th of October 1818, in Dundee

iv Euphemia Lundie, born on the 11th of April 1822, and christened on the 16th of April 1822, in Dundee.

v Elizabeth Lundie, She married David Low on the 26th of July 1852, in Dundee.

4   Margaret Lundie, born on the 1st of May 1788, and christened on the 5th of May 1788, in Dundee

5   William Lundie, born on the 24th of June 1793, and christened on the same date in Dundee.

- - - - - - - - - -

In Dysart

WALTER LUNDIE, burgess of Dysart around 1635 (*Reg. Privy Council*, Series II. VI. 315).

- - - - - - - - - -

ROBERT LUNDIE, burgess of Dysart, was married to Margaret Sibbald. Robert died before March 1627 (*NAS* GD11/115). At this date his son George appears as a witness in a charter by Mr Robert Bruce of Wester Kennet, to Agnes Murray, daughter of Patrick Murray of Perdewis, Robert Bruce's future spouse, in liferent of the half of the lands of Wester Kennet, lands called the Cruihed lands, and Petfoulden, lying in the barony and county of Clackmannan: George is designed "son of the deceased Robert Lundie." It is quite possible that he was the son of George Lundie of Gorthie, as this Robert Lundie, is known to have been involved with business in Lundin as an attorney, and is known to also have a son and heir George.

1   George Lundie, whose details follow.

GEORGE LUNDIE, clerk of Dysart. Initially a servitor to Mr. David Kinghorn he was later the Clerk of Dysart (*Reg. Mag. Sig.*, VIII. 1615). On the 28th of July 1632, he was given a gift of the escheat of David Lundie 'sumtyme of Newhall now of Auchtermairnie,' (*Reg. Signatures*, Liii, fo.271;

NAS, GD50/185/57). He married Janet Broun on the 7th October 1638 (*Reg. Mar. Ed.*). George and Margaret were given a bond by Lord Sinclair of 2000 merks dated the 23rd of May 1648 (*NAS*, GD164/417). George Lundie died before the 14th of November, 1649. He had issue:

1 **Margaret Lundie.** In 1684, she along with her sister was served as heir general to her grandmother, Margaret Sibbald (*Gen. Retours*, No. 6384). In 1694, she was served, along with her sister as heir portioner to the same grandmother, in an annual rent of 10 l. from the lands of Contoun (*Inq. Spec. Ret. Fife*, No. 1600). She married, on the 21st of October, in South Leith, Midlothian, George Henry, minister of Corstorphine. They appear in legal records of the time with regards the bond given to Margaret's parents by Lord John Sinclair. Lord John's son was attempting to avoid payment of this bond to Margaret as their heir, and so Margaret and her husband took action (*NAS*, GD164/417). The Lords of Session gave a decision on the case on the 11th of February 1713. Details of this action can be found in summarised in various accounts of the Decisions of the Court of Session of Scotland. Margaret and George had issue:

a *James Henry*, christened on the 11th of August 1672, in the parish of Corstorphine, Midlothian.

b *John Henry*, christened on the 13th of December 1674, in the parish of Corstorphine, Midlothian.

c *William Henry*, christened on the 19th of December 1675, in the parish of Corstorphine, Midlothian.

d *Janet Henry*, christened on the 19th of January 1685, in the parish of Corstorphine, Midlothian.

2 **Maria Lundie.** In 1684, she along with her sister was served as heir general to her grandmother, Margaret Sibbald (*Gen. Retours*, No. 6384). In 1694, she was served, along with her sister as heir portioner to the same grandmother, in an annual rent of 10 l. from the lands of Contoun (*Inq. Spec. Ret. Fife*, No. 1600).

- - - - - - - - - -

WILLIAM LUNDIE IN DYSART, he is known to have had the following children (*Dysart Reg*).

1 *Male Lundie*, baptised on the 4th of November 1612, before witnesses Patrick Blakature, David Melvill and Gavin Wemyss, presenter of the bairn

2 *James Lundie*, baptised on the 9th of November 1614, before witnesses Sir James Scott of Abbotshall, David Simsone bailie, Michael Law, Robert Allardice, John Law, Andrew – and James Scott "presenter of the ane"

3 *Robert Lundie*, twin brother of James, baptised on the 9th of November 1614, before witnesses Sir James Scott of Abbotshall, David Simsone bailie, Michael Law, Robert Allardice, John Law, Andrew – and James Scott "presenter of the ane"

4 *Richard Lundie*, baptised on the 4th of July 1617 before witnesses: Captain Laurence Sinclair, Richard Lundy and Mr James Aittone.

5 *John Lundie*, baptised on the 28th of April 1619 before witnesses: John Murray of Towmasie, Atton of Kinadie and Walter Cockburn.

- - - - - - - - - -

In Edinburgh

JOSEPH LUNDIE, a spirit dealer, of No. 439 Lawnmarket, Edinburgh, died before the 29th of July 1865 (*Ed. Sheriff Court*).

- - - - - - - - - -

DANIEL LUNDIE, a taylor, in Old Greyfriars Parish, Edinburgh, married Mary Ridley, in New Town, on the 30th of August 1772 (*Reg. Mar. Ed.*).

- - - - - - - - - -

JAMES LUNDIE, a write, in Greyfriars Parish, married Christian Henderson, the daughter of Thomas Henderson, a shoemaker in Calton, on the 16th of July, 1758. They had issue:

1 *Magdalene Lundie*, born on the 13th of April 1759, in Edinburgh Parish, Edinburgh, Midlothian

- - - - - - - - - -

JAMES LUNDIE, a plasterer, in New Kirk Parish, married Elizabeth Fleming, daughter of John Fleming a weaver in Pittenweem, on the 16th of February 1778.

- - - - - - - - - -

In Fawfield

WILLIAM LUNDY IN SOUTHER-FAWFIELD. The first reference I have found to a connection between the Lundie family and this area in the Parish of Kilconquhar, Fife, is around 1522, when William Lundy in Souther-Fawfield, and his wife, Gelis Wemys, appear in the Sheriff Court Book of Fife.

- - - - - - - - - -

GEORGE LUNDIE IN SOUTHERFAWFIELD. Sometime before November 1565, George was put to the horn, denounced as a rebel, and escheated. On the 28th of November 1565, a gift of his goods, along with those of Andro Wilkie and Alexander Walker, both in Methill, was made to a Paterick Fullerton:

> "At Edinburgh, 28th November 1565
> Ane lettir maid to Patrick fullertound, burgess of Edinburgh, his aris and assignais, ane or maa, of the gift of the eschete of all gudis (etc, ut supra No.2425), decreitis and utheris gudis quhatsumevir, quhilkis pertenit to Andro Wilkie in Mothill, Alexander Wlaker thair, and George Lundie in Faulfield, and now pertening, ot (etc) to oure soveranis be reassoun of eschete, trou being of the saidis personis, or (etc) dennuncit rebellis and put to the horn, fugitive fra the lawis, convict or becum in will for thair tressonabill remaining and biding at home fra oure saidis soverains raidis, oistis and armyis ordanit to have convenit at Striviling, Glasgw and Drumfreis."
> (*Reg. Sec. Sig*. V. 2454).

George appears in 1572 as one of several persons testifying at an inquest of retour that John Lundy (4th of Stratherlie), was the lawful heir of his (John Lundy's) late grandmother, Janet Melville, daughter and heir of William Melvill of Carnbee (*Laing Charters,* No. 871).

George died before the 11th of July 1597, as on that date the testament was confirmed of Janet Myrtoun sometime spouse to umpquhile George Lundie in Souther Fafield, in the parish of Kilconqhar.

- - - - - - - - - -

WILLIAM LUNDIE IN SOUTHER-FAWFIELD. On the 20th of June 1604, he was given sasine of an annual rent of 80 merks out of the lands and barony of Lundie by David Lundie in Largo, as bailie in that part an behalf of "a noble man" John Lundy of that Ilk (*Fife sasines*, II fo. 123; *NAS*, GD50/185/57). That same year, on the 1st of November both he and the aforementioned David Lundy in Largo, were witness to a charter by John Lundie of that Ilk to John Lundie of Strathairlie (*Laing Charters* No. 1473).

William had three sisters Isabella Lundie, spouse of James Philip in Anstruther; Margaret Lundie, spouse of Thomas Gray in Fawfield; and Elizabeth Lundie, spouse of William Bredfurd, minister in 'Pitmouat'. William died before the 26th of April 1620, whereupon his three sisters were served as heir 'portionari' of the fore-mentioned 80 merks annual rent from the barony of Lundie (*Inq. Spec. Ret. Fife*, Nos. 304-6). Here William was designed as 'in Sutherfaufeild,' and his sister Elizabeth's husband had by this time passed away.

- - - - - - - - - - -

BARBARA LUNDIE IN SOUTHER-FAWFIELD, was married to Henry Bredfut, in Souther-Fafield. She died on the 14th of February 1625 (*St. Andrews Commissary Court*).

- - - - - - - - - -

In Glasgow

JOHN LUNDIE, pawnbroker and jeweller, at East Clyde Street, Glasgow. He married Elizabeth Stark on the 3rd of December, 1836, in Gorbals, Lanark. He died at Oak Park House, Mount Vernon, near Glasgow, before the 11th of March 1870 (*Glasgow Sheriff Court*). She died on the

10th of July 1888 at Laurel Bank, Uddingston. (*Hamilton Test.*). They had issue:

1   *Elizabeth Lundie*, born in 1844, in the parish of Old Monkland, Glasgow, and died in 1908.
2   *Jessie Lundie*, born on the 3rd of April 1864, in the parish of Old Monkland, Glasgow

- - - - - - - - - -

JAMES BUCHANNAN LUNDIE, pawnbroker, married Janet M'Gilchrist on the 1st of June 1865, in Old Monkland, Lanark. Janet predeceased him, passing away on the 4th of June, 1884 (*Glasgow Test.*). They had issue:

1   *John Lundie*, born on the 10th of March 1866, in the parish of Old Monkland, Lanark
2   *James McGilchrist Lundie*, born on the 17th of October 1867, in the parish of Calton, Glasgow.
3   *Hugh Lundie*, born on the 29th of May 1869, in the parish of Calton, Glasgow.
4   *Albert Lundie*, born on the 24th of February 1871, in the parish of Old Monkland, Lanark
5   *Alfred Lundie*, born on the 18th of May 1874, in the parish of Old Monkland, Lanark

- - - - - - - - - -

In Gott

JAMES LUNDIE IN GOTT, appears in the Records of the Brechin Commissary Court.

- - - - - - - - - -

GEORGE LUNDIE IN GOAT, in 1659 he was given tack of the lands of Goat, in the Lordship of Carmylle (*NAS*, GD45/18/374). On the 11th of December 1663, he was given tack of the lands of Faulleues in the Parish of Monikie (*NAS*, GD45/18/408).

In Hill of Cragie

ROBERT LUNDIE IN HILL OF CRAGIE, was given a bond, registered on the 27th of July 1625, by John Allardice of that ilk, to infeft him in an annualrent of 20 merks under reversion from lands in the sheriffdom of Kincardine, which pertained to John Allardice. They payments were to commence on Whitsunday in 1626, in return for 200 merks. (*NAS*, GD49/418).

- - - - - - - - - -

In Inverurie

ROBERT LUNDIE OF INVERURIE. Had at least one daughter.
1   *Jean Lundie* appears in the register of deeds in 1701, (RD. 2/85/167).

- - - - - - - - - -

This is the only reference to someone of this name being designed as 'of Inverurie,' but there are further persons who were living in Inverurie, and one would presume were connected the fore mentioned Robert and Janet Lundie.

JOHN LUNDIE, son of an Alexander Lundie, was christened on the 25th July in 1719, in Inverurie.

- - - - - - - - - -

Rev. JOHN LUNDIE, minister of Lonmay. According to *FASTI*, he was born in Inverurie around 1726, the son of John Lundie and Anna Farquharson. The minister was educated at Marischall College, Aberdeen, graduating M.A. in 1743. He was licensed by the Presbytery of Aberdeen on the 2nd of August 1749; presented to the parish of Lonmay (Aberdeenshire) by James Hay of Cocklaw, in December 1752; and ordained on the 29th of March 1753. On the 2nd of July 1754, he married Mary Forbes, the youngest daughter of Thomas Forbes of Echt. She died on the 5th of April 1798, aged 77; John himself died on the 28th of April 1807. He was the author of the

1791 account of the parish of Lonmay (*statistical accounts*). At that time his stipend was nine chalders of victual, and 600 merks Scots, or L. 33: 6: 8 Sterling. he is probably the same John Lundie son of a John Lundie, was christened on the 25th of July 1724, at Inverurie; and who on the 15th June 1753, was served as heir general to his father, John Lundy, treasurer of the Burgh of Inverurie. He and Mary had issue:

1   *Margaret Lundie*, born on the 27th of April 1755, died on the 17th of September 1816.
2   *Katherine Lundie*, born on the 6th of May 1758, died on the 9th of August, 1809, at Tanfield.

- - - - - - - - - -

ALEXANDER LUNDIE, in the parish of Inverurie, had the following issue:

1   *Alexander Lundie*, christened on the 8th of December 1738, in Inverurie. He may well be the same Alexander Lundie who married Anne Davidson in 1761 in Inverurie.
2   *Rev. Thomas Lundie*, minister of St. Andrew's Parish, Brunswick County, Virginia. He was christened on the 25th of January 1742, in Inverurie, and studied at Marischal College from 1759 to 1763 (*Kentucky Review*). He married Lucy Yates, in St. Andrews Parish, Brunswick County on the 16th of March 1776. They had issue.
   i   *Thomas Yates Lundie,* born 1777.
   ii   *Elizabeth Bland Lundie,* born 1778.
   iii *William Lucy Lundie*, born 1780.
   iv   *Alexander Ferguson Lundie*, born 1781
   v   *Susanna Randolph Lundie*, born 1787.
   vi *David Greenway Lundie*, born 1789.
3   *William Lundie*, christened on the 1st of April 1744, in Inverurie. He was a watch and clockmaker, and also the first postmaster of the town (*Old Scottish Clockmakers*). He married Elizabeth Robertson on the 24th of August 1802, in Inverurie. William died in 1816, his testament being proved on the 7th of August, 1818 at Aberdeen Commissary Court. His tombstone is in Inverurie Churchyard (*Inscriptions of North East Scotland*). He and Elizabeth had issue:

i William Lundie, christened on the 15th of February 1803, in Inverurie.

ii John Lundie, christened on the 14th of May 1805, in Inverurie.

iii Thomas Lundie, christened on the 10th of April 1807, in Inverurie.

iv Alexander Lundie, christened on the 16th of September 1809, in Inverurie.

v Peter Brown Lundie, christened on the 29th of June 1814, in Inverurie.

vi James Lundie, christened on the 16th of June 1816, in Inverurie.

- - - - - - - - - -

In Leith

ROBERT LUNDY in Leith, was sent barley by the tenants of Kingbarnis between 1502 and 1507 (Exchequer Rolls of Scotland, XII. 207).

- - - - - - - - - -

THOMAS LUNDIE, skipper in Leith. Between 1635 and 1637, he appears in the Register of the Privy Council of Scotland (Series II, VI. 662), with regards the Leith Hospital. He died before the 9th of May, 1638.

- - - - - - - - - -

ANDREW LUNDIE, *mariner in Leith*, was held in captivity in Dunkirk, sometime between 1625 and 1627 (*Reg. Privy Council, Series* II; I., 597).

- - - - - - - - - -

JAMES LUNDIE, mariner in North Leith, married Sophia Wingate on the 7th of June 1700 (with proclamations on the 19th of May). Her father was a mason burgess of Linlithgow. He is probably the same James Lundie, designed mariner in Leith, who was admitted a burgess guildsman of Edinburgh on the 25th of December 1700, by right of admission of Bailie George Mitchell. James and Sophia had issue:

1 *Janet Lundie*, christened on the 4th of October 1702, in the parish of North Leith, Midlothian. She may well be the same Janet Lundie, daughter of a James Lundie, who married James Paterson on the 9th of December 1719, in the parish of South Leith.

2 *William Lundie*, christened on the 21st of April 1706, in the parish of South Leith, Midlothian.

3 *James Lundie*, christened on the 8th of August 1708, in the parish of South Leith, Midlothian.

4 *John Lundie*, christened on the 9th of October 1709, in the parish of South Leith, Midlothian.

5 *Thomas Lundie*, christened on the 15th of July 1711, in the parish of South Leith, Midlothian.

6 *Sophia Lundie*, christened on the 16th of August 1713, in the parish of South Leith, Midlothian.

- - - - - - - - - -

In Montrose

ROBERT LUNDIE, *burgess of Montrose,* was married to Margaret Young. Whilst living in Greenly, they issued letters of reversion in favour of John Allardice, younger, and apparent of that ilk, and Alison Lindsay, his spouse, to an annualrent from the lands of Cloak in parish of Arbuthnot and sheriffdom of Kincardine upon payment of 600 merks. This was done on the 14th of October 1597 (*NAS*, GD49/81). The both died before the 22nd of December 1632 (*Brechin Commissary Court*). They had at least one daughter.

1 *Elizabeth Lundie*. She was married to John Gentilman in Breddiestoun. She was served as heir to her father was served heir to her father (*Gen. Retours*, 1634).

- - - - - - - - - -

In Old Deer, Aberdeen

The connection between the Lundie family and this area of Scotland hails at least as far back as the 1630's and the time of Prof. John Lundie, humanist at Aberdeen University. One of his sons, Alexander, was a lister in Old Deer. Further details of John and his descendants can be read in the previous section. There are however details of a number of Lundies in Old Deer who cannot be directly linked to this family group, but appear none the less in records.

ALEXANDER LUNDIE, was born in Old Deer, and served with the 8th Foot regiment; Duke of York's fencibles, 6th Royal Veteran Battalion, from 1789 to 1816. He was discharged at the age of 37.

- - - - - - - - - -

JAMES LUNDIE, was born in Old Deer, and served with the Aberdeenshire Militia, from 1798 to 1819. At the time of his discharge, he was 48.

- - - - - - - - - -

DAVID LUNDIE, was born in Old Deer, and served with the 2nd Foot Guards from 1819 to 1827. At the time of his discharge he was 26.

- - - - - - - - - -

In Pittenweem

JAMES LUNDIE, was married to Margaret Lessallis before 1613. She died before the 4th of August 1617. (*St. And. Comm. Court*). They had issue:
   1   *Katherine Lundie*, christened on the 13th of September 1613, in Pittenweem, Fife.

A close relation of James must have been Alexander Lundie, who married Eling Lessellis, on the 8th of August 1620, in Pittenweem.

- - - - - - - - - -

JAMES LUNDIE, was married to Agnes Furid (*PRS Fife and Kinross*, VII. 335)

- - - - - - - - - -

JAMES LUNDIE, burgess of Pittenweem, married Anna Richardson.

They had at least one son.

1 *James Lundie,* he was served as heir portioner along with his aunt, Jenna Richardson, to William Richardson a writer (advocate) in Pittenweem, his uncle's son; in three tenements in Pittenweem, and two and a half acres of land within the burgh of Pittenweem; on the 26th of October 1665 (*Inq. Spec. Ret. Fife*, No. 982). He may well be the same James Lundie, a Burgess of Pittenweem, who died before the 9th of December 1665 (*Inq. Spec. Ret.* Fife, No. 985). If that is the case, which is highly likely, he had three daughters who were served as his heir.

i Janet Lundie, served as provisional heir to her father, James Lundie Burgess of Pittenweem, on the 9th of December 1655 in a tenement in Pittenweem (*Inq. Spec. Ret. Fife*, No. 985).

ii Agneta Lundie, served as provisional heir to her father, James Lundie Burgess of Pittenweem, on the 9th of December 1655 in a tenement in Pittenweem (*Inq. Spec. Ret. Fife*, No. 985).

iii Catherine Lundie, served as provisional heir to her father, James Lundie Burgess of Pittenweem, on the 9th of December 1655 in a tenement in Pittenweem (*Inq. Spec. Ret. Fife*, No. 985). She is thought to be the same Catherine Lundie who we see marry Alexander Adamsoune on the 28th of November 1650, in Pittenweem.

- - - - - - - - - -

JAMES LUNDIE *Councillor of Pittenweem*, subscribed to the bond for peace around 1677 (*Reg. Privy Council*, series III; V. 638).

- - - - - - - - - -

GEORGE LUNDY, *burgess of Pittenweem*, was married to Susanna Lumisden. A charter by - Strang, also burgess of Pittenweem, to Susanna, of an acre of land in the Lordship and barony of Pittenweem, shows that George died before 1612 (*NAS*, CH2/833/17).

- - - - - - - - - -

MALE LUNDIE, he had at least two sons:

1 James Lundie, whose details follow.

2   William Lundie, bailie of Anstruther Easter.

JAMES LUNDIE, a baker burgess of Pittenweem, later residing in Anstruther Easter. On the 27th of November 1711, he was served as heir to his brother, William Lundie, bailie of Anstruther Wester.

1   *William Lundie,* a baker burgess of Pittenweem. He was given sasine of half a tenement of land in the burgh of Anstruther Wester, between the minister's manse and the lands of Alexander Stables on the east, the houses of Alexander Scott on the south, the lands of George Rob, William Adam and Henry Lamont on the west and the high common way on the north on the 4th of August 1719 (*NAS*, GD62/308). On the 31st of December 1723, he was served as heir general to his uncle, William Lundie, bailie and baker in Anstruther Wester. This was recorded on the 28th of January 1724. He is thought to have been married to Christian Anderson and had the following issue:

   i Christian Lundie, christened on the 28th of July 1706, in Pittenweem, Fife.

   ii Janet Lundie, christened on the 28th of August 1709 in Pittenweem, Fife.

   iii Ann Lundie, christened on the 4th of March 1711, in Pittenweem, Fife.

   iv Agnes Lundie, christened on the 1st of April 1714, in Pittenweem, Fife.

2   *Alexander Lundie*, married Sophia Walker, the daughter of James Walker cordiner burgess of Pittenweem, later residing in the New North Kirk Parish of Edinburgh. Sophia and Alexander were proclaimed at New North Kirk Parish on the 14th of April 1706, and married on the 19th of April 1706 (*Ed. Mar. Reg.*).

   i James Lundie, christened on the 9th of February 1707, in Anstruther Easter.

   ii Anne Lundie, christened on the 24th of April 1709, in Anstruther Easter.

   iii William Lundie, christened on the 19th of April 1711, in Anstruther Easter.

   iv Rachel Lundie, christened on the 16th of June 1713, in Anstruther Easter.

v Alexander Lundie, christened on the 23rd of December 1715, in Anstruther Easter.
vi Sophia Lundie, christened on the 7th of July 1718, in Anstruther Easter.

- - - - - - - - - -

JOHN LUNDIE. He married Christian Anderson on the 20th of July 1731, in Pittenweem. They had issue:

1 *Sophia Lundie*, christened on the 11th of May 1732, in Pittenweem. Thought to be the same Sophia Lundie who married James Layng on the 9th of August 1754 in Pittenweem.

2 *Agnes Lundie,* christened on the 28th of July 1737, in Pittenweem.

- - - - - - - - - -

JAMES LUNDIE was married to an un-named lady on the 1st of January 1660, in Pittenweem.

- - - - - - - - - -

CHRISTIAN LUNDIE, married Patrick Morton, on the 7th of June 1717, in Pittenweem.

- - - - - - - - - -

In St Andrews

JOHN LUNDIE, *treasurer and burgess of St Andrews.* He married, on the 10th of August 1648, at St. Andrews and St. Leonard's, Fife, Margaret Lentron (*PRS Fife and Kinross*, XXII. 26). John died before 1679, by which time Margaret was married to Alexander Watsone, Provost of Dundee.

1 *Margaret Lundie*, christened on the 11th of September 1649, in the parish of St Andrews and St. Leonards, Fife.
2 *John Lundie*, christened on the 11th of May 1651, in the parish

of St Andrews and St. Leonards, Fife. He must have died very young.

3   *John Lundie*, christened on the 29th of May 1653, in the parish of St Andrews and St. Leonards, Fife.

4   *Jean Lundie*, christened on the 12th of November 1654, in the parish of St Andrews and St. Leonards, Fife.

He may well be the same person as ***JOHN LUNDIE, merchant and bailie of St Andrews***, who died at the age of 44, in 1671. He was buried in St. Andrews on the 20th of March 1671 (*Lamonts Diary*, p 255), and details of his monument were preserved in the book *"An Theatre of Mortality, or a further collection of Funeral Transcriptions over Scotland,"* by Robert Monteith. The details of his tomb are as follows:

B. John Lundie's monument

Hic jacet Johannes Londinus Mercator, ac Balivus
hujus Civitatis; quo obitt Anno Dom. 1671. Ætatis fuæ
44.
Stirpe fatum clara, Justi Veriq; tenacem,
Osoremq; Mali jam capit Urna Virum;
Quem vivum coluere pii, planxere cadentam:
Pronus, quippe, æqua flectere Fræna Manu.

[Here Lies John Lundie, Merchant and Bailie of
this city, who died in the year 1671, aged 44.
Of famous birth, a lover of the truth,
Hater of Ill, now hath this Urne forsooth;
On Life, all good Men lov'd him; now they mourn:
For, from the Right, he ne're aside did turn.]

His is probably also the same John Lundie, whose testament is proved at St Andrews Commissary Court on the 18th of June 1681 (*St. And. Comm. Court*).

- - - - - - - - - -

JOHN LUNDIE, merchant and citiner in St Andrews. He was married to Isobel Lepar. He died before the 8th of December 1626, Isobel before the 22nd of October 1652 (*St. And. Comm. Court*).

- - - - - - - - - -

JOHN LUNDIE, citiner in St Andrews, was married to Helen Monepenny. Helen died before the 17th of April, 1628. They had issue:

1   *Christian*, died before 18th of September 1629 (*St. And. Comm Court*).

- - - - - - - - - -

ROBERT LUNDIE, son of Thomas Lundie in Strathairlie. On the 8th of December 1586, he was bound as the apprentice to David Blair, a sadler in St Andrews, for 6 years. (*St. Andrews Hammermen*).

- - - - - - - - - -

THOMAS LUNDIE, maltman and citiner in St Andrews. He was married to Murray Bessie. He died before the 3rd of February 1606; Murray before the 4th of August 1597 (*St. And. Comm. Court*).

- - - - - - - - - -

THOMAS LUNDIE, was apprenticed to Alexander Napier, a Saddler in St.Andrews, on the 3rd of May 1566, for six years. (*St Andrews Hammermen*)

- - - - - - - - - -

In Strathbenlian in the Means

ANDREW LUNDIE, had at least one son:

1   *Alexander Lundie*, registered as an apprentice to Thomas Wilson, a Lister on the 22nd of July, 1657 (*Ed. Reg. Appren.*)

- - - - - - - - - -

In Weisdale

ANDREW LUNDIE, a miller. He married on the 9th of July 1858, at Arbuthnott, Kincardine Jane Watson. He died before the 3rd of June 1862 (*Lerwick Sheriff Court*). They had issue:

1   ***Janet Lundie***, born on the 23rd of April 1860, in the parish of Arbuthnott, Kincardine.
2   ***David James Lundie***, born on the 19th of December 1861, in Tingwall, Shetland, Scotland

- - - - - - - - - -

Section Seven

Well Documented Individuals

Eric Balfour Lundie.   An international Cricketer for South Africa. He was born 15th March 1888, in Willowvale, Cape Province South Africa and died during the First World War, 12th September 1917, near Passchendale, Belgium.   At the time he was a 2nd Lieutenant in 3rd Battalion of the Coldstream Guards.   He was a right arm fast bowler, and right hand batsman.   He played first class cricket for Eastern Province, Western Province and Transvaal.   His first and only test for South Africa was the 5th test against England at the Crusaders ground, St. Georges Park, Port Elizabeth, South Africa; starting on the 27th February 1914.   In England's first innings he took 4 for 101, the pick of the bowling by far.   One of these wickets included that of the great Jack Hobbs.   England won the test by 10 wickets.   This was the last test before the outbreak of war.   The next time South Africa were to play, 1921, this promising bowler had lost his life.

Francis Walter Lundie.   Born in Alberton, South Australia in 1866. He was president of the Australian Workers Union, councillor of Adelaide City Council for twenty-two years, and councillor of Port Adelaide Council for seven years.   The 'Lundie Gardens' in Adelaide takes its name from him. He died in 1933.

His son Francis John Phillip Lundie fought in both WW1 and WW2.   He held the rank of Corporal in both, and in WW2, served with the 2/27 Australian Infantry Battalion.   Frank J. P. Lundie wrote a number of poems during his time with the 2/27 Battalion.   These were published together in a book entitled "Reveille" in 1946.   The foreword to this book was written by Brigadier Ivan N. Dougherty; stating that as a front line soldier, he believed Corporal Lundie had done a great deal for his country, and that he hoped that his poetry might do a little bit more by providing pleasure to its readers.

Further information on Francis Walter Lundie can be read in "Additional papers of Clyde R. Cameron, comprising his account of the life of Francis Walter Lundie 1866-1933 and his involvement in the Labor Party and Australian Workers' Union"

Frank Lundie, a prosperous stockman and farmer, was born in Canada in 1862, the son of William Lundie, and his wife Edith.   Frank's father, William Lundie was originally from Scotland. His mother Edith is said (in a 1903 biography of Frank) to have been from the State of Maine in the United States of America, but the 1880 US census entry for Frank states that she came from England. This same entry gives Frank as living in Evanston, Uinta, Wyoming, with his occupation as a Labourer.

Frank left home at the age of 14 for Fort Bridger in the State of Wyoming, USA. He spent two years there, working in the construction of railways, whereupon he left for Green River then spending a year farming. After this, up until 1888, he spent a lot of time travelling. The first four years were spent moving between Fort Washakie and Lander, following which he went out of state to Arizona, California and Nevada, returning to Lander in 1886. He is then said to have left soon after for Idaho, where he spent the subsequent two years. During the early period of travel, Frank also spent some time in Colorado, where, on the 29th of September 1879, he was witness to the infamous 'Meeker Massacre.' Here members of the native American Utes tribe killed Nathaniel Meeker (an Indian agent of the White River Utes tribe) and seven members of his Staff. This was in response to Meeker's act of calling in the army to deal with the Utes after they objected to having him try to force them to become farmers.

In 1888 Frank returned to the State of Wyoming, ceased his travels, and started a cattle ranch near to Fenton (a place described as Bighorn Country). This he sold in 1898 and used the proceeds to buy a smaller ranch in the near vicinity. Although he sold the ranch, he kept his cattle, which by 1903 was said to consist of 150 head of Hereford.

The life of Frank Lundie is one of several portraits in the 1903 book "Progressive men of the State of Wyoming." As well as giving basic details of his life up until 1903, it gives a romantic picture of some of the adventures he faced as a cattle rancher. It describes how he has apparently "looked death by violence in the face on more than one occasion, and, sometimes, for days together, every hour has been full of peril." How "Hostile Indians and wild beasts have opposed his progress," with "road agents and other renegades from law and order" holding him up. He is however ultimately described as "being much esteemed as one of the leading representative men" in his part of Wyoming, due to his interest in the general welfare of the community in which he is living.

John Lundie, Mayor of Weymouth. He was elected Mayor of

Weymouth in Dorset, on the 9th of November 1876. He appears mentioned in an article in The Times of the 22nd of September 1877, in connection with an accident at sea when two vessels, *The Avalanche* and *The Forrest* collided. Following this article is a letter of his to the editor:

"TO THE EDITOR OF THE TIMES

Sir, Will you kindly give me space in your columns to reply to the charges made by some of your correspondents as to the neglect on the part of the residents of Weymouth in the manner of the burial of the bodies picked up from the late wrecks of Portland.

Those gentlemen ought, before making so grave a charge to know a little more about the locality at which the bodies were taken ashore and buried – viz., Portland. As that place is possessed of a Local Board of Health (connected with which are gentlemen of wealth and position), and has also the benefit of two resident educated clergymen, besides a considerable number of Dissenting ministers, would it not be thought almost an act of impertinence on the part of the authorities of Weymouth to interfere in any matters purely local? Such at all events is the opinion entertained in this town, and is the decided opinion of myself.

I do not for one moment wish to excuse in any way the wretched manner in which the interments were made, but at all events let the blame fall where it is due.

Your obedient servant,

JOHN LUNDIE, Mayor.

Weymouth. Sept. 20."

Ensign John Lundie, of the Argyllshire Highlanders. On the 13th of February 1692, Ensign Lundie was among the members of the government army who butchered the Clan MacDonald of Glencoe, at Glencoe. It is said that upon the 1st of February Glenlyon, a Captain in the Earl of Argyll's regiment, with Lieutenant Lindsay, Ensign Lundie and six score Soldiers came to Glencoe, where they were met by John MacDonald, son of MacDonald of Glencoe and 20 men. John MacDonald requested the reason for their coming to Glencoe. Lieutenant Lindsay showed MacDonald orders that the soldiers must quarter at Glencoe, whereupon they were billeted in that country, and familiarised themselves with the people of that region. Captain Glenlyon was the uncle of the wife of Alexander MacDonald, another son of Glencoe, and as such was invited to his house on each subsequent day. On the day of the slaughter it is also suggested that Glenlyon, Lindsay and Lundie were all invited to Glencoe's house for dinner that evening. However, first thing on the morning of the 13th, Lieutenant Lindsay led a part of Soldiers into Glencoe's house, killing him and all others around. The soldiers of this regiment then slaughtered any person they came across in the outlying country. The massacre at Glencoe was not a random spur of the moment act of madness, but had been planned long before the troops billeted in the country around Glencoe. It had been sanctioned by government, in order to help subdue to the Jacobitical tendencies of the Highlands, and prevent rebellions against the new government of King William and Queen Mary (*The massacre of Glenco*). The soldiers involved, along with the members of government who gave the orders escaped punishment, as it was difficult to work out who was really responsible for what. The enquiry in to this barbarous act was also hampered as the Duke of Argyll's regiment happened to be posted in Flanders at the time.

This posting to Flanders at the time of the enquiry makes it most likely that John Lundie is the same *Ensign John Lundie*, of the Scotch Guards, who died at the Battle of Landen on the 29th of July 1693. This was a battle fought in the Netherlands, now in the Belgian Province of Flemish Brabant, between the forces of King William III of England and II of Scotland, and those of France, lead by Marshall Luxembourg: The French forces prevailed. John Lundie is listed on the Guards officers Memorial at the Military Chapel, Wellington Barracks, England.

Private Joseph Lundie. Born in 1839, the son of Alexander Lundie, a hand-loom weaver, and Margaret Rae, he served with the Black Watch in India. He died on the 28th March 1911, at 23 Napier Street, Penicuik. He left a widow, Mary Lundie, (m/s Quigley) and at least one son, Alexander, whom was living in Penicuik at the time of his father's death. His obituary from 'The Scotsman,' on the 31st of March that year reads as follows: "Death of an Indian mutineer veteran – The small band of survivors of the affair of Sara Ghaul in the Indian muting has been still further reduced by the death of Pt. Joseph Lundie, whose funeral took place at Penicuik yesterday. Born at

Old Machar, 72 years ago, he, at the age of 18, enlisted in the Black Watch. At his funeral military honours were accorded. A detachment from the Royal Scots at Glencorse being present."

Captain Kenneth Lundin. He served in the Earl of Leven's regiment around 1690, and appears in the register of the Privy Council with regards his involvement in some violence in Edinburgh that year.

"The Lords of their Majesties Privy Councill doe heir by give ordor and warrand to Sir William Lockhart, his Majesties sollicitor, with assistance of Sir Patrick (Home) and Mr. Hugh Dalrymple, advocats, to raise and follow furth a criminal pursuit before the Lords of Justiciary against Captain James Bruce, Lt. David Arrat, Lt. Kenneth Lundie, Ensign Archibald Hay and George Davidsone, souldiers in Captain Denholm's Company, all in the Earl of Leiven's Regiment, and Adreas [?] coachman to the said Earl of Leiven, for the tumult and slaughter comitted within the city of Edinburgh upon the 4th day of November last by past 1690 years."

(*Register of the Privy Council of Scotland*, XVI page 181: (1691))

He appears to have not suffered as a result of this, and appears as a Captain holding a company in Linlithgow in 1698 (*NAS,*, E100/32/8); and a deed registered in 1701, indicates he was a Captain in Brigadier Maitland's Regiment. His connection to a particular Lundie branch is unknown, but a generation after himself, Strathairlie has a son Kenneth, which is the only other person of that name found, and may imply a strong connection with that branch.

Robert Leonard Lundie. Joint Managing Director of the Royal London Mutual Insurance Society. He worked for the company for over 53 years, was appointed a Director in 1945, and managing director in 1951. At the time of his appointment to the later position, the company had an annual income of almost 16 million pounds, and assets of over 93 million pounds. He retired on the 26th of April 1955 (*The Times*, 3rd May, 1945, p8; 11th May, 1948, 26th October 1951; p8; 22nd April 1952, p9; 30th April 1952, p10; 25th April 1955, p19; 25th April 1956, p17). He died on the 5th of

November 1967, at his home in West Wickham, Kent, at the age of 82. His funeral was held at the church of St. Mary of Nazareth, West Wickham, on Thursday November the 9th, at 11.25 am. He was cremated at Beckenham Crematorium (*The Times*, 7th November 1967, p17).

Daughters of the Lundie family

There are a great many daughters of the Lundie/Lundy/Lundin family who appear in the registers of Scottish records alongside their husbands, but of whom no detail is given of their parents/origins. This list is simply a brief summary.

Agnes Lundie, spouse of Henry Ramsay younger of Ardounie, sometime between 1634 and 1651 (Reg. Mag. Sig., IX. 87).

Agnes Lundie, spouse of Robert Auchmoutie. Robert was the brother of Sir David Auchmoutie of that Ilk. Agnes appears as the granter of a bond of Corroboration, registered on the 10th of December 1668 (*Dal*; XXIV. 205).

Barbara Lundie, spouse of Mr Robert Gillespie, minister at Strathmiglo. Barbara appears on record as receiving a bond from David Srimgeour of Cartmore, for 1000 merks, on the 25th of May 1692. Discharged of the said bond was given in July the following year. She appears designed as the widow of Robert Gillespie (*NAS* GD26/4/254). She was given a bond by George Earl of Melvill, for 1000 merks on the 29th of January 1702. They had at least one child:
1   *Margaret Gillespie*. She appears in a writ along side her mother on the 4th of June 1714 (NAS, GD26/4/254).

Christian, spouse of David Kay of Well and Ferry-Port-On Craig. Living sometime between 1600 and 1660 (*PRS Fife and Kinross*).

Dorothy Lundie, wife of Ninnian Liddel of Halkerston. Dorothy appears, designed as Ninnian's widow in a contract between herself and John Pentland in Halkerstoun, of the 9th of July 1573. It would appear as if John Pentland was involved in the slaughter of Ninnian Liddel, and the contract was to remit any criminal and civil action that could be taken against John, in exchange for half of the lands of Halkerstoun (*NAS*, RH4/191).

Elizabeth Lundie, wife of William Stirling of Achyle, later of Coldoche. Elizabeth and William were given a charter of 22s 8d lands of Dunaverig, and 6s 8d lands of Cassafuir, in the Stewartry of Menteith and Sheriffdom of Fife, by Sir Alexander Napier of Edinbellie, in April 1619. They were given sasine of the lands soon after, which was registered (*PRS Stirling*) on the 29th of April 1619 (*NAS* GD430/67). Elizabeth and William (now of Coloche) were still alive in 1641, as a charter by William with Consent of Elizabeth, and William's son Archibald; in favour of William's eldest son James; shows (*NAS*, GD86/561-2)

Elizabeth Lundie, Lady of Wester Fernie. She was twice married. Her first husband was Walter Fernie of that Ilk; her second, David Scot. She appears a number of times in the Sheriff Court Book of Fife 1515-22, after the decease of her first husband.

Euphemia Lundy, Lady Airdrie. She was married to Thomas Lumisden of Airdrie. The burgh records of Dunfermline show that sometime before 1584, by which time Thomas was dead, she let lands to her 'weilbelouit William Lumisdene, persoune of Cleische.' Euphemia also appears twice, 1562 and 1572, in the records of St Salvator's College, University of St. Andrews.

Ewfamia Lundie, spouse of David Wemyss younger of Strathardill, sometime before 1513 (*Reg. Mag. Sig.*, II., 2151).

Helen Lundie, spouse of George Wemyss of Balquharge. Living sometime between 1600 and 1660 (*PRS Fife and Kinross*).

Isobella Lundie, Lady Dury, spouse of George Dury of that Ilk, sometime before 1513 (*Reg. Mag. Sig.*, II., 1717, 3069).

Jean Lundie, spouse of James Buchannan of Sheriffhall. She died before the 29th of June 1633 (*Ed. Comm. Court*). They had at least one son, John Buchannan of Sheriffhall (*Reg. Mag. Sig.*, VII. 1701, 1322).

Jenna Lundie, spouse of David Kinghorn, clerk and burgess of Dysart. She died before the 3rd of February 1657 (*St. And. Comm. Court*). They had at least one child, William Kinghorn, who was served as heir to his mother on the 5th of September 1661 (*Gen Retours*, No. 4495).

Janet Lundie, Spouse of David Moreis of Cowdenbeath. Living sometime between 1600 and 1660 (*PRS Fife and Kinross*).

Janet Lundie, spouse of John Duddingston. John and Janet had one son, and in 1593, they were tenants of the mill and mill lands of Muircambus, in the Parish of Kilconquhar (*NAS*, GD66/1/76).

Janet Lundie, Lady Ardross, spouse of George Dishinton of Ardross, sometime between 1513 and 1546, (*Reg. Mag. Sig.*, III., 870).

Janet Lundie, spouse of James Bruce of Rail. A charter of confirmation, under the Great Seal, from the the 10th of May 1555, confirming a charter by James Bruce of Rail to his grandson William Bruce, names Janet as James's spouse, and reserves her liferent (*Reg. Mag. Sig.*, IV., 994).

Joneta de Lundy, Lady Arnot, spouse of John de Arnot, sometime before 1513 (Reg.Mag. Sig., II., 406).

Katherine Lundie, spouse of David Scot of Petlowie. David was the son of William Scot of Balwaerie. They were married by 1501 (*Act. Lords of Council Civ. Cases,* II 426; III. 259).

Katherine Lundie, Lady Durie, spouse of Robert Durie of that Ilk, sometime between 1513 and 1546, (*Reg. Mag. Sig.*, III., 3061).

Margaret Lundie, spouse of John Brydie, merchant of St. Andrews. Margaret and John were given sasine of a tenement in St. Andrews, called "Wolt lie cros hall" on the 24th of May 1594.

Margaret Lundie, spouse of Thomas Melville of Dysart. She died before the 7th of February 1565 (*Edin. Tests*).

Margaret Lundie spouse of Mr. Robert Bowis, minister at Dundrennan. They were married in Edinburgh on the 11th of February 1668.

Margaret Lundie, spouse of Duncan Strathachin of Glenkindy, sometime before 1513 (*Reg. Mag. Sig.*, II., 3589).

Margaret Lundie, Lady Slains, spouse of Andrew Moncur of Slains, sometime between 1580 and 1593, (*Reg. Mag. Sig.*, V., 1050).

Margaret Lundie, spouse of Michael Scot of Auchtermuchtie. As a result of a contract between David Scot, the son of David Scot of Kinilloch, and Michael and Margaret, from the 20th of December 1604; Michael and Margaret were required to pay David Scot £4000 merks. This they did not do, and were put to the horn for this £4000 merks, and £100 of expenses. David Scot petitioned the Privy Council on the 16th of July 1607, after the horning, as he had still not received payment (*Reg. Privy Council.* Series I. XIV. 513). See also (*Reg. Mag. Sig.*, VI., 2018).

Mary Lundie, spouse of Norman McKenzie, minister at Whithorn. She appears being granted a bond, registered on the 18th of June 1672 (*Dur.* XXX. 408).

Section Eight

Bibliography

A collection of Original Letters and Papers, concerning the affaris of England, from the year 1641 to 1660. Found among the Duke of Ormonde's papers, Thomas Carte M.A.

A Garden of grave and godlie flowers, by Alexander Gardyne [reprinted from the edition at Edinburgh, 1609.] The theatre of Scotish kings, by Alexander Garden [reprinted from the edition at Edinburgh, 1709]. Together with miscellaneous poems by J. Lundie (now first printed) [Edited by W. B. D. D. Turnbull.]

A Short Memoir of James Young, by Alexander Johnston, 1860.

A system of heraldry. Speculative and practical. With the true art of blazon according to the most approved heralds of Europe. Illustrated with suitable examples of armorial figures and achievements of the most considerable surnames and families in Scotland, &c, together with historical and genealogical relative thereto, by Alexander Nisbet.

A testimony to the truth of Jesus Christ, or, to the doctrine, worship, discipline, and government of the Kirk of Scotland By sundry ministers of the gospel in the provinces of Perth and Fife. Printed by the printed by the heirs and successors of Andrew Anderson, 1703.

A sermon preached before the Mayor, &c. of the town of Berwick upon Tweed, on the 13th day of February, 1801, being the day appointed for a general fast, William Stow Lundie.

Acts of Parliaments of Scotland, General index to The

Acts of the Lords Auditors of Causes and Complaints A.D. 1466-1494, London, 1839.

Acts of the Lords of Council in Civil Causes

Acts of the Lords of Council in Public Affairs: 1501-1544, Robert Ker Hannay, Edinburgh, 1932.

Anthology of Scottish Women Poets, An by Meg Bateman, 1991.

Ancient Scottish Weapons, James Drummond, RSA, Edinburgh 1881.

Annals of Dunfermline, The by Ebenezer Henderson

Annals of such patriots of the distinguished family of Fraser, Frysell, Sim-son or Fitz-simon, as have signalised themselves in the public service of Scotland: From their first arrival in Britain, and apointment to the office of Thanes of the Isle of Man, until their settlement as Lord of Oliver Castle and Tweedale in the South, and Lords of Loveth in the North. Edinburgh, 1795

Attorney's Pocket Companion: Or a Guide to the Practisers of the Law: In Two Parts. Being a translation of Law proceedings in the Court of Common-Pleas: Containg a collection of the common forms, beginning with the original, and ending with the Judicial Processes: Together with explainations on several &c's made use of in the proceedings, The by a gentleman of the Inner Temple, 1734.

Autobiography of the Rev. Dr. Alexander Carlyle, Minister of Inveresk: Containing Memorials of the Men and Events of His Time. 1861.

Baronage of Scotland; containing an historical and genealogical account of the gentry of that Kingdom, The begun by Sir Robert Douglas, completed by other hands, Edinburgh, 1798.

Baronetcies of England, Ireland and Scotland, by John Burke Esq. And John Bernard Burke Esq. Second Edition, 1841.

Blairs of Balthaylock and their Cadets, by John Blair, Clan Blair Society 2001.

British Library Public Catalogue, The

British Railway History: An Outline from the Accession of William IV to the Nationalization of Railways, by C. Hamilton Ellis, 1959.

The Burgh Records of Dunfermline, transcribed from the original manuscript volume, courts, sasines etc., 1488-1584, edited by Erskine Beverage, Edinburgh, 1917.

Caledonia, or, A historical and topographical account of North Britain from the most ancient to the present times with a dictionary of places chorographical and philological, by George Chalmers.

Calendar of Charters, 1165-1214, National Archives of Scotland

Calendar of Documents relating to Scotland, preserved in Her Majesty's Public Record Office, London, edited by Joseph Bain, Edinburgh, 1881-88 (IV Volumes)

Calendar of the State Papers relating to Scotland and Mary Queen of Scots, 1547-1603, preserved in the Public Record Office, the British Museum and Elsewhere in England, editede by Joseph Bain

Calendar of the Laing Charters, by The Rev. J. Anderson, 1899.

Catalogues of The National Library of Scotland, main and manuscripts.

Charters of David I, The edited by G. W. S. Barrow.

Charters of the Abbey of Inchcolm, The Scottish Record Society

Chinese Armorial Porcelain, by D. S. Howard, 1974

Chronicle of Walter of Guisborough: Previously Edited as the Chronicle of Walter of Hemingford or Hemingburgh, The Harry Rothwell, 1957.

Clan Donald Magazine No12 (1991)

Commissariat Record of Edinburgh, Register of Testaments, Volumes 1 to 35, 1514 to 1600. British Record Society, Scottish Section, edited by Francis J. Grant.

Commoners of Great Britain and Ireland, enjoying territorial possessions or high official of rank, but uninvested with hereditary honours, by John Burke Esq. 1838.

Compota Thesaurariorum Regum Scotorum: Accounts of the Lord High Treasurer of Scotland, edited by Thomas Dickson (Vol I) and Sir James Balfour Paul (Vol II-XI), Edinburgh, 1877 – 1916.

Decisions of the Court of Session, from its institution til the year 1764. With several Decisions since that period. Arranged under proper titles, in the form of a dictionary, The.

Decisions of the Lords of Council and Session, from June 6th, 1678, to July 30th, 1712, collected by the Honourable Sir John Lauder of Fountainhall.

Diary of J. Lamont, edited by G. K. Kinloch, Maitland Club, 1830.

Dictionary of American Biography Base Set. American Council of Learned Societies, 1928-1936.

Dictionary of National Biography.

Domestic Annals of Scotland, by Robert Chalmers

Dormant, Abeyant, Forfeited & Extinct Peerages of the British Empire, by Sir Bernard Burke C.B., LL.D. 1883.

Durham University Archives Special Collections – Ordination Papers

East Neuk of Fife: its histories and antiquities, geology, botany, and natural history in general, Walter Wood; second edition, rearranged and enlarged, Rev. James Wood Brown, 1887.

Emblazoned an Heraldic Manuscript, by Sir David Lindsay of the Mount (1542). Facsimilie edited by Sir David Lang, 1848.

Epitaphs and Inscriptions from burial grounds and old buildings in the North-East of Scotland, by Andrew Jervise

Essay on Additional Figures and Marks of Cadency. Shewing, the ancient and modern practice of differencing deccendants in this and other nations. More fully and exactly than any thing hitherton published upon this part of harauldry, An by Alexander Nisbet, Edinburgh 1702.

Exchequer Rolls of Scotland

Family Records, by Ashworth P. Burke

FASTI Ecclesia Scottiæ: the succession of ministers of the Church of Scotland from the Reformation, by Hew Scott (1791-1872)

FASTI of the United Free Church of Scotland, 1900-1929, edited by John Lamb

Feudal Britain: The Completion of the Medieval Kingdoms, 1066-1314, G. W. S. Barrow, 1956.

Fife, pictoral and historical: Its people, burghs, castles and mansions, A. H. Millar, 1895.

General Armoury of England, Ireland, Scotland and Wales; comprising a registry if armorial bearings from the earliest to the present time, by Sir Bernard Burke C.B., LL.D. Second edition, 1884.

Going with God. The Biography of Rev. Alexander Caseby, from 1898 until 1991, prepared and edited by his youngest son, Ronald R. Caseby, B.A., D.M.S., C.ED., F.I.P.M., F.B.I.M., Lewes Book Guild, 1993.

Great Historic Families of Scotland, by James Taylor M.A., D.D., F.S.A., 1887

Heads of religious houses in Scotland Scotland from the 12th to 16th Century, Scottish Record Society

Historic Earls and Earldoms of Scotland, by John MacIntosh, LL.D.

History, ancient and modern, of the Sheriffdoms of Fife and Kinross,..., by Sir. Robert Sibbald.

History and Proceedings of the House of Commons of England with the speeches, debates, and the conferences between the two houses, through every session from the year 1660. Faithfully collected from the best Authorities and compared with the journals of Parliament.

History of Stirlingshire, William Nimmo

History of the county of Fife, from the earliest period to the present time, by J.M. Leighton. 1840

History of the house and race of Douglas and Angus, by Mr David Hume of Godscroft, Edinburgh, fourth edition.

History of the shire of Renfrew. Containing a genealogical history of the Royal House of Stewart, with a genealogical account of the illustrious House of Hanover, from the time of their intermarriage with the Stewart family, to the present Period. . . . collected by George Crawford, and continued by William Semple.

Illustrated London News"

In memoriam, Robert Henry Lundie, London, 1895

Index Calendar of Deeds, National Archives of Scotland.

Index drawn up about the year 1629, of many records and charters granted by the different sovereigns of Scotland between the years 1309 and 1413, most of which have been long missing. With an introduction giving a state, *founded on authentic documents still preserved, of the ancient records of Scotland, which were in the Kingdom in the year 1292. To which are subjoined indexes of the persons and places mentioned in those charters, alphebetically arranged, An* by William Robertson Esq., Edinburgh, 1728.

Index Register of Deeds at the National Archives of Scotland.

Index to PRS for Shire of Berwick and Bailiary of Lauderdale, 1617-1780, Vol II

Index to PRS for Sheriffdom of Forfar, 1620-1700

Index to PRS for Sheriffdoms of Fife and Kinross Vol I – 1617 to 1700

Index to the Register of Sasines Aberdeen, 1599-1629 and 1630-1660

Index of Tutories and Curatories Lawful in the Record of retours: 1701 - 1897

Journal of the Very Rev. Rowland Davies, LL.D.: Dean of Ross, (And afterwards Dean of Cork), Edited by Richard Caulfield and Rowland, 1857.

Largo, An Ilustrated History, by Eric Eunson and John Band, 1995

Liber Cartarum Prioratus Sancti Andree in Scotia. E Registro ipso in Archivis Baronum de Panmure hodie asservato. Edited by Thomas Thomson, Bannatyne Club, 1841.

Liber Insule Missarum: Abbacie canonicorum regularium B. Virginis et S. Johannis de Inchaffery registrum vetus: Premissis quibusdam comitatus antiqui de Stratherne reliquiis. Edited by Cosmo Innes, Bannatyne Club, 1847

Liber Sancte Marie de Melros. Munumenta vetusitora Monasterii Cisterciensis de Melros. Edited by Cosmo Innes, Bannatyne Club, 1837.

Life and Adventures of Sir William Wallace, General and Governor of Scotland... printed Glasgow **18..** by J and M Robertson.

Liverpool's Legion of Honour, Birkenhead, 1893

Lundins of Fife by Graham T. Welsh.

MacDonells of Lundie by Norman H MacDonald, Editor

Massacre of Glencoe: Being a Narrative of the Barbarous Murder of the Glencoe Men in the Highlands of Scotland, by way of military execution, on the 13th of February 1692.

Matriculation Roll for the University of St. Andrews 1747 – 1897

Massacre of Glencoe: Being a Narrative of the Barbarous Murder of the Glencoe Men in the Highlands of Scotland, by way of military execution, on the 13th of February 1692.

Medical Who's Who, 1914

Metrical History of Sir William Wallace Knight of Ellerslie, by Henry, commonly called Blind Harry: Carefully transcribed from the M.S. copy of that work, in the advocates' library, under the eye of the Earl of Buchan. And now printed for the first time, according to the ancient and true orthography.

Mitchell Rolls, Scottish Heraldry Society.

Medieval Scotland: Crown, Lordship and Community Essays Presented to G.W.S Barrow, G. W. S. Barrow, 1993.

Memoir of Mary Lundie Duncan; being Recollections of a Daughter: by her Mother

Memoirs of Walter Pringle of Greenknow, by Walter Pringle, Edited by the Rev. Walter Wood.

Memorials of the Browns of Fordell, Finmount and Vicarsgrange. by Robert Riddle Stodart, 1887.

Minute book of the Hammermen Incorporation of St Andrews, 1539-1792.

Minstelry of the Scottish Border, Sir Walter Scott

Missionary Life In Samoa, as exhibited in the journals of George Archibald Lundie during the revival in Tutuila in 1840-41 edited by his mother, Mary Lundie the elder, afterwards Duncan.

National Archives of Scotland [Note that individual manuscript numbers are referenced in the text (*NAS, ----*)]

Noble society in Scotland. Wealth, family and culture from the Reformation to the Revolution, by Prof. Keith M. Brown

Non-Commissioned Officers in the medical services of the British Army, 1660-1960, Sir William Robert Macfarlane Drew, KCB. London, 1968

Notices from the local records of Dysert, Maitland Club, edited by W. M. Muir.

Old Scottish Clockmakers from 1453 to 1850, compiled by John Smith, Edinburgh 1921.

Original Letters relating to Ecclesiastical affairs of Scotland, cheifly written by, or addressed to King James the Sixth after his accession to the English throne, Bannatyne Club, Edinburgh, 1841.

Particular Register of Sasines for the Sheriffdom of Perth.

Peerage of Scotland, containing an historical and genealogical account of the nobility of that Kingdom, from their origin to the present generation: collected from the public records, and ancient chartularies of this nation, the charters, and other writings of the nobility, and the works of our best historians, by Robert Douglas.

Petition for Robert Fletcher of Balinsho, 1st January 1740

Poets of the Church, E. F. Hatfield, 1884

Presbytrie Booke of Kirkcaldy. Being the record of the proceeding of that presbytery from the 15th day of April 1630 to the 14th day of September 1653, edited, with introduction, notes and index by William Stevenson, M.A., F.S.A. SCOT. Minister of Auchtertool, Kirkcaldy: Published by James Burt, MDCCCC

Protocol Book of J. Young, 1485 – 1515, Scottish Record Society

Regestra Regnum Scottorum

Register of Apprentices of the City of Edinburgh 1583 to 1800. Published for the Scottish Record Society, 4 vols; Vol. I, edited by Frances J. Grant; Vol II and III, edited by Charles B. Boog Watson; Vol IV, edited by Margurite Wood.

Register of marriages for the Parish of Edinburgh, 1595 – 1700, edited by Henry Panton M.A., Scottish Record Society, 1905.

Register of marriages for the Parish of Edinburgh, 1701 – 1750, edited by Henry Panton M.A., Scottish Record Society, 1908.

Register of marriages for the Parish of Edinburgh, 1595 – 1700, edited by Francis J. Grant, W.W., Rothesay Herald, Scottish Record Society, 1922.

Register of the Privy Council of Scotland, Series I, II and III.

Registrum Magni Sigilli Regum Scotorum. The Register of the Great Seal of Scotland, Volumes 1 to 3, edited by James Balfour Paul and John Maitland Thomson; Volumes 4 to 9, edited by John Maitland Thomson.

Registrum Monasterii S. Marie de Cambuskenneth A.D. 1147 – 1535 Edited by Sir William Frazer, Grampian Club, 1872.

Registrum Secgreti Sigilla Regum Scotorum. The Register of the Privy Seal of Scotland, edited by M. Livingstone and D.H. Fleming, Edinburgh, 1908.

Retours of services of Heirs, Inquisitionum ad capellam domini regis retournatarum abbreviato, 1544 – 1699, vol I-III.

Retours of Services of Heirs 1700 – 1850

Roll of Alumni in Arts of the University and King's College of Aberdeen: 1596

– 1860, edited by Peter John Anderson, Aberdeen, 1990.

Roll of Edinburgh burgesses and Guild Bretheren1460 – 1841 Scottish Record Society, edited by Charles Boog Watson; printed 1929 and 1930.

Roll of Eminent Burgess of Dundee 1513-1880

Roll of Scottish Arms by Lt. Col. Garye of Garye and Nigg

Rotali Scotiæ

Royal Commission for Architecture and Historic Monuments in Scotland.

Secretaries Register of sasines for the Sheriffdoms of Fife and Kinross: 1603 to 1609.

Scalaronica of Sir Thomas Grey, The

Scotland under Charles I., David Mathew, 1955.

Scot's Compendium or Rudiments of Honour containing the succession of Scots Kings, From Fergus, who founded the monarchy. Also the nobility of Scotland, present and extinct; their titles, marriages, descents ans issue, with all posts of Government: Likewise their Coats of Arms, with those of the Order of the Thistle, perfectly engraved on ninty copperplates. . . 6th Editttion, 1756.

Scots Magazine

Scots Peerage, founded on Wood's edition of Sir Robert Douglas's Peerage of Scotland. Containing an historical and genealogical account of the nobility of that Kingdom, The, edited by Sir James Balfour Paul, C.V.O., LL.D. Lord Lyon King of Arms, Edinburgh 1914.

Scotsman, The (newspaper)

Scottish Arms, being a collection of armorial bearings A.D. 1370 – 1678; reproduced in facsimile from contemporary manuscripts. With heraldic and genealogical notes by R. R. Stoddart, Edingburgh, 1881.

Scottish Biographies, 1938, Thurston *et al.*

Scottish Heraldic Seals: Royal, official, ecclesiastical, collegiate, burghal and personal, by John Horne Stevenson and Marguerite Wood, Glasgow, 1940.

Scottish Historical Review, The

Scottish Nation; or, the Surnames, families, literature, honours, and biographical history of the people of Scotland, The by William Anderson

Sheriff Court Records of Aberdeen, edited by David Littlejohn, New Spalding Club

Sheriff Court Book of Fife (1515-1522), The Transcribed and edited by William Croft Dickison MA. PhD. 1928.

Some Predictions or Prophesies of severals of the Reverend and Worthy servants of the Lord 1769.

South Leith Records. Compiled from the parish registers for the yeas 1588 to 1700; and from other original sources, by D. Robertson, LL,B., S.S.C. Session Clerk

Statistical Account of Scotland 1791-99, ed. Sir John Sinclair

Statistical Account of Scotland 1845

Surnames of Scotland. Their origin, meaning and history, by George F. Black.

Tales of a Grandfather Sir Walter Scott

Theater of Mortality: Or, the Illustrious Inscriptions extant upon the several monuments, erected over the dead bodies, (of the sometime honourable persons) burried within the Gray friars church yard; and other churches and burial places within the City of Edinburgh and suburbs, An : collected and Englished by R. Monteith, M.A.

Theater of Mortality: or, a further collection of Funeral inscriptions over Scotland, An by Robert Monteith, M.A.

Thirteenth Century, 1216-1307, The Maurice Powicke, 1962.

Times, The London edition, archives –1785-1985.

Transactions of the Supreme Court of Michigan 1805-1814, Blume

Wreck of the Isabella, The by David Miller, London, 1995

Index

M

Printed in the United Kingdom
by Lightning Source UK Ltd.
121732UK00001B/165/A